The Civilising Mission and the English Middle Class, 1792–1850

Also by Alison Twells

BRITISH WOMEN'S HISTORY: A Documentary History from the Enlightenment to World War I

The Civilising Mission and the English Middle Class, 1792–1850

The 'Heathen' at Home and Overseas

Alison Twells
Principal Lecturer in History, Sheffield Hallam University, UK

palgrave
macmillan

First published 2009 by
PALGRAVE MACMILLAN

Palgrave Macmillan in the UK is an imprint of Macmillan Publishers Limited, registered in England, company number 785998, of Houndmills, Basingstoke, Hampshire RG21 6XS.

Palgrave Macmillan in the US is a division of St Martin's Press LLC, 175 Fifth Avenue, New York, NY 10010.

Palgrave Macmillan is the global academic imprint of the above companies and has companies and representatives throughout the world.

Palgrave® and Macmillan® are registered trademarks in the United States, the United Kingdom, Europe and other countries.

ISBN-13: 978–1–4039–2040–9 hardback
ISBN-10: 1–4039–2040–0 hardback

This book is printed on paper suitable for recycling and made from fully managed and sustained forest sources. Logging, pulping and manufacturing processes are expected to conform to the environmental regulations of the country of origin.

A catalogue record for this book is available from the British Library.

Library of Congress Cataloging-in-Publication Data
Twells, Alison.
The civilising mission and the English middle class, 1792–1850 : the "heathen" at home and overseas / Alison Twells.
p. cm.
Includes bibliographical references.
ISBN-13: 978–1–4039–2040–9 (hardback)
ISBN-10: 1–4039–2040–0 (hardback)
1. Missions—England—History—18th century. 2. Missions—England—History—19th century. 3. Missions, English—History—18th century. 4. Missions, English—History—19th century. 5. England—Church history—18th century. 6. England—Church history—19th century. 7. Middle class—England—History—18th century. 8. Middle class—England—History—19th century. I. Title.
BV2863.T94 2008
266′.02342—dc22 2008030096

10 9 8 7 6 5 4 3 2 1
18 17 16 15 14 13 12 11 10 09

Printed and bound in Great Britain by
CPI Antony Rowe, Chippenham and Eastbourne

For my mother, Jean Powditch, and in memory of my grandmother, Helen Twells

Contents

List of Figures

Acknowledgements

I have incurred many debts of gratitude during the course of writing this book and the years that preceded it. Many years ago, as a school student in the East Midlands, I was fortunate to be taught and supported in my interests by a number of teachers, including Peter Coatham, Steve Laws, Mike Lewis, Steve Room, John Turner and (the late) Jane Waite. As an undergraduate student at the University of Sussex in the late 1980s, I was immensely inspired by the teaching of Eileen Yeo. The research for this book began as a MA dissertation at Sheffield Hallam University on the missionary Hannah Kilham. I am grateful to (the late) Paul Nunn for encouraging me to study for a PhD, and to the ESRC for funding a three-year studentship at the University of York. Jane Rendall and Edward Royle were the most excellent of supervisors: Jane's scholarly rigour and ability to steer me through unfamiliar territory, and Ted's gentle encouragement, deep understanding of evangelical culture and determination that I should not lose my soul to post-structuralism were very much appreciated and are, I hope, in evidence in the book.

The comments of readers have helped me bring the themes of the book more clearly into focus. I am immensely grateful to Peter Cain and Edward Royle, both of whom have given their time generously in reading the manuscript and provided encouragement and critical feedback at crucial moments. Without Helen Rogers' willingness to read various versions of the manuscript, over many years, and her sustained engagement and faith that it would some day be finished, the book would have rolled into its second decade. As reader of the draft manuscript for Palgrave, Jane Rendall's perceptive comments gave me exactly what was needed to bring the project to completion. I am also grateful for comments given on papers, chapters and specific points by a number of scholars, in particular: Anna Afanassieva, John Baxendale, Antoinette Burton, Joanna de Groot, Kathryn Gleadle, Catherine Hall, Alan Kidd, Maria Luddy, Clare Midgley,

Richard Price, Sarah Richardson, Susan Thorne and Eileen Yeo. I would also like to thank my colleagues in History and English at Sheffield Hallam University who have supported me in what must have seemed like a never-ending project. Thanks also to Sue Salaun, who heroically proof-read the manuscript, and addressed some of the vulgarities of my grammar. All the errors remain, of course, my own. Thanks also to Michael Strang and Ruth Ireland at Palgrave for their editorial assistance and to Geetha Naren of Integra for her support in the final stages of production.

Librarians at Sheffield Local Studies Library and City Archives have been most helpful. Thanks especially to Ruth Harman, Doug Hindmarch, Martin Olive and Mike Spick. My thanks also for the help provided by librarians and archivists at the British Library; the CMS Archive at Birmingham University; the Library of the Religious Society of Friends, London; John Rylands Library, Manchester; the National Portrait Gallery; the CWM/LMS Archive at SOAS; Sheffield University Library; local studies and reference libraries at Chesterfield, Leeds, Liverpool, Manchester, Nottingham and York; and at Collegiate Learning Centre, Sheffield Hallam University, for speedy assistance with so many inter-library loans.

I am grateful for copyright permission to use material initially published as: '"So distant and wild a scene": language, domesticity and difference in Hannah Kilham's writing from West Africa, 1822–1832', *Women's History Review*, vol. 4 (September 1995), 301–318; '"A State of Infancy": West Africa and British Missionaries in the 1820s', *Wasafiri*, no. 23 (Spring 1996), 19–25; 'Colonial discourse and domestic femininity: The British and Irish Ladies' Society, 1822–1828', in Máire Ni Fhlatúin (ed.), *The Legacy of Colonialism: Gender and Cultural Identity in Post-colonial Societies* (Galway, 1998); '"Let us begin well at home": class, ethnicity and Christian motherhood in the writing of Hannah Kilham, 1774–1832', in Eileen Janes Yeo (ed.), *Radical Femininity: Women's Self-Representation in the Public Sphere* (Manchester, 1998), pp. 25–51; '"A Christian and civilised land": The British middle class and the civilising mission, 1820–40', in Alan Kidd and David Nicholls (eds), *Gender, Civic Culture and Consumerism: Middle-Class Identity in Britain, 1800–1940* (Manchester University Press, 1999), pp. 47–64; 'Missionary domesticity, global reform and "woman's sphere" in early nineteenth-century England', *Gender & History*, vol. 18, no. 2 (2006), 266–284; 'Missionary "fathers" and wayward "sons" in the South Pacific', Trev Lynn Broughton and Helen Rogers (eds), *Gender and Fatherhood in the Nineteenth Century* (Palgrave, 2007).

Various friends have sustained me through the process of writing, and I have appreciated their interest in the book and willingness not to talk about missionaries, as well as the usual pleasures that are the stuff of friendship. My thanks and appreciation to Hayley Clouston, Ann Claytor, Dave Mayall, Mary Peace, Eileen Yeo and (again) Helen Rogers. Liz Smith, Irene Reynolds and Hendrika Stephens have provided great care and lovely times for my girls and in so doing have enabled me to continue to enjoy the time spent on this project.

Finally, I have of late read with great interest other academics' domestic acknowledgements. Tony Mancini has never spent a Sunday afternoon walking hand-in-hand through the past imperial sites of Sheffield, and if he has ever read a word I have written it has been on pain of death. But he has taken his share of the routines as well as the pleasures of parenting, given me relief from many a broken night, and done more (far more, far, far more) than his fair share of domestic upkeep and maintenance. He knows how much I owe him, and remains blissfully unaware of how very proud nineteenth-century missionaries would be of his persistent pursuit of (my) domestic reform. Ruby and Madeleine have been oblivious to the book, but have brought many things to it, including a sense of perspective; and both deserve a mother who is a bit more in the world of Narnia, Barbie and girl pirates. My mother, Jean Powditch, has never openly questioned why, though I am sure she has wondered, and has made the process of writing this easier, and contributed to life's daily pleasures, with her humour, domestic support and motherly and grandmotherly love. This book is dedicated to her, and to the memory of my grandmother, Helen Twells, whose stories got me started.

Alison Twells
Sheffield, October 2007.

List of Abbreviations

BMS	Baptist Missionary Society
BFBS	British and Foreign Bible Society
CMS	Church Missionary Society
EM	Evangelical Magazine
LMS	London Missionary Society
SBCP	Society for Bettering the Condition of the Poor
SI	Sheffield Iris
SCA	Sheffield City Archives
SLSL	Sheffield Local Studies Library
SM	Sheffield Mercury
SRI	Sheffield and Rotherham Independent
WMMS	Wesleyan Methodist Missionary Society

Introduction: The Missionary Movement, the Local and the Global

Writing of the Somerset village of Cheddar in 1789, Martha (Patty) More stated that there was 'as much knowledge of Christ in the interior of Africa as there is to be met with in this wretched, miserable place.'[1] The people were 'savages', 'depraved and wretched', 'brutal in their natures and ferocious in their manners.'[2] According to Martha More's more famous sister Hannah, writing to Elizabeth Montagu about her plans for a Sunday school, they were 'so ignorant, so poor and so vicious, that I consider it a sort of Botany Bay expedition'.[3] Indeed, More felt herself to be 'the queen of Botany Bay'.[4] The neighbouring village of Nailsea, introduced to the sisters by its inhabitants as 'Little Hell', drew another colonial analogy: it was 'abounding in sin and wickedness, the usual consequences of glass-houses and mines; and when we cast our eyes round, and meditated on the great singularity of its situation, we could not help thinking it would become our little Sierra Leone.'[5] Similarly, though unaccompanied by the Dante-esque imagery, the More sisters' home village (from 1804) of Barley Wood was inhabited by 'a little colony of colliers' requiring their missionary care.[6] Looking back on the Mendips after a decade of evangelisation and reform projects, the *Reports* of the Society for Bettering the Condition of the Poor continued in the same vein to reflect on the transformation of a region in which there had been 'little to be seen...which could distinguish it as in a civilised society, or within the pale of Christianity'.[7]

I begin this book with Hannah and Patty More's description of their missionary field in Somerset to point to the interconnectedness of languages of savagery and civilisation, heathenism and Christianity, in missionary writing. The Mores' plans for Sunday schools (and later, benefit clubs for women) were cast as a 'civilising mission', a colonising venture which would see Christianity and civilisation implanted in a heathen and savage land. The imagery used by the sisters reflects the flurry of excitement generated by contemporary expeditions, to Sierra Leone in 1786 and of the first fleet to Botany Bay in 1788.[8] It reveals their familiarity with overseas schemes, and suggests their acquaintance with the body of Enlightenment writing about civilisation that had by the 1780s come into common currency.[9] Their descriptions also underscore the scale of the missionary task at hand. Savagery was expected in Australia, Africa or among the 'tomahawking' Native Americans, the subjects of an earlier missionary venture. Indeed, the More sisters' knowledge of all three places centred on a series of moral ills: crime and prostitution, slavery, polygamy and countless other cruelties. It was the existence of savagery and barbarism in England that was shocking to them. The comparison with Sierra Leone and Botany Bay underscored the excitement, the potential and the ultimate horror of the cultural encounter in England's 'heathen' villages.

The missionary philanthropic movement, for which Hannah More was an important pioneer and inspiration, burst onto England's cultural scene in the first two decades of the nineteenth century. Seeking no less than national and global reformation, the movement combined an impressive and astonishingly ambitious array of concerns: to make loyal, moral and industrious subjects out of the working classes at home; to promote 'civilisation' in Africa and other 'savage' regions; to abolish slavery and the slave trade; and to save Hindu and other 'heathen' girls and women from infanticide, ignorance, sati and domestic oppression. Missionary philanthropy became a fully-fledged provincial movement during the 1810s, with the extension of the British and Foreign Bible Society (1804) and the establishment of monitorial and Sunday schools and a range of societies designed for the reform of the English poor. The movement was augmented by the arrival after 1813 of overseas missionary societies, auxiliaries to the 'parent' Baptist, London (largely Independent) and Church Missionary Societies, formed between 1792 and 1799, and forerunners to the formal Wesleyan Methodist Missionary Society (WMMS) (1819).[10] By the 1820s, missionary philanthropy infused English culture, from the domestic lives of individual families, through local and regional networks, to high political campaigns. Encompassing women and children as well as men, it was public and familial, domestic and global, simultaneously involving intimate and very distant concerns.

The Civilising Mission and the English Middle Class is concerned with the popular missionary movement from its beginnings as an evangelical project in the late-1780s and 1790s, to the 1840s and early-1850s, when it occupied a central place in the national culture to become a wider, English civilising mission. Four broad themes are central to the book. Firstly, I examine the significance of missionary philanthropy at home and overseas to the formation of the English middle class. I argue that the networks and technologies of the civilising mission gave shape to middle-class identity and culture, enabling the emergence of a 'social' sphere of cultural intervention and facilitating middle-class claims to greater power and influence founded on leadership of a global civilising project. Men and women played different roles within this movement. While women's participation in missionary philanthropy has long been acknowledged,[11] the nature of their involvement, and in particular their central and active role in the formation of local societies, in the face-to-face work with the domestic poor, as supporters of overseas missions and, underpinning all, as the originators of a scripturally sanctioned expansive 'missionary domesticity,' has been consistently underplayed in previous accounts. A second concern of this book is to remedy this neglect, and in addition to underscore the centrality of the early nineteenth-century missionary wife to the civilising mission overseas.

Thirdly, the book explores the uneven nature of the process by which missionary philanthropy became central to a wider civilising mission. I trace the changing relationship between missions to 'heathens' at home and overseas in the early nineteenth century. These two movements emerged in parallel in the 1790s and early 1800s, sharing personnel, strategies and a broader missionary philanthropic paradigm which located social improvement in individual moral reform inspired by the Scriptures. By the 1830s and 1840s, however, this dual focus was breaking down, increasingly giving way to a new focus on distinct developmental trajectories and environmental and secular paradigms. Further undercut by resistance to the Christian message on the part of missionary subjects, by differences of class and authority within the overseas missionary project, and by the anxiety that the advance of civilisation was no certainty at home, the 1840s and 1850s saw a separation of the two missionary projects.

Finally, *The Civilising Mission and the English Middle Class* seeks to reinstate the centrality of the Bible to the missionary movement and to the world views of nineteenth-century missionaries and reformers. Giving shape to the mission, to interpretations of 'other' peoples and to the roles of men and women as missionaries, the Bible was fundamental to organising understandings of 'the World' and the place of Britons within it.

The middle class and the civilising mission

The missionary philanthropists of the early decades of the nineteenth century were men and women of the newly emerging English middle class. In contrast to the mainly artisan and lower-middle-class origins of overseas missionaries in this period,[12] the men and women who formed the motivating and organising force behind the domestic movements and overseas missions were drawn from among merchants, manufacturers, clergymen, journalists and other professionals. They established the auxiliary societies and committees, raised funds and wrote pamphlets, encouraged and selected overseas missionaries, held public meetings and anniversary celebrations, commissioned deputations and engaged in projects to reform the poor at home. As members of Baptist, Independent, Methodist and Anglican congregations which had been swept up in the revivalism of the

1780s and 1790s, they were largely evangelical, deeply committed to saving the souls of those not currently within the Christian community.[13] Missions also had roots in Unitarian and Quaker communities. These denominations traditionally had stood back from enthusiasm on doctrinal grounds, but were increasingly influenced by Enlightenment notions of education and social progress and the evangelical emphasis on social action as a fundamental marker of Christian lay religious practice and middle-class identity.[14]

That the intersecting memberships of philanthropic and voluntary societies were of considerable significance in the formation of local, regional and national middle-class networks and authority in the early decades of the nineteenth century has been well established.[15] Participation in religious societies and in church and chapel congregations was crucial to developing middle-class identities in this period. Religious belonging bestowed benefits that were both spiritual and social, facilitating economic alliances and marriages and opening up a new world of leisure pursuits. These were of particular importance for Dissenters, who continued to be excluded from positions of power and influence by the Test and Corporation Acts.[16] For philanthropic men, their occupation of key seats on a variety of voluntary bodies soon mapped onto other sites of urban power. Women's missionary commitments also enabled them to participate in a movement for Christian regeneration, centring on their neighbourhoods and, more controversially, the nation.[17] While the middle class was differentiated in terms of wealth, politics or denomination, involvement in missionary philanthropy enabled the development of a shared identity, defined by participation in a progressive project which was both national and global in its reach.

The aim of missionary philanthropy was to produce men and women of Christian character; to infuse the English nation, its cultural life and its polity, with Christian principles and moral systems; and to extend a Christian moral system and community across the globe. The two branches, home and overseas, were part of the same project.[18] Studies of the development of philanthropy in England, however, have neglected its global dimensions.[19] Domestic philanthropy is usually discussed in relation to issues of class and gender formation and the constitution of the public sphere. Denise Riley, Eileen Yeo and others have traced the philanthropic contribution to the development of the 'social' sphere of middle-class intervention,[20] while other historians have focused on the place of men and women within the 'religious' or 'missionary public' and the 'moral sphere'.[21] The Habermasian division of the world into 'public' and 'private' realms has been challenged by those historians of the 'social' who point to a variety of new cultural spaces which made up the public arena.[22] This re-ordering of (multiple) public realms is particularly important for our understanding of the prominence of women in the movement: the 'religious public' and 'social' spheres, partly constituted through the educative, nurturing and disciplinary functions of the domestic world of evangelicals, accommodated women with ease.[23] Global philanthropy, and in particular the practice of 'missionary domesticity', which saw the familial lives of women infused with social and global commitments, adds to our understanding of the overlapping spheres of social formation (see below).[24] Missionary philanthropy was not merely a demonstration of Christian benevolence, therefore, but is best viewed as a middle-class movement for national and global reform which saw the carving-out of a new sphere for social action and intervention.

When studies of missions overseas have moved beyond an exploration of their impact on recipient cultures to examine their role in the creation of an imperial culture at home, they have rarely been brought into the same frame with missions for the reform of the domestic poor. Catherine Hall's pioneering study of the imperial commitments of provincial Birmingham townsfolk, for example, does not explore how abolitionists and missionaries responded to the poor in their midst.[25] But the same men and women who subscribed to overseas missionary bodies, incorporated missionary meetings into their regular cultural calendars and taught their children according to a missionary pedagogy also engaged in attempts to reform the poor at home. Energetic philanthropists from the middle class sought the transformation of the English working class in much the same way as they supported the reform of the 'heathen' overseas. The domestic visit, through which missionaries encouraged reform, Bible reading and donations to the cause, saw the homes of the poor established as a 'contact zone'.[26] Monitorial and Sunday schools were similar missionary 'sites'. These were class encounters, systems for the improvement of the poor. The technologies of reform and the records of missionary encounters – the reports, journals and diary entries – were productive of dominant knowledge about the poor and their family lives throughout the nineteenth century.[27] Part of the 'package' of domestic reform was the encouragement of benevolence on the part of the poor: their missionary offerings were proof of their Christian character and commitment to the civilising project.

The Civilising Mission and the English Middle Class brings together home and overseas missions, exploring in the same analytic frame[28] the ideas, personnel and technologies of reform that in the early nineteenth century made domestic and overseas philanthropy part of the same movement for national and global change. It explores the self-representation of the new middle class as the natural leader of the civilising mission; the class best placed to lead the process of civilisation and Christianisation both nationally and in the wider world. The belief that they occupied a position at the helm of a global project of Christianisation entailed a sense of providential destiny that provided the missionary middle class with claims to greater social influence and political power in England.

Women and missionary philanthropy

Women were at the heart of the missionary philanthropic movement. While many were related, as wives, sisters and daughters, to missionary men, we should not assume that their commitment was derivative; women were independent actors within the missionary public. Many auxiliary societies were formed by women. They subscribed to a range of societies, and worked as collectors, teachers and domestic visitors within the movement. At home, women created a 'missionary domesticity' which, sanctioned by scriptural authority, endowed them with a considerable range of responsibilities. Alongside the duties of child-rearing, the education and management of servants and neighbourhood visiting, evangelical women and girls offered their support to causes across the globe. Missionary women sought to combat women's own ignorance and lack of housewifely and maternal skills; to reform the sexual morality of working-class girls in Britain; and, through steering men away from drink, to create happy Christian families throughout the land. They worked to improve the treatment of enslaved women; to address the universal problem of girls' lack of education; and to address the poor value accorded to women in the 'heathen' world, evident in female infanticide, sati and the seclusion of the zenana.[29] Early-nineteenth-century domesticity was not for many girls and women a dull and confining world, from which they were keen to escape into the relative freedom of a separate philanthropic sphere;[30] rather, it was shot through with social and global concerns.

The 1810s to 1830s were also formative decades in women's work as overseas missionaries. Unlike both the female supporters of missions at home in England and the independent female missionaries who populated the expanded overseas field from the 1860s, most women who served as overseas missionaries in the early nineteenth century originated from artisan and lower middle classes. This may account in part for their neglect on the part of historians who, in their keenness to explore the role of missions as part of an emerging imperial dimension to feminist campaigns for an expanded sphere,[31] have tended to overstate the argument that the overseas missionary of the early nineteenth century was an exclusively male figure.[32] There are a number of factors which serve to obscure women's missionary role in the earlier period. It was certainly the case that men alone could acquire experience of lay-preaching and an apprenticeship to an artisan trade, thereby possessing both the vocation and the skills required for spreading the Word and inculcating the means of civilisation. Only a man was capable of becoming the ordained missionary desired by (and so elusive to) the missionary society directors. Doctrines of masculinity constituted men as capable of independent action on the world stage. For women, both dependant and having dependants, overseas travel was dangerous and, if single, lacking in propriety. Distant climes, purportedly peopled by slave traders, polygamists, widow-stranglers and countless other brutal heathen, were considered to be unsuitable places for white women.

While missionary work was not formally opened to women in these decades, from the 1820s it was seen as desirable that men who travelled overseas were accompanied by their wives. The presence of women would, it was believed, make it more likely that the group would be received in friendship. A wife would provide her husband with home comforts and moral support, hopefully preventing him from going astray. More fundamentally, women could perform crucial tasks that men were unable to fulfil, a realisation that led to the early missions of single women, such as Mary Ann Cook, Hannah Kilham and Maria Newell who journeyed to Calcutta in 1820, West Africa in 1824 and Malacca in 1826.[33] The absence of domesticity and separate spheres was crucial to the missionary and Enlightenment interpretation of other cultures as 'heathen' and 'uncivilised'. As teachers and models of appropriate femininity, missionary women would impart domestic reform and 'civilisation', believed to be vital to the success of the mission and crucial to social progress and global Christianity.

As women's missionary activity at home was crucial to the creation of a new 'social' in the early nineteenth century, so the overseas work of missionary wives had implications for the colonial project. Domestic visitation in particular, was more than an apolitical encounter between the visitor and the visited. That the practice drew upon 'maternal' strategies – the face-to-face encounter, an emphasis on sympathy, influence, example, discipline and instruction – did not feminise the mission or 'soften' the impact of colonialism. It served instead to ensure that domestic, familial and intimate concerns, and technologies which emphasised acquiring knowledge through seeing and conversing, were at the heart of the reforming project, even if such projects were reshaped – 'provincialised' – by their fortunes in different colonial contexts.[34]

Missions, power and colonialism

Would-be missionaries were at the very least interested onlookers to British expansion. Many had their appetites as children whetted by the publicity surrounding the voyages of scientific and navigational exploration in the 1760s and 1770s, especially those of James Cook.[35] During the last quarter of the eighteenth century, they witnessed the early fleets to Botany Bay and Sierra Leone and Britain's rapidly expanding territorial acquisitions in north-east and south-east India, New South Wales, the Cape of Good Hope and on the West African coast.[36] The missionaries who travelled from Britain to India, the Pacific and West Africa in the 1790s were among many Westerners – soldiers and sailors, colonial adventurers and administrators, captives, traders, travellers, explorers and natural historians – who enjoyed an unprecedented access to 'other' peoples in these 'remote' parts of the world as part of an expanding and colonising power.[37]

Much of the writing on overseas missions has been concerned with the extent to which missionaries might be considered 'handmaidens' of British expansion or imperialism. While, as Andrew Porter argues, any general assertion of a close relationship between missions and the actual mechanics of colonial power may be questioned,[38] there can be little doubt that missionaries provided networks and institutions that facilitated contact between indigenous peoples and colonisers. They also created a popular imperial culture at home. It is unhelpful, with regards to the impact of missions, to try to distance missionaries from the harsher aspects of imperialism. To be emphatic about their 'good intentions' must be qualified by the awareness that representations of themselves as civilisers of heathen savages contributed to a wider discourse of colonialism and to assumptions of the superiority of Western civilisation.[39] This not only had a profound impact in Britain and the West, as Edward Said has shown,[40] but could work to devastating effect in the colonies themselves. As articulated most powerfully by Frantz Fanon, the imposition of Western religion and cultural systems could contribute to the destruction of indigenous religious systems and social organisation, paving the way for further colonial exploitation, and affecting the individual psyche and sense of self-worth.[41] Missions were 'enterprises that aimed to dignify and liberate their subjects' but which 'could also contribute to their denigration and dependence.'[42] Eighteenth-century evangelicalism was emphatic about spiritual equality: that all peoples were able to receive God's grace was a foundational principle of the movement.[43] The very nature of the 'mission', with its endeavour to change a culture and to replace it not only with Christian belief and practice but with 'civilised' cultural practices, was shaped by a meta-narrative of social progress which made it a vehicle of the West's 'post-Enlightenment imagination'.[44]

While imported missionary Christianity worked to support a sense of European superiority, it is necessary to consider the variety and complexity of the experiences of missionary subjects. Anthropological studies in particular have produced a wealth of sophisticated accounts. Jean and John Comarrof have drawn attention to the rituals, gestures, rites and 'body work' central to the missionary endeavour to reconstruct the daily lives of their subjects. They have documented the range of responses to the mission, from rejection and avoidance to enthusiastic participation, and the various stages between which saw partial acceptance and a transformation of the original missionary message.[45] Historian Jeffrey Cox is critical of the tendency to confine missionaries to too narrow a range of relationships to indigenous cultures and to ignore ways in which missions were made meaningful and authentic in the new cultural context.[46] Elizabeth Elbourne and others have posed questions as to why some cultures are able to more readily absorb Christian symbols, enquiring into the particular appeal of Christianity to the most powerless, in its promise of equal status or the potential offered for political allegiance or cultural defiance.[47] As Elbourne concludes, despite a 'latent authoritarian potential' there were 'multiple uses of mission' which should not be too heavy-handedly associated with colonialism.[48]

The missionary movement was similarly diverse. Nicholas Thomas' observation that there has been among historians a palpable reluctance to accord any 'plurality of hegemonic and counter-hegemonic perspectives among colonizers and colonized' is, as he suggests, especially relevant to missionary men and women.[49] There were differences between missionaries, shaped by personality, denomination, class, gender, authority, levels of popularity and contrasting and (increasingly) conflicting degrees of humanitarian sentiment. Most of the early missionaries were drawn from the lower-middle and the artisan classes, and although a good number had prior experience of missionary work in Britain, many hailed from communities which may also have been on the receiving end of missionary philanthropy. Missionaries were judged, selected, managed, supported, reprimanded or neglected by a missionary society directorship which spoke the language of brotherhood but which treated them as employees and in many cases seemed to view the men themselves as in need of civilising. To use Ann Stoler's words from a slightly different context, they were regarded little higher than other 'recalcitrant and ambiguous participants' in the imperial project.[50]

The 'heathen' at home and overseas: issues of race and class

That the domestic poor were seen by evangelicals as worthy missionary subjects in much the same terms as 'heathen' overseas raises important questions about contemporary perceptions of 'other' peoples and about historians' reliance upon the categories of race and class. What did representations of the English poor as equal in their depravity to the 'savage' overseas mean in terms of the likeness or difference between different groups of 'heathen'? Did evangelicals see peoples at home and overseas as belonging to separate 'races', and if so, how did the characteristics of a 'race' compare with those of the domestic poor? The changes in the mid-century that, according to the orthodoxy among cultural historians, saw a greater biologising of race and an erosion of the humanitarian sentiment, need to be charted in relation to these earlier developments.

Enlightenment theorising about cultural difference created a space for the advancement of analyses based on the existence of 'different species' and for peoples at 'home' and 'overseas' to be placed within different narratives of change. This is evident in pro-slavery writings of the mid-to-late eighteenth century, such as Griffith Hughes's *Natural History of Barbados* (1750), Henry Home's *Sketches of the History of Man* (1774), and Edward Long's *History of Jamaica* (1774), each of which represented slavery as a natural condition for black peoples. At the same time, the new physical anthropology pioneered by Blumenbach, Linnaeus and Buffon saw ongoing debates – concerning the division of humankind, the permanence and fixity of condition, the possibility of cultural degeneration, the capacity of peoples for development, and the significance of language, climate and environment – which provided a context for the development of more fluid analyses of cultural difference.[51]

While the term 'race' was used by about 1800 to refer to a permanent, fixed, physical or biological type, it also referred to cultural, linguistic, religious groups of people, as well as designating a family line. An ethnic group might also be termed a 'race' or, more frequently, a 'nation'. As Kenan Malik argues, '[t]he idea of "peoples", "nations", "classes" and "races" all merged together. Race often expressed a vague sense of difference and the characterisation of that difference was based variously on physical traits, languages, the aptitude for civilisation and the peculiarities of customs and behaviours.'[52] 'Race' did not, then, refer exclusively to colour and biological difference, as it would later in the nineteenth century, although physical differences were frequently part of the characteristics which were being described and categorised. Its meaning was closer to modern conceptions of the terms 'type' and 'group': Mrs Babar, a much-celebrated Sunday school teacher at one of Hannah More's schools, referred to the people of Cheddar as 'an enlightened race'; Jane and Ann Taylor could even dedicate a volume of poetry to that 'interesting little race, the race of children'; climbing boys might be described as a 'race', as might the poor of a particular trade or area within Britain.[53] 'Race thinking', then, also happened at home.

From William Carey's dismissal in 1791 of assumptions of the 'inhuman and blood-thirsty dispositions' of 'heathen' peoples, biological explanations of cultural difference remained unpopular among missionaries.[54] All peoples, according to the Bible, were members of God's family; the 'heathen' overseas and the poor at home shared moral qualities bestowed upon them by a God who had 'made of one blood all nations of men for to dwell on all the face of the earth' (Acts 17:26). This is not to suggest, however, that non-Christians overseas and at home were seen as equal in their depravity and capacity for change or, indeed, that each constituted an undifferentiated body of peoples and cultures. While, in Susan Thorne's words, sin was a 'great equaliser',[55] within the broad framework of a universal 'Fall', the influence of Scottish Enlightenment 'histories of civilisation' ensured that some cultures were considered more or less savage or barbaric than others.

This new and dynamic theory of historical change had compared contemporary Scotland with older European cultures and newly discovered 'primitive' cultures, particularly those in the South Pacific.[56] Writers such as Adam Ferguson, John Millar and William Robertson concluded that progress towards civilisation was achieved in stages. It involved a transition in the mode of production as all societies moved from hunting and gathering, through stages of pastorage and settled agriculture, to finally arrive at a commercial economy. It further included changes in social institutions, in ideas of justice and property, in custom and culture, and in the role of women.[57] Peoples were categorised on one progressive scale but in terms of differing degrees of deficit. At the pinnacle of civilisation was urban, western Europe, placed there by its commercial, civic and domestic successes and values, happily unhindered by its neighbouring peasant, Catholic and orthodox populations.[58] India was characterised as an ancient civilisation reduced by idolatrous religion to a nation of human sacrifice and widow-burning. The idol worship, promiscuous sexuality and homosexual practices of the South Pacific were mitigated by the absence of corruption by slavery and apparent openness to Western ideas and influence. Fewer peoples were lower than Africans in this scale of civilisation, their 'barbarism' tragically reinforced by slavery and by their blackness which was long associated with disadvantage and degradation.[59] This was, in Brett Christophers' words, 'a discourse of *difference within sameness*. Human oneness was absolute but fractured, temporarily, by sin.'[60]

I am not suggesting that potential missionaries necessarily read Robertson or Millar or the other proponents of Scottish Enlightenment stadial theory. The language of savagery and civilisation and the model of progressive development were, however, in common currency by the 1790s, boosted by the neat manner in which they mapped onto the 'heathen' and the 'Christian' of evangelical discourse. Missionaries and evangelicals refined stadial theory to produce a Christian understanding of social progress.[61] Rejecting the Enlightenment model of organic change to promote a more interventionist formulation, evangelicals believed it was the missionary who could effect change, facilitating the introduction of Christian knowledge, belief and practice to hitherto savage or barbarian cultures alongside wider civilised cultural practices, and thus hastening progress towards civilisation.[62]

If the 'heathen' at home and overseas were understood in similar cultural terms in the early nineteenth century, it has been widely argued that the 1840s saw an increasing popularity of biological understandings of cultural and racial difference.[63] There are a number of problems with this analysis, not least how it sits with the surge in the popularity of missions in the years between the death of John Williams in 1839 and the publication of Livingstone's *Missionary Travels* in 1857. This book contributes to recent research which suggests the unevenness of the rise of 'race thinking' in the nineteenth century. It explores conflicting currents, which see the disillusionment of some missionary brethren expressed in challenges to humanitarianism,[64] alongside plentiful evidence of a continuing commitment to missionary universalism in a vibrant, inclusive and family-based cultural and social movement in Britain. It examines these developments in relation to another complicating factor: the heightening concern for the improvement and containment of the domestic poor during the 1830s and 1840s and the emergence of a competing model of reform which prioritised environmental analyses of the 'condition of England' and methods for improvement which extended beyond the moral reform programme inspired by the Scriptures.

The Bible and cultural history

Our knowledge about missions is derived primarily from the writings of missionaries themselves. Reports were sent home to missionary society directors from men and women in the field, or composed by domestic philanthropists detailing their work at home. Letters were sent to family and friends. Journals, memoirs, biographies and hagiographies were increasingly popular, extracts sometimes finding their way into newspapers and periodicals. These cultural artefacts were created for a range of purposes. They sought to solicit funds or to justify money taken, to encourage further volunteers and to disseminate understanding of and sympathy for the evangelical global mission. They also asserted the agency of the readership within the national civilising project.[65]

The most striking (and yet unsurprising) feature of missionary sources, although one which is often lost in the focus on issues of representation and difference, is the extent to which they are infused with a specifically Christian, evangelical and sometimes millenarian, sensibility. They are emphatic in their insistence on the missionary's fulfilment of their obligations as *Christian* men and women. As Andrew Walls has stated, missionaries were 'representative Christians trying... to do Christian things, things that were specifically, characteristically Christian. They were trying to share the knowledge of Christ; and more than any other group of Westerners in the period of Western expansion, they were trying to make Christian choices and live in a Christian way.'[66] Missionaries shared in what the anthropologist Kenelm Burridge has referred to as 'a metacultural mandate' to extend the love of God to all. They held a 'divine motive', desiring to convert individuals, in the belief that outside of Christ man is lost, and to create a global Christian community which was witness to Christ's work.[67] The global evangelising of the 1790s and early nineteenth century was the result of a Biblical imperative, which saw missionary extension overseas as a natural development once the conversion of the poor at home was accepted as an intrinsic part of Christian duty.[68]

The fundamentally theocentric nature of missions is obscured within much contemporary historiography. Many social and cultural historians of missions repeatedly show themselves to be more comfortable with secular analyses of the missionary enterprise.[69] At worst, the post-modern theoretical frameworks of a secular society see religious faith as standing in for some other, more primary dynamic.[70] At best, historians repeat a few scriptural passages, concerning 'one blood' or teaching 'all nations'. Secular aspects of the mission are certainly important. Artisan and lower-middle-class men and women of the early London Missionary Society (LMS) and WMMS quite possibly felt that mission work accorded them a respect and authority to which they would not be entitled at home.[71] For missionary women, their involvement in overseas work, even as supporters from within Britain, provided them with an expansive sphere.[72] As is the central thrust of this book, the civilising mission was central to the early formation of the middle class in nineteenth-century Britain. But while secular dimensions of mission add greatly to our understanding, they are insufficient for explaining the missionary impulse. *The Civilising Mission and the English Middle Class* seeks to reinstate the Bible at the centre of Christian missionary and philanthropic practice. Missionaries and middle-class Christians had *faith*; they believed the message of the Bible which gave shape to their entire spiritual and material world and an understanding of their purpose within it. Indeed, it is at this point, when we consider the motivations rather than the wider cultural relations of mission, that we may see missionaries as well-meaning people, separate from an imperial project, and the Bible as much more than a cynical justification for the expansion of power and influence.

At the root of the motivation to take the 'good news' to the heathen both at home and in non-Western cultures was the belief that Christ belonged to all of humanity and that his message could be understood by all. The missionary method, beginning with the proclamation, moving through teaching, conversion, baptism and the making of a church community, was grounded in the belief that exposure to the Bible would produce a new Christian subject, transforming individuals and cultures. The job of the missionary was merely to 'set forth the Word of God, and allow its intrinsic power to work.'[73] Missionary beliefs were derived primarily from the Bible: that non-Christians required conversion for salvation, and that their religious systems constituted little more than 'pagan idolatry'; that Western civilisation was both superior to and had a capacity for improving others; and the commitment to the monogenist interpretation of human origins.[74] For missionaries, so 'unambiguously people of the Book',[75] the Bible offered moral guidance and literal truths. It provided an image of the 'heathen' and an analysis of their situation, and supplied a narrative for their salvation in which the missionary could locate him or herself as the agent of change.[76] In their work for cultural reform, missionaries believed that they were ushering in the prerequisites that would enable the second coming of Christ.

Both model and inspiration for the missionary enterprise derived from the work of the apostles. The *New Testament* is a missionary document; the gospels promote different understandings of mission. The emphasis of Luke, for example, is on Jesus's 'boundary-breaking compassion', and in particular his association with the poor, with women, tax-collectors and Samaritans and other marginalised peoples. The 'Great Commission' of Matthew 28:18–20, used by Carey in his *Enquiry* (1792), urged missionaries to 'Go ye therefore, and teach all nations . . . '[77] Foremost of all, the letters of St Paul to the Romans formed the foundational texts for the missionary impulse. Romans 1, written from Galatia to the Roman Christians whom Paul was due to meet en route to Spain and the first of his letters to the Romans, is the passage of the Bible most often quoted by missionary evangelicals.[78] Beginning with Paul's assertion that Jews and Gentiles are equally in need of salvation, Romans 1 provides a strongly-worded indictment of heathen life, describing the thankless, vain and foolish peoples of the world outside of Christendom, whose 'ungodliness' led them not only to 'a reprobate mind', but to lives filled with 'all unrighteousness, fornication, wickedness, covetousness, maliciousness'.

They were 'full of envy, murder, debate, deceit, malignity'; were 'whisperers, backbiters, haters of God, despiteful, proud, boasters, inventors of evil things, disobedient to parents, without understanding, covenantbreakers, without natural affection, implacable, unmerciful...' (Romans 1:29–31). Paul saw those outside the Christian community as utterly lost; all – Jew and Gentile, Greek and barbarian, free and slave, rich and poor – were able to receive 'unconditional love and unmerited grace'. Paul's intention, according to Andrew Walls, was to show 'the whole world under judgement': 'Is he not the God of the Gentiles also' (3:29), thus refers in the late eighteenth and nineteenth centuries to God as 'the God of the heathen also.'[79]

What missionaries saw, on encountering the 'heathen' at home or pagans of another culture, was the world as described in Romans 1, refracted through the lens of eighteenth-century British culture.[80] Paul's depiction of the heathen world informed missionary expectations of their subjects and provided an interpretative framework for their encounters. Idolatry, human sacrifice, sex outside of marriage or between men, widow burning and infanticide, cruelty and warmongering: all of these fell within this frame. Paul was their model and England – the origin of this new movement – inevitably became seen as a chosen nation. By the 1820s, missions were 'emblematic of national virtue'; by the 1840s and 1850s, widespread acceptance of Protestant narratives about chosen communities informed the English civilising mission.[81]

This book does not celebrate missionaries, but strives to understand the mission from the viewpoint of the missionary himself/herself and to take seriously the issue of religious faith. But it does so with an awareness of the challenges presented by post-colonial readings of British history in the colonial period.[82] Missionary documents form part of the imperial archive: if not produced by men and women with a colonising agenda, they were nonetheless shaped by and gave shape to a colonial discourse which, in the words of R. S. Sugirtharajah, was 'informed by theories concerning the innate superiority of Western culture, the Western male as subject, and the natives, heathens, blacks, indigenous peoples, as the other, needing to be controlled and subjugated', or at least, converted and civilised. The very selection of parts of the Bible, originally composed in an imperial arena and translated and interpreted for a nineteenth-century colonial context, reinforced a missionary relationship which sometimes lent itself very readily to colonial domination.[83] Sugirtharajah overstates the relationship between missions and colonial domination, however, and we need also to be cognisant of the places – the many instances – when missionary endeavours failed to go to plan: the enticement of some missionaries by 'heathen' cultures; the loss of control implicit in the translation process, beginning with the struggle for appropriate idioms and ending with the inevitability of independent interpretation; and the challenges to Biblical definitions of 'heathenism' by missionary subjects and converted Christians.[84]

The local, the national and the global

The Civilising Mission and the English Middle Class explores these themes through an examination of the dynamics of mission in a specific locality. The case study here is the provincial town of Sheffield which saw the emergence of a vibrant missionary culture in the early 1800s. Sheffield is not unique: countless towns across the country underwent almost identical developments, albeit of slightly different complexions due to topographical and denominational variations and with different rates of development, often dependent upon the size of the middle class.[85] The town is certainly representative, therefore, although that does not form my main reason for its selection. The wealth of extant sources concerning missionary philanthropy in Sheffield in this period provides an opportunity for the sustained examination, over half a century, of relationships of class, authority and denomination, between men and women, and between domestic philanthropy and the wider framework of the global civilising mission. This approach has much in common with those studies which focus on a specific missionary site or a denominational society, and seeks to address the problem that considerations of the 'local–global axis' seem invariably to have more to say about the impact of Britons overseas than of empire on the home culture.[86] While avoiding the pit-fall of the over-generalisations associated with applications of 'colonial discourse',[87] a case study enables consideration of the ways in which the 'local' is shaped by its relationship with a variety of 'others', through familial, denominational or commercial ties, and in relation to regional, national and global developments.

A word on the language of nation: I have chosen to emphasise 'England' rather than 'Britain' in this book. This has not been an altogether straightforward decision, not least because a similar argument could be made for Scotland. Indeed, a number of Scots, including Thomas Chalmers, George Thompson, Glasgow Bible Society ladies, George Combe and David Livingstone, not to mention the philosophers of the Scottish Enlightenment, appear in the narrative and are, at times, central to the argument. However, not only does the book focus on the English provincial town of Sheffield, but to claim to speak for Britain rather than England would raise issues that are not addressed in this study, such as the relationship between England and the other nations which make up the British Isles, and their complex and different relationships to British colonialism.[88]

The chapters travel between various missionary sites: 'at home' in early-industrial England, and overseas in Ireland, the West Indies, West Africa and the islands of the South Pacific. The destinations are determined by the missionaries and the societies to which they were affiliated. Abolitionist women, for example, had a particular commitment to the West Indies. Hannah Kilham's interest, inspired by Edward Bickersteth and the *Missionary Register*, was in Sierra Leone, and her trip to southern Ireland was enabled by her contacts within networks of London Quakers. The journey to the South Pacific of Congregational philanthropist George Bennet was shaped by the particular involvement of the LMS in that region. The absence of any sustained Sheffield connection to India in this period accounts for the omission of this popular mission field, although reports of meetings of returned missionaries or of William Carey's successes at Serampore provide an important context for the development of a missionary culture.

The book opens, in Chapter 1, with a discussion of the eighteenth-century context for the emergence in the 1790s of the civilising mission. The chapter explores the evangelical revival, the initiatives of the Clapham Sect and, especially, Hannah More's philanthropy in the Mendips, and the development of a 'missionary solution' to the national and international crises of that decade. The chapter introduces themes which structure the rest of the book: the relationship between domestic and overseas missions; the language of savagery and civilisation as a backdrop for a new articulation of the nation's ills and for understanding the English poor; and the critical importance of the Bible in identifying the various 'heathens' and developing a programme for their salvation.

Chapters 2 and 3 complicate the colonial and gender dimensions of early nineteenth-century philanthropy through an exploration of the creation of a missionary culture in Sheffield in the early decades of the nineteenth century. Chapter 2 examines the languages of savagery and civilisation and Christianity and heathenism that informed the new network of Bible, missionary and philanthropic societies in Sheffield, and the similarities between the technologies of mission at home and overseas. It emphasises the centrality of domestic reform – the raising of 'heathen' women – to the missionary movement at home and overseas and to broader strategies for civilisation. Chapter 3 focuses upon the global and missionary context for evangelical family life. I argue that 'missionary domesticity' provided evangelical women with an expansive world in which they had global agency. Through their involvement in missionary philanthropic projects, they helped to give shape to emergent middle-class culture and identity and contributed to the creation of new social and global spheres of cultural intervention.

Chapter 4 moves more decisively into the overseas mission fields to explore the role of women in the early-nineteenth-century overseas missionary movement. It examines the expansive roles of missionary wives in the promotion of domestic reform, and comes to focus upon the extension to Ireland, the Gambia and Sierra Leone of missionary philanthropic practices developed in England. A particular focus is the language of 'home' in the construction of a hierarchy of civilisation which places English evangelical culture at its apex.

Chapter 5 returns home to England, to look at challenges to overseas missionary philanthropy during the domestic crises of the 1830s and 1840s. The first part of the chapter looks at challenges from within evangelicalism: from philanthropists certain that the site of urgent action was at home rather than overseas, with climbing boys, factory children and victims of the New Poor Law. The second part of the chapter focuses upon the urban missionary movement of the 1830s and 1840s: the Mechanics' Institutes, Statistical Societies and city missions. While these drew upon the ideas and practices of the earlier domestic missionary movement, they ushered in some critical changes: regarding the roles of men and women; the relative emphasis given to scriptural and secular education and to moral and environmental paradigms for change; and the dislocation of domestic reform from its global context.

Chapter 6 looks at the packaging for the 'missionary public' at home of the experiences, memoirs and artefacts gathered by George Bennet, a Sheffield philanthropist and LMS supervisor to the South Pacific in the 1820s. The chapter explores two main concerns. Firstly, it considers the obscuring within the missionary narrative of some of the tensions of mission, between missionaries and their subjects, missionaries and directors, and the brethren themselves. Secondly, it argues that the representation of the civilising mission in new civic sites – in museums and through civic memorials, for example, saw the broadening of the missionary public to include men with a more secular interest in civilisation and global change.

The provincial middle class of the early nineteenth century was a missionary class. While relatively few middle-class men and women left England's shores, and a great many were not evangelical, they flocked in their numbers to the new missionary movement. *The Civilising Mission and the English Middle Class* explores the importance of missionary philanthropy for middle-class formation: its significance in terms of networks and organizations; the roles of men and women; the global context for their rise to power; and the relationship between the class and the nation. It examines the fractured, contested and often uneven developments which saw the establishment of an English national civilising mission by the mid-nineteenth century.

Miss means home not [just overseas

1

'One Blood': The 'Heathen' at Home and Overseas in Late-Eighteenth and Early-Nineteenth-Century Missions

The national impulse to mission which saw the emergence of a popular missionary movement in England in the early decades of the nineteenth century was shaped both by long-term cultural and theological trends and by the immediate and intense anxieties of the 1790s. Most fundamentally, English Protestantism had undergone a profound change during the course of the eighteenth century, as congregations within Old Dissent and the Church of England were transformed by their encounter with an intrinsically missionary Methodist movement. By the 1790s, Baptists and Independents, as well as the Anglican Clapham Sect, were leading the missionary movement at home and overseas. Their missionary strategy was further consolidated by the dynamic secular theory of cultural change which, developed by Scottish Enlightenment thinkers, saw all societies moving through distinct stages of development. In particular, the polarity of the 'civilised' and the 'savage' within Enlightenment thought mapped onto the Biblical dichotomy of the 'Christian' and the 'heathen', emphasising the capacity for progress and salvation of all peoples and providing a framework for missionary intervention. More immediately, the years following the French Revolution saw an urgency to marshal new forces of order and authority in Britain. The Terror in France, the dislocation and distress exacerbated by the French Wars, and the rise of domestic radical political activity generated a social crisis which engulfed the nation. Such localised alarm was compounded by global anxieties: worries about Britain's overseas power following the loss of the American colonies, fears of French colonial expansion, the 'ignoble savagery' of newly discovered parts of the world, and expressions of the ideology of the Rights of Man in Ireland and among enslaved peoples of the Caribbean.

This chapter examines the relationship between the domestic and overseas missionary movements in England in the late-eighteenth century. Despite their emergence in tandem, the two movements have rarely been considered together. Missions overseas tend to be explored in terms of their relationship to imperialism: whether or not they were a 'handmaiden' to colonial authority and their role in the creation of an imperial culture in Britain. Philanthropy in Britain, on the other hand, is usually discussed vis-a-vis issues of class and gender relations and identities and the emergence of a social sphere.[1] Yet, their emergence together in the writing and practice of prominent evangelicals in the 1780s and 1790s raises important questions which are key to our understanding of cultural formation in this period: of the relationships between home and empire, race and class, and men and women. Focusing on the missions of Methodists, Independents, Baptists and the Clapham Sect within the Church of England, the chapter introduces some of the most influential missionary practices which, disseminated throughout the nation via sermons, reports and the evangelical press, came to shape local missionary cultures and practices.

The first concern of the chapter is to establish the close relationship between the evangelising of the 'heathen' at home and overseas in the early missionary movement. The Methodists, both in the 1730s–1740s and as a mass movement in the 1780s and 1790s, pioneered missions to the British poor and to non-Christians in America and the Caribbean. By the 1790s, the Baptists and Independents within Old Dissent were, under the influence of Methodism, emerging from decades of quietism with a commitment to take the gospel to the 'heathen' at home and, via the conduits of the newly formed Baptist Missionary Society (BMS hereafter) (1792) and London Missionary Society (LMS hereafter) (1795), to peoples in India and the South Pacific. At the same time, members of the evangelical Anglican Clapham

Sect, disquieted by some aspects of nonconformist practice but sharing many aspects of their missionary impulse, launched new projects at home and overseas. Their abolitionism, support for the Sierra Leone scheme (1786), the Church Missionary Society (CMS hereafter) (1799) and the ultimately successful campaign to open up India to missionaries (1813) were complemented by the leading roles taken by evangelical Anglicans in a range of societies at home: the Sunday School Movement, the Society for Bettering the Condition of the Poor (1796), the Religious Tract Society (1799), the Vice Society (1802) and the British and Foreign Bible Society (BFBS hereafter) (1804).

The chapter then considers the consolidation in the mid-1790s of a missionary solution as the driving force for the reform of class relations at home and 'primitive' cultures overseas. This was an elite-led Christian cultural revolution, which emerged from a range of encounters and clashes of denomination, Scriptural interpretation, and attitudes to irregularity and respectability. The Clapham Sect and, especially, Hannah More (1745–1833), the Somerset-based philanthropist and writer of didactic literature, drew upon Biblical exegesis to transform aspects of Pauline theology into a model for missionary practice. Focusing on religious, cultural and moral reform led by the middle class, this accorded a central role to middle-class women. Proponents of the new missionary practice sought, through Bible teaching, domestic visiting and school teaching, to instil in their missionary subjects Christian knowledge and practice, virtues of cleanliness, industriousness, frugality and moral independence, a commitment to the 'separate spheres' of men and women and an acceptance of the ordained nature of social hierarchy. Through the wave of overseas missionary activity in the 1790s, the values and practices of the mission to the poor at home were extended to all peoples throughout the world.

'Like Cherokees and Mohawks, but more wicked': early Methodist missions

Overseas expeditions and voyages of discovery, and the social theory that issued from such travels, formed an important context for the missionary movement throughout the eighteenth century. Prior to the appearance on western horizons of the Pacific and Australasia in the 1770s and 1780s, the more established 'new world' of the Americas formed the focus of overseas missionary attention. A site of considerable excitement and potential for Enlightenment theorists and evangelicals alike, America and the Native Americans formed a crucible for ideas about the origin and progress of humankind and the possibilities for Christian conversion.[2] The Society for the Promotion of Christian Knowledge (1699) and the Society for Propagating the Gospel in Foreign Parts (1701), both formed in the new climate of religious toleration which (following the Act of Toleration of 1689) allowed dissenters to worship but not to hold public office, promoted missions in America alongside those in Britain.

By the 1730s and 1740s, the mantle of missionary pioneer had passed to the Methodist movement. Beginning as a religious society in Oxford in the 1720s, Methodism was inspired by Welsh and trans-Atlantic revivalism and by Moravian missionary enthusiasm in continental Europe. John Wesley and George Whitefield engaged in missionary tours across the nation, holding prayer meetings, visiting the sick and distributing religious literature as a means of regenerating the Church of England from within. Wesley had served a missionary apprenticeship in America, travelling to Georgia with the SPG in 1735. There he met David Brainerd, the celebrated missionary to the Native Americans, and Jonathan Edwards, leader of the Great Awakening in Massachusetts, who had provided a powerful stimulus to Wesley's own missionary work in Britain.[3] Wesley took evangelical Christianity to the people by means of open-air and field preaching and cottage meetings. Services in meeting rooms and chapels were similarly accessible: seating arrangements depended upon early arrival, not the purchase of a pew, and hymn singing and a rejection of sermonic essays reiterated the emphasis on popular participation. The missionary impulse shaped the movement's distinctive religious calendar of prayer meetings, love-feasts, watch-nights and visiting; open to all, the one requirement was the desire of converts 'to be saved from their sins'.[4]

Despite these early adventures, Wesley's was a domestic mission. With George Whitefield, and assisted by itinerant preachers, Wesley paid particular attention to those inhabitants of the industrial villages, mining communities and market towns located on the routes between Tyneside, Bristol and London. In its bid to educate, discipline and reform the populace, the Methodist missionary strategy was at once authoritarian and democratic, and as such pre-empted that of later missions.[5] The policing of members was often undertaken by Wesley himself: questions to be discussed at meetings dedicated to self-examination were set by him, and his *Directions given to Band Societies* (1749) banned smoking and the consumption of alcohol, the use of the pawnbroker and the wearing of jewellery, and promoted a 5 a.m. call to worship.[6] At the same time, the cellular or 'class' system of organisation, whereby small groups of same-sex converts met regularly to examine their souls and assess their spiritual development, promoted lay responsibility. Those class members who failed to submit themselves to the rigorous programme of discipline could be expelled from the Connexion.[7]

The nature of this 'reform', in particular its capacity to provide an alternative to the revolutionary politics of the century's end and instil a work discipline which fitted workers for capitalism, or conversely, to bolster the burgeoning radical movement through the development of moral and social discipline, has formed one of the most contested issues in the history of the movement.[8] There was certainly widespread belief among contemporary Methodists that the rules, discipline and promotion of literacy and education had a civilising impact on the membership. Wesley's favoured colliers of Kingswood, near Bristol, were known prior to their introduction to Methodism for 'neither fearing God nor regarding man; so ignorant of the things of God that they seemed but one remove from the beasts that perish.'[9] At a meeting in Whitehaven in the 1780s, Wesley concluded his assessment of the well-to-do congregation by comparing them favourably with the miners whom he now so obviously esteemed: 'they behaved with as much decency as if they had been colliers.'[10] According to Thomas Bewick, drawing on contemporary notions of savagery, Methodism on Tyneside had 'greatly civilised a numerous host of semi-barbarians, the pit-men and others employed in the pit works. These seemed like Cherokees and Mohawks, but they were more wicked.'[11]

While Wesley agreed that the Cherokees and Mohawks did indeed require 'civilising', he was reluctant to pursue overseas fields.[12] This was left to Thomas Coke, author of the 1783 pamphlet *Plan of the Society for the Establishment of Missions among the Heathen* and superintendent of Methodist missions in America (1784) and Antigua (from 1786).[13] Coke's desire was to bring into the mission a range of different 'heathen' peoples. His 1786 *Address to the Pious and Benevolent* proposed an annual subscription for the support of missionaries in 'the Highlands and adjacent Islands of Scotland, the Isles of Jersey, Guernsey and Newfoundland, the West Indies, and the Provinces of Nova Scotia and Quebec.'[14] Similarly, his *Account of the Rise, Progress, and Present State of the Methodist Missions* (1804) placed the 'Negroes in the West-Indies' alongside the Scots, Welsh and Irish. None were sufficiently civilised: while 'myriads' among the Welsh were 'still in spiritual darkness' and Irish Catholics only gradually emerging from the 'depths of superstition and vice', Scottish highlanders and islanders, Coke wrote, were 'little better than the rudest barbarians'.[15]

Old Dissent and 'all the world'

Thomas Coke's catholic missionary enthusiasm reflected the surge of interest in the 1780s in peoples overseas. Nevertheless, the formalisation of missions within Methodism came some years later, with the formation in Leeds in 1813 of the first Methodist Missionary Society and the establishment of the (national) Wesleyan Methodist Missionary Society in 1819.[16] Wesley's lack of support meant that, prior to 1813, overseas missions were generally the province of the Baptists and Independents. These denominations, traditionally characterised by insularity and quietism, had been profoundly changed through their encounter with Methodist enthusiasm to become the leaders of the revivalism of the 1780s and 1790s.[17] The combined influence of Philip Doddridge and Isaac Watts; the greater openness promoted by ministers from the Northamptonshire and Leicestershire Association and the Baptist Bristol Academy and Western Association; and the example offered by Jonathan Edwards in America: all contributed to the extensive debate among Baptist congregations on the 'Modern Question': the extent to which the converted were responsible for taking the gospel to the unconverted. Andrew Fuller, minister in Kettering from 1782 to 1806, preached on *The Gospel of Christ Worthy of all Acceptation* (1785), later developed into a lengthy book, in which he rejected the hyper-Calvinist belief that the unconverted were depraved and therefore could not be expected to repent in response to the gospel.[18] Fuller, along with William Carey, a shoemaker from Paulesbury, Northampton, who ministered at chapels in Northamptonshire and Leicester, and John Ryland, also a minister in Northamptonshire before his move to the Bristol Academy in 1793, participated in monthly prayer meetings which assumed individual moral responsibility for salvation, for one's own and for that of others.[19] As members of Baptist associations embarked on preaching tours in England, William Carey's *Enquiry into the Obligation of Christians to Use Means for the Conversion of the Heathens* (1792) extended evangelical principles to all non-Christians.[20] The BMS was formed in 1792 and Carey made his subsequent journey to India to found the Serampore mission in 1793.[21]

Independent congregations had been undergoing a similar transformation. This shift was influenced by Philip Doddridge's acquaintance with Whitefield, the contribution of Calvinistic Methodism to the general expansion of Congregationalism, and a more outward-looking approach, evident in a changing style of preaching and the popularity of the hymns of Isaac Watts.[22] Local associations, encouraged by individual ministers such as George Burder, David Bogue and Rowland Hill, had promoted prayer meetings from the early 1780s. Future directors of the LMS, Bogue and Burder were originators of the 'Plan for Promoting Knowledge of the Gospel in Hampshire' and the 'Warwickshire Association of Ministers for the Spread of the Gospel, both at Home and Abroad' (1793). They evangelised also 'through the dark corners' of Dorset, Cornwall and much of southern England and the Midlands.[23] John Eyre, Joseph Hardcastle and Rowland Hill were also involved, variously, with the Village Itinerancy Society (1796), which aimed to evangelise towns and villages throughout the country with the support of the newly formed Hackney Seminary, the BFBS (1804) and the Hibernian and Irish Evangelical Societies.[24] The London Itinerancy Society began as an LMS representative became acquainted with 'the benighted state of the village of Dullwich'.[25] Old academies were revitalised, and new ones, such as that at Rotherham in 1795, were formed.[26] By the 1790s, theological shifts had seen the emergence of 'moderate Calvinism', adherence to the Armenian belief that grace was available to all rather than just to a chosen elect.[27] This, alongside the emphasis on the doctrine of assurance, whereby believers enjoyed the security of knowing, rather than struggling with, their individual commitment, ensured that an increasingly activist and inclusive Congregational practice shared a great deal with that of the Particular Baptists and Methodists.

The Scriptural passages cited by Carey in his *Enquiry* (1792) invoke the missionary duty of the true Christian in an expansive world. The text is prefaced with St Paul's statement of spiritual equality:

> There is no difference between the Jew and the Greek: for the same Lord over all is rich unto all that call upon him. For whosoever shall call upon the name of the Lord shall be saved. How then shall they call on him in whom they have not believed? and shall they hear without a Preacher? And how shall they preach except that they be sent?
>
> (Romans 10: 12–15)[28]

Other passages, drawing on Matthew's Great Commission and the gospel of Mark, refer to the duty of Christians to address peoples, or nations, of the world: 'Go and teach all nations' (Matthew 28:19); 'Go into all the world and preach the Gospel to every creature' (Mark 16:15); 'Lo, I am with you always, to the end of the world' (Matthew 28:20). Carey adheres to the Biblical and monogenist framework favoured by evangelical and Enlightenment theorists alike: the various 'heathen' overseas and the poor at home shared moral qualities bestowed upon them by a God who had 'made of one blood all nations of men for to dwell on all the face of the earth' (Acts 17:26). Affirming Paul's message to the Athenians, Carey takes his self-justification from the words of the apostle: 'Be not afraid, but speak, and hold not thy peace...' (Acts 18:9). He evokes the patriarchal examples of Abraham, Isaac and Jacob, and even finds evidence that the heathen were to be found by travelling over the seas by ship.[29] Such themes were taken up in the Autumn of 1795 by Independent founders of the LMS, or the Missionary Society, as it was known until 1818.[30]

Although Calvinists had moved away from the notion of the 'chosen' in strictly theological terms, the missionary movement had implications for the self-understanding of English Christians. To the Reverend Thomas Raffles, the young preacher recently arrived at Great George Street, Liverpool, who gave the LMS anniversary sermon in London in 1814, the nation – and here Britain and not just England – had been placed by God in the privileged position of missionary to the world:

> Whilst all the political world teems with wonder; whilst tyrants, the victims of unbounded ambition, have been unconsciously fulfilling the divine decrees; whilst the groans of slaughtered thousands have reached us from afar, who has not turned with rapture to Great Britain, the Missionary, - the Bible Society, - the Instructress of the globe, - the Ark of freedom, - the Asylum of liberty, - the Couch on which outcast monarchs may recline at ease? Who does not cherish the delightful hope that God is about to make Great Britain, by her Bibles and her Missionaries, the herald to prepare the way for the second coming and universal reign of the Messiah?[31]

In the 1790s, the status of the British nation as 'chosen' was in the process of becoming apparent. But despite being placed closer to the apex of civilised life as a nominally Christian country with so many inhabitants who had been chosen for the purpose of saving souls, 'civilisation' in Britain was by no means guaranteed. Indeed, while peoples overseas might be more depraved, they were frequently seen by missionaries as more rewarding subjects than the domestic poor. The mere ignorance of the former was contrasted with the wilful refusal of many among the poor to achieve respectability, despite having advantages bestowed upon them on account of their easy access to a Christian education. In the words of a London Itinerancy Society representative, 'the transition from the view of the deplorable state of the Heathen abroad to that of the Heathen at *home* is easy and affecting.'[32] As stated by William Carey four years earlier, 'there are multitudes in our own nation, and within our immediate spheres of action, who are as ignorant as the South-Sea savages'. This was not proof against extending overseas. Indeed, 'our own countrymen have the means of grace, and may attend on the word preached if they chuse it . . . ', whereas others had no Bible or ministers, 'nor any of the advantages which we have', but were quite clearly capable of improvement.[33] Carey included in his volume tables detailing the numbers of pagans in the world, and argued that barbarism was no good reason for leaving them alone, and in fact might be a good reason for taking the Gospel to them; 'Gauls, Germans, Britons – all barbarians at the times of apostles' had all become Christian only through being evangelised.[34] All peoples were fallen, whether heathen or nominal Christian, and were thus at the mercy of God's wrath and in need of His redemption. All were capable and worthy of help. Through their own good will and the guiding hand of the missionary, whose duty it was to go out into the world and spread the 'good news' of Jesus Christ, the importance of justification by faith and the knowledge of the wrath of God, they were to be made fit for the great occasion of judgement day.

The missionary impulse: collaborations and conflicts

As Andrew Porter has recently argued, missionary enthusiasts of different denominations were members of overlapping networks. Carey's *Enquiry* (1792), taken by many to be the starting point of modern missions, brought Baptists into the evangelical missionary community already inaugurated by the Methodist Thomas Coke.[35] Carey and fellow members of the Northamptonshire and Leicestershire Association and the Bristol Academy were connected, by ties of family and friendship, to prominent Anglicans; Wilberforce and Thornton were amongst the early subscribers to the BMS. Carey's letters from the first Baptist mission station at the Danish settlement of Serampore, north-east India, were read by Thomas Haweis and David Bogue, inspiring the two Independents to join discussions with other interested parties and so begin the meetings which led to the formation of the LMS in 1795.[36] Haweis later participated in the meetings of the Anglican Eclectic Society, a forerunner to the CMS, while Thomas Coke and John Ryland exchanged thoughts on missionary matters with members of the Clapham Sect and the Church of Scotland.[37] Independents worked alongside Calvinistic Methodists and Presbyterians in the London-based Missionary Society; Methodists were recruited to the LMS with the first party of missionaries to the South Pacific in 1796–1797, and missionaries reported considerable support from members of other denominations. For Bogue, this coming together of Church and Dissent represented the 'Funeral of Bigotry', the title of his sermon at the opening meeting of the LMS in 1795.[38]

If such connections point to an emergent common culture, motivated by a 'pan-evangelical impulse'[39] and desire to co-operate, they should not suggest a completely homogenous movement. Denominational antagonisms continued to be important, especially between Anglicans and Methodists, the latter finally breaking from the Church of England on John Wesley's death in 1791. Despite Hannah More's predilection for Methodist Sunday School teachers (see below), many Anglicans expressed a continued unease with aspects of Methodist practice. Most notable were their objections to 'enthusiasm' and to the breaches of parochial obligations involved in itinerant preaching and outdoor assemblies. With frequent incursions by itinerant preachers into their parishes, these had long disturbed the established church. From the 1790s, the rapid growth of the Methodist Movement and its appeal within the lower orders caused considerable alarm.[40] Methodism's overlapping constituency with political radicalism and the apparent proximity of popular religion to the language of the 'Rights of Man' raised concern over the movement's 'irregularity' and the potential disloyalty of its adherents.[41] Such fears occasioned the withdrawal of Anglicans from the Wesleyan-dominated mixed-denominational Sunday schools in the early 1790s.[42] Many evangelical Anglicans continued to be cautious and denominationally defensive; they were soon to be insisting on the inclusion of the Catechism in the BFBS Bible, as well as establishing the Religious Tract Society (1799) and the Society for Promoting Christianity Among the Jews (1809) as *Anglican* bodies. While sharing a core of beliefs about evangelicalism and missionary practice with most Independents and Baptists within Old Dissent, as well as most Methodists and General Baptists within the New Dissent, Anglican and Claphamite missionary politics were much more intricately involved with the politics of loyalism and the need for social cohesion after 1789.

Antagonisms extended beyond the Methodist/Anglican breach. Unitarians, while keen supporters of philanthropic initiatives, were consistently opposed by all Trinitarians. Many Wesleyans, Particular Baptists and Anglicans declined to give support to the (London) Missionary Society, the latter deterred by the early sympathies of some Independents with French Republicanism, while the former were hostile to Congregationalists collecting money from Methodists.[43] Moreover, the years following the French Revolution saw continuing suspicion on the part of the Establishment of any reforming project; this extended beyond alarm at the radical sympathies of some Methodists, to also challenge the wisdom of any evangelicals, including Anglicans, engaged in projects for the education of the masses.[44] Old and New Dissent, including the leadership of the BMS and LMS, were situated in a more uncertain relationship to the social hierarchy. This was not only through the need to deal with radical sympathies among the rank and file, but because of their criticisms of the Test and Corporation Acts, among other Establishment practices.

The early missionaries who travelled to India in 1792 and Tahiti and Tongatabu in 1796 were also on the receiving end of considerable criticism,[45] although here denominational issues were frequently conflated with those of social class. As befitted their lower middle-class or artisan backgrounds,[46] most men (and their wives) had usually been involved in missions to the 'heathen' at home prior to their recruitment to serve in foreign climes. Many had experience as Sunday school teachers, while some were lay preachers. These men, who had not the advantage of the missionary culture that galvanised the next generation of missionaries, felt themselves to have received a particular calling, maybe inspired by the lives of David Brainerd or Jonathan Edwards or by the preaching of a particular minister.[47] Most among them were not ordained, but saw themselves as 'godly mechanics': respectable men who, while having skills to impart, were primarily concerned with Christian conversion; many intended to become ordained once they were established as part of the mission.[48] While their domestic missionary experience was considered good practice for their work with the 'heathen' overseas, their unequalness to the task was widely recognised, not only by critics of evangelicalism but also by directors and fellow missionaries. The first mission to the South Pacific was a dismal failure, with some men abandoning the mission. Zachary Macaulay was exasperated by Methodist missionaries he encountered in Sierra Leone, expressing his alarm at their eccentric preaching and ridiculing their wives for their 'doleful lamentations' and 'bitter complaints' that they could not find pastry shops nor gingerbread for their children in Freetown, contrary to the promises of Dr Coke.[49]

A more 'respectable' missionary practice had been forged by the 1810s, a result of education prior to departure and, increasingly, the selection of missionary couples. For this to happen, however, a shared missionary project had to emerge from the tensions and denominational differences of the 1790s. As I discuss below, events of the 1790s allowed moral reform and the civilising mission to be newly articulated during that decade.

'A sort of Botany Bay experiment': Hannah More and the missionary solution

The shared missionary solution that emerged during the 1790s took shape in the context of the very particular anxieties presented by the French Revolution and the pressures of war-time. Led by the Evangelical Clapham Sect, Christianity was promoted as a bulwark of national security and Anti-Jacobin morality.[50] The 'Claphamites' were a group of powerful and influential men associated with the Clapham congregation ministered by John Venn. They included among their number local residents Henry Thornton, William Wilberforce and Zachary Macaulay, extending to Josiah Pratt, editor of the *Christian Observer* (1802) and the *Missionary Register* (1813) and to more distant brethren such as Thomas Gisborne in Staffordshire and Thomas Babington in Leicestershire. Hannah More, currently developing her missionary philanthropy in the Mendips, was the sole independent female of the group.[51]

Claphamites are perhaps most famous for their overseas projects and abolitionist commitments. Wilberforce, Thornton and Zachary Macaulay were key figures in the Sierra Leone scheme (1786), the Sierra Leone Company (from 1791) and the CMS (1799). Wilberforce, the mouthpiece of abolition in Parliament, was assisted in his political campaign by Macaulay who, as governor of Sierra Leone in 1794–1795 and 1796–1798 and secretary of the Sierra Leone Company from 1799, gathered evidence about slave operations in West Africa.[52] Macaulay also facilitated the early work of the CMS, which saw the arrival in West Africa of the first (German) missionaries in 1804. Fellow Claphamites Charles Grant and John Shore (later Lord Teignmouth) used their positions within the East India Company to ensure the prominence of the campaign for missionary extension to India, which gathered momentum in the lead up to the renewal of the East India Company Charter in 1813.[53]

A number of prominent Claphamites had been involved in domestic reform initiatives in the 1780s. Wilberforce had with Thornton been a patron of Robert Raikes' interdenominational Sunday School Society, formed in 1785. Wilberforce was also a member of the Philanthropic Society and had encouraged King George III's proclamation against vice (1787–1788). A prelude to the formation of the Society for the Suppression of Vice (1802), this society supported measures to end practices such as duelling, drunkenness, the lottery and some of the more violent and bloody popular sports and amusements, and to promote Sabbatarianism, and drew support from Lord Teignmouth, Macaulay, Thornton and John Venn and others.[54]

Most importantly for this chapter, the year prior to the French Revolution had also seen the onset of Hannah More's missionary activism. The former actor, playwright and bluestocking was at this time distancing herself from the London theatre scene which had provided the context for her earlier work, to create a new social circle. This included the evangelical Reverend Thomas Scott, the Bedfordshire Sunday school teacher Sarah Trimmer, slave trader turned evangelical abolitionist John Newton, the abolitionist essayist Thornton, and Wilberforce, who soon became an intimate friend.[55] In 1788, More assisted Thomas Clarkson in a canvas of Bristol opinion, his first mission for the newly formed Committee for the Abolition of the Slave Trade. Her poem, *Slavery*, was published alongside Newton's *Thoughts upon the African Slave Trade* to coincide with the first Parliamentary debate on the trade in the spring of that year.[56] More's *Thoughts on the Importance of the Manners of the Great*, similarly intended to spur readers to activity, was also published during 1788. This was explicitly addressed to those 'persons considerable in reputation, important in their condition of life, and commendable for the decency of their general conduct' who, More believed, could remedy the absence of 'real religion' within society. Hoping to urge to action the 'multitudes of well-meaning people who would gladly contribute a mission of Christianity to Japan or Otaheite, to whom it never occurred that the hairdresser whom they are every Sunday detaining from church, has a soul to be saved,' More pressed for reform among all sectors of society:

> Reformation must begin with the GREAT, or it will never be effectual. *Their* example is the fountain whence the vulgar draw their habits, actions, and characters. To expect to reform the poor while the opulent are corrupt, is to throw odours into the stream, while the springs are poisoned.[57]

The evangelical mission was to the wealthy and powerful as well as the poor.

The Cheddar School, encouraged by Wilberforce's expressions of horror at the situation of the villagers and enabled by his financial support,[58] was the first of a range of schools and other projects which sought to restructure community relationships. Its aim was not to abolish poverty; More adhered to the Scriptural insistence on the necessity of the poor in society. Rather, the school aimed to promote dignity in poverty, to turn people away from radicalism and towards a Christian understanding of social hierarchy, and to revitalise relationships between the well-to-do and the poor. Teaching children to read the Bible (they were not to learn to write[59]) was a gift, which was good for the rich to give and for which the poor were to be grateful. Hannah and her sister, Martha (Patty), deployed an unsophisticated pedagogy in their bid to elicit improved behaviour: clothing, food and Sunday school anniversary prizes were given to children, while white woollen stockings (hand-knitted), five shillings in money and a Bible were given to women of 'good character' upon their marriage, as well as the more traditional lying-in benefit to those pregnant women who could offer proof of their married status. The Friendly and Benevolent Societies for women, which provided some practical relief and a caudle (a hot and spicy drink of ale or wine mixed with egg yolks) after childbirth, encouraged domestic skills and more general wifely virtues.[60] Treats of tea and cakes and similar 'Simple pleasures' were believed to 'have their use in civilising them'.[61] Club Feasts and children's dinners were held annually, at which sermons were given by the local clergy and 'Charges', either praising the women or reprimanding them for their bad behaviour were, in punitive maternal fashion, read out by More herself.[62]

We have seen that the More sisters considered their philanthropy in the Mendips as a colonial project which they compared to both Botany Bay and Sierra Leone.[63] They were shocked by the depravity and wretchedness of the people; they were 'savages', 'brutal in their natures and ferocious in their manners', and with no more knowledge of Christ than would be encountered in Africa.[64] Importantly, it was not only the very poor who were deserving of the appellations of savagery. Hannah More was upset at the coarseness and vulgarity of the farmers, and the absence of any civilising influence among them in the form of a resident gentry or middle class. On visiting Congresbury in 1791, More's ethnographic discourse identified the enlightenment and evangelical scales of progress: 'we made a visit, and found the poor divided into two classes – the very poor, and what is called gentleman farmers, wealthy, unfeeling, and hard; and, though not in the same state of *barbarity* with our other villages, yet quite as far from *Christianity*.'[65] In order to gain permission to set up a school, the sisters had to woo the farmers, especially the 'chief despot' of each village: in Cheddar this was a man 'who is very rich and very brutal; so I ventured into the den of this monster, in a country as savage as himself... '.[66] Another of these 'rich savages', a Mr Hydes, More described as a 'profligate, abusive, depraved... proud man [and] haughty sinner'.[67] During the later Blagdon controversy, as farmers obstructed her missionary ventures, she felt herself to be 'battered, hacked, scalpelled and tomahawked' after their brutal and un-Christian assaults.[68] Farmers who broke this mould were the exception. At Yatton, for example, an unusual farmer sent his children to Sunday school; he 'was the phenomenon – a pious farmer, well behaved and sensible'; his 'civil behaviour was extremely new to us.'[69]

It was no accident that More embarked on her domestic philanthropic adventures among the Somerset poor in 1789. Comparisons of the poor at home with peoples of Botany Bay and Sierra Leone drew not only on the wider colonial context but expressions of 'savagery' across the Channel. The language of savagery and civilisation continued to inform More's loyalist didactic literature of the 1790s. Her first pamphlet, 'Village Politics' (1793), sought to deter working men from joining radical societies in expression of their support for French revolutionary principles. Republicanism is represented and undermined through the character of Tom Hod, a politically naïve labourer, ignorant of the demands of a successful, commercial, civilised society.[70] In this key pamphlet of the Loyalist backlash of 1792–1793, More deploys the humorous counter-arguments of Jack Anvil to argue that civilisation was necessarily founded on tradition and on inequalities of property: it was 'for every man to pull down every one that is above him, till they're all as low as the lowest.' Telling Hod that he 'quarrel(s) with Providence and not with government', Anvil asserts that hierarchy is natural and ordained by God: '…the woman is below her husband, and the children are below their mother, and the servant is below his master.'[71] In this she entered into debates about the deserving and undeserving poor, about 'want', wage levels and the motivation to work, which were reinvigorated in the writings of Burke, Bentham, Eden, Paine and Malthus and others in the context of the poor harvests, high prices and high rates of poor relief of the 1790s. The poor were essential to the national good through their hard work and, in a Smithian sense, their ability to buy consumer goods. If they failed to pull their weight or had their incentive to work further undermined by poor relief, they were a threat to individual prosperity and to the nation.[72]

As with More's philanthropy, the Cheap Repository series extended beyond the concern to counter political radicalism to develop an extensive programme of cultural reform.[73] A wide range of tracts present young men and women indulging in plebeian customs and pastimes that were believed to be incompatible with civilised society. Their fate lay either in a happy moral reform or an unhappy end, as suggested by the subtitle to 'The Story of Simple Sally:…shewing how from being Sally of the Green she was first led to become Sinful Sally, and afterwards Drunken Sal; and how at last she came to a Melancholy, and almost hopeless end; being therein a warning to all young women both in town and country'. 'Black Giles the Poacher', subtitled 'Some Account of a Family who had rather live by their Wits than their Work', ends with the death of Giles, an idle thief who accuses a good and honest man of poaching apples from the garden of the respectable Widow Brown. A companion story, 'Tawny Rachel', is the tale of Giles's gypsy wife who, representative of all 'cheats, impostors, cunning women, fortune-tellers, conjurors and interpreters of dreams', connived her way into farmers' kitchens, playing on people's ignorance and superstitious fears in order to extract money and silverware; she is despatched to Botany Bay for her punishment.[74] Botany Bay features again in the story of Betty Brown the orange seller, in which a greedy employer tries to persuade the honest Betty to cheat her customers.[75] While undoubtedly part of the same project as her *Thoughts* of 1788, More now has a double audience: the missionary subjects themselves and the middle class, whom she encouraged to become leaders of a national missionary philanthropic movement.[76]

While the Cheap Repository Tracts were undoubtedly aimed at a poor readership, their reception is almost impossible to gauge. Certainly More went to a great deal of trouble to understand the techniques of those 'vulgar and indecent penny books' of popular literature, in order to make her stories more attractive to their audience. She even went so far as to encourage some future authors to meet with hawkers to learn their selling and distribution strategies.[77] From 1796, the tracts were further distributed through charity schools, the army and navy, prisons, workhouses and factories. We know little about what the poor actually made of them: whether they were read with interest, or indeed whether they were read at all, or merely left on a shelf, used as door-stops or became the focus of ale-house derision for their simplistic portrayal of poor people.[78] What is clear, however, is that the tracts were popular with members of the upper and middle classes. Some were addressed specifically to them, presented in nicely bound volumes.[79] More took just as much care in the delineation of their civilising roles. The irresponsible, vain, superficial, philosophising Mr Fantom, for example, is contrasted with the kind and charitable Mr Trueman, his tax-paying, church-going, Bible-reading friend.[80] Similarly, in 'The Two Wealthy Farmers', it is the family of Farmer Bragwell who come to the sticky end. Unlike Mr and Mrs Worthy, whose household was a model of good order and organisation, and who were regular attenders at Church and attended to their servants' education, Bragwell was interested in little beyond making money while his wife dedicated herself to ensuring their daughters had sufficient accomplishments to marry well to become gentlewomen.[81]

Philanthropic women and the Corpus Christianum

The most positive and indeed pivotal role in More's missionary vision is accorded to middle-class women, the activities of many of whom reflect her own bid at a female-led missionary cultural revolution in the Mendips. Although the poor were to take responsibility for their own uplift and improvement, their reform required that they be visited, scrutinised, taught to read the Bible and to acquire simple housekeeping skills. As wives and domestic managers, middle-class women were best placed to perform this role: they had skills to impart, and their maternal roles provided the requisite balance of sympathy and discipline. In this, as Kathryn Sutherland has pointed out, More was influenced by the emphasis on the relative roles of the sexes in the 'histories of civilisation' of the Scottish Enlightenment.[82] Women's active domesticity was seen to be an essential component of civilisation. As Adam Smith had argued, women's responsibilities for private domestic consumption and the rearing of responsible male citizens placed them in a central role in the negotiation of the competing demands of self-interest and civic duties which characterised commercial society.[83] In polite society, reading circles, salons and tea parties were all believed to contribute to the reform of domestic manners which was deemed essential to the improvement of public and political life; the 'domestic' was a civilised social space which allowed women to be involved – on certain terms – in current affairs.[84] 'The Cottage Cook; or Mrs Jones's Cheap Dishes', later titled 'A Cure for the Melancholy; Shewing the way to do much good with little money', 'The Sunday School', and its sequel, 'The Story of Hester Wilmot' all recruited the active civilised Christian domesticity of middle-class women to a central role in the reform of poor women (and through them, their husbands and families) hitherto lost to slovenly habits and immoral ways.[85]

But while influenced by Enlightenment thought, More's female domesticity was primarily Scriptural. Women's roles as missionaries drew upon a contested interpretation of the Bible, taking as role models Lydia, Priscilla, Tryphena, Tryphosa and other women known to have played an important part in the promotion of Christianity, in the circles of St Paul. As More undoubtedly discovered, finding female role models in the New Testament was more than a case of just 'searching the Scriptures'. Feminist theologians have argued that the difficulties of presenting Jesus to the patriarchal cultures of Jews and pagans meant that the second-century apostles played down the role of women in his ministry.[86] Women's presence is scanty, much diminished from their historical involvement in the fellowship of Jesus; a diminution epitomised by apostolic treatment of Mary of Magdala who, through her presence at the resurrection and commissioned by Jesus to missionary work, fulfilled the criteria of apostleship, but was all but written out of the Gospels.[87] Paul nonetheless referred to missionary women: Junia and Priscilla were members of established missionary couples; Mary, Tryphena, Tryphosa and Persis were commended by him for having 'laboured' for the cause; Euodia and Syntyche also 'contended' beside him. He made reference to wealthy converts who were patronesses; to Chloe, the 'purple manufacturer'; and to various leaders of church-houses: Apphia in Colossae, Lydia from Thyatira, a businesswoman who began a church in Philippi, and Nympha of Laodicea who led 'the church in her house'. In giving Phoebe the titles of *diakonos* and *prostatis* which, when used for men, meant minister or deacon, Paul indicated that she was his co-missionary.[88]

Similarly, the controversial injunctions, issued by Paul and Peter, which represent women as subservient to their husbands, also require interpretation.[89] New Testament scholars have argued that the Bible was not written to 'tell it how it was', but to convince an audience of Jesus' message; as such it produced particular representations of the role of women. Gerd Theissen has insisted that Paul's mission to a socially differentiated, urban world (in Corinth) provided him with church communities and potential converts that were fundamentally different from those receiving the Jesus movement in Palestine. His co-missionaries were not itinerant charismatics but community activists, and the churches themselves were mixed in terms of wealth and status. Theissen suggests the term 'love-patriarchalism' to denote the household and congregational structure promoted by Paul to accommodate such complexity. In this, all were spiritually equal, but there were accepted inequalities and women, children and slaves were governed by male members of the household; any potential friction was reduced by 'an obligation of respect and love' on the part of the dominant partner. As Theissen notes, this was not based on theology but on a slippage into the language of nature.[90] Feminist theologians have tended to place rather more emphasis on 'patriarchalism' than 'love', however, noting that this system represented a development of early Christianity, away from the egalitarian and counter-cultural characteristics of early communities and other cultist associations, to become from the second century the orthodoxy.[91]

More addresses these issues in her two-volume biography of St Paul (1815). In a short section, she sought to counter the disenchantment expressed by some women with Paul's teachings; a friction which, she (no doubt rightly) assumed, was based on his emphasis on women's subordination, silence and shamefacedness.[92] Not only did Paul have many valued female friends, she argued, but his views proved that he held women in high esteem. Referring to his statements about women's dress, she wrote that Paul seemed to be 'of the opinion, that the external appearance of women was an indication of the disposition of the mind; and this opinion, it is probable, made him so earnest in recommending these symbols of internal purity.' He objected to certain personal decorations because they were 'the insignia of the notoriously unworthy females of his time.' More concludes that 'it may be fairly presumed, that he never thought it could be construed into a hardship' to be cautioned against such garments and decorations.[93] Sometimes 'modern' women required such a dressing-down. In 'The White Slave Trade' (1805), More indicted the slavery to fashion of 'the wives, daughters, aunts, nieces, cousins, mothers and grandmothers even of these very zealous abolitionists themselves'.[94] Indeed, it is fascinating that More, a nineteenth-century Bible Christian, can insist in terms very similar to those of modern theologians, that Paul's injunctions need to be understood in their cultural context.

St Paul's popularity with More and other evangelicals lay in his illumination of daily Christian conduct and the development of a Christian moral system and social body, the Corpus Christianum.[95] Paul had occupied an interesting position, as a converted Jew and missionary in a complex, urban world. It is quite possible that the issues he faced as a community leader, arising from the social differences among the congregations and his struggles with conscience, imperfection, clashes of interest, resistance and conflict, both communal and internal, account for his popularity with late-eighteenth-century and early-nineteenth-century evangelicals. Hannah More was particularly concerned to elucidate a blueprint for a Christian society, found in Paul's missionary practice and everyday Christian observances: his morality and strictness and his emphasis on 'searching the Scriptures' for spiritual influences and guidance in personal activity.[96] She assumed that such day-to-day expressions of Christian faith were distinguishing characteristics between Christian and heathen cultures. While 'heathen' belief systems were merely concerned with intrigues between deities, Pauline Christianity supplied a body of morals and a governing system, thus ensuring that 'the meanest believer' was at an advantage over the 'most enlightened heathen philosopher'.[97] Women had a particular role to play in the development of the Corpus Christianum. As mothers and missionaries they could ensure that the spheres of politics and culture and ecclesiastical matters were not separate but were overlapping, and that Christian principles directed all areas of society.

More's body of work between *Strictures on the Modern System of Female Education* (1799) and her only novel, *Coelebs in Search of a Wife* (1809), all share similar concerns with the role of women in the shaping of a Christian society. *Strictures* reaches back to the arguments first presented in *An Estimate of the Religion of the Fashionable World* (1790), with its emphasis on domestic decay, the dangers of the 'World' and public amusements, of imagination and an 'ill-directed Sensibility'. Here More argues that women should 'come forward and contribute their full and fair proportion towards the saving of the country'.[98] Her *Hints towards forming the Character of a Young Princess* (1805) extended to the (future) sovereign her concern with the 'Importance of forming the Mind' and henceforth the Christian character of 'women of rank and fortune'. Here, More argues the mind of the leading royal ('even [that of] a female sovereign') 'should be trained to embrace a wide compass', including deportment, domestic habits, choice of society and raising the tone of conversation;

extending to a sense of morality developed through knowledge of history and geography; and an understanding of the relationship between Christian principle and the laws of the land. An appreciation of the 'Necessity of religion to the well-being of States', and the importance of religious institutions and especially the Church of England, would ensure that (in an interesting choice of phrase) '"Kings become nursing-fathers, and Queens nursing-mothers" of the visible Church'. For women, in families and at the head of the nation, More's emphasis was on 'Christianity as a Principle of Action':[99] the day-to-day striving for a Christian character, both personal and national, inspired by the doctrines and duties 'searched for' in the Scriptures.

More's anti-revolutionary politics have given her a reputation as an arch-conservative defender of the *status quo*, and as a consequence she has suffered neglect among historians. Most recently, Anne Mellor has rightfully, if simplistically, rebutted claims by social historians that More's work can be reduced to a simplistic class-based oppression.[100] More subtly, and in a less celebratory vein, Christine Kruegar suggests that More should be seen as a social prophet, in the mould of other eighteenth-century women preachers such as Mary Bosanquet and Mary Elland.[101] Her enthusiasm for St Paul and ability to draw from his writings a set of principles of action which would give shape to the Christian social body support this view. But More's vision was wider than this. Her missionary practice was informed by theories of civilisation and by the Bible to promote cultural reform, the development of a Christian social body and the domestic reform of women as a missionary solution to national and international ills. More was, therefore, more than a locally based methodistical woman prophet. Her model for missionary reform was to be extended throughout the world, by abolitionists, the Cheap Repository Tracts[102] and members of the missionary societies. Without leaving Britain's shores, Hannah More was a global missionary.

More's missionary writing and reform projects in Avon and Mendip villages provided a blueprint for a new generation of evangelical philanthropists. By 1798, as the Cheap Repository Tracts wound down, More's version of missionary reform was promoted across a number of sites. The Society for Bettering the Condition of the Poor (1796) prioritised cultural reform, Bible reading and female domestic reform, concerns that were soon evident in the practices of Sunday schools, the monitorial system of education (1797 and 1798) and the BFBS (1804). Bolstered by the writing of Bentham and especially Malthus, these were all, in Eileen Yeo's words, 'systems for the mass production of improvement'.[103] To this end, a proposed 'narrow utilitarianism' sought to inculcate discipline and self-sufficiency with a broad concern for inspection and surveillance and an emphasis on domestic reform and 'moral restraint', which equated the comfort, happiness and survival of the poor with the progress of the nation.

Whether located in Britain, Tahiti or the rural areas surrounding Calcutta, early missions adopted a very similar structure, combining methods of Christian education with a programme for 'civilisation', or cultural reform. Overseas missionary communities would begin by holding public meetings, providing Biblical instruction, Sabbath schools and Benevolent Societies and building churches and chapels to accommodate the new congregations. Solid houses with windows and with separate living and sleeping quarters were built, often as part of new village settlements, in West Africa, the Pacific and the Caribbean. Improved habits concerning dress, deportment, eating and sleeping, were also encouraged and appropriate gender roles were promoted, involving the acquisition of artisan and agricultural skills for men, and domesticity, in skills, dress and demeanour, for women and girls.[104] Detested practices, including promiscuity, homosexuality, infanticide, cannibalism and human sacrifice in the South Pacific, and sati, idolatry, pilgrimage and the exposure of the sick and dying in north India were also to be rooted out.[105] For most within the missionary movement, there was no clash of interest between Christianity and civilisation. Enlightenment and civilisation were unthinkable without Christianity and moral reform. Christian conversion, it was believed, would necessarily lead to the abandonment of savagery and the adoption of civilised cultural practices, and thereby to the progress of civilisation and Christianity on a global scale.[106] At home, missionary subjects were also seen to suffer not only from an absence of religious knowledge, but from a more fundamental cultural deficit. Programmes for reform involved a thorough-going assault upon aspects of the traditional culture: attendance at fairs, participation in blood sports and the practice of St Monday; pursuits and pastimes such as dancing, miming, music, wrestling and boxing, were all deemed to encourage ungodly behaviour. Domestic reform was of paramount importance, as women were encouraged to be frugal and clean, moral and industrious, to send their children to Sunday school and keep their husbands from the public house.

Conclusion

While missions were not new to the 1790s, moral reform and the civilising mission were newly articulated in that decade, as a groundswell of grassroots missionary activity drew in all Protestant denominations. Global evangelising of the 1790s and early 1800s was the outcome of a Biblical imperative: extension overseas, enabled by new opportunities for visiting hitherto remote regions of the world, was a natural development once the conversion of the poor at home was accepted as an intrinsic part of Christian duty. In Britain after 1789, the missionary solution was successfully steered by Hannah More and other members of the Clapham Sect. Working in conjunction with evangelicals and social reformers of other denominations, they popularised the belief that a missionary movement could inculcate moral restraint and domestic reform, and perform a role in the surveillance of the poor, thus contributing to social cohesion. The Claphamites and their supporters were able to appropriate the more positive aspects of Methodism while simultaneously engaging with their anxieties about popular religion. In so doing they forged a polarity in popular evangelicalism, between the 'respectable' on the one hand, and the 'irregular' and 'disorderly' on the other. At the same time as differences fractured the movement, the shared missionary impulse enabled points of connection and places to work together. The existence of equivalent societies across and within denominations suggests that denominational loyalty was compatible with shared beliefs and principles for action.[107]

In the first two decades of the nineteenth century, the missionary solution was widely adopted in the English provinces. While it began as a movement of elite members (although never, as Roberts suggests, driven entirely from the homes of the Gurneys and Frys in Spitalfields and Earlham)[108] missionary philanthropy soon became a mass provincial movement. As will be shown in Chapter 2, respectable evangelical men and women leaped aboard the missionary project. Alongside the swelling congregations which saw the flurry of church and chapel building in the 1790s and early 1800s, the formation of missionary societies provided important sites of collaboration for those – largely middle-class – evangelicals anxious to address the concerns of global irreligion and of Methodist and working-class 'irregularities'. Missionary practice came to create new networks through which a broad middle-class culture began to take shape.

2
Charity Begun at Home: Missionary Philanthropy and the New Middle Class in Sheffield

The first two decades of the nineteenth century saw the establishment of an expansive network of missionary philanthropic societies in England. The Society for Bettering the Condition of the Poor (SBCP), formed in London in 1796, spawned provincial auxiliaries and promoted a range of related reforming bodies. The extension of the British and Foreign Bible Society (BFBS) (from 1804), the establishment of monitorial and Sunday schools and a range of societies designed for the reform of the English poor, and the arrival during the 1810s of the auxiliary denominational missionary societies saw the consolidation of a popular missionary philanthropic movement. As I have shown in Chapter 1, domestic philanthropy was from the outset intimately connected with overseas missions. Frequently inspired by the commitment of missionaries to taking the gospel overseas – sometimes as a reaction against the perceived neglect of the 'heathen' at home, and often self-consciously promoted as part of the same global project – domestic philanthropy was acutely informed by the global civilising mission. The significance of the overseas and domestic missions, however, lay in more than their emergence in parallel in the 1790s and their shared personnel and strategies. During the early nineteenth century, the civilising mission came to supply a framework for middle-class self-representation as the carriers of global civilisation and social progress at home.

This chapter seeks to complicate the colonial and gender dimensions of early-nineteenth-century philanthropy. It explores the emergence of a public missionary culture in the

Yorkshire town of Sheffield in the first two decades of the nineteenth century. My concern in the first part of the chapter is with the small group of middle-class men who took a formative role in the development of the new philanthropic movement and emerging civic culture of early-nineteenth-century Sheffield. Philanthropic networks were a key part of men's social and civic identities. Benevolence was a central characteristic of a reformed, Christian middle-class manliness which prided itself on its sensitivity, morality and guidance to others.[1] As has been effectively demonstrated by R. J. Morris, philanthropic societies were among the multitude of associations – the book clubs, economic, scientific, political and religious societies – which were formative of the new male middle-class networks in London and the provinces. Their (often overlapping) memberships acted as a 'broker' of potential areas of conflict between men of different wealth and religious and political affiliation, enabling collaboration and the development of a shared public middle-class identity.[2] Positions of status within the missionary philanthropic movement mapped onto other sites of civic authority. The chapter begins with an examination of the context for the formation of the Sheffield SBCP in 1804. It addresses the new 'science of the poor' and changing attitudes to poverty, the 'French threat', and the global civilising mission. It explores the overlapping personnel of the range of new societies and, focusing on the Lancasterian and Sunday schools, discusses the representations of class and civilisation in contemporary reports and local histories which identified the missionary middle class as leaders of civic and national progress and overseers of a project of global change.

Missionary philanthropic strategies and networks were made not only in masculine arenas, but in a 'social' sphere which was extensively peopled by women and fundamentally shaped by the concerns of the 'domestic'. The representation of liberal philanthropic men as the sole architects of the culture of voluntarism and social progress in the English town is problematic.[3] In the second part of the chapter, I argue that domestic visitation, widely associated in histories of philanthropy with the work of the Glasgow divine, Thomas Chalmers, and the city missions of the 1830s and 1840s, had its genesis in women's domestic reform and home visiting within the missionary philanthropic societies of the 1800s and 1810s. It was this early practice that established familial and domestic issues at the core of the missionary agenda and the associated 'social' sphere of the nineteenth century. Domestic visiting did not represent an occasional excursion into the 'social' world by women who were helpmeets to men or who sought escape from 'colourless and restrictive' lives.[4] To the contrary, it amounted to a social movement which, shot through with ideas of civilisation and Christian progress, formed a key part of the confrontation between the evangelical middle class and popular culture that emerged from the crises of the 1790s and early 1800s.[5]

Middle-class men and philanthropic networks

Sheffield's philanthropic spark was ignited in 1804, as four men, recently acquainted through their positions as Overseers of the Poor, made the decision to form a Society for Bettering the Condition of the Poor. This group, termed the 'Four Friends', (Figure 1) comprised James Montgomery (1771–1854), newspaper editor, poet and hymnodist of rising reputation; Samuel Roberts (1763–1848), a manufacturer of silver plate and later campaigner on behalf of climbing boys, paupers and factory children; George Bennet (1774–1841), who had recently acquired a considerable inheritance which had made him a wealthy man; and Rowland Hodgson (1774–1837), another gentleman of independent means. Other men were present on the fringes of the group, most notably the cutlery manufacturer Thomas Asline Ward (1781–1871).[6]

Over the next two decades, the 'friends' were overwhelmingly influential in a range of voluntary bodies in Sheffield. The Aged Female Society, formed in 1810 for the purpose of systematising the activities of the various Female Friendly Societies for elderly single women and widows that had been in operation since the end of the eighteenth century, saw Hodgson, Bennet, Roberts and Montgomery (Figure 2) sharing the positions of chair, treasurer and secretary.[7] Montgomery and

Figure 1 'The Four Friends': George Bennet, Rowland Hodgson, James Montgomery and Samuel Roberts. (Courtesy of Sheffield Local Studies Library, s09433.)

Ward attended the meeting, also in 1810, to form the Sheffield Auxiliary Bible Society and at which Dr Steinkopff and the Reverends John Owen and Joseph Hughes of the parent BFBS were present.[8] They were also present at the gathering in the house of the Quaker John Hoyland in November 1812 to establish the Sheffield Bible Association, the 'active wing' of the Bible Society.[9] Bennet and Montgomery are lauded in their obituaries and in local histories for their roles in the Sunday School Union (1812), a federation of Sunday schools associated with the Congregational and Methodist chapels in Sheffield. Both men worked as Sunday school teachers, chaired meetings, wrote reports, addressed anniversary gatherings, and were generally involved in the supervision of the activities of the Union; Bennet also held Social Tea Meetings for Sunday school teachers at his Highfield home.[10] The 'friends' displayed collective energy and enthusiasm in the formation of denominational missionary societies: the Baptist and West Riding (LMS) Auxiliary Societies and the

Figure 2 James Montgomery. [B. Holl (Engraver). Courtesy of Sheffield Local Studies Library, s08148.]

Wesleyan Methodist Missionary Society (WMMS), were formed in 1813, and the Church Missionary Association (CMS) in 1816.[11] The longevity of their association with the aforementioned societies is impressive.[12] During the 1820s they participated in a second wave of activity which saw the formation of the Literary and Philosophical Society (1822), the Anti-slavery Society (1824), the Mechanics' Library (1823) and Mechanics' Institute (1832).[13]

The Sheffield Society for Bettering the Condition of the Poor was inspired by the London society of the same name, formed in 1796 by Wilberforce, Shute Barrington and Thomas Barnard. The Society operated in an essentially missionary mode, with similar organisations soon emerging at Clapham and Cork (1799), Edinburgh (1801), Bath and Oxford (both 1802). The Society publicised in its *Reports* a variety of 'models, inventions and experiments' believed to facilitate reform as part of its promotion of the 'science of the poor': methods for heating soup kitchens, machinery to replace climbing boys, systems of domestic visiting, the procurement of cottage gardens, whitewashing of cottages, dietary economics and a range of local initiatives, including Sunday schools in Berkshire, friendly societies in County Durham, village shops in Oxfordshire and spinning schools in Rutland.[14] All such 'accounts', many of which were written by Barnard, his wife, or prominent evangelicals such as Thomas Gisborne, were presented in the same 'scientific' format, consisting of a description of the scheme, followed by 'observations' and a summation, as if deduced from an experiment.[15]

While the London SBCP emerged out of the membership of the Proclamation Society and shared the concern to encourage the well-to-do to reform the poor, its immediate stimulus had been the war with France and the bad harvest of 1795–1796.[16] Concerned to alleviate distress, the Society sought to address the bad habits which it believed exacerbated poverty, in particular the lack of agency on the part of the poor to improve their conditions of life. Agency was understood as a moral quality, latent in all people and finding expression only within the context of a Christian life. An individual who lacked agency was not merely idle but, following Malthus, who famously moved away in his second expanded edition of his *Essay on Population* (1803) from his initial emphasis on the role of natural disasters in the control of populations to introduce the notion of 'moral restraint',[17] potentially indigent and therefore a threat to national prosperity and beyond that to civilisation itself. A member of the Bible Society, Lancaster's Committee, and a supporter of workers' savings banks, the parson's intervention was less dramatic than is sometimes represented. His advocation of charity which 'makes itself acquainted with the objects which it relieves' and which 'enters into their houses, informs itself not only of their wants, but of their habits and dispositions' chimed in with philanthropic practice.[18]

The Sheffield Society for Bettering the Condition of the Poor echoed the analyses of the parent SBCP in London in locating poverty in the dispositions of the poor. Poverty was not material, but a product of mind. It could be genuinely ameliorated only by the 'moral and mental' change which would see the poor take responsibility for their improvement. Other factors, it was conceded, exacerbated a culture of pauperism. The 'improvident habits too commonly indulged in' by the poor were often the result of a bad start in life rather than an inherent failing. Poverty itself mitigated against motivation: it 'blunted and almost destroyed' the 'energy and cheerfulness so necessary to industry and domestic economy', and produced a 'languor of dependency, ... which almost paralysed any effort to surmount such depression'.[19] But it was human weakness and immorality that were believed to exercise the most debilitating impact upon individuals, preventing them from seeing, or even desiring, the possibility of improvement. Countering the predilection for 'indiscriminate charity' which was believed to have characterised the eighteenth century, the Sheffield SBCP provided philanthropic support for the independent action of the poor, 'seconding the efforts of the Poor on their own behalf'.[20]

That the SBCP was formed in 1804 hints at the place of the philanthropic venture within a wider response to radicalism and the panic about an imminent French invasion.[21] Sheffield was certainly a town ripe for missionary intervention. The home of the cutlery trade, it was notorious from the 1790s for a working class with considerable sympathy for political radicalism. The appearance of the Sheffield Society for Constitutional Information in 1792, a precedent by a few months to the London Corresponding Society, and the demonstrations over the next decade against enclosure, the war, taxation and the price of bread, and in support of political reform, all signified profound alarm for the town's well-to-do.[22] The discovery that there were many radicals among the town's Methodists, including members of the more restrained Wesleyans as well as the democratic and schismatic New Connexion (1797), added to the mood of anxiety.[23] The Volunteers had been formed in 1792, and George Bennet and Samuel Roberts became early, and representative, members. Montgomery's conservatism was less fully-fledged. As his 'Ode to the Volunteers' suggests, it was the edginess of the authorities, rather than an expansive radical sympathy, that saw him incarcerated in York Castle on two occasions in 1795–1796.[24]

The political threat in Sheffield was exacerbated by the noted cultural and geographical separateness of the working class from the town's respectable elements. On the one hand, was the perceived absorption of the poor in a popular culture which centred on the pub and other unruly pastimes. On the other, physical separation, largely a result of Sheffield's geographical organisation as a collection of small industrial villages established along the rivers running through the town, was believed to foster insularity.[25] (For Sheffield's industrial east end in the early nineteenth century, see Figure 3). Even the 'little mester' system of

Figure 3 Sheffield from Attercliffe Road, 1819. [G. Cooke (Engraver), E. Blore (Artist). Courtesy of Sheffield Local Studies Library, s11421.]

industrial organisation within the predominant tool and cutlery trade was viewed as problematic. Characterised by small units of production in domestic and small-scale workshops, it was noted for its flexibility, as men were not tied to one master but were frequently able to set up independently, often sub-contracting work to apprentices. Allowing men to become both employee and 'little mester', the trade was worryingly without a strong employer-class.[26]

Indeed, the town's middle class was small. Sheffield was neither the 'midland metropolis' of Birmingham nor the home of a sizeable manufacturing and merchant class comparable to that of the cottonopolis across the Pennines.[27] The occupations of some among the 'friends' nonetheless point to the late-eighteenth-century developments within the occupational elite. The production of crucible steel and silver plate led to the growth of a substantial merchant–manufacturer interest. The arrival in 1787 of the *Sheffield Register*, one of the new provincial middle-class pro-reform newspapers [later to become Montgomery's *Iris* (Figure 4)], marked the beginnings of a professional elite as well as an emergent culture of polite society.[28] While the involvement of the big industrialists in bourgeois voluntary culture developed with the coming of the 'steel giants' from mid-century onwards, public life in early-nineteenth-century Sheffield was dominated by smaller manufacturers and professional men.

Sheffield's philanthropic community was profoundly shaped by the experience of religious revival. Evangelicalism had been powerfully received in Yorkshire in the 1780s and 1790s, among both artisans and the more well-to-do. Methodism was particularly strong in Sheffield, its rising status represented in the opening of the opulent Carver Street chapel in 1803.[29] James Montgomery, raised as a Moravian and who had been a student at Fulneck School while his parents worked (and died) as missionaries in the Caribbean, was heavily influenced by the Sheffield Methodist community.[30] Roberts, although an Anglican, had been taken as a child by his mother to hear Whitefield preach on Sheffield Moor, and retained a great sympathy for the movement.[31] Bennet's nonconformity was that of Old

Figure 4 Iris Office, No. 12 Hartshead. (Courtesy of Sheffield Local Studies Library, s16815.)

Dissent: after a dissolute youth he had become a 'serious Christian' and prominent member of Queen Street Congregational Chapel, built in 1790 and, with Reverend James Boden (of the LMS) at its helm, soon the hub of Sheffield evangelicalism.[32] Indeed, the interdenominational make-up of the 'four friends' reflected the fortunes of Anglicanism and Old and New Dissent in the town where, despite the arrival of the evangelical Thomas Sutton as Vicar of Sheffield in 1805, nonconformity triumphed well into the mid-century.[33] While Rowland Hodgson remained with the Church, another notable philanthropist, Thomas Asline Ward, was in the first decade of the century moving away from his Anglican roots towards Unitarianism, and was thus a representative of Sheffield's small but immensely influential community of rational Dissenters at Upper Chapel.[34]

Sheffield's evangelicals cherished a culture of inter-denominationalism. As Montgomery stated on the occasion of the first WMMS meeting in the town in November 1813, missionary activity was a site on which individuals of different status and denominations could collaborate; despite their differences, they were not 'discordant' but were 'blended till they are lost, like the prismatic colours in a ray of pure and perfect light'.[35] Some 'blending' is evident: the relationship between the Anglican National School Society and nonconformist Lancasterians, for example, fraught with competition and bitterness across the country, was in Sheffield extremely cordial. Montgomery and Hodgson, the latter secretary of the local National District Society, promoted both schools. The Lancasterian Schools accommodated Anglican children prior to the building of the National School in 1813.[36] Their common purpose was expressed in the 1818 *Report* of the Boys' Lancasterian School, which claimed 'these respectable institutions [not] as opponents, but as fellow helpers in the same great cause of humanity and kindness.'[37] In the same spirit, pupils from the (separate) Anglican Sunday school were able to join with the Sunday School Union for part of their annual anniversary celebrations and processions from 1816.[38]

The global civilising mission was central to the evangelical identity and practice of Sheffield's cultural elite. Montgomery's work as journalist and poet provided a rich backdrop for the town's missionary endeavours. With Bennet and Roberts, he was an active supporter of the first wave of abolitionism which saw the ending of Britain's involvement in the slave trade in 1807. His reputation as an evangelical poet was soon to be established with the publication in 1809 of *The West Indies*, a panoramic poem which celebrated the transformation of the 'heathen' African, worshipper of 'demon-Gods, in hideous forms', into the 'happy pilgrim' of the Christian world.[39] A second epic poem, *Greenland* (1819), which preceded his prolific concentration on prose and shorter missionary poetry during the 1820s, combined an exploration of Scandinavian and Icelandic lore and Romantic descriptions of landscape with the celebration of the

Moravian 'moral revolution' which had successfully reclaimed a population 'almost universally, from idolatry and barbarism'.[40] Montgomery used the pages of the *Sheffield Iris* to promote sermons and collections for missions, visits of missionaries and 'native converts' and news of Christian progress across the globe.[41]

Subscription lists appended to the Annual Reports reveal the extensive participation in the voluntary network of middle-class men and – as will be discussed below – women.[42] For middle-class men, philanthropic societies were critically important 'new arenas of social power'.[43] They were significant in establishing a form of authority – as negotiated, based on expertise and grounded in moral righteousness – and a sense of involvement in a progressive movement. New local, regional and national networks, established via the circuits of voluntary association and shaped by the global civilising mission, formed civic sites from which to contest the authority of the traditional elite. Positions of authority within the hierarchical committees of voluntary societies came to map onto other sites of authority within early-nineteenth-century towns. The principal seat-holders within voluntary associations – the chairmen, treasurers and secretaries – occupied important positions as Overseers of the Poor, town trustees and members of the committees for street-lighting and highways, gas and water companies, and of the General Infirmary and Dispensary, all of which were central to the administration of urban affairs prior to incorporation.[44] Achievements were celebrated in appropriately public ways. Road names and public buildings reflected their status, as did the 'Montgomery medal' at the newly opened School of Design. Busts and paintings were placed in the Cutler's Hall and Bluecoat School, and statues and memorials constructed for display in the town. Samuel Roberts was commemorated by a stained-glass window in the Anglican Cathedral, while Sheffield General Cemetery became home to posthumous monuments to George Bennet's missionary triumphs in the South Seas (see Chapter 6) and to James Montgomery (Figure 5).[45]

Figure 5 James Montgomery's Monument, Sheffield General Cemetery. (Now situated outside the Anglican Cathedral. Courtesy of Sheffield Local Studies Library, s07702).

The monitorial system and global civilisation

The reports of the Lancasterian and National schools and the various inter- and denominational Sunday schools, state most clearly the importance of the global civilising mission as a reference point within domestic philanthropy. Interestingly, the monitorial system had dual origins in missions to the 'heathen' at home and overseas. The Reverend Andrew Bell's Male Asylum, stimulus for the Anglican National Society, was established in Madras in 1797 to provide a basic education for children of British soldiers and Indian mothers; while Joseph Lancaster's

Borough Road school opened in a poor area of south London the following year.[46] Lancaster branched outwards: his lecture tours and the formation of the Lancasterian School Society (1808) saw the adoption of his methods in schools established by philanthropists throughout the country; following the formation of the (renamed) British and Foreign School Society in 1814, his methods became popularised in mission schools overseas.[47] As Lancaster's schools expanded to the empire, so Bell's system was brought home. British Anglicans, opposed to the non-denominationalism of the Lancasterian system[48] and fearful that nonconformists were leading the way in matters of national education, formed the National School Society in 1811 and began the process of establishing schools in towns throughout Britain.

The monitorial system in Sheffield, which saw the opening of a Lancasterian Boys' School in August 1809, had first been promoted by Montgomery in the *Sheffield Iris* in 1807, and received further stimulus from Lancaster's visit to the town in February 1809.[49] The new school catered for boys and, prior to the opening of the Lancasterian School of Industry for Girls in 1815, girls, of all denominations.[50] The system was unremarkable for the content of the curriculum, combining religious instruction with spelling, reading and writing; girls, like those supervised by Lancaster's sister, Mary, at Borough Road, were instructed in needlework.[51] As Richard Johnson has noted, the Lancasterian and National schools shared a 'common language' of 'habit', 'order' and 'restraint' and represented an opposition to aspects of a popular culture which were identified as deficient and disorderly.[52] The position of the teacher on a raised platform at the front of the class allowed him to survey monitors and pupils. The use of unpaid child monitors as schoolmasters' assistants presented to all children the possibility of becoming a monitor and, it was believed, allowed them to internalise authority, rather than merely having it imposed upon them. Children were given rewards for good behaviour and beating was avoided, although punishment was ministered through a variety of other means.[53] The requirement to dress simply, cut hair short, arrive at school looking neat and clean, attend a place of worship on the Sabbath, and the later imposition of a fee, on the grounds that little value was placed 'on that which costs nothing to obtain', established the terms of their children's attendance most likely to have an impact upon the parents.[54] This system was subsequently adopted in the National Schools, opened in 1813,[55] and across the range of popular Sunday schools which formed the Sunday School Union (1812).

The author of the first Annual Report of the Methodist Sunday school, represented the provision of popular education as evidence of Britain's lofty place on the scale of civilisation:

> In every civilised nation of the world, whether antient [*sic*] or modern, the education of youth has been regarded as an object of the greatest importance. As men have emerged from barbarity, they have gradually risen to the invention of arts, a sense of propriety, and a love of social order; and with the discovery of science, parental and filial affection have acquired greater strength and tenderness, children have experienced more of their parents' care.[56]

The poor were capable of responding to such improvement, according to the Sunday School Union Report of the following year, precisely because of their higher starting point in the scale of civilisation:

> If Negroes, Greenlanders, Esquimaux, and Hottentots, the rudest and wildest barbarians, to whom the very use of letters was at first incomprehensible, eagerly and easily learn to read and write at any age... how can it be doubted, that even the most ignorant persons in this country may soon be taught the rudiments of common education, wherever there is the will to become scholars, since they begin with advantages of previous knowledge unheard of by savages.[57]

When compared to other missionary subjects, it was argued, the English poor were well placed to reach civilisation, with the assistance of their more Christian and civilised teachers and cultural mentors.

For girls, civilisation demanded that they acquired the domestic skills of kitchen and house work, laundry and needlework alongside the reading, writing and scripture lessons they shared with boys. The Reverend James Mather, minister at Howard Street Congregational Chapel, in a speech canvassing support for the girls' school in Sheffield prior to its opening in 1815, called attention to

> the advantages, which must result to Families, to Society and to the rising generation, from female education. Females were never designed by Providence either to draw the sword in the field of battle, to push the bayonet, or to storm the redoubt; but their stations are not less important. They stay at home: and while they do this, they stamp their own character on the families where they reside; and so great is Female Influence, that every society with which they are connected derives its character from them. Where the word of God is not known, Women are regarded as little better than beasts. And what are the Men in such places? Are they not mere savages? But in those places where woman occupies the place which the Lord has allotted her, the Men are rational, affectionate and kind.[58]

Women were responsible not only for the next generation of citizens, but also for male members of their families: only the domesticated working-class woman would ensure that her husband and sons wanted to spend their leisure hours at home rather than indulging in drink and vulgar recreations. In Montgomery's words, 'the peace of society depends so much upon the morals of the lower class of females'.[59] Middle-class concerns about working-class females came even closer to home, as women and girls were employed in middle-class households: 'As servants, they nurse our children, and have our property, our peace and our comfort in their hands.'[60] Domesticity was both the mainstay of society and a hallmark of progressive Christian civilisation, a signifier of British superiority to 'savage' races throughout the world.

The *Reports* of the Sheffield Boys Lancasterian School continued to negotiate the fear that to provide education for the poor rendered them vulnerable to seditious literature, unfitting 'the Children for becoming domestic servants... generat[ing] in them a spirit of dictation and a habit of command, that it tends to render them at once idle and insolent'.[61] But the message from sermons and *Reports* of the schools and Sunday schools was overwhelmingly positive in tone. Boys formed the majority of the 'thoughtless, headstrong children', some of whom had gambled and been involved in riots or in prison, who subsequently displayed 'diligence, steadiness and integrity'. Joseph Gilbert's sermon at the first anniversary of the Sheffield Sunday School Union in 1813 articulated the civilising impact of schooling on boys who became 'successively honest, industrious and orderly servants; prosperous mechanics or tradesmen; affectionate husbands; and finally discreet parents bringing up their children in the fear of God, and teaching them the knowledge of truth.'[62] The Union expanded to include a number of Schools for Young Men, designed to stem 'youthful depravity' and keep them away from the sorts of 'degradations' that finally resulted in imprisonment or transportation to Botany Bay.[63] A Lancasterian education was similarly believed to inculcate in male pupils obedience to parents and an understanding of 'civil duties', 'respect to superiors', 'reverence to authorities' and 'honour to the king', amounting to 'a spirit of order, industry and enlightened loyalty amongst the labouring classes of society'.[64] In some cases, despite having to leave to go to work, they had found their way back to the school, crying and begging to be readmitted. Letters of gratitude, written to the committee by parents and ex-pupils, were incorporated within the narrative of progress, a final vindication of the rightfulness of those who had campaigned for the extension of instruction to the working class.[65]

The annual reports publicly paraded stories of success with the girls. The sponsors felt reassured that the two hundred who left annually were 'carrying knowledge, principle, order, religion, [and] happiness' into their own families and those where they were employed, although due to the pressures of finding employment most girls stayed at the school for less than two years.[66] Tales abound of 'careless, inattentive, disobedient' girls transformed into godly young women, paying greater attention to cleanliness and decency, and demonstrating 'an increase in affection, prompt and universal obedien tion to parental authority'. The subse 'domestic felicity' rendered home 'what earthly paradise'. Other model pupils incluc and crippled children, those who converte bers, and others less fortunate who had a upon the teachers, and those whose dying w Lord'.[67]

Despite the clarity of their aims and wishes, the success or otherwise of the monitorial schools is notoriously difficult to measure. Indeed, parents often preferred the flexibility provided by local dame schools or the very popular Sunday schools. The latter, run by the same philanthropists, were less expensive, with fewer rules and no charity-like uniforms, and were more compatible with the rhythms of a working life. In the case of Red Hill and Allen Street Sunday Schools in Sheffield, they had the added attraction of teaching writing.[68] The Reports suggest an awareness that successes were partial, that 'only like the scattered grains of corn promiscuously rising from a barren soil, or like the fruit transported from its native climate and forced in its growth by artificial power . . . we do not expect perfection however we desire it.' As implied by such images of cultivation, the educators believed themselves to be 'sowing for a future harvest'. Moreover, through the activities of the BFSS, which saw (mainly Quaker) women supporting mission schools in 'heathen' nations, they were to enable the 'harvest of the world', as the extension of civilisation beyond 'the shivering children of the north' was to be taken to 'the black, the brown, and the tawny offspring of the East and of the South'.[69] While such claims warrant greater scrutiny and will be discussed later in this chapter, the certainty of the authors, often expressed in the Biblical language of sowing and reaping, is striking. Schooling was part of an inevitable march of progress which, by the early nineteenth century, had placed England near to the peak of civilisation.

Women, domestic reform and the visiting system

According to her contemporary Lucy Aikin, the 'rage' for domestic visiting was inspired by Hannah More's character, Lady her popular novel *Coelebs in Search of a Wife* (1809).[70] *Coelebs* helped to nurture philanthropic commitment, estic reform was already at the heart of missionary prac- ice, brought to the attention of the philanthropic community by More's work at least 10 years earlier.[71] By the time of the publication of *Coelebs*, the practice was being taken up by the provincial women members of the auxiliary Bible Societies who determined to extend the focus of the BFBS from supplying Bibles in mother tongues for missionaries working overseas or in non-English speaking areas of the British Isles, to include reform at home.[72] Within a few years, domestic visiting was also practiced by the auxiliary missionary societies, as agents combined canvassing for monetary contributions with the promotion of reform in the home. By the 1820s, visitors were frequently members of a range of associations, including the new monitorial school societies and others concerned with the reform of inmates at lodging houses, the infirmary, the workhouse and the prison.[73]

The first domestic visiting committee had been formed, perhaps not surprisingly, at Clapham in 1799. The committee, in the early days involving men as well as women, had divided working-class areas into eight districts to enable a systematic approach to the neighbourhood. The visitors promoted domestic reform and were concerned to investigate the lives of the poor, to inform themselves of 'the *circumstances* and *character* of every person within their district…' This, they believed, would enable a more thorough knowledge of the conditions of poverty and foster better relationships between the poor and themselves. Adopting an embryonic social scientific method, observations and changes were recorded in a journal. The visitors were supported by lady sub-treasurers, a 'medical gentleman' who provided advice on inoculations and medical issues, and by two women in paid employment: a lady who taught knitting and reading at a school for girls in the vicinity, and a poorer but respectable woman – 'clean, assiduous and skilled in cookery' – who held the stores for the sick.[74] Following this pattern of organisation, the Sheffield SBCP formed a Committee of Visitors in 1807, during which year 135 families were brought under their 'care' by weekly visits.[75]

It was the face-to-face nature of the domestic visit that was believed to be so valuable as a strategy for reform. The encounter with godly ladies was similar in its effects to the assumed impact of reading the Scriptures: exposure to the 'benign and civilising influence' of their social superiors would create an 'abstract Christian subject with similar attributes of behaviour and belief, regardless of cultural conditions, material environment, or pre-existing religious beliefs.'[76] Central to this change was the stimulation of agency and responsibility. As explained by Hannah Kilham, author of the Annual Reports of the Sheffield SBCP, it was the mind alone, that 'seat of principle and spring of reason', that could bring about a desire for change: 'Our endeavours must be directed to their *minds*, to their *principles*. We must lead them, if possible, to think and feel for themselves wherein their best welfare consists . . . ' Material relief was discouraged, except in the case of the sick or women in their 'confinements', where meat was provided for broth. Instead, the 'great object' of domestic visitors was 'to induce and to second the exertions of the poor on their own behalf', 'to incite in them additional solicitude for the proper support of their own character.'[77] This was to be achieved through 'affectionate conversations'. As Kilham elaborated in the 1813 *Report*:

> To prevent evil, it has often been remarked, is both better and easier than to remove it. The sudden renovation of a destitute dwelling, or the clothing of an indigent family by gratuitous supplies, may indeed arrest the attention by the contrast it presents, and be admired and applauded as the fruit of compassion; but to meet the poor by kindness and encouragement *before they are sunk into absolute indigence* – by friendly attention, advice and assistance to stimulate and support their good intentions and endeavours, is a conduct which having its influence on the *minds* of the poor, as well as on their circumstances, will be far more beneficial in its effects, than that in which the *agency of the individuals themselves* is not called forth for the improvement of their condition.[78]

Kindly, maternal and nurturing, examples of piety and morality, lady visitors believed themselves to be equipped to combat what they saw as the confusion, stagnation, misery and unbelief of working-class homes and the fundamental lack of agency that prevented positive change.

Descriptions of the passivity of missionary subjects prior to their introduction to the lady visitors are most overwhelming in the Reports of the Society for Aged Females (1810), the second Sheffield society to adopt the visiting system.[79] Sketches of 'typical' lives tell of women 'worn down with personal slavery and long suffering', unable to support themselves, originally because of inadequate parents, who had forced them to become 'household slaves' and to miss out on an education due to their responsibility for younger siblings; or because of a poor choice of husband who, either due to misfortune or his improvidence and immorality, had been unable to protect his dependants from falling on hard times.[80] The Society conceded to provide material relief for elderly, pious widows who were no longer able to work for a living, but saw its main duty as working 'to animate, support, and encourage' the women to take responsibility for their well-being.

The promotion of 'comfort and welfare', 'industry, economy and order' in the working-class home required instruction as well as influence.[81] Kilham's solution was to lend books 'in which are examples of piety' and to distribute tracts, composed by herself, which addressed domestic and religious themes, in the hope that their display in the homes of the poor would act as additional stimuli to their improvement. *Family Maxims* (1817), a small book designed to be displayed in the homes of the poor, exhorted the poor to hard work, 'self-discipline', 'honesty' and 'neglect': 'Retire early to rest, and be "early to rise". Industry promotes health, order and happiness'; 'Use every endeavour to make home a scene of happiness'; and 'Wholesome food, decent clothing, and a decent dwelling are all to be desired if we value health and comfort; but these may all be spoiled and lost by idleness and neglect'.[82] The Sheffield ladies also supplied lime with which to whitewash houses, and a number of women were loaned equipment and materials for spinning and knitting, their produce placed for sale in a shop in the town. Women were encouraged to deposit weekly savings with the Thrift Club, in order to eventually purchase subsidised household commodities such as rugs and blankets. Through holding their own Deposit Books, they were to learn how to be in control of their family's finances.[83] Kilham, a Quaker school-teacher, also saw such visiting as an important element in the education of young middle-class girls, and sometimes enlisted the help of pupils at her school when making her visiting rounds. In her autobiography, Mary Howitt recalled a time as a 12-year-old pupil when she accompanied her teacher on visits to areas of 'broken-up ground and half-built ruinous houses'.[84]

Domestic visiting involved Sheffield's lady visitors in a process of 'strict investigation'. As part of their rounds, they made enquiries concerning the circumstances of the household, especially the employment of the occupants and religious education of their children. This strategy, a derivative of the new 'science of the poor', had been praised in Clapham for enabling the visitors to become 'better qualified to afford them judicious relief, and to distinguish between the deserving and the worthless', and in Sheffield assisted in the delineation of the 'barrier between poverty and indigence'.[85] It was believed to enable the Society to target the many women who could be 'elevated above their former degraded condition' and to facilitate identification of those who were 'indolent, vicious and profligate', believed unlikely to rise above the 'filth, extravagance or listlessness' of their condition and who were therefore unworthy of assistance.[86] Empiricist methods were valued for their professed neutrality. Hannah Kilham insisted that philanthropists were 'disinterested participants', merely exposing the facts about individual lives through 'bringing the general state of poor families into view'. Homes, like the prisons she visited in Sheffield and Wakefield, were 'receptacles of sorrow out of sight' that needed to be explored and brought into public view.[87] 'The first step towards bettering the condition of the poor', she wrote,

> is to *know* what that state really is, and this by persons who have judgement and feeling to improve their condition, and

> have the power to be instruments to its improvement. The state of the poor will be best *known by seeing them* in their own houses, and *hearing from themselves* the affecting detail of their sufferings and privations.[88]

Seeing, exposing, knowing: these processes were not impartial but were critical to classifications of the poor as deserving or undeserving, respectable or indigent. Despite the emphasis on allowing the poor a degree of self-representation, the process of 'hearing from themselves' was in tension with the educative, leading role accorded to middle-class visitors. It was the ladies who had the necessary 'judgement and feeling', the moral authority, with which to clearly see and accurately assess the situations of the poor.

Agency was similarly expressed strictly in terms of that believed by the middle class to be appropriate for the poor. Any evidence of a shift to a cheerful, animated, resigned-but-combative attitude to poverty found its way into the SBCP and Aged Female Society Reports. These celebrated the 'increased attention in the mothers of poor children to a decent and creditable manner of clothing their families' and the 'increased cleanliness in their dwellings, and decency in their appearance'.[89] 'A great change for the better is evident in the domestic habits of the humblest classes here', wrote the author of the 1821 *Report*: 'a more general attention to cleanliness and domestic comfort is very obvious; and the visitors have the consolation to see much improvement in the care of infants and in the education of children.'[90] Working-class women may indeed have become more active, but the agency accorded them by visitors was recognised only in terms of a proximity to middle-class ideals of femininity. It was only through adopting the domestic practices of middle-class ladies that working-class women were seen to have had their agency restored.

Annual Reports of voluntary societies are cultural artefacts, produced with the intention of displaying the work of the society and affirming its purpose, as well as accounting for the spending of subscriptions. Their structure underlined the participation of members who, as names on lists of subscribers or suppliers of domestic vignettes, became agents of conversion and reform.[91] The reports constructed a public knowledge of poverty, based on an identification of poverty and immorality as inherent in the dispositions and 'cultural deficit' of the poor. Their emphasis on moral reform precluded any discussion of the material circumstances which exacerbated poverty in the early-industrial period: the shift from a rural to urban environment, the inadequacy of the family wage and the erosion of familial assistance, the neighbourhood safety net and of paternalist forms of charitable assistance or public relief. Obscured too are the survival strategies of the poor by which they might 'fit themselves into the positions required by the donors at the moment of the transaction and then to apply the gift (as far as they were able) to their own real needs.'[92] That 'some remain in filth, extravagance or listlessness', and others show instances of indifference and resistance, are hinted at in footnotes or in occasional warnings to the ladies to visit in pairs and take the necessary care.[93] Lurking beneath the positive, progressive trajectories of the Reports, these are suggestive of the anxiety that the poor would fail to provide 'the return "gift" ' expected of them: the 'status of being deserving.'[94]

Despite their delight at instances of personal transformation and expressions of agency, it was never the intention of the visitors that working-class women should become too much like themselves.[95] The aim of domestic reform was not to eradicate poverty; that was, according to the Bible, neither possible nor desirable. The authors of the *Ninth Report of the Female Friendly Society for the Relief of Widows and Single Women* (1817) reproduced a lengthy quotation from a speech by Joseph Hughes, secretary of the Bible Society, in which he dismissed as 'impious and absurd' attempts to challenge 'that mysterious economy, which presents the offspring of the same Almighty Parent in situations so unlike and unequal.' Hughes explained:

> The difference between individual and individual may often be reduced, and the endeavour to reduce it on a plan both practicable and prudent, is at once indicative and productive of the sublimest virtues; on the part of the elevated it implies condescension and kindness; on the part of the

> depressed, it awakens the hope and the gratitude, which attach in some degree to human benefactors, but supremely regard the Almighty.[96]

It was the *effort* to reduce the 'difference', the missionary relationship itself, that was most valuable. It reflected well upon the philanthropist and stimulated in the poor a desire for betterment, a respect for their social superiors and gratitude for the acts of a benevolent God. Philanthropy thus enabled the 'conversion' of the 'apparent evil' of poverty into an 'occasion of infinite good', and all without disturbing the natural (and Biblical) presence of the poor.

Women and the missionary public

If domestic visiting was thus far unproblematic, its adoption by the Bible and Missionary Societies of the 1810s introduced new dynamics and areas of contention. The Bible Societies formed throughout the country as a result of the national lecture tours undertaken by the Reverends John Owen and Joseph Hughes and Dr Charles Steinkopff soon sprouted an 'active wing', an often female-dominated auxiliary, committed to gathering contributions and the delivery of Bibles and Testaments to the homes of the poor.[97] On these visits, the women promoted domestic reform in much the same manner as the SBCP. In Sheffield, where the original Bible Society had been formed in 1810 and the Bible Association in 1812, Montgomery emphasised the compatibility of domestic reform and the scriptural blueprint for living provided by the Bible. Writing in the *Sheffield Iris* in 1819 of the '18,000 families previously destitute of the Scriptures' and who now benefited from being visited 'at their houses, not here and there, but by house-row, from street to street', Montgomery reassured his readership that:

> The religion of the Bible will have taught its readers not only their duty towards God and their neighbour, but will have caused a change of life, conversation, and habits, correspondent with the change of heart which is its first, and last, perfect

> work. Industry, order, cleanliness, economy, sobriety, with looks, and words, and deeds of kindness, will have succeeded indolence, confusion, dirt, waste, riot, swearing, selfishness, quarrelling and fighting.[98]

Personal transformations were noted, as domestic abodes were turned from 'dungeons', individuals made the transition from recipient to small-time benefactor, and the poor generally were 'become better children, apprentices, labourers, fathers, mothers, relatives, friends, neighbours, citizens and subjects.'[99]

Montgomery's pronouncements were supported by C. S. Dudley, the BFBS's first domestic agent who travelled the country assisting thousands of ladies in towns throughout Britain to organise to their greatest efficiency.[100] In his *Analysis of the System of the Bible Society* (1821), Dudley insisted upon the compatibility of domestic reform with Bible distribution: 'The advantages of cleanliness, sobriety, and economy', he wrote,

> – the duty of loyalty, and subordination to their superiors – the importance of having their children educated, and of learning to read themselves – and the blessings attending a state of independence and freedom from pauperism, may be, and in numerous cases are suggested, without the slightest departure from the fundamental principle of the Bible Societies.

He insisted that ladies made such suggestions with delicacy, encouraging rather than remonstrating, and demonstrating patience in the face of ignorance. The success of the method was supported by further vignettes: of women who had so felt the benefit of buying their own Bible that they were now subscribing in order to be able to give a Bible away; of the 'comfort' of being able to contribute a regular shilling to the Society; of a child reading the Bible to her dying mother; and an old woman buying a Bible for her grandchild.[101]

There was nonetheless a critical and controversial difference between the work of the BFBS (and the missionary societies as they emerged in the next few years) and the visiting committees of the SBCP, the Aged Female Society and other similar organisations. The distribution of Bibles and collection of money for the missionary fund involved a financial exchange, which was problematic on two fronts. Firstly, the reconstruction of the poor as benefactors within the missionary relationship, an important innovation by the Bible Society, led to claims that the poor 'are *oppressed* by the contributions required of them, and that they are induced to give what would be better spent on their families'.[102] Evangelicals maintained that the agency of the poor, demonstrated in their contribution to buying a Bible was part of the process of civilisation. The making of regular payments towards purchase or part-purchase of a Bible required making choices, forward planning, careful thought and frugality. Its distance from indiscriminate charity clearly cheered philanthropists: as Dudley explained, 'a *gratuitous* distribution could not satisfy the minds of those who wished to counteract the degrading influence of Pauperism, to check the progress of Infidelity, and to extend the empire of Religion and Morality.'[103] 'By such conduct', he explained, 'the poor are elevated from the ranks of beggars, to that of the benefactors of mankind'. Dudley quoted Thomas Chalmers to support his point:

> It brings up their economy to a higher pitch, but it does so, not in the way which they resist, but in the way which they choose. The single circumstance of its being a *voluntary* act, forms the defence and the answer to all the clamours of an affected sympathy.– 'You take from the poor?' 'No, they give.' – 'You take beyond their ability?' – 'Of this, they are the best judges.' – 'You abridge their comforts.' – 'No, there is a comfort in the exercise of charity: there is a comfort in the act of lending a hand to a noble enterprise.'[104]

Benevolence was important for a healthy Christian society. In James Montgomery's words, the willingness of the Sheffield poor to donate their 'mite' to public collections and to the Bible Associations reflected the 'privilege to do good, as well as to receive it, and their *duty* to exercise that privilege'.[105]

If asking the poor to contribute to the purchase of their own Bible was controversial, asking them to give financial assistance to the evangelising of the 'heathen' elsewhere was even more problematic. Missionary societies had been formed throughout the country from 1813, many in response to Basil Woodd's tour and the sermons and publicity surrounding the campaign to include support for missionaries in the renewed charter of the East India Company. Yorkshire saw a particularly impressive missionary explosion, beginning with the formation in Leeds of the West Riding Missionary Society in 1813, and in Sheffield an auxiliary Juvenile Missionary Society (also LMS, 1813), Methodist Missionary Society (1813) and the Church Missionary Association (1816).[106] Missionary Society supporters countered charges of 'oppression' of the poor through their emphasis on the 'reflex principle': that supporting missions overseas revitalised individual religious commitment and so assisted in the popularity of the home churches.[107] The Reverend Richard Watson (1813–1833), a founder member of the WMMS in Leeds in 1813, and its secretary from 1816, explained at the meeting founding the Sheffield WMMS:

> Charity to the Heathen is charity begun at home. This is not difficult to prove. We cannot take a step towards evangelizing the Heathen, without entering into many inquiries as to the extent of our moral wretchedness; and such inquiries are eminently useful to ourselves... [I]f, by comparing our light with the darkness of the Heathen, our riches with their poverty, we learn to prize these blessings more, and to use them better; then, Sir, Missionary efforts will prove a blessing to us, to our Societies, and to our country, and *charity to the heathen will be charity begun at home.*[108]

Even if the people had few blessings bestowed upon them, they would know their superiority to the 'heathen' overseas.

It was not only the contributions of the poor that excited opposition, but the role of women in extracting them. While men publicised the cause and raised funds, most vigorously through the missionary anniversary, a week-long event of sermons, speeches and collections, it was women who usually canvassed local neighbourhoods to promote domestic reform and solicit funds.[109] For some, this financial exchange – to use Howsam's term in relation to the BFBS, 'Bible transaction' – required little comment.[110] Dudley played down the degree of the woman missionary's transgression in making the seemingly conservative point that all public exposure devolved on men, while women's weekly visits, lasting an hour at the most, did not detract from their domestic duties or forfeit their delicacy. But for some, the participation of lady philanthropists in soliciting financial contributions saw women trespassing into a potentially unfeminine territory and led to a new set of anxieties about feminine propriety and respectability. The nature of women's participation – 'the zeal and spirit, the forwardness and intrusive boldness of an active member of a Ladies' Bible Association' – raised fears as to how it was possible 'to retain the softened diffidence and virgin modesty which form the great charm of the female bosom.'[111] Such antagonism required more than a degree of justification, and led into direct engagements with the meaning of the 'public' and women's relationship to it.[112]

While the 'public' in Dudley's use of the term certainly referred to a world of men, he frequently gave voice to the view that the 'religious public' was a suitable place for women.[113] His *Analysis* of 1821 drew upon accounts of women Bible-sellers from throughout the United Kingdom. The ladies of the Paisley Female Bible Association drew inspiration from the Bible to argue that the public needed women's influence:

> It is becoming in women as well as in men to aid so valuable a purpose. It is equally the duty of females to believe and obey the Gospel; and if Mary chose that better part which shall not be taken away, even the doctrine of Jesus as the one thing needful: if Lydia attended to the things spoken of by Paul; and if Priscilla assisted in teaching Appollos the way of GOD more perfectly; surely it is the duty of female Christians now to follow the examples; and not only to be religious in private, but in public also, encouraging by secret prayer and public exertion every pious undertaking.

Ladies from Glasgow also remembered 'the Marys and Priscillas, the Tryphenas and Tryphosas', the women who aided St Paul to give 'active cooperation in the cause of the Gospel'. The authors of the *Sixth Annual Report of the Glasgow Auxiliary Bible Society* drew more explicitly on the stadial context of their work. Quoting from an Address from the prelate of the Protestant Episcopal Church of America to the Female Bible Society of Philadelphia, they urged all to:

> Look at the condition of women in the countries where the religion of the Gospel is unknown; and in all the arrangements of domestic life will be found a comment on the position. Can it then be out of the sphere of your sex, to be actively engaged in disseminating a system of truth and morals, which has so excellent a bearing immediately on your interests; and, through you, on whatever contributes to the rectitude, to the decorum, and to the rational enjoyments of social life?[114]

The women of Paisley signal the 'religious public' as a suitable place for women; here, a feminised Christian public is seen as essential to civilised society.

Conclusion

Missionary philanthropy gave rise to a new public sphere and civic culture in early-nineteenth-century England. Membership of philanthropic societies enabled the rise to prominence of middle-class men, the formation of cultural networks within the middle class, the development of a 'social' sphere of activity and the articulation of an identity as the carriers of civilisation. While men played a central role in establishing the structures of the philanthropic movement and promoting the voluntary society in a civic forum, the new social sphere was not solely equated with a masculine public world. It was fundamentally shaped by the domestic sphere and much of the work with the poor 'on the ground' was undertaken by women. Neither prominent nor celebrated, their identities gleaned from the lists of subscribers or their activities outlined in memoirs and autobiographies, missionary women energetically promoted domestic reform, distributed Bibles and canvassed for missionary donations. Women revised the focus of the Bible Society to include 'home' as well as 'overseas', and played a pioneering role in the practice of domestic visiting in all philanthropic societies. This occupation was more than an apolitical encounter between the visitor and the visited: it was a class encounter, one of a number of systems for fostering improvement among the poor, which identified the working-class home and family as a 'contact zone' and became the principal mechanism in the production of knowledge about poverty throughout the nineteenth century.

Underpinned by theories of civilisation and social progress, domestic visiting and the wider practice of missionary philanthropy had a global dimension. Philanthropists developed their missionary strategy with close reference to missions overseas, drawing on 'civilising' practices alongside Christian instruction, cultural change and domestic reform. The language of civilisation enabled domestic missionaries to gauge social progress in England, measure the capacity of the poor at home to be improved by Christian instruction, insist upon the domestic rights of English men and explain women's extended philanthropic role. By the mid-1810s, the missionary middle class in England had assumed a role as overseer of national reform and a position at the helm of global change. The cultural ambitions of the early nineteenth-century middle class thus paved the way for the imperial ambitions of the nation in mid-nineteenth-century England.

3

Missionary Domesticity and 'Woman's Sphere': The Reads of Wincobank Hall

While the public voluntary society was of considerable importance in bringing together sympathetic men and women to create a missionary movement, a second very social 'site' operated to construct a collective missionary identity. The family was of great significance for evangelicals. The household had been spiritualised as part of the Protestant Reformation, as male heads of household were given a special responsibility to direct the religiosity of other household members. The earthly family was seen as an extension of the heavenly family, and relationships between husband and wife, parents and children, and employers and servants were believed to have been ordained by God. According to nineteenth-century readings of St Paul's Epistle to the Colossians, the male head of the household was to be a caring husband and father, intimately involved with family life. Women were dependent and subordinate, offered salvation through marriage and motherhood, but able through philanthropy to negotiate the boundaries of their 'sphere' and assume responsibility for the moral regeneration of the nation.[1] Children, at the centre of the evangelical family, were to please the Lord through obeying their parents; growing up in the 'nursery of virtue', their future moral characters would be shaped in domestic life. The family was bound together by religious practice in the home, such as family prayers, Sunday Bible reading, and the keeping of spiritual memoirs.[2] The home was the place in which most children developed their religious belief and practice, in which their spirituality was nurtured and their sense of mission inspired.

This chapter contributes to the ongoing 'relocation' of the domestic sphere of nineteenth-century England. Traditionally represented as a separate and secluded space, in counterpoint to the public world, the home is now understood to occupy a more complex relationship to both public and private domains. This reassessment has particularly, although not exclusively, focused on Unitarian and Quaker women.[3] Evangelical women have yet to find a secure place within 'public' religious culture. In particular, historians have had little to say about the work and family lives of female philanthropists in relation to the 'missionary public' in this period.[4]

In this chapter, I advance the concept of 'missionary domesticity' to explore the social nature of evangelical family life and the areas of overlap between women's domestic duties and missionary philanthropic commitments. The chapter begins with an examination of evangelical childhood and the missionary household through a focus on the early years of the Read sisters of Wincobank Hall, Sheffield. Mary-Anne, Eliza, Catherine, Sarah and Emily Read were born into a well-to-do Congregational family which was to be at the heart of Sheffield's new missionary culture. During the 1810s and 1820s, they participated in a wide range of missionary philanthropic activities. Their play and leisure pursuits, formal education and neighbourhood life, were informed by an evangelical pedagogy which was profoundly shaped by the notion of the 'heathen other' and by global missionary concerns.

The expansiveness of the missionary domesticity of Mary-Anne Rawson (née Read) is explored in the second part of the chapter. By the 1830s, Rawson was a well-known anti-slavery activist and supporter of missionary reform at home and overseas (Figure 6). Her missionary philanthropy made her part of a broad social movement which sought reform for a range of domestic cultural practices and which focused with some intensity on women. I am particularly interested in the relationship between Rawson's missionary domesticity and her lack of concern for the 'woman question', expressed in her retrospective

Figure 6 Mary-Anne Rawson, far-right, second row. The Anti-Slavery Convention, 1840. (Painting by Benjamin Robert Haydon, Oil on Canvas, 1841. Courtesy of the National Portrait Gallery, London, NPG 599.)

dismissal of the furore over the acceptability of women's participation at the 1840 World Anti-Slavery Convention in London. In the later nineteenth century the imperial context was of considerable significance for the emergence of feminism and women's demands for an extended sphere, enabling opportunities for the development of women's professional skills and facilitating a sense of British womanhood as leading a movement for the global advancement of women.[5] In the 1830s and 1840s it provided instead a framework for an anti-feminist politics. For Rawson, and her friend Ann Taylor Gilbert, mistress of a very different form of missionary domesticity, the 'domestic' was not equated with confinement or a smallness of sphere. Rawson, and Gilbert in her rejection of Anne Knight's letter canvassing support in 1849 for the enfranchisement of women, clearly asserted that their understanding of themselves and other women as primarily and rightfully 'domestic' did not mean seclusion from worldly commitments. Instead it placed them at the core of the evangelical project to create a new Christian society.

Making Christian children: the evangelical mother's mission

The first two decades of the nineteenth century saw a particular encouragement given to children's participation in public evangelical culture. Correspondent with the growth of women's bible and missionary associations and the work of women as Sunday school teachers, children also joined the missionary movement. The first Juvenile Bible Society, established in 1804 in Sheffield by 15-year-old Catherine Elliott, was promoted as a model to be emulated.[6] The parent body of the British and Foreign Bible Society (BFBS) received collections from Sunday schools from 1808, and its first official children's association was formed in Southwark in 1812. Through this society, two thousand Sunday school pupils raised the sum of £2115 in the first eight years of its existence. In 1821, C. S. Dudley composed a set of rules for use by children's Bible Societies, which included the organisation of a committee, with an elected treasurer, regular meetings and a requirement of a minimum contribution of 1s a month. Parallel developments were afoot within the denominational missionary movement, as Anne Burton of Ashby-de-la-Zouch organised the first Wesleyan Methodist Missionary Society (WMMS) children's association in 1814. By 1820, children's associations were operating across the nation. The use of children was in part strategic, as adults found it hard to refuse a request from a child for a donation to the missionary fund. But children, in their innocence and purity, were believed to be peculiarly placed to lead erring adults to salvation.[7]

The popularity of public missionary developments is reflected in the family life of Mary-Anne (1801–1887), Eliza (1803–1851), Catherine (1804–1865), Sarah (1806–1829) and Emily Read (1807–1883), and their little brother Edmund (1815–1873).[8] Their parents, Joseph (1765–1837) and Elizabeth (1778–1865) Read, both came from established Independent backgrounds and were enthusiastic participants in the evangelical revival. Joseph, who inherited with his brother John the family gold and silver smelting works in 1802, was a member of Queen Street Congregational Chapel, the building of which in 1784 had been supported through subscription by his father, Joseph Read senior. He also supported Rotherham College, opened in 1795.[9] Elizabeth, whose father Ebenezer Smith had trained for the ministry in London before returning to Chesterfield to become a partner in the family's successful iron foundry, taught a Sunday School class at Soresby Street Congregational Church in Chesterfield. It was at this chapel that Elizabeth and Joseph conducted much of their courtship.[10] From their marriage in 1800, the Reads lived in Attercliffe, Sheffield's burgeoning industrial quarter, moving out to rural Wincobank in 1816. They were prominent members of Sheffield's evangelical community, and typical of the well-to-do townspeople who made up the constituency of Independent congregations.[11]

The little Reads' public benevolence started young: Mary-Anne, Eliza, Catherine, Sarah and Emily were all enlisted by their mother as very small girls to help with running Sunday school classes at Attercliffe's Zion chapel.[12] Indeed, public evangelicalism was in these years very much a family affair. As Mary-Anne recalled in her 'Memorials of James Montgomery', it was as a family that the Reads attended the first meetings of the Sheffield Bible Society in 1812 and the Missionary Society in 1813. For the duration of the latter event, Joseph Read had rented rooms in the centre of town, so that his wife and daughters could enjoy socialising with friends from around the region and hear all of the missionary speeches, including the Reverend John Campbell's tales of the conversion of the 'Hottentot'.[13] In 1812–1813, years marked in Sheffield by a flurry of evangelical activity, the family became active in the newly formed Sunday School Union. Over the next few years they offered their support to the Society for Bettering the Condition of the Poor (SBCP), the Society for Superseding the Necessity for Climbing-Boys, the Aged Female Society, the Bible Society, the Girls' and Boys' Lancasterian Schools, the Hibernian Society and the missionary societies. In 1817, following their move to Wincobank Hall, the elder girls established a Sunday school. As members of the Sheffield Juvenile Missionary

Society and the SBCP, they began visiting the homes of the poor in their neighbourhood, taking gifts of pin-cushions, garden produce and tracts, reading from the Bible, collecting for missions and persuading them to send their children to Sunday school.[14]

The public missionary society rarely provided the initial inspiration for a child's developing interest in missions, however, whether at home or overseas. Rather, it was an evangelical commitment nurtured within the home that directed children into the public society and forged an enduring missionary identity. Responsibility for the early education and moral and spiritual development of children fell to the mother. While fathers were often lovingly involved in their children's lives, participating in play, religious instruction and the enforcement of discipline, mothers managed the routines of the nursery and oversaw the maturation of children.[15] For evangelical mothers, 'parenthood...was a mission'.[16] Children were believed to be in need of special protection from 'the world' and its corrupting capacities: sin was both within and all around, encouraged by popular culture, the indulgences of the rich and the aspirant amongst the middle classes and, for Dissenters, the association of Anglicans with worldly pastimes.[17] Adherence to the belief that children were inherently sinful led some evangelicals to promote 'rigorous...cheerless and over regimented' child-rearing practices, in which excessive discipline was used in a bid to break the will of the child.[18] But for many others, the religious and moral education they provided was protective and gentle.[19] Belief in the malleability of the child's character and that adult morality was shaped in childhood, that 'as the twig is bent, the tree will incline', meant that, in order to develop the necessary internal constraints, it was essential that children were exposed to positive influences and beneficial external impressions.[20]

Elizabeth Read, herself a member of a large and loving family, placed a firm emphasis on affection and encouragement as well as discipline, on fun and games and an education including but extending beyond religious instruction and family worship.[21] Morality and religion were, however, at the core of her maternal concerns. Her dairies and letters written to her daughters on their birthdays reveal how she fretted over the state of their souls, prodding their religious sensibilities and encouraging them to examine their religious feelings.[22] When, in 1819, 16-year-old Eliza became the first of her children to experience a conversion, Elizabeth was overwhelmed with relief and pleasure: 'That a child of mine should come forward, to avow herself on the Lord's side, and take a decided part in religion, is more delightful to me than I can express...'[23] Writing to the more worryingly wilful Mary-Anne later in the year, she talked of the 'awful, yet endearing responsibility of that tender relation' between mother and child, of the knowledge that her love was not enough to secure their happiness and 'eternal interests', and encouraged her elder daughter to follow the example of her pious younger sister.[24]

Happy English children and the 'heathen other'

The development of her children as Christian subjects was for Mrs Read underpinned by a missionary pedagogy. She believed that the British people, on account of the evangelical revival and various correspondent cultural changes, had a privileged access to salvation. As she wrote to Mary-Anne on her twelfth birthday in 1813:

> You were born in a Christian land, you are privileged Sabbath after Sabbath to hear the glorious gospel from a faithful and affectionate servant of Jehovah; you have books put into your hands calculated to arouse your attention to your eternal concerns.[25]

She urged her elder daughter to reflect upon, and to be open to, such religious influence. Writing nearly a decade later to eight-year-old Edmund in praise of his decision to become a missionary collector, Elizabeth Read deployed a missionary metaphor in her bid to gently cajole the little boy into showing the enthusiasm of his sisters for benevolent practices. Insisting that he should contribute his own money, lest he might enjoy the pleasure of collecting more than he cared for the 'poor heathen children', she wrote:

> I hope you begin to feel sorry for those little children who live in countries where they never hear anything about God, and Jesus Christ; where they have no Sabbath-days, no Bibles, and their parents are so ignorant and so wicked that they teach them nothing but what is foolish and naughty.[26]

Benevolence was seen as an early sign of an individual's future commitment as well as an important training in religious habits.[27] Collecting for the missionary society was an important factor in enabling a contrast between Edmund's goodness and the 'naughtiness' of 'heathen' children, whose parents were unqualified to attend to their spiritual development.

Elizabeth Read's rather tame admonition of 'heathen' parents who failed to give Christian guidance to their children demonstrates restraint and gentleness when compared to some of the images in the evangelical press. In 1812, for example, the editors of the *Evangelical Magazine* encouraged English children to empathise with the heathen child of the evangelical imagination and recognise their own privileges as Christians through a terrifying story of 'Hindoo' parental neglect. 'Many offer up their children to a river, which they worship as a god, putting the poor little children into baskets, and throwing them into the water to be devoured by crocodiles... O could you behold some of these scenes, surely you would exclaim:

> Lord, I ascribe it to thy grace,
> And not to chance as others do,
> That I was born of Christian race,
> And not a Heathen or a Jew.'[28]

By God's grace, it was English children who had been chosen for salvation; and must now demonstrate their gratitude by assisting in the conversion of others.

If the images offered to children were designed to frighten them into evangelical submission, denominational magazines also offered rather more gentle guidance to young parents in establishing familial roles, family worship and the practice of philanthropy. The popular *Evangelical Magazine* reflected on a range of essential topics, providing articles 'On Family Worship' and 'Paternal Admonition', 'Thoughts on the Importance of Catechizing Youth', 'Encouragement to Pious Parents', 'Good Advice to a New Married Couple' and 'Free Thoughts on the Propriety, Importance, and Advantages of Family Meetings'.[29] An edition for September 1810 contained a supplement on 'Relative Duties', which drew upon Paul's Epistle to the Colossians to outline the responsibilities of different family members. Wives were to submit 'unto your own husbands, as unto to the Lord', and husbands should love their wives as themselves, and provide for their own households: if a man failed to do so, he was 'worse than an infidel'. Parents were to nurture their children, who in return should 'obey your parents in all things, for this is well-pleasing to the Lord.'[30] These were supported by a variety of texts in the early years of the nineteenth century, including health manuals, such as the new editions of Buchan's *Domestic Medicine* and his more populist *Advice to Mothers* (1803), which presented an ideal of active femininity and underscored the seriousness of marriage and motherhood.[31] Novels and conduct books, such as Hannah More's popular *Coelebs in Search of a Wife* (1809) and Ann Martin Taylor's *Practical Hints to Young Females* (1815), prepared women for the serious business of domestic management and motherhood.[32]

Elizabeth Read expressed her commitment to missionary domesticity in the family life she created at Wincobank Hall, to which the family moved in 1816 (Figure 7). This was a rambling rural idyll, situated in 120 acres of woodland, orchard, vinery and pasture on Sheffield's northern edge.[33] In 1817, the same year that Mrs Read had the family's globes repaired and purchased a copy of Sarah Trimmer's *Scripture: History and Selections*, her husband Joseph turned the laundry room into a chapel. Equipped with a newly built pulpit and a Bible presented by George Bennet, the family hosted religious services for local people, conducted by students and tutors from nearby Rotherham College.[34] Supported by their membership of a range of local, regional and

Figure 7 Wincobank Hall and Grounds. (Courtesy of Sheffield Local Studies Library, s05891.)

national missionary societies, the girls now began their local philanthropy, becoming acquainted with the north Sheffield poor through their Sunday school and domestic visiting.

The Read children's developing missionary identities were chronicled in family magazines, produced by the girls from 1817. Variously titled 'The Wincobank Remembrancer', 'The Family Repository' and 'The Wincobank Repository', these were informal versions of a genre that was fast becoming established as a means of moral instruction.[35] They contained humour, riddles and short moral tales: for example, the stories of Ned, the boy who wished he was a crow so that he would not have to suffer in the knowledge that God could read his thoughts, and Eleanor, the naughty girl who procrastinated; and the dialogue between Matthew Hopeful, a recent convert and regular chapelgoer, and John Goodenough, who failed to realise that it was not enough to dig his garden, weed his onions and lead a good and quiet life.[36] Under the editorship of Eliza, more space was given to reflecting upon sermons and upon the girls' roles as agents of the improvement of others. A short contribution to the 'Family Repository' of April 1819, for example, described a visit to local cottages for the purpose of distributing tracts, encouraging Sunday school attendance and collecting donations to the Missionary Society. At one cottage, the author reported, a mother enthused about the positive effects of their Sunday school, which not only prevented her children from getting into bad company but ensured that they came back clean and enthusiastic about their lessons; Sunday schools, she exclaimed, were 'the best thing that ever happened to poor people.' In another, usually dirty, abode inhabited by subscribers to the Missionary Society, the sisters recorded with delight their discovery that as a result of the recent conversion of the husband, his wife had recognised the value of cleanliness and domestic order.[37]

It is not possible to know the precise influences on individual maternal pedagogies or the Read sisters' education as, apart from the work by Mrs Trimmer, there is no other mention in extant records of books they had read. But we can at least safely guess that the children read the books of Jane and Ann Taylor; not only do Sarah's poems of the 1820s replicate the structure of their work (see below), but the younger of the sisters became a friend and neighbour after her marriage in 1813 to the Sheffield Congregational minister Joseph Gilbert. Similarly, extant material from the period of Miss Dinah Ball's term as governess at Wincobank Hall reveals both the priority given to global missionary concerns and the girls' familiarity with the content and style of missionary writing. Miss Ball had previously been a teacher at a private school in west London, where she had received 16-year-old Mary-Anne in 1817, and arrived at Wincobank following a rather dramatic recalling of the wilful elder daughter a few months later. Mary-Anne had admitted, nay flouted, in a letter home to her mother that she had participated in card-playing, visited the theatre and attended an Anglican service, activities which caused the strict Dissenters considerable consternation. Rather than dismissing the services of the respected teacher, Miss Ball was summonsed to Wincobank Hall by Elizabeth Read, where she could teach Mary-Anne and the younger girls under their mother's watchful eye.[38]

Dinah Ball went on to publish a pamphlet in the early 1820s promoting missionary activity. *The Missionary Society, A Dialogue,* sees Tom, an agricultural labourer, stimulated to find out more about missions by an encounter with some 'young ladies' who had asked him for a donation to their missionary society. As his desire to find out more about their cause unfolds, the piece introduces the noble aims of the local missionary society in a language thought appropriate for the poor. Asking 'Mr Preachwell', the local minister, about the 'heathens', the innocent but ignorant Tom receives the following reply:

> Oh! You cannot think, Tom, what a world we live in. Our own country is only like one ear of wheat to that whole field. There are eight hundred millions of people in the world, and more than half of these people are Heathens; that is, they worship false Gods... They live over almost the whole of Africa, one quarter of the Globe. They are spread over the greatest part of America, another quarter; and a great many large kingdoms of Asia, a third of the Globe, are full of Heathens.

Preachwell continued, explaining the horrors of 'heathen' worship, and of cultural practices such as sati and infanticide, and of the wonderful changes inspired by missionaries in India, the South Pacific, Africa and the West Indies. The pamphlet ends with Tom and his friend Harry's decision to donate to the missionary society the money they had been saving to spend at the fair.[39]

Such stories taught middle-class children about their own place in society, and about class relations more broadly. Conveying 'the sincere milk of the word' rather than lapsing into the realm of fantasy,[40] it was here that children learned about the 'heathen other' of the evangelical middle-class imagination and, in Matthew Grenby's words, were 'schooled' in 'the charitable impulse'. Such fictionalised accounts taught children the rules governing nineteenth-century philanthropy: the requirement on the part of the donor to assist independence and not to create a dependency; the importance of being able to discriminate between real and feigned needs; the significance of personal alms-giving in the local community; and the place of self-sacrifice in the transition to adulthood.[41] They highlighted the value of the missionary practice of young ladies, helping missions overseas while assisting in the assault on popular culture at home. By the 1820s, Ball's story was one of few pieces of missionary fiction available to young girls, and replicates themes introduced by Mary Martha Sherwood in the first missionary novel, *The History of Little Henry and His Bearer* (1814). Here, it is the daughter of an English clergyman in India who converts an English boy, who had been brought up by his (male) Indian nurse. Henry's emergence from 'heathen darkness' culminates in his attempt to convert his carer, thus mirroring hopes for the missionary movement in India.[42]

Mary-Anne Read's 'Missionary Atlas', a collection of maps drawn in 1819 depicting the state of missionary activity throughout the world, was a likely product of Miss Ball's teaching. This was revised by Catherine in 1822 and presented to George Bennet on the eve of his journey to the South Pacific. The Reads hosted Bennet's farewell party and, as discussed in Chapter 5, the family maintained correspondence with this long-standing family friend during his travels. Bennet liked Catherine's emphasis on the progress rather than the slowness of global Christianisation, represented by her use of gold stars to highlight mission stations. He expressed his appreciation in verse:

> The dark places of earth are with cruelty fraught,
> There horrid oppressions abound;
> And iniquity often for virtue is taught
> By heathens to heathens around.
> But God has declared that light shall arise
> to those in the shadows of death;
> That the Gospel a passage shall win throu' the skies
> Nor in vain be expended his breath.

Heathenism was so widespread that people talked of searching in vain to find nations belonging to God. But, with her missionary map 'Miss Catharine [*sic*]' had: '... repainted the globe; / Cloth'd the stations of missions in Mantles of Gold, / and the rest in obscurity's Robe.'[43]

Bennet also inspired Sarah Read's *Journal of a Voyage from Gravesend to Madeira*, also supervised by Miss Ball. Written in the form of a letter to a friend, the journal details impressions of the 'barbaric' customs of the 'deep chocolate'-coloured people of Halifax Bay, who had teeth and parts of fingers removed as children to ensure that they could tolerate pain. Sarah discusses the ornaments of feathers, flowers, beads and shells with which people in 'Otaheiti' adorn themselves, and refers to the indolence of the men, who allow women to feed them from spoons.[44] In its careful attention to the morality and customs of the people, as well as geographical details of distances and directions, the wildlife and vegetation of specific islands, Sarah's Journal reveals the author's familiarity with the content and style of missionary writing.

In his letters from the South Pacific, George Bennet played a role in the instruction of the young Edmund, who was a little boy of seven at the time of his departure in 1822. Bennet sought to interest Edmund in the subject of missions, sending the little boy shells which were ostensibly a present from a young Tahitian boy, named John Williams, after the missionary, who was attending the mission school. These gifts were in return for flowers and peacock feathers that Edmund had collected from the garden at Wincobank, and which had accompanied presents sent by Elizabeth Read to be given to King Pomare and his family. Bennet's letters to Edmund display a tone of avuncular interest, telling him of the coronation of the new King of Tahiti, himself a young boy of Edmund's age and a Christian, and encouraging the little boy's own reflections on his faith and the peculiar privilege of the child in England. Writing on the occasion of Edmund's imminent departure for his first boarding school at Mansfield, Bennet quoted a verse from the hymn by Ann Taylor Gilbert:

> I thank the goodness and the grace
> Which on my birth have smiled
> And made me in these Christian days
> A happy English child.[45]

Childhood and children feature prominently in Bennet's later letters to Joseph Read from India in 1826, where he praised his friend's daughters, reflecting upon the 'blessing' bestowed on girls by an evangelical education: 'The poor creatures, the Ladies who have either been educated in these countries altogether or have only been sent to England for a few years of instruction are so vapid, so ignorant of anything worth knowing, so vain . . . ', he wrote of English women in India. To him, their 'frivolous pursuits' and 'mental as well as corporeal indolence' made them far inferior to the active, usefully feminine evangelical Christians.[46]

The theme of the privilege of the English child was addressed in poetry composed by Sarah Read in the context of the anti-slavery campaign of the mid-1820s. One untitled poem is structured around a conversation between a mother and her young son after the child had seen a notice for an anti-slavery meeting pinned to the churchyard gate, and was bursting with questions concerning slaves and slavery. Following her explanations about the horrors of the Middle Passage and life on West Indian plantations, the mother appeals to her child's ability to empathise, comparing his daily freedoms with the work, poor conditions and punishments experienced by slaves:

> When you returned from school on Thursday night
> You said you did not feel inclined to play,
> How in your garden did you take delight
> As you were wearied from the sultry day;
> And yet you'd had no labour to perform,
> Nor any exercise to make you warm.

Horrified by this knowledge and assured in his capacity for moral influence, the child resolves to persuade his father to abandon slave-grown sugar: 'I think that I can do some little good . . . I know he'll do it – if he thinks it right'.[47] The poem was possibly written to assist Mrs Read in her attempts to inspire in Edmund a sense of Christian global responsibility.[48]

'A Tale of Woe', also written by Sarah, affirmed the author's faith in the power of British missionaries to effect global change. The story of a young boy snatched at the age of 14 from an idyllic African landscape and forced onto a slave ship bound for the Americas, this is a tale in which white men have 'black' hearts, are unable to see the grief and pain of their captured African brothers, and in which black men do not yet know of the 'friend on high' who cares for the slave and can answer their prayers for mercy. 'The Recaptured Negro' takes a similar format, featuring a male narrator who reflects from a slave ship on his happy life in Africa, expressing his own pain through his thoughts of his mother's broken heart. Represented as a vulnerable human being, articulating his desire for freedom through memories of domestic happiness, the enslaved man is constructed in the image of the evangelical ideal of the sensitive, feeling male. The poem concludes with his liberation by the efforts of a British anti-slavery vessel and 'recapture' by a missionary who promises him freedom through Christian education.[49]

By their early adulthood, a sense of themselves as missionaries was placed at the centre of the consciousness of the Read sisters. The 1820s saw their continued involvement in a range of local evangelical bodies, including the SBCP, the Campaign for Superseding the Necessity for Climbing-Boys, the Sunday School Union, the Hibernian Society and the Bible and Missionary Societies. They also subscribed to national societies, including the Tract Society, the BFBS, the London Missionary Society (LMS), and the Society for the Promotion of Christianity Among the Jews. A family magazine of August 1826 suggests the breadth of their interests and the degree to which the girls' social lives were structured around missionary pursuits. Written for their paternal aunt, Ann Read, then residing in Devon, the magazine informed her that 'three of the blooming daughters of Joseph Read' had been present on the occasion of the consecration of Attercliffe Church in July,[50] and that Sarah and Emily, who had attended the Bible Society meeting at Chesterfield in August, were organising a bazaar for the Ladies' Hibernian School Society and planned to send profits made from the sale of honey from their own bees to the Society for Promoting Christianity Among the Jews.[51] With responsibilities for domestic reform, the emancipation of slaves in the West Indies, and the evangelisation of the Irish and the Jews, the Read sisters occupied an expansive sphere. Pursued from within their own home and local community, the civilising mission provided evangelical girls and women with a powerful sense of their own agency and influence in the world.

Missionary domesticity: Wincobank Hall

Wincobank Hall was established during the 1820s as an informal centre of evangelical activity and benevolence, both locally and within a national network of evangelical nonconformity.[52] The Reads offered respite to friends and acquaintances in need of a stop-over on missionary tours of the north of England or on long journeys back to London and the south, to those invited to speak on the occasion of a missionary meeting or a Sunday school anniversary, or to weary missionaries experiencing the disorientation and exhaustion which often accompanied the return to England.[53] As is revealed by Rawson's 'Treasury of Pen and Pencil Memorials of Absent Friends', visitors to the family home in the mid 1820s included many prominent evangelicals, such as Ann and Joseph Gilbert, Josiah Condor, John Angell James, Thomas Raffles and William Ellis, the latter recently returned from the South Pacific.[54] William Wilberforce, Robert Moffat, William Lloyd Garrison and, later, Frederick Douglass also enjoyed the hospitality of the family.[55]

During the 1830s and 1840s, Mary-Anne Rawson built on the missionary domesticity created by her mother to establish Wincobank Hall as a centre of philanthropic reform. She had returned with her infant daughter Elizabeth in 1829, leaving the Nottingham home she had shared with her husband William Rawson from their marriage in 1828 until his death from tuberculosis in July 1829.[56] Living with her mother and two unmarried sisters, Catherine and Emily, the 1830s saw Rawson preoccupied with the ladies' anti-slavery campaign, the founding of which in Sheffield in 1825 had involved her and her mother Elizabeth as members of the first committee. In the years before her marriage, she had participated in the energetic rounds of activity that had made women abolitionists the most visible activists in their neighbourhoods, engaging in fund-raising, tract- and pamphlet-distribution and house-to-house canvassing in support of the 1826 campaign for abstention from slave-grown produce.[57] In the early 1830s, Rawson was soliciting contributions to *The Bow in the Cloud* (1832), her collection of poems and short stories by many prominent abolitionists, as well as writing pamphlets in support of immediate abolition, collecting signatories for the 1833 petition and generally following the activities of the more radical Agency Committee which culminated in abolition in August 1833.

In 1837, Rawson again stepped up her anti-slavery and missionary commitments, becoming a founder member of the Sheffield Ladies' Association for the Universal Abolition of Slavery, established in support of Joseph Sturge's Birmingham-based Central Negro Emancipation Committee to campaign against the apprenticeship system.[58] Through her contacts with Sturge and his sister Sophia, Rawson took a lead in coordinating the British support for the Thompson Normal School, in the 'free village' of Kettering, Jamaica. Established in 1840 by Baptist missionary William Knibb and his wife and daughters, the school trained Jamaican girls and young women as teachers.[59] Under Rawson's direction, the ladies in Sheffield held fund-raising bazaars, made collections of materials for needlework and supplied books for rewards for pupils at the school. They also coordinated the national subscription which by 1840 saw money coming in from ladies' associations in towns throughout England and Scotland.[60]

Extant letters from Mary-Anne's daughter Lizzie Rawson (1828–1862) to her cousin Mary Eliza Wilson (1830–1851) are testimony to the missionary focus of life at Wincobank. The daughter of Eliza Read, the only one of Mary-Anne's sisters to marry and have children, Mary Wilson and her six siblings lived in Nottingham, where they were active missionary philanthropists,[61] before moving to Torquay in 1841 on account of their mother's ill-health. Mary-Anne was admiring of Eliza's missionary domesticity, as her children participated, with varying degrees of enthusiasm, in missionary bazaars, tea-parties, prayer meetings, and the running of their own missionary shop.[62] Alongside chat about fabric for pinafores, commiserations over the death of a pet rabbit, competition over height and skipping, and their hopes that 'aerial machines' might be invented and so bring them closer, Lizzie and Mary regularly exchanged missionary news.[63] The 1838 *Appeal for Slaves*, partly written by her mother on behalf of the Sheffield Ladies'

Association for the Universal Abolition of Slavery, was sent to Mary by Lizzie, along with snippets of information about the campaign and, especially, the popular abolitionist George Thompson, friend of Mary-Anne's, of whom Lizzie was particularly fond. Lizzie sent Mary articles written by Thompson and shared her memories of days spent in the Peak District or in London with his family. In return, Mary engaged in a regular leg-pulling on account of her cousin's 'imaginations and fancies and ravings' about 'precious Mr T'.[64] The two girls followed the progress of Robert and Mary Moffat, LMS missionaries in southern Africa, and whom both had met, Lizzie expressing her relief that their party had reached their Kuruman mission station in safety. On other occasions, Lizzie described a lecture she had attended at Brightside Exhibition Room on the subject of the Niagara Falls, where the lecturer and his companions had dressed up as Native Americans, beating a drum and dancing. She told her younger cousin of her participation in missionary meetings in Sheffield, where she learned about missionary progress in China or about 'the present beliefs of the Jews', and of her busyness with the accounts of the Hibernian School Society.[65] Such activities reflect the general paraphernalia of missions which, by the 1830s and 1840s, was becoming increasingly centred upon the young.

Domestic missions necessarily formed a regular feature in Lizzie's and Mary's correspondence. From the late 1830s, as Chartism again placed the condition of working people on the reform agenda, Rawson became more involved in domestic missions. Teetotal lectures and teas at Wincobank were described with pride by Lizzie. Working-class fathers were the particular target of the Wincobank Total Abstinence Society (1840), and were invited to regular festivals to hear celebratory speeches by reformed drinkers and to partake of dinners of roast beef and plum pudding, enjoyed after singing George Thompson's 'Teetotal Joyful'.[66] Rawson's evening class for local men, set up in the hope that the desire for an education would keep them away from the 'slavery of wine and ale', might be taken as indicative of the self-assurance of middle-class philanthropic women. A verse adorning the school-room wall proclaimed their vision of desirable plebeian masculinity, reiterating the message of the 'Joyful':

> Smoking, feasting, fretting,
> Brandy, beer and betting,
> Will kill the strongest man alive.
> But water, air and diet,
> Domestic peace and quiet,
> Will make the weakest man to thrive.[67]

In a most evocative image of her desire to 'domesticate' working men, Rawson demonstrated the growing of hyacinths in ale-glasses, thereby suggesting an alternative, rather more fragrant, use.[68]

In 1841, funded by the British and Foreign School Society, Mary-Anne opened a day school for local children (Figure 8). Local families invited to the opening celebration in April 1841, sang Ann Gilbert's hymn, especially composed for the occasion,

Figure 8 Wincobank Nondenominational Chapel and School, 1841. (Courtesy of Sheffield Local Studies Library, s05103.)

which expressed a wish that 'children yet unborn' should be saved from 'ignorance and vice forlorn.'[69] The school consolidated the family's long involvement in running Sunday schools for local children, where they not only taught Bible-reading, but prepared girls to become servants in their home.[70] Mary-Anne, Mrs Read and Emily taught writing and arithmetic to all children, and needlework and knitting to the girls. The requirement of children to be punctual and polite, to develop table manners, habits of cleanliness and adopt a simplicity of dress, necessarily relied upon their parents, who were required to provide plates, mugs, knives and forks, as well as contributing copybooks and clean pinafores, and a payment of 2d each week. Parents also attended the anniversaries, at which lines of children, the little girls neatly dressed in white and carrying bouquets of flowers, engaged in orderly procession.[71]

For Rawson, the causes of abolition, overseas missions, temperance and domestic missions were intertwined. The family's own conversion to teetotalism had been inspired by William Lloyd Garrison who, dining at Wincobank on his British 'tour' at the time of the Anti-Slavery Convention of 1840, had initiated what became known in the family as the 'protest against the decanters'.[72] It was through the participation of parents in children's schooling and anniversary celebrations that the wider community would, it was hoped, be converted to temperance and to the values of the school. Indeed, Mary-Anne Rawson's domestic philanthropic activities at Wincobank throughout the 1840s might be seen as an endeavour to establish her own version of the Jamaican 'free village'.

Missionary domesticity and woman's sphere

The place of Wincobank within such national and international movements provided Mary-Anne and her daughter and nieces with a strong sense that they were participants in world-changing events, the impetus for which derived less from formal politics than from their missionary domesticity. Rawson's activities pronounced the evangelical family, and at its heart missionary women, as the very originators of the new Christian social body. As she had argued in 1827 during the women's campaign for the immediate abolition of slavery, it was the location of slaves within God's family, within the family of Man, and the emphasis of abolitionist women on familial abuses and reform, that formed the strongest arguments for abolition and for the duty of Christian women to stand firm against the objections of the gradualist male leadership of the movement:[73]

> We ought to obey God rather than man. Confidence here is not at variance with humanity. On principles like these, the simple need not fear to confront the sage; nor a female society to take their stand against the united wisdom of this world.

Pre-empting criticism of their independent stance, which had certainly been forthcoming from the very top of the movement, the Sheffield women claimed that 'No views of policy, no regard to worldly interest, must here interfere.'[74] After abolition their actions would be justified, as slaves came together as families, overcoming the physical separation enforced by the plantation system and developing familial bonds and sentiments:

> Sweet will be the tumult of affection, full will be the fervours of that meeting, when the cords of slavery shall snap, and the husband shall rush to the arms of his wife, and the wife to her husband's; the mother to her babe's, and the babe to his mother's; and each then first shall clasp them as their own.[75]

Patterns of 'civilised' family life – a subject on which women had greater knowledge and authority – were to be the happy outcome of women's participation.[76]

Ten years later, in the midst of the anti-apprenticeship campaign, Mary-Anne Rawson and the Sheffield ladies again argued that only abolitionist women could bring about a true, moral, global reform. *An Appeal to the Christian Women of Sheffield*, co-authored by Rawson in order to publicise the formation of the Sheffield Ladies' Association for the Universal Abolition of Slavery in 1837, implored 'Christian daughters, wives and mothers' to

> "Remember them that are in bonds, as bound with them." Oh! if we were bound with them, how should we wish others to feel and act for us? If our parents, brothers, sisters, husbands and children, were bound with them, could we turn away from the discussion of the subject, as a political question in which we had no interest? Yet mark the words, "As bound with them". Here we take our stand, and regard it as a decidedly religious question.[77]

Such a concern with the immorality of slavery did not involve encroaching upon the male 'public' world. Women were, in Rawson's words, 'happily excluded from the great theatre of public business, from the strife of debate and the cares of legislation'. Their contentment stemmed from the belief that such exclusions did not prevent their deployment of the moral influence that was to have profound social implications, leading to the 'envelop(ing) ... in a moral atmosphere' of the 'whole earth'. The commitment to 'keep alive and increase zeal at our firesides' was of far more fundamental and far-reaching consequence than anything undertaken by politicians.[78]

It was during the anti-apprenticeship campaign of 1838 that Mary-Anne Rawson incurred the disapproval of male and female anti-slavery activists in Sheffield when, following the neglect of the men's society to organise public events and invite speakers from the Central Negro Emancipation Committee, she went ahead and organised them herself. In the events that followed, six Anglican ladies resigned and the men's committee expressed its disapproval of her actions. In response, the remaining ladies announced that they found such 'interference' on the part of the men 'uncalled for', stating that they represented 'an entirely independent society'.[79] As Clare Midgley has argued, implicit criticism of the male leadership of the campaign is suggestive of a relationship between the anti-slavery movement and mid-nineteenth-century feminism, at least in its providing 'a public questioning of male authority, an assertion of independence, and a recognition that their [women's] views were not adequately represented by men.'[80]

Such open acts of defiance were, however, unusual for Mary-Anne Rawson. There are in her papers very few other instances in which she challenges prescriptions of appropriate feminine behaviour. On occasions where she felt aggrieved by the procedures adopted by the men in her philanthropic circle, such as their decision to hang James Montgomery's portrait, the commissioning of which she had suggested, in the dark and secluded rooms of the Literary and Philosophical Society, she simply made her disappointment known. When women were excluded from the public celebrations of Montgomery's retirement in 1825, Rawson merely acknowledged the fact, busying herself with the suitably feminine activity of organising the fund for the Montgomery mission station in Tobago, the Caribbean island on which his missionary mother had died.[81] Even when the exclusion of women at the 1840 Anti-Slavery Convention had resulted in bitter disputes between American and British delegates, Rawson, despite her friendship with Lloyd Garrison and with some of the radical American women, retrospectively expressed the view that 'both parties have made the question respecting women's rights of too great importance.'[82]

Rawson's disinterest in the feminist politics of the 1840 convention was a feature of her evangelical missionary domesticity. It coincided with other profoundly anti-feminist moments in the late 1830s and 1840s, including the great popularity of Sarah Stickney Ellis's espousal of women's domesticity in her *Women of England* series (1839–1843),[83] and Ann Taylor Gilbert's negative response to Anne Knight's invitation to join her fledgling campaign for women's suffrage in 1849.[84] These women, members of overlapping social and religious networks, were all involved in the movements for abolition, working-class education and temperance. All three were missionary activists, advocates of the education of girls and of 'full and useful lives' for women, and supporters of domestic reform in England and overseas. Mary-Anne Rawson, like Ellis and Gilbert, was a creator of a missionary domesticity which she believed to be fundamental to global reform.

This, then, was no cloistered, restricted domestic life. Indeed, for some evangelical women, missionary domesticity involved *too great* a volume of work. If Mary-Anne Rawson's lack of concern for the 'woman question' derived from an absence of a feeling of grievance concerning women's sphere, her friend and co-abolitionist Ann Taylor Gilbert (1782–1866) sought scriptural authority to *restrict* her too-extensive missionary duties. Certainly Gilbert's familial responsibilities were very different from those of Rawson. In contrast to Mary-Anne, who had a single child and, as a widow, no wifely duties, as well as a ready network of familial support, Ann's marriage in 1813 to Independent minister Joseph Gilbert (1779–1852), pastor at Sheffield's Independent Nether Chapel and tutor at Rotherham College between 1813 and 1817, saw extensive duties as a minister's wife in Sheffield, Hull (1817–1825) and Nottingham (1825-until the death of her husband in 1852). She assisted her husband with his correspondence each afternoon, as well as receiving guests and providing for a succession of young male boarders. She combined these responsibilities with caring, in the early years of her marriage, for her husband's orphaned niece, Salome, as well as mothering eight children of her own, born in the 11 years between 1814 and 1825.[85] Indeed, if anyone can rebut Frank Prochaska's claim that women's burgeoning missionary philanthropy was the result of their having more time on their hands, it is Ann Gilbert.[86] She came to find that her domestic life was so busy, that both the writing she had pursued prior to her marriage and any sustained participation in the religious public beyond the domestic realm eluded her.[87] Although she managed to play an active role in Nottingham Anti-Slavery Society, and was energetic in gaining signatories for the 1833 petition, she reminded Rawson in 1838 that 'You have not so great a pressure constantly weighing you down.'[88]

Ann Gilbert believed that women's sphere of responsibility had widened since her grandmother's day, and that the expectation that a Christian woman would engage in missionary and benevolent work, however desirable, made her workload almost unmanageable.[89] Her biography of her husband Joseph, written after his death in 1852, is peppered with commentary on the roles of the sexes that, quite superfluous to the narrative, reveals this to be a central and constant preoccupation in Ann's life. Her discussion of the pace of their lives in Hull is followed by the reflection that

> We cannot suppose that, in the sight of God, there are in reality anywhere, clashing duties. To his eye a line exists, which it is happy for us if we can discern, between the public and the private; and few, after the minister, have greater need or interest in ascertaining it than the minister's wife. Willing and happy as she should be to do her utmost abroad, it cannot be questioned that her first business is at home. Too much, as I have thought, is expected from many, probably having large families and small assistance, by whom that station is occupied.[90]

Ann had undoubtedly felt herself to be on the receiving end of such criticism for not taking an active enough role 'out of doors', and a clearer demarcation of the boundaries of the private would thus have been comforting, as well as justifying a reduction of her workload.

Indeed, Gilbert struggled to find a scriptural basis which would limit her public duties. As expressed in her famous declension to Anne Knight's invitation to participate in the early suffrage movement, she could get no further than discussing the extensive nature of Biblical injunctions '"to guide the house", "to bring up children", "to entertain strangers", and to descend to the humblest kindnesses', the duties marked out for women by 'apostolic authority'. Each of these duties was capacious. Bringing up children required that women were to 'do much, even politically', as it was a mother's 'duty to instil *principles* into her children – principles affecting all the great questions – Freedom; Slavery; Justice; Humanity; War; Monopoly; Private Judgement; Voluntaryism, with as many more as may be thought of...'

Looking after the house and hosting visitors saw Ann creating a successful missionary domestic life, of a similar order to that of Rawson. As her 'Autograph Album' from the 1820s and 1830s reveals, the Gilberts entertained eminent ministers, philanthropists and missionaries, many of them giving a visiting sermon to Joseph's Hull and Nottingham congregations. These included John Philip, LMS missionary in southern Africa, who stayed with the Gilberts in 1827, during a tour of Britain for the purpose of drumming up support for his campaign against the ill treatment of the 'Caffer and Hottentot'. He returned in 1836, this time accompanied by Jan Tzatzoe, the 'Caffer Chief' who had travelled with him to Britain. John Browne, Presbyterian minister and evangeliser of the Highlands, John Angell James, evangelical minister at Carr's Lane, Birmingham, and the Reverend Dr Thomas Raffles of Liverpool all made their visits in the late 1820s, as did Richard Knill, missionary to India, Ceylon and Siberia who had recently settled in St Petersburg. Most eminently, the Gilberts received William Ellis and Robert Moffat who, along with the 'martyred' John Williams, were the most popular missionaries of their generation.[91]

As she confessed in the same 1838 correspondence to Rawson, Gilbert was unable to invoke scriptural authority in 'drawing the line correctly between *in door* and *out of doors* business'.[92] She resorted instead to the concept of division of labour, 'the great secret of order and progress' and the general busy-ness of women as wives and mothers. 'So long as houses have insides as well as outsides', she wrote:

> I think that the female head will have enough to do, even, I might also say, irrespective of the numerous demands now making upon her by benevolent and religious societies. To these she does feel it is her duty to attend, but they make a large addition to "women's work" as understood by our grandmothers; still, with a warm heart and managing head, much of this sort may be accomplished, but it seems to me to form the boundary line of her out-of-doors business... Supposing she do this well, wisely, effectively, and see to it at the same time that dinners come *secundum artem*, that shirts have buttons

> (and buttons shirts) – that everything, in short, within the homestead is "done decently and in order" – she will have, to my thinking at least, enough to do![93]

For Gilbert, not only would women taking a Parliamentary role go against the Scriptures, complicate government and take up precious time, but women's missionary domesticity provided a world that was simply *big enough*.

Missionary mothers and public men

Mary-Anne Rawson shared with Ann Taylor Gilbert a sense of her capacious and far-reaching missionary domesticity. She reflected on the relationship between public identities and missionary domestic life in her 'Memorials of James Montgomery', written in 1857. In this unpublished volume, Rawson drew upon sketches, photographs, letters and her own personal reminiscences of James Montgomery, the Sheffield philanthropist and poet, who was also a family friend.[94] The particular subject of her discontent was John Holland's *Memoirs of the Life and Writings of James Montgomery*, published in seven volumes in 1854–1856.[95] Rawson feared that Holland, despite a long acquaintance with Montgomery, was an inappropriate biographer and of insufficient Christian feeling to appreciate fully his subject's character. This was for her, borne out in his failure to locate Montgomery's public role – his pioneering involvement in the formation of Sheffield's civic culture and his place within a national literary culture – within a familial and missionary context. Rawson framed her account with a representation of Montgomery as a missionary: the child of missionary parents, fulfilling the promise of his 'missionary spirit', despite the disappointment of his schooling at Fulneck and the aberration of his early detour into radical politics during his employment as clerk and book-keeper for Joseph Gales, editor of the *Sheffield Register*.[96] Discussing a letter he sent to her family in 1814 informing them of the visit to Zion Independent Chapel, Attercliffe, of a Moravian minister from Fulneck and a missionary recently returned from Labrador, Rawson writes: 'it seems quite in character that this should be the first, and his letter on sending Testaments to China, the last of his notes to us; for he possessed pre-eminently a missionary spirit.'[97]

Rawson's narrative moves backwards and forwards between reminiscences of Montgomery and events of significance within her own life. She recalled the excitement generated by Montgomery's first public speech, his 'coming out publicly as an evangelical Christian', on the occasion of the first anniversary of the Sunday School Union at Nether Chapel in 1813. She enjoyed tales of the conversion of the 'Hottentot' by a returned missionary at the meeting of the West Riding branch of the LMS, held in Sheffield, at which Montgomery made his first missionary speech. Her memories of childhood picnics at Matlock Bath with her parents, Montgomery and George Bennet brought to mind later visits at significant times in her adult life, as a young wife or with her baby daughter Elizabeth, in the months which followed the death of her husband. Her memories of the annual Climbing-Boys' Dinner at which Montgomery often presided reminded her of the compassion of Elizabeth, who had befriended a young climbing-girl at one such event. Montgomery's commitment to Moravian missions enabled her to state her own disapproval of their apparent complicity in the slave trade, while her acknowledgement that Montgomery sometimes despaired at what he called her 'extreme notions (and) ultra views' – her support of total abstinence, immediate abolition and the ending of the death penalty – allowed her expression of her own, quite different opinions. Her pleasure at hearing Montgomery's hymn, 'A Children's Temple Here We Build', written for the opening of Wincobank day-school in 1841, reminded Rawson of his participation in the celebrations of that day. In his participation in the social and religious life of her family, James Montgomery was a member of an extended family of evangelical writers and lay-persons who took Wincobank Hall as their 'family' home. Placing Montgomery's story within her own domestic context, Rawson's 'Memorials' can be read as a corrective to the marginalisation of the 'domestic sphere' and of women within mainstream biography, and an affirmation of her belief in the importance of the evangelical family and missionary domesticity in the making of 'true' missionaries and 'public' men.[98]

Mary-Anne Rawson's commitment to missionary domesticity was delightfully confirmed in her old age in her relationship with her nephew, Henry, a product of her sister Eliza's successful evangelical family life and her own guiding role. Henry had been the 12-year old to whom Rawson had written in 1845, in a letter which will entertain many a mother of sons, to express her disapproval that he had named the hyacinth she had given him 'the Great Conqueror'. She informed him that she had named her own, more appropriately, after her 'favourite ladies' in British history, and suggested that he might like to research them: 'the Lady Rachel' (Russell), the subject of a painting at his Oakhill home in Torquay, sitting 'by Russell's side under the judgement seat'; 'the Lady Jane' (Grey) after 'a learned and gentle woman who challenged a popish priest'; and 'the Lady Griseld', the Patient Griseld celebrated by Chaucer, the perfect wife, daughter, sister and mother who had no published account of her life. We do not have a reply from Henry, and know not if he heeded his aunt's advice, but, as Henry Joseph Wilson (1833–1914), Liberal MP for Holmfirth (1885–1912), an energetic campaigner, with his wife Charlotte, against the Contagious Diseases Acts and, on the domestic front, a solid supporter of his daughters' independence and education, he was later to become living confirmation of the power of evangelical women to produce good and public men.[99]

Conclusion

In a letter to his niece Mary Eliza Wilson in 1843, Edmund Read, by now the manager of the family's silver smelting company in Sheffield, concocted a missionary and domestic tale. He claimed to have only just escaped the 'blood thirsty hands' of roving 'Indians', who were 'breaking up their Wigwams' and making their way southwards for the winter, towards the Wilson family home in Torquay. While the 'Indians' were 'savage barbarians', they were also 'absurd creatures', their absurdity underlined by their choice of a 'squaw' for their 'chief': 'I think that when persons ape what they neither are nor can be, it is best, as far as possible, to treat them with silent contempt', Edmund wrote, 'I should have much more respect for the Squaw Chief, were she to lay aside her feathered headdress and leopard skin robes to look after the Pots and Pans and other domestic concerns.'[100] No doubt inspired by the lecture at Brightside Exhibition Room a few months earlier,[101] Edmund's letter confirmed the place of savagery and civilisation as a theme in the children's play. At a more serious level, his comments about the social organisation of the 'tribe', and in particular the public and leading role of a woman, underscores both the harsher language of savagery that emerged by the 1840s and the belief in the more civilised nature of family life in England.

But while 'civilised' women were 'domestic' women in nineteenth-century England, Mary Eliza Wilson and Lizzie Rawson knew, as did their mothers and other evangelical women, that this was no secluded domesticity. Women's work 'indoors' may have been ordained in the Scriptures and supported by a 'scientific' division of labour, as well as made necessary by their extensive domestic responsibilities, but their commitment to missionary domesticity ensured that their responsibilities were expansive and wide-ranging. Missionary women educated children in political and global concerns, hosted missionary events and welcomed prominent evangelicals and returned missionaries into their homes. They participated in domestic philanthropy and assisted in the missionary project to uplift the position of 'heathen' women across the globe. To this end, they campaigned against slavery and supported the building of schools, the training of female teachers and the education of girls across the globe. Through their missionary philanthropy, evangelical women acquired knowledge about, and adopted very public positions on, 'the world'. Missionary domesticity was profoundly implicated with social and global concerns. It was central to ensuring that Christian principles ran through all spheres of society, and contributed to the new sphere of the 'social' as a site of cultural intervention. It was integral to the construction of middle-class 'social selves' and the collective identity of the evangelical middle class. It created for middle-class women an expansive and commodious world, far removed from the stifling, cloistered, over-upholstered domestic environment that has come to caricature nineteenth-century female society.

4

'Bringing about the World's Restoration': Missionary Women and the Creation of a Global Christian Community

Heathenism and savagery were bound up in the evangelical imagination with domestic cruelty and women's oppression, and the necessity for domestic reform was in evidence all over the globe. In India, home to the first mission station of the Baptist Missionary Society (BMS) and the destination of the pioneering independent female missionaries of the 1820s and 1830s, the low status accorded to women was believed to prevent social change. As suggested by Jemima Thompson in her 'Survey of the condition of woman in heathen countries' (1841), missionaries identified child marriage, the despotic power of the mother-in-law, a lack of regard for the mother among her sons, female infanticide and sati as obstructive to social and religious progress, while their seclusion in the zenana made Indian women especially inaccessible to male missionaries. In China, polygamy, poor education, foot-binding, female slavery and the sale of widows underscored the savage core of an otherwise cultured and lettered people. Women in the South Pacific, like those in North America, were believed to need guidance into the home. Too little differentiation between their roles and those of their menfolk, it was believed, had resulted in a lack of respect for women, who shouldered the burden of heavy labour and were treated as sexual slaves. Finally Africa, long associated in the Christian imagination with heathenism and slavery, was characterised by polygamy, believed to undermine all natural familial ties and responsibilities and to result in the subjection of women and cultural degradation.[1] Despite the different manifestations of women's domestic oppression, it was widely agreed in the missionary movement that happy wives and mothers were exceptions in the heathen world. The reform of woman's lot was of fundamental importance to the civilising mission. It could not, however, be undertaken by missionary men alone.

This chapter explores the prominence of domestic reform in women's overseas missionary practice in the 1820s and early 1830s. The argument that the overseas missionary of the early nineteenth century was an exclusively male figure has been overstated in recent accounts. Valentine Cunningham states the case most strongly, with his assertion that missionary work overseas 'was clearly perceived as a task performed by men that women merely supplemented. Missionary was a male noun; it denoted a male actor, male action, male spheres of service'.[2] While the overseas field was not formally opened to independent female missionaries until after 1860, the 1820s and 1830s were formative decades in women's work as overseas missionaries, witnessing the widespread acceptance of the missionary wife and the early missions of single women, such as Mary Ann Cook, Hannah Kilham and Maria Newell, who journeyed to Calcutta, West Africa and Malacca, respectively, between 1820 and 1826.[3] Reports from the mission field represented wives as primarily committed to domestic work, but the duties that this entailed were extensive. Letters, memoirs and news items disseminated in the missionary press tell of women performing many tasks deemed crucial to the global progress of Christianity and civilisation.

The first part of the chapter argues that the women who participated in the first missions of the 1790s–1830s were active missionaries. Women's missionary work was geared to address the absence of domesticity that featured so prominently in evangelical critiques of 'heathen' cultures. Missionary women ran schools, taught Bible classes and Sunday schools and instructed girls and women in domestic skills. They promoted modesty and a reformed attitude to dress and taught needlework. They set up tract societies and visited the sick and elderly, and learned languages to facilitate all of these activities. They encouraged attendance at chapel, and promoted the rites of baptism, marriage and Christian burial. In addition, they raised their own families and supported those of struggling and ailing colleagues.[4,5] In these tasks, they drew upon skills acquired in the missionary movement at home, particularly as visitors and Sunday school teachers. They took inspiration from Biblical precedent, engaging in acts of teaching which were sometimes very close to preaching, and believed themselves to be building a global Christian community. While missionary men could teach 'heathen' men artisan skills, help them to build new village communities and supervise the Christian development of their rulers, only female missionaries could, in all propriety, gain access to 'native' women and perform the essential work of raising womankind.

Hannah Kilham's work as a missionary pioneer in Ireland and West Africa in the 1820s and 1830s is the focus of the second part of the chapter. Kilham, a Quaker from Sheffield, was an experienced philanthropist prior to her first trip to Gambia in 1823. She has been celebrated by various biographers and historians as a pioneering woman, who broke the confines of feminine domesticity to carve a useful role for Western women as educators and missionaries and who successfully challenged attitudes to the education of African girls.[6] Her emphasis on mother-tongue teaching and her published studies of West African languages have also been seen as pioneering and progressive,[7] leading her to the heart of debates about Africa's capacity for progress and the relationship between missionaries and their subjects. Yet these achievements were in tension with a representation of other cultural groups as in need of her civilising care. While Kilham made important interventions in the debates concerning cultural and biological differences to assert the fundamental likeness of all members of the family of man, at the same time her deployment of a language of maternalism and descriptions of the domestic situations of women contributed to the construction of a hierarchy of civilisation.[8] Domestic reform enabled missionary women such as Kilham to subvert the discourse of domestic femininity through the export of 'Western' notions of domesticity to overseas settings, while at the same time serving to reinforce the new understandings of cultural hierarchy which were emerging in early-nineteenth-century Britain.[9]

Missionary women and global Christianity

Women worked as missionaries from the outset of the overseas movement in the 1790s. They travelled with their husbands to form the first BMS mission to India (1792), the ill-fated London Missionary Society (LMS) mission to Tahiti, Tongatapu and the Marquesas (1796) and with the Methodists and the Church Missionary Society (CMS) to West Africa at the end of the decade. Although not independently selected, women's involvement was considered beneficial to the missionary project, ensuring a happier reception and providing home comforts for missionary men. As teachers and models of appropriate femininity and representatives of the monogamous family, missionary women would impart domestic reform and civilisation. LMS Candidates' Papers from the 1810s state explicitly that capable and hard-working wives helped the selection of their husbands and fiancés. Given the 'considerable influence' of women in 'promoting or retarding the success of the missionaries themselves', stated the Board, 'it becomes the duty of the Directors to examine and to judge whether they possess the views and qualifications which are suitable to the services in which they are to be engaged.' Although women were to be primarily responsible for the missionary household, 'the time which can be spared from domestic affairs, shall be devoted to Missionary Purposes, more especially among the female heathen and their children, both in promoting their civilisation . . . and their religious instruction.'[10] In the words of the directors of LMS, they would exhibit a 'model of a little society under useful regulations, and of a Christian church with its beneficial discipline.'[11] By the late 1810s, it was widely accepted that missions, as well as missionaries, needed wives.

Evangelical women did not become missionary wives merely through the chance of marrying missionary husbands. Many held long-standing ambitions. As suggested by the diary of Mary Ann Middleditch, it was difficult for unmarried women to admit their missionary desires. Mary Ann, who worked as a

Sunday school teacher and tract distributor in Biggleswade and Wellingborough in the late 1820s and early 1830s, first confessed her interest in working as an overseas missionary after reading Statham's *Indian Recollections* in Spring 1830, writing in her diary that 'I *have* almost fancied myself there.'[12] In a letter to a friend, she expressed her envy of an acquaintance about to go to Ceylon as a missionary wife:

> Your dear friend Miss Daniel, is highly favoured; is she not? O, how I *envy* – would I say *envy* her? Oh! how I should *enjoy to partake* of her privilege. What is so honourable, or delightful, as the work of a Missionary.[13]

In a later correspondence, she adopted a confessional tone: '*in confidence,* my mind has lately been much exercised about Missions – and I have been much harassed, lest I should have acted wrong.' Choosing not to work as a missionary felt like a refusal to help God; yet wanting to go also involved a transgression of what was acceptable for a single woman: '*Remember, this letter is to be shown to no one*'. Her desire to work as a missionary became a constant preoccupation for Mary Ann, even on one occasion inducing a case of 'hysterics' following a rousing missionary meeting. In November 1833 she informed her parents of her wishes and shortly afterwards found the key obstacle in her path removed when she met John Hutchins, who was to join William Knibb and Thomas Burchell on their return to Jamaica in April 1834. It was the sign she wanted: after a hasty marriage, she travelled with Hutchins to the West Indies, settling to a short missionary life at Savanna-la-Mar. After her death (in childbed) in November 1838, the Reverend Thomas Abbott wrote: 'She possessed in so eminent a degree a Missionary spirit, that her fitness for the important station she filled, must have been manifest to the casual observer...'[14]

Prior to their marriages, would-be missionary wives worked as collectors, Sunday school teachers or Bible society visitors. They were sought out as partners in the missionary life; or indeed, like Mary Ann Middleditch, did the seeking themselves.[15] Elizabeth Parks, for example, who became the wife of the Reverend William

Harvard, Wesleyan missionary in (then) Ceylon from 1814, had worked in Hoxton as a Sunday school teacher, a visitor to sick children and distributor of religious tracts, and had been 'looked upon as a future female Missionary' by ministers of the Society in London. Mary Ann Chambers, sister of Hiram Chambers, himself a missionary candidate for the Indian field, wrote letters to her brother at Gosport Academy in December 1816 expressing her desire to engage in overseas work: 'how does my soul anticipate the day when I shall leave my native land, and enter upon that blessed work!' In February 1817, within a fortnight of meeting the Reverend James Coultart, Mary Ann had married him and was on her way to missionary wifehood in the Caribbean. Margaret Morley, teacher at a Wesleyan School near Doncaster and a visitor and collector for Bible and Missionary Societies, experienced a particular calling on attending the anniversaries of the Wesleyan Methodist Missionary Society (WMMS) and British and Foreign Bible Society (BFBS) in London in 1823. Shortly afterwards, she met Benjamin Clough, a missionary who was soon to return to India; within a month, he had asked for her hand.[16] Eliza Clarkson distributed tracts, attended missionary meetings, collected for the missionary society and was generally immersed in missionary concerns in Hull in the 1830s. Her first diary entry about becoming a missionary came on 1 August 1834, the day of slave emancipation: 'I think I could freely spend, and be spent, in the Missionary cause, were I called. There is much labour there.' The following year, H. B. Foster asked her to marry him, and she accepted in the full knowledge of his wish to become a missionary: 'I am anticipating the time when I shall take some small part in these labours with you . . . ' Married in July 1839, the couple arrived in Jamaica in January 1841, where until her death 20 months later, Eliza was, in her husband's words, 'the sharer of a missionary's toils'.[17]

It was sometimes the case that entire families of evangelical sisters and daughters engaged in the missionary cause. When in 1818 Martha Cobden was invited by her sister, the wife of William Reeve, (LMS) missionary in Karnataka, India from 1816, to help out at the Bellary mission station, she took over domestic concerns, opened a small boarding school, and began to learn Canarese. In 1821, having acquired a taste for the missionary life, Martha married the Reverend George Mundy, travelling to Chinsurah, Bengal, where she learned the language, opened a school for girls, and taught domestic skills to young ladies. A third Cobden sister became Mrs Archibald Murray, missionary wife in India.[18] Selina MacDonald and Deborah Stevens, wives of Alexander MacDonald and Charles Stevens, respectively, missionaries in the South Pacific from the 1830s, were daughters of evangelical Congregational minister, the Reverend Ezekiel Blomfield. Two more of their sisters were married to missionaries in New Zealand. Similarly, three sisters of the Hitchcock family were married to Aaron Buzacott and Charles Hardie, both stationed in Tahiti from the late 1820s and mid-1830s, respectively, and James Sewell, missionary in India from 1838. Given the importance of familial participation in missionary events and the significance of missionary commitments in domestic and social lives, one can well imagine the excitement with which sisters planned for such marital adventures.

Despite a keen recognition of their importance by both male relatives and missionary society directors, official missionary reports and many published memoirs downplayed the scope of the role of the missionary wife. William Ellis denied a full missionary status to his recently deceased colleague Mary Williams in her obituary in 1852. She possessed 'many of the essential qualities of a *good missionary's wife*,' he wrote, '...to be more than this she did not aspire, and less she never was.' Ellis did not diminish the value of women's work, however: 'It is easy to trace the effects which follow teaching a native woman to read, and to write, and to use the needle; or a man to use the hammer and the saw, to provide himself a better house, and a more fruitful garden, but', he continued:

> it is not easy to estimate the vastly more beneficial effects produced on uncivilised communities, by the perpetual daily example of a well-ordered, consistent, Christian family; and it is here that the influence of a missionary's wife is clearly seen, and powerfully exercised.[19]

While celebrated by Ellis as offering nothing more energetic than example and good domestic management, we learn elsewhere of the range of duties that Mrs Williams performed: she learned the language, held Bible meetings, encouraged women to wear bonnets and taught them to cut and sew gowns.[20] Like Ellis's own wife, the long-suffering Mary Mercy Ellis, who travelled with him to Tahiti, Huahine and Bora-bora where she taught Christianity and domestic skills to women and girls, Mrs Williams' activities were fundamental to the evangelical conception of mission and global Christian progress.[21] Mary Williams, it seems, 'was no less assiduous in her department than her husband was in his'.[22]

Indeed, the two Marys and the domestic revolution that they pursued in the South Pacific also made a success of a hitherto failing mission. As I discuss in Chapter 6, despite some outstanding early volunteers, the first missionary cohort to the area had produced a number of outlandish failures, and it was the arrival in 1817 of a new team of missionary couples that was believed to rescue the mission. Including the Williams and Ellis families, the new group was soon notoriously at odds with the older brethren, and the issue of domestic propriety was central to their critique. They were horrified to find missionaries and their wives living in basic houses which they described as 'bird cages'. The dress of the established missionaries, or lack of it, their general dishevelment and various accommodations to indigenous culture, were all condemned, as was the perceived wildness of some among their children;[23] and all this before the lack of conversions had even been considered. This reaction, as Niel Gunson has suggested, was fuelled by culture shock, and the new missionaries' criticism of their brethren ignored neglect by the LMS in London, for which the evidence is considerable.[24] They also ignored the domestic successes of some within the first group: Hannah Crook, for example, an indefatigable teacher of girls, had introduced bonnet-making and made baptismal gowns, and later became a midwife to royalty.[25] Determined to make their mark through establishing a more respectable, domestic mission, Williams, Ellis, Threlkeld, Orsmond and others moved to the neighbouring islands of Mo'orea, Huahine and Raiatea, where their wives played an important role in the construction of the new bourgeois missionary domesticity.[26] When George Bennet and Daniel Tyerman arrived in the islands on their supervisory visit with the LMS in 1822, they were quick to identify the importance of wives in enabling cultural change.[27]

The promotion of missionary domesticity, like the mission more broadly, was a precarious enterprise. That the women on the receiving end of the mission did not always receive Christianity in the manner intended, will be discussed in the next part of the chapter. Missionary domesticity was sometimes further challenged from within the missionary family itself. There were many instances of women suffering poor physical and mental health, and numerous occasions when children adopted behaviour which, in the words of Lancelot Threlkeld, 'stopp[ed] the peace of a parent's breast.'[28] Private letters from the South Pacific, for example, tell of errant behaviour: of boys choosing to become circumcised and of both sexes becoming tattooed and engaging in premarital sexual activity.[29] This situation was not much improved with the founding of the South Seas Academy on Eimeo in 1824. Indeed, missionaries later sent their children to school in Auckland or Sydney, while others left them with relatives in Britain. This represented not only a profound personal anxiety, but potentially undermined the entire basis for the mission. Children were the product of the new Christian community, but were more influenced by their 'heathen' peers than by the Christian culture their parents had striven so hard to create.[30]

Hannah Kilham's domestic mission

Hannah Kilham's pioneering missionary work in Sheffield, Ireland and West Africa in the 1810s–1830s contributes to our understanding of women's sphere within the civilising mission and to the interconnections between projects at home and overseas. A convert to Methodism in 1794, she joined the New Connexion in 1797,[31] marrying its leader and becoming a Sunday school teacher in Nottingham. Back in Sheffield following her husband's death, and with a daughter and step-daughter to care for, Kilham (Figure 9) opened a school and made a final

Figure 9 Silhouette Portrait of Hannah Kilham. (Courtesy of The Library of the Religious Society of Friends, London.)

denominational move in 1804, when she joined the Society of Friends. In the same year, she became a founder member of the Sheffield Society for Bettering the Condition of the Poor (1804) and over the next decade became active in a range of other societies, including the Sheffield Bible Association, the Society for Visiting and Relieving Aged Females and the Girls' Lancasterian School. On top of committee and visiting responsibilities, she attended Balby Quaker Meeting and wrote numerous reports and a number of tracts and pamphlets.[32]

Kilham operated within the nonconformist tradition in which all believers, including women, received God's message in their own hearts and were accorded the power to speak, preach and, indeed, to protest. She was assured of her possession of spiritual equality and, as her denominational shifts suggest, of her right to stand up to authority in the process of being true to herself and to God. Her thoughts about travelling to Africa, inspired by the publicity surrounding Edward Bickersteth's journey to Sierra Leone, and first expressed in her diary in 1816, were not unproblematic. While there was greater fluidity in their understanding of gender roles among early-nineteenth-century Friends than in other nonconformist sects and denominations,[33] Quaker ideas of active female religiosity quite emphatically did not stretch to envisioning a single woman leading a missionary party to 'heathen' Africa. Even within the Committee for African Instruction, formed in 1820 to promote Kilham's proposal to travel to West Africa to find suitable young men to be trained as missionaries in England,[34] and which later became the first mixed-sex committee within the Society of Friends, there was considerable hesitation about a woman travelling alone.[35] The group arranged for William Singleton, a Quaker schoolmaster from Sheffield, to be despatched to assess the situation in West Africa in 1821, while Friends at home canvassed a suitable male companion.[36] Eventually making her first trip to Gambia in 1823, Kilham and Ann Thompson, a Quaker from Cooladine, Ireland, were accompanied by two obligatory males, Richard Smith, a Quaker land surveyor from Staffordshire who had previous experience of American missions, and John Thompson, Ann's brother, without a missionary commitment but a keen and burly lad who, it was believed, would provide protection for the women.[37] Ironically, both men were dead before Kilham returned home in 1824.

A traditional hostility to missions within the Society of Friends also impeded Kilham's journey to Africa. Many Quakers rejected the missionary emphasis on the written text of the Bible as at odds with the belief in the inner light and divine ministry. Traditionally a quietist sect, the Friends placed emphasis on the quality of individual faith, and Quaker meetings were often conducted in silence, in the belief that God only spoke to a still and receptive soul.[38] The early nineteenth century had seen movement away from an exclusive emphasis on the inner light, as some Friends were influenced by the evangelical revival to become involved in the BFBS (1804), civic philanthropy and the Lancasterian system of education. Quaker women became aware of women's work overseas through their participation in the Ladies' Committee of the British and Foreign School Society (1813), which provided training to women teachers in Britain and to early female missionaries.[39] While many Friends continued to resist so explicit an engagement with 'the world', a group with evangelical sympathies led by Joseph John Gurney, William Allen and Luke Howard, shared Kilham's sentiment that Quakers needed to be more outward-looking, to turn their attention to their less 'polished' brothers and sisters overseas.[40]

The missionary impulse nonetheless placed Kilham and her friends in a marginal position within the Society. When she presented her ideas to form a school of West African languages in England at the 1819 Yearly Meeting, she encountered considerable hostility from members within the main body of Friends.[41] In her *Address to Friends* (1820), she sought to address Quaker antagonism, offering an assurance that she accepted the 'sound and charitable principle... that the heathen to whom the outer knowledge of the gospel has not reached, do not necessarily perish for want of it.' However, she argued, the operations of the slave trade had produced obstacles, a 'mental darkness', which prevented Africans from each seeing their inner light. 'Will any feeling mind', she asked:

> therefore deny that the outward knowledge is profitable in addition to the inward?... [C]onsidering that these *are* men, who have *minds* to be instructed, and *souls*, for whose sake as for our own the blessed redeemer came into the world... have we, in the Society of Friends, yet done for them all that is in our power to do?[42]

To many Quakers, however, her plan to train men to evangelise their own peoples suggested that she was not a linguist and an educator, as she insisted,[43] but a missionary tinged with Methodist enthusiasm.

Hannah Kilham eventually made three trips to West Africa, travelling to Gambia in 1823–1824 and to Sierra Leone in 1827–1828 and 1830–1832. Prior to 1823, however, stymied by obstacles of both gender and denomination, she turned her attention to two missionary projects closer to home. Firstly, she became involved in the education of Sandanee and Mahmadee, two West African men she had sought out on the River Thames. From Gorée and the banks of the Gambia, respectively, both men were enslaved, the property of a merchant at Gorée, and were working as sailors in London. They agreed to teach Kilham the rudiments of the Wolof and Mandingo languages,[44] and in return were given a Christian education.[45] Kilham's second project saw her travel to Ireland in 1822, as a representative of the newly formed British and Irish Ladies' Society (BILS).

Wretched cabins, little palaces: domestic reform in Ireland

The British and Irish Ladies' Society for Improving the Condition and Promoting the Industry and Welfare of the Female Peasantry in Ireland was established in 1822 as an offshoot of the London Committee, set up to coordinate relief across Ireland as famine followed a very wet spring and the subsequent rotting of the potato crop.[46] As its full title suggests, the BILS was interested in permanent improvement rather than temporary relief. Inspired by the philosophy and practice of the Society for Bettering the Condition of the Poor (SBCP), supporters of the society in London included philanthropists with an extensive experience of missionary work, including Elizabeth Howard, Anne Fry and Sarah Trimmer.[47]

In Ireland, the BILS shared membership with other missionary societies, but differed in its primary focus on domestic reform rather than the distribution of the Scriptures.[48] Active in promoting moral reform but free from clerical influence, the society was unique in bringing together middle-class women with the Anglo-Irish female gentry who traditionally dispensed relief throughout Ireland.[49] The relative 'absence of gentry and the want of a middle-class in society' was identified by Kilham as the reason why the condition of the poor was so miserable in

Ireland: they had no example to look up to, and could 'frequently pass on from youth to age without seeing anything of order, cleanliness, and industry, superior to what their own hovel presents.'[50] The organisation canvassed the patronage of aristocratic ladies in Ireland and supported the establishment of district associations. By 1823, 135 auxiliaries had emerged across Ireland, expanding to 254 across 29 counties in 1824. Like the SBCP in England, the ladies engaged in visiting and investigation into the lives of the poor, placing great emphasis on 'going into their dwellings and seeing... with our own eyes.'[51] In counterpoint to Catholic charity, the BILS helped to create missionary philanthropy as a middle-class Protestant movement in Ireland.[52]

The BILS identified the 'wretched cabin' as the locus of Ireland's ills. The home was the site and origin of poverty and immorality: the 'apathy and listlessness', 'despondency, dependence and idleness' which were believed to characterise the 'indolent' Irish peasant could all be 'traced back to the miserable habits in the midst of which he is born and bred'. Even drunkenness, Hannah Kilham confirmed, was the product of domestic failure, the result of 'their wretched condition at home.' Catholicism was a factor here, though we deduce this from the tone of the writing and its compatibility with other accounts rather than any explicit attack on the Roman church in Ireland. Catholicism was nonetheless believed by evangelicals to assist such disorder, fostering an unhealthy society characterised by indolence, passivity and a lack of responsibility.[53] These were disasters of circumstance and not of nature. Indeed, Kilham respected the care and concern that the Irish people showed each other: '... there is a feeling of generous kindness in the Irish peasant that shines and is beautiful amidst all the depressing circumstances with which he is surrounded', she wrote. The peasant relieved of his poverty was a supporter of neighbours in trouble; and even when they were 'nearly naked', he sent his children to school.[54]

The ladies made the philanthropic provision of assistance dependent upon women's 'moral reaction', evidenced by their commitment to domestic reform. The accounts of local associations, such as that from the parish of Castlemagner in County

Cork in 1823, specified the importance of a 'return'.[55] Attention was to be given to household cleanliness, airiness and annual whitewashing (believed to ward off typhus); pigs should be banished from the house. The ground next to the home should be levelled and weeded, and vegetable and flower plots constructed, with the manure heap located at a healthy distance. Children were to be clean and orderly, and mothers encouraged to wear 'a short jacket and apron, such as is used in the west of Scotland, and which are better adapted to household work, and less wasteful of cloth, than the long slatternly gown generally worn in Ireland.' Only when inspection had shown these to be fulfilled were households deemed eligible for spinning wheels, flax, wool, linen and flannel and nets for fishery.[56] In supplying women with the means to improve their livelihood via 'useful employment', the ladies acknowledged the particular vulnerability of women to economic distress. The BILS arranged for them to sell clothing and articles to newly opened shops and a Repository in London and buy other goods 'requisite for their health and comfort' at a subsidised rate.[57] Their policies attested to the belief in the superiority of such domestic organisation, and contested the increasingly popular belief in England that Irish people were naturally 'lazy, bigoted and ungrateful', suggesting that through the inculcation of 'virtue and piety' and 'habits of industry, cleanliness and an attention to domestic duty', Ireland could be transformed.[58]

Kilham sought to further assist change in Ireland with her *Thoughts for the House*, created for display in the homes of the poor (Figure 10). Four sheets, each decorated with a fancy border, depict peasant families engaged in useful employment, such as spinning, knitting, and bonnet- and basket-making, in clean, sparse and well-aired homes. Like Kilham's *Family Maxims*, published in 1817 for use among the English poor, the text exhorts women to send their children to school and to concentrate on making a good home. 'It is by doing useful things', urges one, 'a little and a little, that a man will in time make a barren spot beautiful, and a woman make her house tidy, snug and pleasant.' 'When the mother of a family is conscientious, kind, cheerful, neat, orderly, and diligent', proclaimed another, 'she will be

Figure 10 Hannah Kilham, 'Thoughts for the House', *Report of the British and Irish Ladies' Society* (1826). (Courtesy of The Library of the Religious Society of Friends, London.)

doing good to the whole house – every day.'[59] Such sentiments were echoed in the *Reports* of the BILS: 'Whatever tends to create industry and civilisation among the females will be found to influence the whole family.'[60]

In addition to women, Ireland's 'future mothers' were to receive training in domestic skills and 'moral feeling' in newly established schools.[61] In 1827, the British and Irish Ladies' Society set up a Model Infant School in Longford, and it was hoped that its example would be replicated through the nation. Both sexes were to learn skills in knitting, plaiting and basket-making; the boys were also to garden, while girls hemmed and sewed and stayed behind after lessons to clean up.[62] The focus on domestic and manual skills was to be supplemented by shorter periods devoted to religious education, play and instruction in reading and writing. As skilled and virtuous labourers and domestic workers, Ireland's children were to be instruments of national regeneration. Among the texts from which the children were to be taught were Hannah Kilham's *Scripture Selections* and *First Principles of the Christian Religion*, suggesting Kilham's belief that exposure to the same methods would benefit the heathen poor in England and the Catholic Irish.

The *Reports* of the BILS, written in the narrative style of missionary reports, abound with joyful accounts of the 'wretched and disconsolate' becoming 'cheerful smiling faces'; women who had become more clean and self-respecting; who would now willingly walk miles to each others' houses in order to spin; whose motivation enabled them to work all night long. 'A spirit of industry has been excited', proclaimed a contribution from Waterford, 'and the generality of our poor women seem as if awakening from a long dream of depression, indolence and wretchedness.'[63] An account from Carlow emphasised the impact of employment in making previously 'filthy' cabins 'clean and comfortable.'[64] Kilham endorsed such accounts. 'It was cheering', she wrote following a day's visiting with the Countess of Clare, 'to see the industry, cleanliness and comfort that could be found in a cabin...'[65] Attention to the habits and moral principles of mothers and 'future mothers of the families of Ireland' was producing a 'gradual' but nonetheless 'real advancement in moral feeling' which, it was believed, 'was calculated to have the most extensive and desirable effects on the habits of the rising generation.'[66]

The relationship between the missionary and missionary subject is, of course, much more complex than that allowed by the above interpretations. The women on the receiving end of the mission often used charity to quite different ends from those intended. This is suggested by the following typically energetic account of the personal transformation of a Limerick woman whose cabin, on their initial visit, was reportedly 'dyed with smoke, and hung with spider's webs... [and] the colour of the floor had evidently not been seen for a long time past.' The visitors discussed her response to their offers of assistance, reporting that their suggestion that they could provide the necessary lime for whitewashing was received 'languidly', the woman stating that she would prefer to be given the price of the lime, with which she would buy potatoes. However, when the ladies offered to lend her a spinning wheel, 'her countenance brightened up in a moment, and she earnestly replied "Ah! If you'll lend me a wheel, and let me spin, I'll whitewash and do anything you please!"' She promptly applied to the Board of Health for whitewashing materials, expressing her desire that her home should be cleaner before they called again.[67] This is suggestive of a more complex system of exchange. While it is difficult to hear voices other than those of the missionaries themselves, instances such as this reveal that although some aspects of the civilising mission were accepted as of benefit to them, Irish women did not concur with the ladies' interpretation of their lives.[68] For this woman at least, a spinning wheel meant employment, money, food, a degree of independence, and not moral regeneration.

For the Protestant ladies, the experience of Irish homes contributed to a hierarchy of civilisation. Kilham reported the 'dwellings' of the Irish poor as characterised by a particular wretchedness, a depravity on a scale unknown in England. 'I do not conceive it possible', she wrote in her journal,

> for any language or picture of destitution to have conveyed to any mind the impressions received from the actual sight of the peasantry, as they at present exist. The wretched cabin built by the hard-straining efforts of extreme poverty, is destitute of almost everything that could mark any attainment of civilised life.[69]

Only the heart-felt response and energetic activity on the part of ladies could remedy the domestic disorder which was responsible for the nation's position at a lower stage of civilisation. Making some concession to the efforts of the people to combat their poverty, Kilham, as Lucas Balfour later reflected, was engaged in the task of 'raising human beings into a state to provide themselves with the accommodations of civilised life', the need for which was as great in the south and west of Ireland as in 'Africa or the wilds of America.'[70]

On her arrival in Gambia in December 1823, less than a year after her unflattering descriptions of Irish cabins, Kilham compared African 'huts' – 'so close, and dirty and comfortless – so unlike what we could desire to see as human habitations' – with cabins in Ireland, concluding that 'degraded as are the poor peasantry of Ireland, they are in some respects much better prepared for improvement than the Jolas are.'[71] She returned to this theme a few weeks later, writing that she longed to 'see the people here put in the way of forming better dwellings, many of the *poorer* Irish cabins I have seen are like little palaces in comparison with some of these African huts.'[72] This description of Irish homes had little bearing on Kilham's experience of them. It served rather to emphasise Africa's position in a hierarchy of civilisation, constructed in terms of the proximity of a cabin, hovel or hut to the comfortable home of the Christian English woman.

African huts: Gambia and Sierra Leone, 1823–1832

Despite Kilham's assessment of the state of homes in Gambia, she had absolute faith that with missionary intervention, domestic and social progress would occur. Early experiences confirmed this expectation. While initially unpromising, Kilham's meeting with the 'Alcaide' (El Kadi)[73] of Bakau soon after their arrival in December 1823 was soon interpreted as a positive sign of a capacity to change. Their association had begun badly: such had been the eminent African's interest in the missionary project that he had forgotten about the first planned meeting, and was not at home when they arrived for their introduction. When they finally met, Kilham was unimpressed: he had 'a straw hat on his head; his whole appearance was uncouth, and expressive of listlessness and apathy. As I looked at him', she wrote, 'I could not but sigh to think how very, very far remote these people are from a state of civilisation...'[74] This feeling was reinforced by his antipathy to English education. While accepting that others might wish to send their children to the mission school, he had no interest in educating his own children in English: 'He taught them Arabic at home', Kilham wrote, 'and others at Birkow did the same for their children; and he thought their learning Arabic was sufficient!...OTHERS MIGHT DO AS THEY LIKED'; she wrote, the punctuation and capital letters serving to underscore the extent of her horror.[75]

This negative impression was counteracted, however, by the El Kadi's request that the visitors should build a stone house for him as well as for themselves. That he had articulated a wish for a 'better habitation' in which to live was promising on two counts: it indicated that he had a capacity for envisaging progress; and that he had understood the centrality of domesticity to civilisation. 'We were really glad to hear him make the suggestion', Kilham wrote, 'not merely for the reasonableness of his wish, that white men should thus give proof of their benevolence; but also that he should EXPRESS A WISH TO HAVE A BETTER HOUSE TO LIVE IN.' This, she concluded, would put him on the road to civilisation.[76]

Kilham was also encouraged by her work with children. She had been certain of the capacity for improvement of African people from the day she set foot on the Gambian shore. Looking around her at the potential subjects of her mission, she reported that 'the countenances of many of the natives' looked 'interesting and intelligent, and bespeak a mental soil that would well repay a friendly and liberal cultivation.'[77] Kilham and Ann Thompson had been initially disappointed to find that Bakau was not a Wolof-speaking area, and had to change their plans and open schools at Bathurst, the boys taught by Sandanee, if they were to put her books to the test.[78] Kilham emphasised the speed with which the children learned to read in the Wolof language: 'With regard to intelligence', she wrote in Gambia in 1823, 'we do not find the black girls in any degree behind the mulatto, or white children, so far as we have had the opportunity to judge'.[79]

Kilham knew that she had to be better acquainted with the domestic situations of ordinary Africans if she was to make a true assessment of Gambian potential for change. As she confessed in her journal, this was not as straightforward as in colder climates: 'as they were out at the door, there was little occasion to enter the huts, but I went in one or two,' she wrote, without comment on whether or not her entry was invited. Kilham's 'sighs of sadness' at these visits were not at the more easily remedied domestic 'laxity and indolence' of the women, but at the fundamental and structural place of polygamy within society. A barbaric system which 'unhinges these strong and endearing connexions of domestic life', polygamy was believed by Christians to place women in a 'dreary bondage and degradation ... both in body and mind' that was akin to slavery. The foundation of such customs on primitive social organisation at least suggested that African 'barbarism' was not an immutable fact, however, and like other practices, such as slavery, the division of labour and popular cultural expressions such as the Joulah dance that had so disgusted Hannah Kilham, it could change.[80] Indeed, within a few days of opening the school at Bathurst, she was delighted to encounter married women expressing an interest in her needlework classes. Unable to participate because of their accompanying small children, she 'made them presents of workbags, &c. that they might manage their needlework at home.'[81]

Kilham's positive experiences in Gambia were reinforced by her short excursion to Sierra Leone in February–April 1824. Here, she was cheered by evidence of domestic improvement. Many of the 'liberated Africans' had built themselves 'firm stone-houses, with piazzas to them, and gardens behind.'[82] Her delight echoed that of Singleton who, visiting homes in Regent's Town in April 1821, stopped to admire the 'sofas, covered with clean print, or the country cloth; tables, forms, or chairs; and, especially, I noticed in each house a corner-cupboard with its appropriate crockery ware. The beds and sleeping rooms are remarkably neat and clean ... '[83] Kilham was impressed with the ease with which missionary wives, and in particular Maria Macfoy, the American-educated African wife of the (West Indian) superintendent of Freetown, taught domestic skills, transforming African girls into 'clever cooks, house-maids and laundresses'. The 'African FEMALE', she wrote, might 'in time be led to regard with desire and admiration ... [the] domestic order, decency, quietness, [and] cleanliness' of Christian family life.[84]

Kilham was further impressed with the children's learning at the mission schools. At the 'free village' of Leopold, she met a little boy who had learned to read the New Testament in six months, and at Charlotte encountered a six-year-old girl who could read 'the account of the sick and palsy restored' after only 15 months instruction.[85] Writing to William Allen, Kilham declared there was 'no inferiority in the African mind.'[86] Kilham went on to criticise those Europeans who claimed certainty of African inferiority based solely on encounters with 'a few of those who have been slaves, or mostly beggars' and who hadn't witnessed the 'bright, intelligent countenances of many of the children.'[87] She insisted that in Africa the impact of slavery was of such magnitude that it was impossible to conceive of the peoples' true potential. Slavery had inhibited individuals and damaged relationships between family members and different cultural groups; it had produced a society which was locked into barbarism. 'It is very unfair and a great aggravation to the cruelty,' she wrote in a letter to the *Missionary Register* in 1824,

> to reflect on the victims of it, as LACKING ABILITY for any other station than that which they have been suffered to fill...I am fully convinced that it is not any inferiority in the African mind or natural capacity that has kept them in so depressed a state in the scale of society, but the lack of those advantages, which are, in the usual order of Providence, made use of for the advancement and improvement of human beings...I do not think that even here [Sierra Leone], Africans have had a fair trial of what they might be, had they had the same advantages in education, and circumstances connected, which Europeans have been favoured with.[88]

Kilham's experience of children's learning in Africa thus led her straight to the heart of contemporary debates within Britain about cultural and biological difference and Africa's capacity for improvement.

Kilham's assessment of Sierra Leone was of particular significance as Britons expressed fears that the infant nation had not yet 'exhibited all those encouraging marks of advancement, either in civil or religious knowledge, which have been anxiously desired'.[89] Sierra Leone had been the focus of a sustained excitement among evangelical Christians since the 1780s, when British hopes for African improvement had come to focus on the newly established settlement.[90] It was here that the first Christian Church in West Africa had been formed, by men and women arriving from London and America.[91] The CMS took

Sierra Leone as its first mission field, and from 1816 the combined efforts of Edward Bickersteth, its secretary, and the newly appointed governor Charles MacCarthy, kept the colony in the evangelical gaze with the establishment of 'free villages' for the settlement of 'liberated Africans'.[92] MacCarthy built churches and mission schools, and ordered bells, clocks, prayer books and weathervanes from England, along with Sunday attire of hats and bonnets, gowns and petticoats, trousers and braces.[93] While such fashioning of the Christian community in the style of European Christianity placed Sierra Leone at the heart of Christian Africa, the slowness of subsequent attempts at conversion saw a waning of interest in Britain.[94] In her accounts, Kilham adopted a by-now familiar missionary teleology, in which stereotypical descriptions of 'savage' men and women were put alongside evidence of their improvement. This was crucial for publicity, but also for self-belief if contributors to missions and missionaries themselves were to see a role for themselves as the agents of positive change.

Kilham's contention was that African development could occur only through a missionary commitment to mother-tongue teaching of the Scriptures. She had made her first trip to Gambia in 1823 with the intention of trying out her books *Ta-Re Waloof, Ta-re boo Juk-a: First Lessons in Jaloof* (1820) and *African Lessons* (1823). These books, both of which had emerged out of her work with Sandanee and Mahmadee, were written in English and a phonetically 'reduced' version of Wolof. They began with a few 'leading words', a basic vocabulary of objects, parts of the body and religious terms, such as 'heaven' and 'ALLA, The Supreme being, God', before progressing to full sentences and finally to parts of the Scriptures. *African Lessons* also contained moral tales, questions and answers on the Scriptures and 'family advices'.[95] That these were reproductions of her earlier publications used with the British and Irish poor indicates Kilham's belief that Christian truths had a universal meaning and that people underwent the same process in order to acquire them.[96]

In her promotion of mother-tongue teaching, Kilham was operating within an established missionary tradition. The evangelical association of language and religious understanding had an early precedent in the practice of the Charity School movement in England, Scotland, Wales and Ireland in the early eighteenth century.[97] Later overseas missionaries had drawn upon this tradition. Most famously, William Carey, Baptist missionary to India from 1793, whom Kilham met whilst visiting her friend Elizabeth Rowntree at Scarborough in 1827, translated the Bible into more than 40 Indian languages and dialects.[98] In Africa, early transcriptions were undertaken by Edward Brunton of the Edinburgh Missionary Society and Melchior Renner and Gustavus Nylander of the CMS, who translated parts of the Scriptures into the Susu and Bullom languages.[99] Kilham's own *Specimens of African Languages spoken in the Colony of Sierra Leone* (1828) was a substantial piece of research, containing lessons in 30 African languages.[100] It was the result of her labours in the villages of Sierra Leone in 1827–1828, where she combined research trips to schools in the 'free villages' with Maria Macfoy with opening her own school at Charlotte, in the mountains above Freetown, teaching in Mende and Yoruba. Kilham also opened a book stall, selling her own textbooks and Ann Gilbert's *Infant School Hymns* as well as publications from the Religious Tract Society.[101] Kilham's work in the field of mother-tongue teaching suggests the expansiveness of women's missionary work. Teaching from the Scriptures placed her alongside missionary wives, while publishing her own books also located her as part of a largely male community of philologists. During her first visit to Gambia, for example, Kilham met the acclaimed philologist T. E. Bowditch, whereas in Sierra Leone during the early 1830s she worked alongside Methodist John Raban, who was studying the Aku and the Igbo languages.[102] She also sent her books across the globe to Lancelot Threlkeld, missionary to the aborigines in Australia and who was producing scriptural translations and grammars in the Awabakal language.[103]

Kilham elaborated on the benefits of mother-tongue teaching in her *Report on a Recent Visit to Sierra Leone* (1828), which details her evolving appreciation of the complexity of issues involved in teaching the Scriptures. She contested the practice of presenting children with English texts without any translation. The words were 'mere sound', she wrote, and produced a 'barbarous broken form' of English; 'although many learn in time to *read* and *spell*, those who are thus circumstanced cannot be expected to *understand* what they read'.[104] Such an approach, she wrote in her journal, led to:

> the mere repetition of prayers, and attention to certain outward forms ... a false rest, wherein the mind is left untouched and cold, the tempers and dispositions wayward and uncontrolled by that renewing influence which can alone introduce harmony, and order, and true love.[105]

Evangelical attention to 'feeling' and inner transformation demanded a more rigorous practice of translation. Kilham's contention was that 'the estimable treasure of the Scriptures' could be made accessible 'to all the tribes of our African brethren who are or may be within our reach'. 'By opening up the doors for intelligible communication with the people, through the native languages', she wrote on her last trip in 1830,' ... it will soon be discovered that Africans have the power to cultivate, and the disposition to improve, that would well repay the Christian labours of their European brethren.'[106]

During the 1820s, missionaries became more aware of the complexities of translation. Experience was beginning to suggest that mere exposure to a mother-tongue Bible did not produce Christians, and that the process involved not only language reduction but the translation of meaning. William Singleton, Kilham's Quaker predecessor in Gambia and Sierra Leone, had grappled with this issue.[107] Methodist missionary John Morgan, while happy that the 'recaptured' Africans with whom he worked in Gambia were so receptive to hearing the Bible, was concerned that his account of the New Testament was understood in terms of the 'greegrees [amulets], charms and superstition' of the indigenous culture.[108] As Kilham later articulated in a somewhat exasperated register, 'the whole of the heathen population of the Colony would press to the Baptismal font, if we would receive them there on an understanding that Baptism is of all

Greegrees the best.'[109] The issue of idolatry raised similar concerns. 'The dear children give a name as applied to the Supreme Being', Kilham wrote:

> yet, so far as we understand them, they have not been taught to look to Him as the Creator of all things, and with but little knowledge of a peoples' views on these Sacred Subjects, I could not adopt a name said to be the Divine Name, from the fear that we should be receiving only the name of an Idol.[110]

Indigenous interaction with Christianity was obviously shaped by existing beliefs.[111] It was increasingly recognised that, however careful the translation, converts may not receive the gospel in the way intended by the missionaries. The very proliferation of translations of the Bible diminished missionary control and heightened their anxieties about the integrity of their subjects.[112]

Kilham's vision for West Africa saw Africans ultimately taking responsibility for evangelising their countrymen and women. While British missionaries had a role as teachers, living with and working alongside the people, it was African Christians, educated at mission schools in their own languages and employed as teachers in village schools, who would 'promote by friendly Christian communication, the instruction, the civilisation, and the evangelising of the people on this continent.'[113] In Britain too, Kilham hoped to see groups of African girls taught by domestic missionaries before returning home as teachers to 'contribute to the advancement of the Female character on the coast of Africa'.[114] In her forceful support for 'native agency', Kilham engaged with the widespread missionary anxiety concerning the integrity of African conversions: whether, in the words of a contributor to the *Missionary Register* in 1831, they were resting on 'insecure foundations'.[115] While much missionary writing of the 1820s swings between an enthusiastic parading of conversions and an anxious hand-wringing about their quality, Kilham argued, quite possibly with Sandanee and Mahmadee in mind, that a Christian education remained worthwhile even if converts were to engage in 'subsequent misconduct'.[116] For her, setbacks were an inevitable part of the progress of Christianisation in a part of the world which had been so impeded by the slave trade. Far from suggesting that Africans could not be educated, they merely pointed to a longer process of civilisation, which required continued supervision by Europeans.

Kilham drew on a familial metaphor to articulate the relationship between Britain and West Africa: 'Our great duty towards Africa', she wrote:

> is to strengthen the hands of the people *to promote each other's good*... It is the Africans themselves that must be the Travellers, and Instructors, and Improvers of Africa. Let the Europeans aid them with Christian kindness, as senior brethren would the younger and feebler members of their Father's family.[117]

Through care and education by missionaries, African people were to achieve adulthood. Writing in 1831, she expressed the complexity of this relationship, in which missionaries too had things to learn:

> As superintendents and directors, we should ever bear in mind that we are fellow-probationers with the dear children,... all other distinctions seem lost in the contemplation of this.[118]

While criticising representations of African people as inferior and insisting on their own probationer status in the eyes of God, Hannah Kilham drew on languages of superintendence and parenthood which undercut her insistence on spiritual equality. Sierra Leone, she claimed, was in 'a state of infancy' and required the guidance of British men and women. Thus, while her lamentation that 'native teachers require so much oversight' and ensured a 'low quality' of educational provision if left to run schools by themselves did not prevent her from leaving her own school at Charlotte under the care of African teachers as she travelled around the colony, she arranged for frequent visits from Freetown, 'leaving the way for an European, should one be disposed to take the charge.'[119] A familial relationship between Britain and West Africa thus ensured an important role for English men and women within the missionary enterprise.

Africa, and especially Sierra Leone, represented for Hannah Kilham the possibility of creating a new, ordered, Christian world.[120] During her work in England, in between her journeys to West Africa, Kilham was frequently depressed by the extent of heathenism at home. Her work in the 'rookeries' of St Giles and Spitalfields, for example, areas known as 'Little Dublin' or 'The Holy Land' on account of extensive Irish migration and favourite early-nineteenth-century philanthropic destinations, left her discouraged and downhearted.[121] 'There is much to do in England', Kilham lamented in 1826. '...Surely throughout the world we should include our own country as well as those more distant. Many sit in heathen darkness even here.' Indeed, the British poor were 'in some respects, more difficult subjects for instruction than many are in these so-called heathen lands...they would want the same care even from the beginning in the attempt to civilise and Christianize them, if we might be permitted as instruments in such a cause.'[122] Returning to her hierarchy of homes, Kilham declared that the 'peasant system in Ireland, with all its miseries, is beautiful in comparison with the wretched habit of living in the garrets of St Giles.'[123] Irish cabins were simultaneously 'wretched', 'palatial' and 'beautiful', and her assessment of them worked to emphasise their need for missionary attention as well as to signal the global nature of the Christian mission. On her 'cloudy days', the free villages of West Africa, organised around the home, church and mission school, to become centres for the diffusion of Christianity within the continent, offered Hannah Kilham a sense of unprecedented and tremendous possibility. As she wrote in *The Claims of West Africa* in 1830, 'What a field does Sierra Leone present!'[124]

Conclusion

By the second half of the nineteenth century, a fundamental change had occurred in the identity of the overseas missionary. The artisan and lay preacher of the 1790s had given way to a greater number of lower middle-class men among missionary candidates, their success in the mission field partly based on the respectability and propensity to teach domestic reform of their wives. By the 1860s, independent women were also travelling overseas, and were soon outstripping men in terms of numbers of missionary applications.[125] The 1820s and 1830s were formative decades in this transition. Female missionaries were during these years acknowledged to be in possession of a range of skills crucial to the civilising mission.[126] Women sang hymns, recited prayers and taught Scripture to women and children, instructed in domesticity and needlework, and exerted influence over fathers, sons, brothers and husbands as well as, they hoped, their missionary subjects.

Drawing on Biblical precedent and scriptural authority, missionary women of all evangelical denominations assumed the right to exempt themselves from some of the limitations imposed by nineteenth-century notions of feminine propriety in Britain. Beginning their missionary careers at home, the domestic poor formed the basis of their understanding of the moral and environmental location of poverty and the critical role of domestic reform in promoting progress and improvement. In their excursions into the 'heathen' world, they maintained women's association with the home, representing missionary domestic life as central to Christian advancement throughout the world. Their skills and commitment to domestic reform were fundamental to the reformulated missionary movement, in which the process of turning dwellings, huts and cabins into homes was central to the construction of a global Christian community. In the words of Jemima Thompson, hoping in 1841 to persuade more women to put themselves forward for missionary duties, woman 'was first in transgression. Let her be foremost in bringing about the world's restoration!'[127]

5
Trembling Philanthropists? Missionary Philanthropy under Pressure

Missionary philanthropy provided a cohesive identity for the early-nineteenth-century middle class, but not all aspects of the movement were supported evenly and in equal measure. From their inception in the 1790s, there had been vociferous critics of overseas missions in the pro-slavery and anti-evangelical lobbies who questioned the capacity of 'heathen' peoples to receive God's grace and challenged the authority of missionaries to preach the gospel. Most famous is editor of the *Edinburgh Review* Sidney Smith's dismissal of William Carey and his colleagues as 'little detachments of maniacs'. As discovered by Carey, the 'consecrated cobbler' of Serampore, this antagonism was sometimes as much about social class as about nonconformist irregularity.[1] These criticisms tended to be voiced by individuals rather than movements until the 1820s, when a sustained critique of overseas missions developed, as radicals contested the focus on overseas at what they perceived to be the expense of the poor at home. Criticism also emerged within the middle class, where the assault came from two directions: within evangelicalism, from those domestic philanthropists keen to prioritise reform at home; and from medical men and urban philanthropists, many of them Unitarian, who issued a profound challenge to the focus of missionary philanthropy on a moral locus of change and its pre-eminent position in civic culture and politics.

The missionary movement came under intense pressure during the 1820s–1840s. These were tense decades, witnessing the stepping up of campaigns for Parliamentary reform and criticism of political economy and capitalist production. Owenism, the Anti-Poor Law Movement, the Ten Hours Movement and, especially, the arrival of 'physical force' Chartism after 1837, underscored the urgent need for new strategy for reform. The ensuing 'condition of England' debate ensured widespread awareness that the domestic reform of working-class women was not sufficient to save the nation, and attention turned to methods, religious and secular, through which to 'remake' working-class men. Two broad movements emerged, united in their focus on England, but bitterly opposed in their relationship to political economy and their visions of civilisation.

Since the 1790s, movements for the reform of the 'heathen' at home and overseas had shared strategies and personnel, and had informed and inspired each other. But the concern that overseas missionary enthusiasm was inclined to eclipse philanthropy at home was also a powerful impetus for the domestic movement. The primacy of the overseas mission was challenged most intensely by members of the campaign on behalf of climbing boys and later by the anti-Poor Law and factory movements. The first part of the chapter explores this dynamic in the context of the breach which occurred in Sheffield's missionary philanthropic community from the mid-1820s between those supporters of climbing boys who were primarily associated with the abolition of slavery and Samuel Roberts, who moved instead towards the anti-Poor Law and Ten Hours movements. Roberts, who with James Montgomery, George Bennet and others had played a key role in the development of Sheffield's missionary culture in the first two decades of the nineteenth century, had by the 1820s begun to resent the focus on slaves and the 'heathen' overseas and the neglect of the poor at home.

The 1820s and 1830s also saw the coming to the fore of a competing model of social change which emphasised environmental and biological factors in different relationships to moral reform and prioritised secular as well as Christian education. The main supporters of the new movement were groups of urban professionals, keen to make their mark and assert their status in the civic arena. Medical men in particular ushered in new social analyses and with them a model of civilisation which centred on 'physical civilisation' alongside moral reform. The second part of the chapter explores the interplay between moral reform, environmental change and (occasionally) ideas of biological fixity in the writing and reform practices of supporters of urban missions in the north of England in the 1820s to 1840s. It examines the promotion of natural science and political economy as a solution to poverty and radicalism and the reshaping of the working-class male character in a new range of reforming institutions grouped around the Mechanics' Institutes and Domestic Missions.

The missionary philanthropic framework of stadial global development, from heathen savagery to Christian civilisation, was shared by missionary philanthropists, Tory evangelicals and medical men. But there the joint project came to an end. Notions of civilisation formed contested territory in the 1820s and 1830s. Critics of overseas missionary enthusiasm redefined both the meaning of civilisation and the means for reform and threatened to force a separation between the missionary movements at home and overseas. The support for the new urban missionary movement in particular saw the contraction of the space in civic culture occupied by the older generation of missionary philanthropists, and their influence correspondingly diminished. While the older philanthropic societies continued to operate, and overseas missions flourished, these were increasingly at a distance from the hub of power in many urban centres. At the same time as it enjoyed pre-eminence in some urban elites, within others, and not only those where its foothold had been traditionally less secure, the missionary philanthropic model was under assault.

Little black climbing boys: the early evangelical critique of overseas missions

As support grew for anti-slavery during the 1820s, the use of the symbolism of slavery was judged expedient by radical and reform movements, to develop the argument that the slavery of the working class at home was worse than that in the West Indies. Sheffield philanthropist Samuel Roberts' (Figure 11)

Figure 11 Samuel Roberts. (Courtesy of Sheffield Local Studies Library, y00358.)

public disagreement with anti-slavery occurred in 1824, some years before Richard Oastler's more famous 'Yorkshire slavery' protest. Its focus was the campaign to prevent chimney sweeps from using little boys to clean chimneys. Begun by London philanthropist Jonas Hanway in the 1770s, the campaign was inaugurated as a national movement with the formation of the Society for Superseding the Necessity for Climbing Boys in 1803.[2]

The formation of the Sheffield Society in 1807 by Roberts, James Montgomery and other associates of the Society for Bettering the Condition of the Poor, had been accompanied by imagery of slavery and stories of the 'stolen child'.[3] Roberts' poem 'The

Chimney-Sweeper's Boy' (1807), based on a story reported in the *Sheffield Iris* in October 1804 of a four-year-old climbing boy in Bridlington whose 'air and manners' had attracted the attention of two philanthropic ladies, became increasingly suffused with abolitionist imagery in its various re-workings. His final version included descriptions of the slave-like conditions of the child's employment and the piety of the small boy who, rattling up the chimney and stopping to pray at a mound of soot outside the master bedroom, is overheard by the mistress of the house and his voice recognised as that of her lost son.[4] Montgomery's editorials in the *Sheffield Iris* further embedded the campaign in discourses of slavery and civilisation. His pleas to women to desist from employing 'the little black climbing boy' and to opt instead for the new sweeping-machine emphasised the colour of the children. Exploitation by brutal master sweeps undermined the tradition of the 'freeborn Englishman' and threatened England's civilised status: 'Consider too the honour of your country. Cowper said, "Slaves cannot breathe in England", yet many slaves as there are in France and other nations, there are none like our climbing boys. Rescue them, ye fair, rescue Britain from this foul disgrace.'[5]

Direct comparisons with colonial slavery were prominent during the 1817 campaign, which aimed in the short term to change the law regarding the age at which children could become apprentices (from 8 to 16 years), and to provide regular new clothing and moral and religious education for boys who continued to be employed. Eventually, the campaign sought to prohibit the use of climbing boys altogether. In his harrowing essay in support of the Sheffield petition, 'On the Employment of Climbing Boys', Roberts suggested that the plight of the boys was even worse than that of West Indian slaves, on account of the victims' youth and trust in their protectors:

> The poor African negro is kidnapped and sold, but it is by strangers, or by foes. These children are kidnapped and sold, and that by their own countrymen, and by their own parents. The negroes are selected for their strength, and consequent power of bearing hardship; these poor children are chosen

> for their youth, small stature and consequent inability to sustain labour. The negro slaves are for the greatest part arrived at years of man or womanhood, and therefore able to bear considerable fatigue without injury to their natural constitutions and frames; but these *British Slaves* are *invariably children*, both male and FEMALE, and are totally unable to bear the common degree and employment of adults, without falling sacrifice to it.[6]

Britain, Roberts argued, was a peculiarly blessed and prosperous nation: the ongoing peace, the development of liberality and charity and confidence in government all put the nation in an enviable position. But there were evils at large which threatened civilisation, and none were more in need of purging than the failure to protect children.[7]

For some supporters of the regulation of the hours of labour of the poor, the blackness of climbing boys secured their preferential treatment: 'The black faces of the little climbing boys have excited the compassion of many charitable people,' wrote the author of an 1817 pamphlet, people who 'remained quite unmoved' by 'the hard work, the hard fare, and the mutilated bodies of the poor children at the cotton manufactories. How *impartial* and *discriminating* is such *charity*!'[8] The blackness of the boys, articulated in an eclectic and undifferentiated use of discourses of ethnicity, enabled an easier denunciation of the system. Climbing boys, 'the most oppressed of Britons', were 'young Africans of our own growth'.[9] 'There is a Caste amongst us,' claimed Roberts, '. . . a Caste branded and shut out from the society of their fellow creatures.'[10] Another testimony likened the hardening of children to a life of 'privation, hardship, and pain' as like that among 'the American Indian, [who bore] it with indifference.'[11]

In his contribution to the 1817 petition, we see a glimmer of Roberts' later critique of evangelical commitment to abolitionism and overseas missions. Dismissing the argument that the climbing boys were happy, Roberts compared them to the people of Greenland who, claiming they did not want the Gospel, only recognised their own heathenism and depravity after the persistence of Christian missionaries in their attempts to educate them.[12] 'We send forth missionaries to endeavour, at the risk of their lives and the certain loss of all that we consider as comforts, to Christianize the heathen of the torrid and the frigid zones,' he wrote, and 'yet we suffer these poor black children in our native land, to live and die in worse than heathen darkness.'[13] Climbing boys, Roberts argued, were similarly depraved by their cruel treatment and conditions, and yet were not the subjects of a celebrated missionary enterprise at home.

Roberts pursued this theme in his contribution to *The Chimney Sweeper's Friend and Climbing Boys' Album* (1824). This volume of factual evidence, poetry and prose aimed to bring new publicity to the campaign after the failure of the Bill of 1819.[14] For most of the contributors, immersed in the new phase of popular abolitionism, slavery formed the most ready comparison to the plight of the climbing boys. It was implicit in many of the factual contributions: the testimonies of doctors and surgeons, which exposed the falls, the burnings, suffocations, deformed limbs and deaths from cancer known to have befallen climbing boys; the descriptions by architects and builders of the construction of chimneys; and the evidence from sympathetic master sweeps, which detailed the flouting of the 1788 Act. For contributors of poetry and prose, colonial slavery was the main point of reference. Mary-Anne Rawson's poem begins with the death of a woman following the abduction of her son to be sold as a 'little English slave'; before dying himself, the child finds his way to his mother's grave. Barbara Hofland's tale sees the sons of a widow and deserted wife sold into this 'worse than Egyptian bondage', where they are maltreated, eventually escape, but die from a fever. In his contribution, Bernard Barton pleaded with fathers, mothers and Britons, to assist 'childhood's helpless race' and abolish the 'dire disgrace' of 'HOME-BRED SLAVERY!'[15] (Figure 12).

Roberts, who had become an active and independent-minded member of the Sheffield Anti-Slavery Society on its formation in the same year, was the only contributor to the album to criticise the evangelical preoccupation with abolition and overseas missions. His 'Petition of William Sampson' drew upon a letter

Figure 12 A climbing boy begging well-to-do passers-by to hear his plea. Illustration from James Montgomery (ed.), *The Chimney Sweepers' Friend and Climbing Boys' Album* (1824). (Courtesy of Sheffield Local Studies Library.)

published in the *Sheffield Iris* during 1823 from a young man and ex-climbing boy in Roberts' acquaintance, who claimed that the equivalent ill-treatment of poor English children would not be acceptable overseas:

> If similar atrocities, among the barbarous customs of Hottentots and Hindoos, were recited at any of our missionary meetings, the audiences would shudder in horror; yet we tolerate them at home, and it seldom occurs to the most humane or reflecting among us, that towards one class of children at least, we ourselves are coolly, deliberately, remorselessly cruel as the most depraved and ignorant heathen, – and that, not from mistaken notions of piety, but out of tenderness to our fine carpets, or veneration for our crooked chimnies.[16]

Repeating such sentiments in Montgomery's edited volume, Roberts was a lone voice in his criticism of missionary sensibility.

Within a decade, as the anti-slavery campaign enjoyed overwhelming success, Roberts found himself engaged head-on with the arguments of the abolitionists. His *Address to British Females* (1834) appealed to women's sensibility before providing a dramatic testimony to their lack (he supposed) of integrity and the limits of their philanthropy.[17] In 1837, his adversary was George Thompson, the popular anti-slavery lecturer, speaking at a meeting in Sheffield. Referring to Sampson, his deformed and stunted companion, Roberts' rhetoric was deliberately chosen to shock and offend:

> Slavery! What is any other slavery to this? This is no nigger. This child was not a picaninny sold by a strange slave-trader in a foreign market. No! This lovely, unoffending child, was sold when little more than seven years of age, *by his own father*, for two guineas, in this land of liberty, in this slavery-detesting town... Pray, Christian Ladies and Gentlemen, what would you have to say for yourselves?[18]

Like William Cobbett, who linked slavery with industrialisation and made the charge of hypocrisy against the abolitionist 'humanity' men,[19] Roberts railed against the enslavement of children to produce the wealth and dubious 'civilisation' of the nation. Abolitionists needed to look to their own neighbourhoods: 'First cast out the beam out from thine own eye [Matthew 7:5]... The abolition of slavery should thus begin with the 'HOME origin of the system!'[20]

Roberts' argument that climbing boys existed in worse conditions than slaves in the Caribbean brought him into conflict with fellow campaigners, most notably William Wilberforce, with whom he had corresponded regularly over many years. While he supported the climbing boys' campaign, Wilberforce confessed to feeling 'a little scandalized at your calling their case an evil not less grievous though less extensive than that of the negro slaves.' Such a view, he argued, was based on an 'inadequate idea of... [the] real enormity' of slavery; not unusual amongst people who were well-informed about slavery, but who tended to look only for 'extraordinary instances of cruelty' and thereby missed the day-to-day 'habitual immorality and degradation' of peoples denied religious instruction or the domestic benefits of marriage.[21] But like Richard Oastler and G. S. Bull, his more famous counterparts in West Yorkshire, Roberts' objection was not just to the hypocrisy of abolitionists, but to the primacy given by them to political economy and to new understandings of freedom, progress and civilisation.[22] These, he argued, enabled their turning a blind eye to the ravages of capitalism at home. Wilberforce illustrated the point perfectly when, disputing Roberts' defence of the pre-1834 Poor Laws, he stated his agreement with the views of the arch-opponent of the Poor Laws, Thomas Chalmers.[23]

Chalmers (1780–1847), the Glasgow divine whose speeches and writings on poverty and the Poor Laws had first impressed English reformers and politicians in 1817, was celebrated in the 1820s for his missionary 'solution' to urban poverty. In his Glasgow parish, Chalmers sought to create a new type of urban community based on Scotland's rural system of parochial relief, in which the kirk and larger landowners were responsible for giving assistance to the poor. He divided the parish into districts, appointing to each a trained deacon with responsibility for home-visiting in order to encourage self-help and neighbourly assistance. As Brown has argued, this was 'a class-oriented agency': very few working-class parishioners held seats in the Church, and the missionaries were drawn from amongst the middle class in the community.[24] The system aimed to create affective bonds between the poor and the well-to-do which, Chalmers maintained, would occupy the 'mighty unfilled space between the high and the low', enabling the two classes to meet not 'in an arena of *contest*' but 'on a field where the patronage and custom of the one party are met by the gratitude and goodwill of the other…'[25] Roberts would support this invocation of traditional rural relations. But Chalmers' prime target – and the source of his popularity in England – was poor relief. His plan was to phase out assistance as people learned techniques of self-sufficiency, thereby tackling the problems of indigence and dependency identified by Malthus as a threat to civilisation.[26] Chalmers' 'Christian economics' drew many parallels with the system of missionary philanthropy already established in the English provinces.[27]

A 'repugnant perversion of traditional Christian values': political economy, Christianity and civilisation

While political economy was a 'supplementary revelation' for some Christians, for others it was a 'repugnant perversion of traditional Christian values'.[28] In Roberts' words, it was a 'half-French, half-Scotch imp of darkness',[29] derived not from the Bible but from secular philosophy. A man-made system, it offered no providential design and, in providing a secularised economic law, gave no space for moral imperatives or for love or charity.[30] The poverty created through the abuses of the factory system was the result of a worldly, avaricious and mechanistic philosophy. The New Poor Law not only sought to replace the parochial, home-based nature of relief, but went against the religious obligation to relieve the poor. Such poverty was destroying the organic social harmony of the old society, encouraging the abdication on the part of the rich of their responsibility, and the corresponding pauperisation of the poor. The web of rights and obligations, of paternalism and deference, consolidated within traditional institutions of aristocracy, church and land, was being undermined, and society was becoming atomised as relationships based on tradition and experience dissolved.[31]

Roberts' proposal was for a return to the traditional social relations that had shaped English civilisation. The most truly Christian period of English history, he claimed, was that in which the Old Poor Law had flourished. An embodiment of 'humanity', 'policy' and 'justice', it had enabled England's rise to greatness, and produced the auspicious circumstances of kingdoms 'in by far the most civilized quarter of the globe'. As a result, the English were the 'most refined, most religious, the most moral, and the most happy people on the face of the earth.'[32] The Old Poor Law, with its aim 'to relieve the poor at the expense of the rich', was contrasted with its successor, which 'expressly declared to add to the incomes of the latter by reducing the relief afforded to the former'.[33] On account of such greed, respectable widows, industrious families and old infirm couples found themselves incarcerated in the workhouse, where they remained due to the 'apathy of the middle classes of society, and particularly of the professed Ministers of the Gospel of Christ...'[34] Roberts decried the Poor Law as a 'Savage enactment', railing against: the 'Poverty prison', 'the Test and Pest House – the Temple to mammon, to Satan, and to Moloch'; the criminalisation of the poor in the big workhouses, built by Lord Althorp to house them 'like the most criminal galley-slaves'; the religious crime of 'putting asunder' man and wife; the Bastardy Laws which encouraged child murder and allowed the 'greater villain' to go free; the access given to doctors to the bodies of paupers who ended up on the dissecting table; and the whole 'concentration of JOBBERY and ROBBERY' in the new occupations of guardians and commissioners.[35] 'There is no system, nationally enacted, whether among pagans or savages,' concluded Roberts, 'so opposed to the laws of God and of Christ, as the Poor Law Amendment Bill.'[36]

Roberts believed that Britain's tolerance of oppressive child labour and retreat from paternalism saw the nation regressing to a position uncomfortably close to barbarism. In a pamphlet addressed to Lord Morpeth, published to coincide with the Commission of Enquiry into the factories in 1833, Roberts trotted through a history of child exploitation to conclude with England, where 'grave debates...carried on, with earnestness, and without remorse, by 658 wise great men, divided into two strongly opposed parties – the twelve-hourians and the ten-hourians', all of whom failed to see the real issue: whether in a civilised society children should ever be dragged from their beds by their suffering mothers to go to work; whether parents should ever be induced 'to sacrifice the health, the limbs, the lives, the souls of their helpless, feeble, unoffending children, both male and female'.[37] The continuance of child labour in England had grave implications for civilisation: 'Thus has been continued and increased, one of the vilest systems of Slavery that ever disgraced any, I was going to say, Christian country. No! *any* country, however savage, on the face of the earth.'[38]

'Pluck out first the beam out of thine own eye': missionary priorities

Such were the conditions at home, and yet religious men and women continued to harp on about Christianising 'heathen savages' in other parts of the world. While Roberts did not doubt the desirability of overseas missions and expressed praise for the impact of missionaries in the South Seas in stamping out infanticide,[39] he believed wholeheartedly that missionary reform needed to begin at home. He directed his anger particularly at those anti-slavery and missionary-supporting Dissenters prominent amongst the factory-owning employers of little children in the West Riding:

> Pluck out first the beam out of thine own eye, and then thou mayest perhaps be able to see more clearly to cast the mote out of thy neighbour's eye! Rely not on your sending of millions of Bibles to the poor of this and other lands. No! You are hereby adding insult to oppression, you steal their material bread which they need and famish, and then you pretend to send them the <u>Bread of Life</u>, of which you stand yourselves in so much greater need... Rely not on the army of missionaries which you have sent, and are sending, out to convert the heathen nations to Christianity. No! They ought to begin at Jerusalem. There seems work enough <u>here</u> for the present for all of them.

In this analysis, those who were most familiar with God, were among the worst of sinners: 'The heathen who know not God, cannot sin as you (who have always known Him) are sinning... No! No! call them back, the ignorant heathen want them much less than the God-insulting, poor-oppressing Christians.'[40] The people who most needed conversion were factory owners and other participants in the exploitation of the poor.

Roberts' critique of abolitionist and missionary enthusiasts was part of the newly sharpened high Tory paternalism that emerged in response to the 'evangelicisation' of political economy and the public prominence of Liberal Tories such as Sumner, Blomfield and Chalmers.[41] Like Richard Oastler (1789–1861) and George S. Bull (1799–1864), the most prominent philanthropic campaigners for children and the poor during the 1830s, Roberts' anti-abolitionism was polemical. He was in fact a prime mover in the shift in emphasis of the Sheffield Anti-Slavery Society from gradual to immediate abolition and also supported, in principle, missions overseas.[42] Likewise Bull, a Church of England curate in Byerley, Bradford, was not opposed to evangelicalism in foreign parts: he had been a schoolmaster in Sierra Leone with the Church Missionary Society in the early 1820s.[43] Oastler, the flamboyant figurehead of the factory campaign in Yorkshire's West Riding, was a Methodist preacher and Bible Society visitor, and had been a supporter of anti-slavery at least since 1807.[44] As Oastler wrote in his first 'Yorkshire Slavery' letter to the *Leeds Mercury*, he had no 'difference in principle' with the abolitionists, but differed in his 'want of application of the general principle *to the whole Empire*'. He wanted the focus to be brought back home; or for abolitionists to at least stop off in Bradford en route to the West Indies, in order to witness the 'scenes of misery, acts of oppression, and victims of slavery' in the neighbourhood, 'even on the threshold of our homes.' When they declined, he decried them as 'hypocrites': 'praying people' who 'took care their work people should neither have time nor strength to pray'; who justified the employment of children on the grounds that labour 'reserve[d] them from "bad company"' and 'prevent[ed] them learning "bad habits"'; professors of religion and reform 'striving to outrun their neighbours in missionary exertions, and would fain send the Bible to the farthest corner of the globe...'[45]

Oastler, like Roberts, did not want for the British poor the freedom pursued for the Caribbean by abolitionists. The abolitionists' post-emancipation vision saw ex-slaves transformed into 'free labourers', selling their labour to the plantation owners, thereby receiving an incentive to work hard and to provide for their families. Women were to be domestic workers, keeping the home and educating children, with the help of the mission schools, to become good Christians. But as was apparent in Britain, workers were thrown entirely upon their own resources, obliged to work at whatever price they could command, often selling the labour of their children to survive. Separated through necessary migration from their neighbourhoods and kin, made anonymous through urban living and culture, they no longer had recourse to either the Old Poor Law or to the cohesive communities of which it was part.[46] Oastler's key concern was not to extend the abolitionist vision of 'freedom' to the English poor, but to challenge liberal doctrines and the general dominance of the values of political economy: 'Sink your commerce', he roared in a speech at Leeds' Union Inn in December 1831, 'and rise Humanity, Benevolence and Christianity.'[47]

The Bible supplied both the language and imagery for Roberts' analysis of poverty. He combined the Scriptural insistence that the 'poor shall never cease out of the land' (Deuteronomy 11:15) with the inclusiveness of Luke: 'When thou makest a feast, call the poor, the maimed, the lame, the blind...' (Luke 14:13).[48] Such relationships were critical for the production of generosity and compassion and the fulfilment of duty, which were the foundations of a moral society.[49] As Roberts reiterates throughout his pamphlets, 'the most essential practical part of Godliness and Christianity, of the prosperity of kingdoms, and the salvation of mankind, (declared in all parts of the Bible), is being kindly, affectionate and liberal to the poor.'[50] But alongside the gentler New Testament love for children – 'It is not the will of your Heavenly Father that one of these little ones should perish' (Matthew 18:14) – he invoked the Old Testament to damn the oppressors of the poor and justify his own speaking out. 'He that oppresses the Poor to increase his riches shall surely come to want' (Proverbs 22:16), Roberts predicted in *England's Glory*. In *England's Passing Bell* (1834) he cited Jonah 3:7–10, to present God retracting his promise to 'do unto them', to ensure that they perished, on evidence that they had 'turned from their evil way'. 'The wicked are turned into Hell', he thundered in *Mary Wilden* (1839), 'and all the nations that forget God. For the needy shall not always be forgotten' (Psalms 17–18). The frontispiece of *The Pauper's Advocate* (1841) uses three biblical quotations to establish the terms of its argument: 'Am I not a man and a brother?', echoing Deuteronomy 1:16, borrows from the colonial anti-slavery campaign, while Malachi 3:5 introduces vengeance upon the oppressors: 'I will be a swift witness against false swearers and against those that oppress the hireling on his wages – the widow and the fatherless, and that turn outside the stranger from his right, and fear not *me*, saith the Lord of Hosts.' Protest is justified through Isaiah 58:1: 'Cry aloud, spare not, lift up thy voice like a trumpet...'[51]

Tory philanthropists shared a great deal with radicals in their resistance to liberal abolitionists and supporters of overseas missions, not least in their use of the Bible to support their analysis of oppression.[52] The emphasis of Roberts, Oastler and others on the father as protector and provider for his family struck a chord with the desire of working-class men as husbands and fathers.[53] Both represented Christianity as incompatible with support for free trade and laissez faire. Many radicals shared the Tory fury at what Cobbett had called the hypocrisy and 'cant' of the 'humanity people'.[54] The disruptions by Chartists of anti-slavery meetings, such as those in Norwich in 1840, were part of a stylised response to abolitionist priorities, which neither meant that radicals were pro-slavery nor precluded them from sympathising with the slaves.[55] From both radical and Tory perspectives, political economy was the cause of widespread poverty, and was responsible for the abuses of the factory system.

But very different models of civilisation were at play in Tory and radical political cultures. Although Roberts claimed to speak on their behalf, the representation of poverty and governance by the 'pauper's advocate' was very different from that put forward by the poor themselves. As Eileen Yeo has shown, the 'science of society' developed by the early co-operative and socialist movement rejected evangelical political economy, adopting instead a definition of civilisation and progress founded upon the happiness of the general populace. Rebuffing James Mill's argument that radicalism 'would be the subversion of civilised society, worse than the overwhelming deluge of Huns and Tartars'[56], Owenites produced 'a new theory of civilisation' in which regression to barbarism could be avoided by proper management of the excesses of industrialisation, where labour was rewarded and profits shared, and public utility was prioritised over 'production'.[57] Roberts' 'radicalism' amounted to a kindly and affectionate protection of the poor, who were not to have a voice in the governance of the country, or any rights except the civil right to receive the Old Poor Law payments from their social betters. They were to be educated in 'true Christian principles' and so understand their ordained place within society.[58] 'Like everything proceeding from a wise, a powerful, and a good God', Roberts wrote in opposition to the Mechanics' Institute in 1832,

> the gradations of ranks in civilized life, is perfectly adapted to produce the greatest good. You know that in the human frame, each member is fitted to and essential in its particular office, to the welfare of the whole body. The feet as well as the head.[59]

The Tory vision of civilisation was a backward-looking vision, entrenched in a memory of traditional social relationships and hierarchies, founded on paternal ties and responsibilities which were rooted in fixed and localised relationships based on the permanence of the land. While it was acknowledged that some landowners were corrupt, the system was believed to be fundamentally right; bringing manufacturers within its bounds, persuaded of their paternal duty, saw 'a spiritual regeneration within existing relations.'[60]

When in 1839, Mary-Anne Rawson requested from Roberts' a financial contribution to the fund for the Thompson Normal School, established by Baptist missionaries in Kettering, Jamaica,[61] he was unequivocal in his reply. Her scheme, he told her, was too grand, and anyway, the most pressing need was at home.

> They have decreed that for no crime but helplessness – infancy – old age – poverty – that they are to be cast into Prison – clothed and have their heads shaved as felons – fed with coarser food than bread, in quantity too small to sustain

> nature, parted from their wives, their husbands and their children – kept from serving God ... The same rulers as set the slaves free. Do then let us begin at home – there is – thank God – nothing else so bad as this in the wide wicked world – I wish that Mr Thompson would take this up.[62]

The situation at home was such that it was essential to turn away from the excitement – and convenience – of overseas missions. Political economy and the factory system were undermining established relationships, based on deference and care. For Roberts, a Tory and an Anglican, this was a social catastrophe, a theological error, and involved the undermining of English civilisation.

Roberts was predictable in his opposition to domestic missionary projects of the 1830s and 1840s. His objection to the Mechanics' Institute, opened in 1832, was on the now familiar grounds that people needed to acquire 'true Christian principles', not secular knowledge.[63] The 'assembling of large numbers of young men' was dangerous, especially in such tumultuous times, and a 'doctor-ridden' management committee was undesirable.[64] The Domestic Mission, formed in 1840, was attacked on the grounds that traditional philanthropy in the form of the Aged Female Society and the Bettering Society tried to address the causes of poverty, whereas contemporary professionals were more interested in showier exertions: fever wards, Magdalene Asylums, paid missionaries.[65] But Roberts' Tory protest was losing out by the 1830s, making way for a model of society and social change, driven by moral, environmental and material analyses, which was even more challenging for missionary philanthropy.

Medical men, phrenology and the challenge of science

The threat posed by medical men to the missionary model of social change was apparent to philanthropists from the mid-1820s. James Montgomery had confronted the issue in a paper on phrenology delivered to the Sheffield Literary and Philosophical Society in 1827. This was published in the *Iris* two years later to coincide with the visit to Sheffield of the famous

Austrian phrenologist Johann Spurzheim.[66] Montgomery's focus was 'On the Phrenology of Hindostan' (1824), a paper by Dr George Murray Paterson, surgeon to the East India Company and member of the Edinburgh Phrenological Society. Paterson argued that the average Indian skull was the size of that of a 15-year-old European and that his capacity for improvement was correspondingly limited.[67] Montgomery, who had previously defended phrenology against the assertion of Sir William Hamilton of the Royal Society of Edinburgh that it led to 'fatalism, materialism and Atheism',[68] objected to Paterson's analysis on the grounds of methodological weakness and, most fundamentally, because his unsupported conclusions contradicted Christianity and undermined the possibility of social progress.

Montgomery's argument centred on the capacity for improvement of nations or peoples. Even if the 'Hindoos' were presently a sorry race, he argued, phrenology could not account for their earlier Golden Age, exhibited in the archaeology, history, language, Scriptures and law which Orientalist scholarship had made visible to the British public. It was clear that Indian men, over the ages, had degenerated from 'men of mighty bone and intellect' to become 'puny' and effeminate. Disputing Paterson's argument that a 'mildness and passive softness' of character could be deduced from the bumps on their heads, Montgomery drew attention to the practices of infanticide and widow-burning to conclude that Indian men were 'more desperately and deliberately cruel than any animal on earth.' Montgomery maintained that 'the premeditated suppression of their intellectual energies' by religion, the caste system and oppressive governance were to blame for India's decline.[69] With proper Christian command, India could again progress.

Montgomery concluded his attack on Murray Paterson with reference to Africa, a continent where, he assumed, there were 'no memorials of remote antiquity' to suggest a previously impressive level of cultural attainment. Agreeing with Paterson that the 'Negro crania' was not like a human skull, he claimed that its bumps nevertheless suggested positive characteristics: of philoprogenitiveness, concentration, hope and veneration, if not other more desirable qualities. Moreover, 'negroes' living in England *had* been improved, coming to excel in art, science, morals and politics. As evidence, Montgomery cited recent missionary success in Africa, and in particular the Christian conversion of Sandanee, the young West African man associated with Hannah Kilham (see Chapter 4), who had described to him a dream of the Day of Judgement. This, Montgomery claimed, indicated that Sandanee had internalised and understood the Christian message.[70]

Montgomery was not against phrenology *per se*, but against its application to suggest that people were unable to improve. His opposition was to its use:

> Like Hindooism, a system of castes, ... [whereby] every tribe of mankind, by fatality of organisation, were doomed to be, through all changes of society, savage, semi-barbarian, or civilised, the same as their fathers had been in one or another of those stages.

This was at odds with the evidence of history: 'What should we deem the ancient Greeks and Romans to have been, were we to judge them by their living descendants in Turkey and the Ecclesiastical States of Italy?' It also denied the possibility of Christian perfection. 'Let then, phrenology be established (if it can be),' he continued,

> by plain and positive facts, and the Christian need not tremble for his religion, nor the philanthropist for his hope of the ultimate Civilisation of every class of the human race, whatever be their present darkness of mind, depravity of manners, or preposterous developments of skull.[71]

Here Montgomery identified the enormity of the threat posed by the 'science' to the missionary philanthropic paradigm.

In his reply, Corden Thompson, the lecturer in physiology at the Sheffield School of Anatomy and Medicine who had been responsible for organising Spurzheim's visit, picked away at each of Montgomery's arguments. The facts remained, he wrote, that '[w]hatever instruction is imparted to a poor idiot with a defective forehead, or, if the language please, with an unhappily modelled and grotesque skull, he will not be found as capable of improvement as another whose cranium is better and differently formed ...' He concluded:

> That there exist nations with small and defective brains, and which, therefore, so long as this organization continues, are incapable of rising in the scale of intellect, remains an *incontestable fact*. Ages and ages have rolled over their heads, and they still continue in precisely the same state.

This did not, as Montgomery had feared, 'impugn the truth of religion'; just as with the 'many hundreds and thousands who are born in Christian countries with defective brains and are therefore doomed to perpetual imbecility', national differences were 'the will of the Creator.' Thompson slips from the varied fate of individual English men, some of whom have the capacity for development and some of whom do not, to the submerging of all Africans and Indians within a national stereotype: 'But who will pretend to expound to us, why one man has one brain given to him than another? Or why one nation excels another in this respect? It is a *fact* ...' Education equivalent to that provided for the intelligent was, in such cases, useless. While some Britons may be unable to emerge from uneducated, barbarian darkness, Thompson maintained, the 'Hindoos' and the 'Negroes' were consigned, as nations, to flounder within it.[72] The threat posed by the phrenological model was most acute to overseas missions, but the denial of the capacity of all peoples to improve had fundamental implications for missionary philanthropy.

Phrenology occupied a fleeting moment in the history of science and social theory in Britain, but it is nonetheless significant for revealing some of the tensions in the urban reform agenda. As Roger Cooter has shown, the widely discredited 'pseudoscience' of the 1810s and early 1820s enjoyed widespread support by the early 1830s, especially after the tours of Spurzheim and the popularisation of Combe's *Constitution of Man in Relation to External*

Objects (1828). Phrenology was utilised by liberal social reformers to enable a radical attack on hereditary power and wealth; it asserted that all people might realise the talents bestowed upon them by their newly discovered moral and intellectual faculties and lay claim, via education and ultimately the franchise, to a higher status and greater influence.[73] In celebrating the intellect, phrenology gave support to the supposed value-neutrality of scientific and medical knowledge, and also conferred status on those, often doctors, who explained the science to a wider audience within the civic arena, such as the membership of the Literary and Philosophical Society.[74] However, as well as drawing on phrenology to support liberal reforms, some supporters were simultaneously using the science to draw a distinction between the characteristics of individuals in Britain, and those pertaining, in the language of Thompson, to different nations.

Secular knowledge and the Mechanics' Institute

In Sheffield, as in other industrial regions, doctors were currently forming a new interest group.[75] The Sheffield Medical and Surgical Society (1820) and, more importantly, the School of Anatomy and Medicine (1828) and the Medical Institution (1829), reflected the new profile of doctors as an increasingly unified group and political force in the town.[76] Their emergence as an influential group, enhanced by their role in the cholera epidemic of 1832, was based largely upon the application of a 'medical model' to social problems and the subsequent construction of the domestic poor as their area of expertise.[77] The means by which the English poor might be improved was a question for the new social reformers in a way that it had not been for evangelicals reliant on Bible learning and domestic improvement. Physicians and surgeons were prominent in the Literary and Philosophical Society (1823), to which they frequently lectured on matters of social and scientific interest.[78] They played a key role in societies established for the reform of working men: the Mechanics' and Apprentices' Library (1824), Mechanics' Institute (1832) and the Town Mission (1840). While old-style missionary philanthropists were both formative and active in these new societies, their character was shaped by a predominant concern with experimental science, environmental paradigms and statistics.[79]

The scattered seeds and distant harvests which formed the evangelical imagery of Christian progress was replaced in medical analyses of society by a semi-industrial language of moulding, solidifying and creating stability among a 'mass'. No doubt inspired by the industrial context of the metal trades in the town, such imagery appeared in the discussions which preceded the opening of the Sheffield Mechanics' and Apprentices' Library in 1824. Dr Arnold Knight, physician at the General Infirmary, warned of the vulnerability and instability of the working man who, in times of hardship, could too easily be led into crime or politics. In such circumstances, he was 'a savage, and reckless of consequences, with a settled conviction that whatever change may take place, to him at least it must be for the better, he is ever ready to engage in any wild or lawless enterprise.'[80] Knight's association of poverty with savagery and changeability contains an implicit contrast with the stability and premeditated thought process of 'civilised' people. While another Sheffield doctor, George Calvert Holland, was able to announce with some confidence in 1829 that 'the savage is chiefly regulated by instinct and necessity, and the member of civilised society by reason',[81] savagery and civilisation refer in Knight's usage not to differences between cultures, but to potential gulfs within the social body at home. The physician's comments are about context rather than nature: some circumstances are conducive to savage behaviour; some forms of knowledge can temper that tendency.

Supporters of education for working men believed that, through imbibing Christian, rational and scientific knowledge, men would develop a moral and intellectual framework which would enable an internal stability of mind. This would in turn lead their values and behaviour to become more settled and predictable and enable them to deal in a civilised fashion with adverse conditions, rather than being open to the influences of rabble-rousers.[82] As argued by Henry Brougham in his influential *Practical Observations upon the Education of the People* (1825), the content of such an education must focus on the development of a man's understanding of his own 'true' circumstances and the 'usefulness of knowledge' adapted to his life.[83] Rather than baffling him with theory and philosophy of science, education was to be appropriate to his needs, abilities and possibly his cranial bumps. In Thomas Chalmers' words, using a colonial analogy, it was a case of 'let[ting] down' knowledge as to 'the capacity and station of the Hindoos'.[84] The Sheffield Mechanics' Library, with its clear rules and collection of scientific, biographical and religious texts, would assist with this process of civilisation.[85]

Supporters of the Mechanics Institute in 1832 championed secular education and its compatibility with Christianity and civilisation. In the words of the Reverend Thomas Allin, a 'solid and useful instruction' would not only divert men from 'sensual and vicious pleasures', but would pave the way for a true Christian understanding of life and make their minds 'gentle, generous, amiable, and pliant to government'.[86] They were to 'be taught to comprehend the real dignity of all useful employments' and to 'learn to look upon the distinctions of society without envy or servility....' Men were to be provided with the 'means of comparing their own actual condition bad as it may be with the worse condition of the previous generation and the still worse condition of men less advanced in civilization.'[87] The sense of satisfaction that life was improving was reinforced by a varied lecture programme, which included the voluminous Dr Charles Favel's contributions on 'The Social Conditions of the Working Class', 'Political economy' and 'The Pernicious Effects of Spirit Drinking', alongside scientific discussions and a host of examinations of local industrial diseases. The Institute established a museum, a laboratory and a library, and organised soirees, tea parties, railway excursions and exhibitions of art and nature.[88] In the context of the opening of the Operative News Room and Political Reading Room in 1832, an attack on the School of Anatomy in 1835 and the emergence of the Sheffield Radical Association and finally Chartism in 1837, these were designed to protect working men from 'the poisoned arrows flying all around'.[89] They would also direct their developing political consciousness, ensuring that their aspirations were contained within the terms of the newly popularised forms of political economy.

That working men frequently did not share the equation of political economy with 'useful knowledge' or its representation as being in their interests has been well-documented by historians. Struggles for control ensured that some institutes became part of a wider radical culture.[90] But of the 700 Mechanics' Institutes which proliferated during the 1820s–1840s, an increasing number were formed as part of a wider middle-class urban missionary vision, which included allotments, Botanical Gardens and parks in urban areas.[91] The new urban mission pursued the remaking of working-class culture through secular as well as Scriptural education, the promotion of participation in civic culture and, increasingly, through changes to the 'physical civilisation' of the homes and neighbourhoods of the poor.[92]

To further explore the significance of the wider urban missionary movement in challenging missionary philanthropy, we have to cross the Pennines, to Manchester and Liverpool, to consider the activities of the Town and Domestic Missionary Movements. While a Town Mission was formed in Sheffield in 1840, it employed just two missionaries and few sources survive.[93] The membership of the Domestic Missions in Liverpool and Manchester grappled with issues similar to those which tested the supporters of the Mechanics Institute in Sheffield. These two missions provide a wider canvas on which to explore the shift to environmentalism and the separation of homes and overseas missions that characterised the new domestic philanthropy of the 1840s and 1850s.

The 'wants of mankind at home': 'physical civilisation' and domestic missions

The domestic missionary movement of the 1830s and 1840s was split along denominational lines and it is the Unitarian Domestic Missions which mainly concern us here. The first of these was established in Spitalfields in 1832 by Unitarians inspired by the visit to Britain of the New England cleric, Joseph Tuckerman. It was followed by missions in Manchester (as the Manchester Ministry to the Poor in 1833, becoming the Manchester Domestic Mission in 1836), London, Liverpool, Bristol and Birmingham between 1833 and 1840.[94] Although Unitarians were keen to work in an interdenominational capacity, Trinitarians refused to join with them and, in response, established the evangelical Town Missionary Movement.[95]

There were many similarities between the evangelical and Unitarian missions. The main aim of both missions was to spread Christianity and civilised domestic practices among the poor through 'aggressive ... domiciliary visitation'.[96] 'Agents' read from the Scriptures, assisted in the purchase of Bibles, encouraged children to go to Sunday school and their parents to attend a place of worship, visited the sick and dying and testified against all open sin and immorality.[97] Non-sectarianism was at the heart of their practice: Leeds and Manchester Town Missions, both established in 1837, stated explicitly that their purpose was 'not to proselytize, but to evangelize'.[98] This was essential if missionaries were to be able to approach Roman Catholics, the disinterest and sometime outright hostility among whom saw Liverpool missionaries adopting the Douay edition of the Bible while some among them were reading in Irish.[99] Missionaries extended their operations to other designated needy groups: boatmen on rivers and canals, for example, and women and 'infidel' socialists attending Knott Mill Fair.[100]

Missionary Reports followed a familiar format, with descriptions of the sorry state of the people followed by happier stories of success. Accounts detail depravity and blasphemy: swearing, Sabbath-breaking and licentious behaviour, adultery, drunkenness and violence among the many disinterested people. Missionaries were sometimes subjected to violence ('not unlike that which the first Missionaries had to endure'): a number had been bruised, stoned and threatened with death.[101] Although a fine line was negotiated between detailing the instances of difficulty (too many and people might think missions a hopeless cause) and proclamations of success (too emphatic and the job was considered done and did not require further donations),[102] the predominant feature is the prolific listing of success stories: of drunkards who had joined the Temperance Society and were saving for a Bible; immoral women, rescued from prostitution and in some cases placed in the Probationary House or in service; women with starving children, ignorant boatmen, Jews and Catholics, an Owenite, even a blind paralytic, all had recognised their sinfulness and found comfort in passages in the Bible, some going on to enjoy obligatory happy deaths.[103] Like depravity and distress, progress was a quantifiable commodity, and the use of tables and statistics detailing the numbers of visits made, tracts distributed and meetings held for prayer and religious instruction reflect the earlier participation of many members in the Statistical Societies.[104]

There were important differences between the urban missions and the earlier visiting societies. The first concerned the employment of paid agents, all of whom were male. The London Mission employed the largest number, its 40-plus visitors working for 36 hours a week, visiting (the same) 500–550 families each month.[105] Other missions were far less ambitious and well-supported: there were originally four visitors at Leeds and Liverpool, and just two in Sheffield. This aspect of the work of the missions made them rather less comprehensive than the Bettering and Bible Societies of the 1810s, which had seen teams of (unpaid) female missionaries visit the homes of the poor to promote a range of domestic reforms. The payment, Donald Lewis convincingly suggests, was intended to give missionary work greater appeal and status among evangelical men. Women's dominance of voluntary visiting acted as a deterrent to masculine involvement and impeded the possibility of professionalisation. Women, no longer engaged in the systematic visiting or in amassing evidence and compiling statistical tabulations, formed Ladies' Branches, for the purpose of raising funds.[106]

A second area of difference between the missions of the 1830s and their predecessors was that, unlike the earlier bible and visiting societies, the reports contain no explicit references to the global context of their work. Overseas missions were rarely mentioned, any reference made in passing.[107] For a growing number of people in the 1830s and 1840s, immersed in cholera, urban squalor and industrial disease, overseas missions were viewed at the very least as a distraction from more pressing concerns. It was an 'error' to lose oneself in 'the contemplation of human degradation at a distance,' wrote G. C. Holland, a Unitarian and

Figure 13 Dr. George Calvert Holland. (Courtesy of Sheffield Local Studies Library, s08691.)

physician to Sheffield's General Infirmary (Figure 13). Discussing the impact on the Sheffield Mechanics' Institute of enthusiasm for overseas missionary projects, he suggested that:

> The consideration of this subject would almost lead us to regret, that we might have looked to remote regions for a field, on which religion might exercise her influence and teach important truths, when the millions at our own door were vicious in their habits, wretched in their condition, and ignorant, not only of spiritual truths, but of the simplest rudiments of knowledge ... We honour the benevolence that commands the Universe in its view, but the first duty of benevolence, is to study the wants of mankind at home.[108]

Holland's dismissal of overseas missions came in 1842, the year in which, as we will see in Chapter 6, George Bennet's memorial was erected in Sheffield General Cemetery and a range of well-attended jubilee missionary meetings held in the town. Missionary philanthropy, while honourable, should not in his view detract from the urgency of the situation at home.[109]

Thirdly, while we must not under-emphasise the place of secular education in early domestic missions, the new missionary movement placed it as central to its strategy. Some went as far as Holland in Sheffield, whose criticism of missionary philanthropists and domestic church extension developed into an advocation of a 'civilisation-first' philosophy: 'It is good to build Churches', he wrote,

> but a preparatory step is necessary – to impart the principles of knowledge, and these will not shoot up in the understanding simply from the increased facilities of worship. We must first teach the mind to think – supply it with the means of thought, and thus a basis of intelligence will be formed for the reception of religious impressions. The union of the two will confer a much larger amount of benefit upon society than either alone... The world is much less in need of proselytism than intelligence.[110]

Secular learning was the basis for the education provided by the Mechanics' Institutes associated with the domestic missions. It was opposed to the missionary philanthropic ideal, which saw 'civilisation' as emanating from Scriptural understanding.

The final difference between the Domestic Missions and their evangelical counterparts, past and present, was that the former pushed at the boundaries of moral individualism and introduced a more material analysis of poverty and domestic reform. The emphasis of the evangelical Town Missions, tediously repeated throughout the 1830s and 1840s in their Reports, was the moral impoverishment of the poor. References to material hardship are remarkably few.[111] Only the London Mission openly questioned their method, although it was not within the scope of their strictly philanthropic paradigm to produce a new approach.[112]

In contrast, the new Domestic Missions were the originators of a much more challenging, material analysis of poverty. The concern for the personal, spiritual and moral dimensions remained, but the missionaries perceived a much more complex relationship between home and society, grappling with the tension between what Cullen has termed moralism and environmentalism and opening the way for critical discussions of wages and political economy and a challenge to a vision of civilisation based on the machine, the factory system, commerce and labour discipline. Thus, the Liverpool Domestic Mission, employing the extraordinary Reverend John Johns, a 36-year-old ex-poet and apparently a popular visitor among the poor, soon moved away from an exclusive concern with 'spiritual nourishment' to an examination of the physical, bodily and material needs of the people. Cellar-dwelling and slum improvements, loan societies, juvenile savings banks, a Mechanics' Institute and Library, Ragged Schools, libraries, museums and allotments were all deemed essential to the moral improvement of the poor. Johns, critical of other (proselytising) charities, confirmed the need for shorter hours and gradually reached the conclusion that 'physical civilisation' and social reform required state involvement.[113]

The significance of the Manchester missionaries in pushing subscribers to the Domestic Mission towards a more material understanding of poverty has been discussed by John Seed.[114] The reflective, respectful and eloquent reports of missionaries John Ashworth (1833–1836), George Buckland (1836–1841) and John Layhe (1841–1856) challenged the employers' 'scepticism' with accounts of the impoverished situation of the 'many sober and hardworking families' unable to escape economic factors beyond their control. While candid about the failings of the poor and acknowledging that individual aptitude could make a difference, they concluded that it was 'in vain to recommend education, or even religion, to such as are in want of the first necessaries of life.'[115] Buckland's missionary addresses in the depression years of 1837–1842 appealed directly to subscribers, asking them to consider poverty 'from whatever causes it may be induced, as detrimental to the moral and religious interests, as it is to the physical happiness and constitution of man,' and arguing that all poverty was remediable, including the domestic depravity of the Irish, whose conditions of life and 'standard of comfort' had to be raised before 'any sensible amelioration, either moral or physical, can be effected.' To be prevented from turning to Chartism, the people needed more model villages, such as those already provided by a number of Manchester manufacturers, and a range of reading and conversation societies, Sunday schools and Mutual Instruction Societies, public gardens and other 'healthful amusements'. But they also required shorter hours with no reduction in wages, as part of the 'clearing away of the plague-spots which are the bane and disgrace of our modern civilisation'.[116]

Traditional missionary philanthropy was under challenge. The emphasis on bodily nourishment and environmental improvement, suggested by Holland's use of the term 'wants', competed with spiritual and moral reform to offer a challenge to traditional missionary philanthropy. The focus on the local poor, taken to the extreme in some 'scientific' studies which differentiated between peoples at home and the 'savage' overseas in terms of their capacity for change, potentially prised apart the dual focus on the domestic poor and the 'heathen' overseas. These challenges may have been less worrisome were it not for the central position of the new urban missions within the civic landscape from the 1830s. Doctors and urban missionaries may have remained subscribers to the missionary societies and attended public meetings, but Chartism, local government, state education and the Corn Laws had become the abiding concerns of the day. The weakening of the missionary philanthropic power-base within civic culture meant that the new urban philanthropy required careful negotiation by missionary philanthropists if their movement was not to become thoroughly unfashionable, feminised and marginal to the civic scene.

How did missionaries respond to this challenge? That many worked alongside doctors and other professionals in the new urban missionary movement, whilst also giving energy and commitment to their overseas concerns, suggests that they did not consider a focus on the material condition of the urban poor to be incompatible with missionary philanthropy. As long as domestic missionaries merely questioned the focus on overseas and not the monogenist basis of the movement, it could be met with a reiteration of the missionary position. It was when biological arguments came to the fore that missionaries felt compelled to respond, as James Montgomery had to Corden Thompson in 1827. As we will see in Chapter 6, missionaries viewed the biological argument as the most seriously undermining and took time in their writing to refute entirely arguments that people could not be saved. For James Montgomery, a founder member of the Mechanics' Institute and its secretary in 1834, civilising and Scriptural concerns could complement one another, although he 'fought many battles...to keep out fiction and infidelity' to ensure a Christian context.[117] While undoubtedly the target of G. C. Holland's anti-missionary comments in the early 1840s, Montgomery pressed ahead with plans for George Bennet's memorial, hymns for the missionary meetings at Exeter Hall and a missionary tour of Ireland in 1843, and continued his involvement with the SBCP, Aged Female Society and the Bible Society as well as with more secular educational activities.[118]

But a further response was to more readily acknowledge the role 'civilisation' played in missions. Many of the strategies of reform proposed – domestic reform, literacy, artisan skills for example – were simply and straightforwardly compatible with the message of the Bible. At home, as we shall see in Chapter 6, the ease with which missionary concerns lent themselves to ethnographic displays in the new museums or to celebrations of a more secular civic pride ensured a flexibility and longevity within the movement.

Conclusion

During the 1820s to 1840s, missionary philanthropy encountered challenges, from evangelicals and domestic missionaries and urban reformers concerned to re-focus on the poor at home. Tory paternalists issued polemical anti-missionary statements as part of their wider critique of urban capitalist society. Missionaries and their supporters were to them just one more group who had abandoned the cause of the domestic poor; whose mistaken priorities were enabling the rise to power of profiteering manufacturers who had no concern for England's tradition, its wider population or its established civilisation. Doctors, merchants, manufacturers and ministers who formed the Lit and Phils, Mechanics' Institutes and domestic missions further countered the voluntarist and evangelical foundations of missionary philanthropy with their emphasis on secular reform and, increasingly, state intervention.

I have argued in this chapter that it was the second of these movements which had a lasting impact on missionary philanthropy. The new movement introduced paid male missionaries, who displaced women visitors within the movement. Secular education and the environmental paradigm had the potential to detract from the Bible and the emphasis on the moral locus of reform. The focus on the reform of the working-class man, his family and environment blurred the hitherto well-established dual focus of missionary philanthropy on the 'heathen' at home and overseas, leading to a separation of the two branches of the missionary movement; home and overseas were no longer automatically part of the same project. This separation made space for different trajectories of development to emerge. During the 1840s, traditional missionary philanthropy lost its pre-eminent position in civic culture and politics. New professionals, men empowered by a catalogue of reforms, from the Repeal of the Test and Corporation Acts (1828) to those concerning municipal government (1835 onwards), concentrated on questions concerning the condition of the English nation: the response to Chartism, poverty, sanitation, the need for education. While support for overseas missions continued to grow in the 1830s and 1840s, it was at times a parallel development, engaging women and children and philanthropic men, and occasionally overlapping with the concerns of the new group within the civic elite.

The missionary philanthropic framework of stadial global development, from heathen savagery to Christian civilisation, was shared by missionary philanthropists, Tory evangelicals and medical men. But there the joint project came to an end. Notions of civilisation formed contested territory in the 1820s and 1830s.

Critics of overseas missionary enthusiasm redefined both the meaning of civilisation and the means for reform and threatened to force a separation between the missionary movements at home and overseas. The support for the new urban missionary movement in particular saw the contraction of the space in civic culture occupied by the older generation of missionary philanthropists, and their influence correspondingly diminished. While the older philanthropic societies continued to operate, and overseas missions flourished, these were increasingly at a distance from the hub of power in many urban centres. At the same time as it enjoyed pre-eminence in some urban elites, within others, and not only those where its foothold had been traditionally less secure, the missionary philanthropic model was under assault.

6

'A Christian and Civilized Land': The English Missionary Public and the South Pacific

By the 1830s and 1840s, missions formed a staple of middle-class cultural life. Missionary propaganda poured home to England, to be disseminated in the evangelical press and new periodicals, missionary memoirs, biographies and hagiographies. The movement continued to grow: the proliferating auxiliary societies saw men, women and children engaged in energetic rounds of visiting, fund-raising and publicity.[1] Sermons and speeches by returned missionaries, often accompanied by testimonies from native converts, drew sizeable crowds, while the spectacular and vast meetings at Exeter Hall from 1842 captured the jubilant mood of the missionary public. This 'great paraphernalia of missionary activity'[2] ensured that John Angell James' claim in 1849 that the 'church on earth' had become 'one vast Missionary Society' was no overblown statement.[3] But the civilising mission was popularised beyond the church and chapel. In these years, missionary contributions to natural science, ethnography and theorizing about the relationship between commerce and civilisation were embraced by a wider audience, as representations of English men and women as agents of global civilisation became matters of local civic pride and national virtue.

This chapter examines the popularisation of the missionary narrative in the first half of the nineteenth century. Its focus is the representation in Sheffield of the London Missionary Society (LMS) South Pacific mission between 1820 and 1842. Sheffield had a particular association with the 'South Seas' through George

Bennet (1775–1841), a prominent local philanthropist, who journeyed to Tahiti in 1821 on a two-and-a-half-year supervisory tour of the LMS's Pacific mission stations.[4] Bennet's voyage presented opportunities to Sheffield's philanthropic elite, who were eager to forge a more intimate acquaintance between the townspeople and the significant characters and events of the mission. Bennet's close friend James Montgomery was peculiarly placed, as poet and newspaper editor, to shape public opinion, and played a key role in disseminating missionary intelligence from Bennet's letters. Montgomery also edited Bennet's memoirs,[5] arranged for the display of Polynesian artefacts in the Lit and Phil Museum and celebrated Bennet's achievements on his death in a monument erected in the General Cemetery in 1842.

The focus of the first part of this chapter is the stories told and untold about the South Seas mission; the public representations of Christian progress and the obscured dynamics of mission. In their writing about the South Pacific, Bennet and Montgomery represented the peoples of the Pacific Islands as 'babes in Christ', younger siblings to their older evangelical brethren from whom they received Christian guidance and care. The familial metaphor enabled engagement with competing discourses of racial and cultural difference: the celebratory account of the 'noble savage', first popularised by the publication of the journals of Captain Cook and other navigational explorers from the 1770s and which was enjoying a resurgence in the 1820s; and newer arguments for the essential inferiority of 'primitive' peoples. Bennet and Montgomery emphasised instead the positive role of missionary intervention in countering savage depravity and hastening the progress of 'infant' cultures as they made the transition to civilised societies.

This was, however, a selective and partial view of the mission which obscured various conflicts within missionary relationships and disruptions to the happy family order. These involved the 'heathens' who refused to adopt Christian belief and practice, the island elites who embraced Christianity falteringly and unevenly, and those errant sons of mission, whose abandonments and transgressions proved that missionaries too were capable of disappointing. While such anxieties of conversion made space for the appearance of a harsher approach to race and cultural difference from the 1840s, the usual missionary solution was to stretch the philanthropic paradigm to accommodate the range of disappointments. By the mid-1830s it was widely acknowledged among Christians that they were working within a longer time frame, that the process of global conversion might take generations and would involve complex processes of translation rather than a brief encounter with the message of the Bible.

Rather than witnessing the thwarting of their project by the new biological racism of the 1840s, missionary supporters at home were able to extend the appeal of the civilising mission beyond the traditional missionary public. The second part of the chapter seeks to problematise claims that the harsher approach to cultural difference, evident in the writing of Thomas Carlyle and Robert Knox, had extensive purchase among ordinary middle-class men and women.[6] The South Seas had long engaged those with an interest in science, and the missionary enterprise acquired a wider audience, particularly among liberal men who were distant from evangelical enthusiasm, through civic representations of civilisation. The ethnographic displays in the new museums, and in Sheffield the civic monument which celebrated both Bennet's missionary adventures and English civilisation, established the process of guiding 'heathen' children towards Christian adulthood as the responsibility not of individual missionaries or even missionary subscribers at home, but of the English nation.

'A moral miracle': evangelical representations of the South Pacific

In Sheffield General Cemetery there is a weathered and disintegrating memorial to George Bennet (Figure 14). Funded by a public subscription organised by James Montgomery and the Sheffield Literary and Philosophical Society and constructed in 1842, some months after his death, the memorial celebrates Bennet's missionary status (Figure 15). The north face carries Bennet's claim that, 'having made an honest comparison of multitudes of persons of nearly all climes, colours and

Figure 14 George Bennet. (Courtesy of Sheffield Local Studies Library, s08614.)

characters', he had found no religion 'so just to God, so true to man' as Christianity. On the south side, Bennet is depicted in a scene of missionary triumph: standing against a background of palm trees and cacti, his right arm rests on a globe, he has a Bible in his hand and a broken idol at his feet.[7] The South Pacific, represented in terms of a romantic landscape and the depraved, morally degraded state of its people, is celebrated as a missionary success story. The authoritative, cultivated figure of George Bennet, and by extension England's philanthropic elites, are agents in the process by which Christian and civilised practices are bestowed upon the 'heathen' world.

Figure 15 George Bennet's Memorial, Sheffield General Cemetery. (Courtesy of Sheffield Local Studies Library, s07654.)

Bennet's memorial was erected at the peak of national public missionary enthusiasm. The final year of Robert Moffat's time on furlough, 1842 saw the celebrated missionary continue to draw rapturous crowds.[8] The huge children's meetings at Exeter Hall were organised in Easter 1842 by the London and Baptist

Missionary Societies. Here, 5–6000 children and other guests listened to an array of distinguished speakers, and witnessed the presentation of Sarah Roby, the Bechuana girl convert, and three blind Chinese girls reading the Scriptures in Braille. They sang hymns specially written for the occasion by James Montgomery and Ann Taylor Gilbert, the latter expressing sympathy for 'heathen' children taught to worship a 'wooden God' and suffering to see 'their mother burnt before their eyes'.[9] An avalanche of missionary writing for children occurred in the 1840s and 1850s. The Church Missionary Society's *Juvenile Instructor* was first published in 1842, followed four years later by the Baptist *Juvenile Missionary Herald* (1846), which sold 45,000 copies each month. These periodicals encouraged children to engage in neighbourhood visiting and collecting, saving for their missionary boxes and raising money through other means, perhaps from making fancy goods to be sold at bazaars.[10] As these examples suggest, this was a family-centred culture, inclusive of women and children and developing their agency in important ways.

While families would have to travel to London to witness so impressive a spectacle as the Easter meetings, there were rich missionary cultures in the provinces. Sheffield was no exception. The *Report* of the Church Missionary Association for 1842 notes the increase in contributions from previous years,[11] while newspaper reports celebrate successes and describe the large audiences attracted by returned missionaries.[12] The *Sheffield and Rotherham Independent* of 2 April 1842 informed its readership that Nether Chapel, one of the venues for the LMS anniversary meeting that year, had been 'crowded to suffocation', as supporters gathered to hear missionary intelligence from southern Africa and Russia. John Philip conveyed the good news that African people were now 'dressed in British manufactures', living in 'decent houses', tilling their enclosed and newly cultivated gardens, and willingly travelling some distance to worship, while Mr Stallybrass, lately returned from Siberia, reminded the congregation of how much still remained to be done. Large numbers also came together for the missionary breakfast the following day.[13] The Wesleyan Missionary Society Anniversary Meeting and Baptist Half-Centenary Jubilee celebrations in October of the same year saw a good turn-out at the tea meetings, while large crowds converged to hear the testimony of William Allen, a converted African from Sierra Leone, and the account of John Clark, missionary in Africa.[14] The following month, Sheffield was host to the celebrity missionary Robert Moffat, as he brought his lecture tour to a close prior to his return to Africa. Nether Chapel was again filled with people eager to hear the eminent missionary's account of plans for that 'great blank', the African interior, 'yet untrodden by civilised man, or the foot of the Missionary.' Moffat thrilled his audience with descriptions of 'savage' men 'tamed by the gospel' and of the general progress of civilisation. Requesting donations of 'Tools and Implements of Sheffield manufacture, for both Moffat's own comfort and with which to instruct the natives', the editor of the *Independent* sought to involve the townspeople in the missionary enterprise.[15] Reports from the liberal *Sheffield and Rotherham Independent* reveal the considerable and growing interest in India in 1840s – an interest which eclipsed that in any other missionary location and which suggests the shifting nature of the colonial gaze.[16]

Enthusiasm for the Pacific mission had climaxed just prior to the erection of Bennet's memorial, with the publication in 1837 of John Williams' *Narrative of Missionary Enterprises in the South Seas* and the public hysteria surrounding Williams' murder at Erromanga two years later.[17] Such excitement was the product of decades of missionary propaganda. During the first 30 years of the nineteenth century, the evangelical periodical press offered a glowing and sanitised account of Christian progress in the South Pacific, in which the dismal failures of the first missionary group were repackaged as a story of tentative success and overwhelming promise.[18] The conversion in 1812 of Pomare II, the Tahitian 'king',[19] was followed by his return to Tahiti from exile in Eimeo (Mo'orea) in 1815, committed to fighting a Christian holy war against the 'heathen'. In 1816, Pomare announced the abolition of idolatry and organised spectacular bonfires of abandoned idols and the donation of his family idols to British museums.[20] Pomare's baptism in 1819 and his promise of a Christian education for his infant son, born in 1820, further confirmed the missionary potential of the region. Scriptural translations consolidated this trend, as Henry Nott and John Davies, with the help of Pomare, produced a spelling book, a Tahitian Catechism and St Luke's Gospel.[21] Christian progress in the islands inspired the expansion of the LMS to India, Ceylon, Africa, the West Indies and New Brunswick and the formation of auxiliary missionary societies throughout Britain. The groundswell of Christian conversions in Tahiti and Eimeo in the 1820s and missionary extension to the islands of Huahine, Raiatea and Bora-bora (known to the British as the Society or Leeward Islands) all fixed the evangelical gaze on the South Pacific. Missionaries on furlough, such as Williams and Ellis in the 1830s, enjoyed considerable popular enthusiasm; Bennet himself returned home in 1829 to a 'torrent of missionary engagements, public and private'.[22]

Evangelical enthusiasm had dramatically replaced an older secular excitement which had accompanied the early public reception of knowledge about the South Sea islands. In the 1770s, the voyages of James Cook (1728–1779) and Louis Antoine de Bougainville (1729–1811) brought the islands and cultures of the Pacific Ocean into view, fuelling an interest in the West that was both popular and scholarly.[23] Absent from the studies of classical literature, untainted by the slave trade, by wars or prior contact with Europeans, Enlightenment thinkers believed the indigenous cultures of the Pacific to represent the first stage of human society and to present ideal material for the study of man. In France, Denis Diderot (1713–1784) used de Bougainville's account of Tahiti to develop a Rousseau-esque critique of the artifice, corruption and repression of modern civilised life.[24] In Britain, Scottish philosophers, such as Lord Monboddo in his six-volume *Origins and Progress of Language* (1773–1776) and Lord Kames in *Sketches on the History of Man* (1774), drew upon Tahitian material to discuss theories concerning the impact of climate on social development, the genealogy of different languages and the stadial theory of social development.[25] William Alexander utilised the journals of Joseph Banks and George Forster in his *History of Women*.[26] Tahiti supplied the raw material, therefore, for the emergent social sciences and provided the impetus for the disciplines of anthropology and philology.[27]

Hawkesworth's best-selling *Account* (1773) of Cook's voyages inspired popular enthusiasm for Tahitians and their neighbours, who were represented as romantic, dignified and harmonious peoples, their culture uncorrupted by the greed, commercialism and restrictive sexual morality of Western civilisation.[28] Along with Bougainville's *Voyage autour du Monde* (1771), the book gave rise to a 'Polynesian vogue' in eighteenth-century Britain and France. The fashionable and well-to-do cultivated a taste for 'Tahitian' toys, jewellery and tattoos, 'Polynesian' wallpaper and 'South Sea' lakes. Coleridge's *The Rime of the Ancient Mariner* (1798) represented literary interest in the region, while the sex shows of a London prostitute named Charlotte Hayes, based on voyeuristic descriptions of public sexual activity drawn from the journals of explorers and sailors, were indicative of a less than highbrow enthusiasm.[29]

By contrast, the Pacific Islands were far from paradise for evangelical Christians. Many missionaries had read Cook's work in their youth,[30] and saw the peoples of the South Seas as among the most morally depraved of humankind. In his sermon to the newly formed Missionary Society in September 1795, the evangelical rector Thomas Haweis agreed with assessments of the natural beauty of the islands and of characteristics encouraging to missionary success. Basing his sermon on Mark XVI 15:16, 'Go ye into all the world, and preach the gospel to every creature', Haweis argued that Polynesian people were uncorrupted by excessive dealings with Europeans, were free from 'persecuting government, [with] no Brahmanic casts to oppose, no inhospitable climate to endure, a language of little difficulty to attain, and of vast extent, with free access, and every prejudice in our favour'. But the overwhelming characteristics of the people were those of moral and spiritual degradation. Describing the 'new world' which 'hath lately opened before our eyes', Haweis warned against seeing the region as resembling

> the fabled Gardens of the Hespirides, – where the fragrant groves which cover them from the sultry beams of the day, afford them food and clothing; whilst the sea offers continual plenty in its inexhaustible stores; and the day passes in ease and affluence, and the night in music and dancing. But

> amidst these enchanting scenes, savage nature still feasts on the flesh of its prisoners, appeases its Gods with human sacrifices – whole societies of men and women live promiscuously, and murder every infant born among them.[31]

Haweis's focus on idolatry, human sacrifice, cannibalism and infanticide, placed against the backdrop of an idyllic Tahitian landscape, became a convention of missionary writing.

For James Montgomery, now a poet of national renown,[32] the South Pacific combined shocking depravity with a marvellous opportunity for Christian labour. Montgomery had long celebrated missionary successes in the South Seas in the *Sheffield Iris*.[33] Appreciation of his commitment reached as far as the missionaries themselves: Henry Nott's home in Papiti, Tahiti, was called 'Montgomery House'.[34] Montgomery urged the people of Sheffield to share in the Christian project by supplying Bennet with donations of Sheffield hardware: edge tools, cutlery, Britannia metal and saws, scissors, razors, fish-hooks. These, he maintained, were needed in the South Seas, along with earthenware, cooking utensils, paper for tracts and children's books, looking glasses, linen and bed furniture, and would serve as appropriate gifts to bestow on potential converts and friends.[35] Such was the abundance of gifts from Sheffield that Daniel Tyerman later complained that they put Bennet and himself in an unequal relationship, particularly as it seems that the Sheffield man refused to let him participate in their distribution; as a result, Tyerman felt obliged to give away his clothes.[36]

Montgomery sought to maintain local interest in the voyage by publishing snippets from Bennet's letters. These were sent with a returning missionary or a passing whaler to himself, the Reads, Rowland Hodgson or Bennet's nephew Edward MCoy, for distribution within missionary circles. Dwelling on his domestic arrangements and state of health, Bennet's letters also invited their recipients to identify with missionary concerns. To Elizabeth Read, he wrote of Sunday school teaching, and expressed a wish that her devout second daughter Eliza might have been present at the May missionary meeting at the large Royal Chapel, in Papara, Tahiti. Edmund Read, a young boy of six years at the time of Bennet's departure, exchanged gifts with a young mission boy named John Williams, and received details of the coronation of the new King Pomare III in April 1824. With his pretty crown in crimson silk and satin, and gold lace coronet with pearls and a cross, Bennet likened the child-king to Edward VI. As Bennet informed Catherine Read, he had presented Pomare III with the scarlet portfolio she had given to him at his farewell party, with the intention that it be used by the boy to carry the Bible and a copy of the new laws of the land at all future processions.[37]

With Montgomery's careful editing, Bennet's news was disseminated by the *Sheffield Iris*. In November 1824, months after he had given over two columns to mourn the deaths of the Queen and King of the Sandwich Islands, who had contracted smallpox whilst visiting London, Montgomery printed extracts from letters which celebrated the increasing numbers of converts in Eimeo and Huahine and the coronation of Pomare III. A poem written by Bennet and sent to Elizabeth Read expressed his sorrow on leaving Tahiti and his joy at 'what God has done' for the islanders, who were now under the 'universal sway' of the gospel. This was placed alongside Bennet's sensational account of his 'perils' among the 'cannibals' of New Zealand, a story of near-death at the hands of the Maori, who had murdered and allegedly eaten the captain and crew of an earlier vessel unlucky to have sailed into the same harbour. Descriptions of 'savages' with 'faces, already hideous from their *tatauings*, [and] rendered even more so by their anger', who brandished axes and spears and 'rais[ed] warsongs, accompanied by the most horrid gesticulation', contrasted to startling effect with the gentle, subdued, Christian island of Tahiti.[38]

Bennet's letters were a resource for Montgomery's public speeches. At the anniversary of the Sheffield Sunday School Union in 1826, he drew on an account of the prevalence of infanticide in the Pacific to inform a few thousand local children of the treatment of children in 'heathen' cultures.[39] This formed part of a regular evangelical diet of terrorising tales, in which children were asked to imagine losing their parents to cannibalism, being eaten by crocodiles on the banks of the Ganges, or simply being struck dead in Sheffield in God's expression of anger at their disobedience.[40] Montgomery's aim was to instil in the pupils a sense of their sinfulness, and to develop their gratitude at being 'happy English children' in a Christian country. The lack of subtlety, if not violence, of evangelical attempts to influence children maybe also point to the deep-felt anxiety about the state of civilisation and Christian commitment at home.

Bennet and Tyerman's *Voyages and Travels* provides an extended articulation of the missionary narrative. The opening verse from 'The Star in the East', by evangelical author Josiah Conder, introduces Tahiti as a 'moral miracle', as the 'rude marae' (a site of worship and human sacrifice) became the 'full-toned Psalm of Christian praise', and

> Savage dialects, unheard
> At Babel, or at Jewish Pentecost,
> Now first articulate divinest sounds,
> And swell the universal Amen.[41]

Voyages and Travels documents the growth in Christian religious practice in the islands: the swelling congregations at the newly constructed chapels and schools; the increasing numbers of people opting for Christian burials, marriages and baptisms; the formation of prayer meetings and charitable societies; the ability and willingness of the people to answer questions on various points of the Scriptures, and to discuss the positive changes in their lives resulting from their conversions to Christianity.[42]

Christian conversion involved the renunciation of previously held religious beliefs and their associated cultural 'abominations'. Bennet and Tyerman's discussions of idolatry, infanticide, human sacrifice, promiscuity and homosexuality veered between denunciation, fascination and praise for the Christian-inspired cultural change. The missionaries, simultaneously appalled by and incredulous at the peoples' belief in the power of idols, made numerous visits to recently abandoned maraes (ceremonious sites) from where they made collections for the LMS museum in London. In scenes symbolising a re-enactment of the story of

Elijah, they participated in ceremonies at which the structures were destroyed, pushed over cliff-tops and into the sea in scenes of Christian triumph.[43] The renunciation of infanticide was also seen as emblematic of the islanders' capacity for change. On their first Sabbath in Tahiti, Bennet and Tyerman had been informed by missionary Henry Nott that three quarters of all babies born on the island were murdered at birth. Such was the scale of the practice that there was a relatively small number of people in the 10–20 years age range, a population trend that was apparently reversing since the establishment of the mission. The regret of hitherto 'heathen' women who had killed babies, was celebrated as a crucial signifier of the positive impact of Christianity, as the ideals of a civilised society were ushered in.[44]

The moves towards 'civilised' family relationships were measured by the missionaries in terms of the care provided for children, the desirability of monogamy and a new attitude to choosing marriage partners, as people became increasingly concerned to acquire a greater knowledge of characters and minds.[45] Men placed a new value on their roles as providers for their families, as loving husbands and affectionate fathers who expressed their domestic authority in an appropriately restrained and legal manner. Discouraged from tattooing their bodies and from idleness and conflict, they were responding to entreaties to soberness, frugality and industry. They were learning 'useful arts', such as carpentry, with which they made sofas, beds and other comfortable furniture for their homes. Families moved into new settlements of plastered dwellings with windows and separate living and sleeping accommodation. They were beginning to sleep at night rather than during the day and to eat in moderation and at regular intervals.[46] Bennet's description of progress at Huahine summed up the change, as a previously itinerant people abandoned their former homes to their pigs, and since their occupation of 'humble, but neat dwellings' near to the bay had become changed in their character and manners:

> While these village erections are thus coming forward, a new form of society is growing up with them ... The gospel may be said to have first taught them the calm, enduring, and endearing sweets of home, which their vagabond forefathers, and

> many of themselves, hardly knew to exist, till the religion of Him who had not where [sic] to lay his head, taught them how good and how pleasant a thing it is for brethren to dwell together in unity, instead of roving like fishes, or littering like swine.[47]

Women too were believed to be starting to inhabit their correct sphere. The absence of female domesticity featured heavily in the missionary critique of Polynesian culture. While in the Pacific Islands women did not do the same work as men – in Tahiti and Hawaii, for example, women were more likely to make mats and barkcloth, collect shellfish, and care for infants – it was widely believed that women were insufficiently domestic and that neither sex worked hard enough. But they were becoming able domestic managers who took pride in their homes. They were taking up needlework and Western styles of dress, and 'modesty, cleanliness and neatness' were increasingly 'characterising their deportment, their persons, and their apparel.' Many were wearing bonnets; higher-class women wore full English dress of gowns and bonnets, even shoes and stockings, at least on a Sunday. New items of dress and habitation were indicative of progress to some converts, as well as missionaries. In the words of Mahamene, a native of Raiatea: 'Look at the chandeliers over our heads; look at our wives; how becomingly they appear in their gowns and bonnets.'[48]

It should be noted, however, that women also presented for missionaries the most difficulty in terms of maintaining the Biblical paradigm for understanding Polynesian culture. The low status of women underpinned evangelical and ethnographic accounts of savage societies. In the South Seas, women's exclusion from idolatrous ceremonies and the ritual murder of those who transgressed this taboo, their prohibition from eating certain foods at feasts, customs surrounding childbirth, and the 'chaotic' nature of Polynesian sexual relationships, all pointed to the savagery of the people.[49] Bennet and Tyerman could find ample evidence to support this analysis.[50] But the deputation occasionally encountered practices which seemed to contradict their analysis of female disempowerment. They registered surprise on discovering that women could propose marriage, and that the marriage of a woman of higher rank to a lower class man did not affect her status. 'On the public causeway', they wrote, in disbelief, 'she goes first, and he, without ever imagining himself degraded, treads in her steps'. The warrior status of Queen Tiramano who, despite being ill with a haemorrhage, had led her people in a heroic march against idolatry armed with a musket, could be celebrated only when her identity as a follower of Christ was secure; a Christian soldier, she was both 'a Deborah' and 'a Mary in the house, sitting at Jesus' feet'.[51] The evangelical paradigm which insisted upon women as fragile creatures exploited by men, their morality and virtue inhibited in a savage society, was challenged implicitly, if not explicitly, in their writing.[52]

Domestic reform fostered values of orderly living which, seen to emanate outwards, had a reforming impact on public life. It was claimed that indigenous forms of entertainment, such as 'licentious' dancing, cock-fighting and cruel sports, were abandoned, and feast times, previously characterised by 'surfeiting, drunkenness, debauchery, quarrelling and murder', became pleasant occasions. This, it was believed, was partly due to the civilising presence of women who were newly participant at such events. A public festival at Raiatea in December 1823 was quite a spectacle, with 241 sofas and over 100 tables, an awning of cloth, much food, and people dressed in their best attire. Dinner was followed by addresses, during which the 'feasting, their improved dress, their purer enjoyments, their more courteous behaviour, the cleanliness of their persons, and the delicacy of their language in conversation' were compared with 'their former gluttony, nakedness, riot, brutality, filthy customs and obscene talk'. Civil society, the polity, codes of laws and the legal system were also undergoing a transformation.[53]

'Nothing behind our own countrymen': God's family on earth

Voyages and Travels presents the reception of Christianity and civilisation in Tahiti in the context of a familial missionary relationship. The language of childhood abounds in Bennet and

Tyerman's account: the people were taught, as younger children, by their older Christian brethren. They described living happily 'amidst a people, lately savages, now Christians – Christians in their infant state'.[54] On another occasion, they write of the 'eagerness' and 'patience' of 'these babes' – the people of Eimeo – for the 'sincere milk of the word'.[55] 'From the King, through all inferior gradations of society', Tahitians were established as a 'surprisingly teachable' people, quick to express their new-found piety and sorrow at their earlier sins. In Lovett's words, they were 'babes in Christ'.[56] Polynesian capacity for progress was reiterated through comparison with the poor at home. 'As to original capacity,' wrote Bennet and Tyerman,

> we cannot doubt that the reclaimed Savages, who are receiving instruction of every kind as little children, need not to be ashamed to measure their standard with that of the bulk of mankind in civilised countries.

'In mental capacity and discernment', Bennet wrote, 'they are nothing behind our own countrymen, so far as their talents or their taste have yet been put to proof.'[57]

The emphatic nature of evangelical representations of missionary subjects as members of God's family was in response to recent attacks on the Pacific mission. Most immediately, Bennet and Montgomery felt compelled to respond to slights from Otto von Kotzebue (1787–1846), a Russian naval captain who had visited Tahiti and the Sandwich Islands during a navigational exploration of the Pacific. Kotzebue's *A Voyage of Discovery* (1821) and *A New Voyage round the World* (1830) provided a damning account of the corrupting influence of Europeans on previously unspoiled Polynesian peoples. The Russian claimed that Pacific peoples, characterised by their gaiety and unrepressed attitudes to sexuality, were being spoiled by commerce, competition, unfamiliar diseases and the forcible introduction of a debased Christianity. 'A religion like this', he wrote:

> which forbids every innocent pleasure and cramps or annihilates every mental power, is a libel on the divine founder of

> Christianity... (I)t has given birth to ignorance, hypocrisy and a hatred of all other modes of faith, which was once foreign to the open and benevolent character of the Tahitians.[58]

In his introduction, Montgomery challenged Kotzebue's assessment of the missionary impact and disputed the Russian's revival of the notion of noble savagery, warning against the confusion of the 'state of nature' of the Pacific Islanders with a 'state of innocence'. Kotzebue, he maintained, was one of a number of visitors to the Pacific who had been seduced by the idea of unrestrained pleasure and who was consequently blind to the brutalities of Polynesian cultures. Montgomery challenged wrong-headed romanticism throughout the volume, claiming to reveal the 'real condition' of the people prior to the arrival of the Christian mission: the despotism, infanticide, murder and cannibalism which amounted to 'a state of nature fallen FROM innocence'.[59]

Much more threatening in the long term than Kotzebue's spirited defence of noble savagery was the increasingly popular explanation for human variety and cultural difference which focused not on Biblical principles and monogenism, but on biology. Montgomery had also to confront the argument that peoples of the Pacific and 'primitive' peoples generally were naturally inferior and could not be improved. He had defended the monogenist view in the *Sheffield Iris* on the occasion of the visit to London in 1824 of the King and Queen of the Sandwich Islands, challenging 'those who talk of Blacks not being fit to be intrusted with freedom' to 'study the[ir] character and conduct' as model Christian converts.[60] Much of his prose and poetry during these years was dedicated to defending the principle of missionary universalism against such hostility.[61]

It was a member of the Hawaiian royal party of 1824, a chief named Boki, who formed a sustained focus of anti-missionary propagandising in the 1820s. The *Quarterly Review* had published a letter, allegedly written by Boki, in which he accused the missionaries of corruption. Drawing upon Kotzebue's evidence to make the case that Pacific peoples remained unchanged by Christianity because they lacked a capacity for civilisation, the

Quarterly ridiculed both Boki and the missionaries. The fullest response came from the missionary William Ellis, an ex-tutor of Boki, who used his knowledge of the structures of the Hawaiian language to assert that the letter was a forgery.[62] Ellis argued that Kotzebue's experience of 'loving' the Tahitians only 'for their licentiousness' limited his understanding, and it was the missionary, having lived among the people, learned their language and observed their customs, who could form the 'more just and accurate conclusions' about the change in the islands.[63] Operating within the tradition of ethnographic writing in which observation and experience formed the basis of true knowledge, the expertise of the missionary allowed him to make a true assessment of a peoples' degradation and their capacity for improvement.[64]

The missionary model of God's family was reinforced in the remainder of the *Voyages*, which follows Bennet and Tyerman on their extended journey home. After leaving Tahiti, the men visited mission stations in Hawaii, New Zealand and New South Wales, where they articulated different degrees of infantilisation, seeing peoples with lesser exposure to Christianity as children awaiting instruction. The people of Hawaii, despite the American missionary presence on the island, had been less successfully won over to Christian cultural practices and exhibited a much greater 'ignorance, vice and wretchedness' than was found in Tahiti and the Society Islands. The Hawaiians practised infanticide and prostitution and, flying flags over their homes which were initially taken by the missionaries to be of a sacred nature, advertised dram shops. They displayed 'a disgusting scantiness of dress', lived in 'wretched native hovels', slept for much of the day, played cards and were 'gross feeders', scrapping over their food. 'They are slow learners', wrote Bennet and Tyerman, 'and will be, till Christianity, with its civilizing influence, gains possession of their minds by purifying their affections.'[65]

Bennet's and Tyerman's abhorrence at Hawaiian culture extended to members of the royal family, whom they felt to be inferior in 'manners and intelligence' to ordinary Christian Tahitians. It was at this point in their travels that the missionaries provide the richest and most sustained evidence of shock at cultural difference. They were horrified at the appearance of the Hawaiian queens who, covered in flowers and ferns on their first meeting, were over six feet tall and had two or three of their front teeth 'barbarously dismantled'. The women showed no public decorum or shame: they ate without using cutlery and immodestly combed their hair in company. While the Tahitian women were engaged in sewing and other useful activities, the Hawaiian queens and their attendants lounged around in 'idle luxury' or indulged in inappropriate exertions. They were caught enjoying being pushed in a wheelbarrow by 'two stout men', for example, before traipsing off to fetch bundles of rushes from the swamps to cover their floors. They were, wrote Bennet and Tyerman, 'as unashamed of their honest labour, in this instance, as of degrading amusement in the other.'[66] The king and his chiefs were similarly idle, spending their days 'loitering and looking about with vacant eyes, or humming a low, dull, monotonous air without melody, as though they know not what to do with themselves.' 'Indolence', declared Bennet and Tyerman, was a 'national sin of the people', and was expressed in a particularly irreverent fashion whilst at chapel. At one service the king had 'lain full length on a bench, resting his head on one attendant whilst being fanned by another', while the ladies 'sat and lolled in a group ... from time to time handing a pipe about themselves.' During one of Ellis' sermons, the chiefs had again 'flung themselves upon their backs, on the floor, lolling or dozing with utter indifference'; at the end of the service, the king had marched out 'swinging his stick about with an air of barbarian dignity.'[67]

Bennet and Tyerman's hierarchy of civilisation was confirmed at their next port of call: the Methodist mission station at Whaarongoa Bay, New Zealand. Here, their party endured the most harrowing experience of their journey as they found themselves in a confrontational situation with a group of Maori men and believed that they were to be killed and eaten in a cannibal feast.[68] But while the Maori were 'savage and filthy', their appearance, manners and violence all evidence that they occupied a considerably lower level of civilisation than did the South Sea

Islanders, they became 'magnificent barbarians' as Bennet and Tyerman reached Sydney and encountered the 'abject natives' of New Holland. Australia's blacks, in the missionaries' estimation, were dirty, idle, slovenly and superstitious; they were practitioners of infanticide and given to drink, violence and cruelty to their wives; 'the lowest class of human beings', they were less civilised than even the 'Hottentot'. However, such a reference to the southern African Khoi evoked a sense both of the degradation of native Australians and of their capacity for improvement, for while the humanity of the 'Hottentot' had been questioned by white Europeans they were now in the process of conversion to Christianity:

> The Hottentot and the Negro have proved themselves men, not only by exemplifying all the vices of our common nature, but by becoming partakers of all its virtues; and, that the day of visitation will come to the black outcasts of New Holland also, we dare not doubt.[69]

'Degraded as they are', wrote Tyerman in a letter to LMS director George Burder, 'they still have souls...as vigorous as our own.'[70] As an expression of their faith in the potential for change, the deputation supported the proposal of Lancelot Threlkeld to establish a mission to the aborigines near to Sydney.[71]

The missionary model of cultural difference received further confirmation in Australia, where the presence of the 'worst class of white men' inspired Bennet and Tyerman to reflect upon the Christian maturity of Pacific peoples. Bennet was appalled by English and Irish convicts, whom he described as 'repulsive' and 'miserable', with the 'looks of fallen beings'. White settlers, whose inhumanity saw them 'rejoice and have them [the blacks] killed off a thousand times sooner than have them instructed and civilised', were no more civilised than their aboriginal hosts.[72] Writing to Governor Brisbane about the condition of native Australians, Bennet and Tyerman noted with some irony that 'those are the most degraded, who are brought into contact with their civilised invaders!'[73] Indeed, Threlkeld refused to preach to white settlers, on the grounds that they were the more barbaric and that to do so would compromise his commitment to aboriginals: 'no man can serve two masters, I cannot serve the Blacks and the Whites'.[74] Hope was present, however, in the children of convicts attending the Paramatta Sunday school, who wept for their parents' sins.[75] It was exposure to Christianity, not colour or biological capacity, that determined the civilisation of a people.

Voyages and Travels presented an uncomplicated account of the South Seas mission as an evangelical success story, as the missionary labours of God's elder children led their younger siblings to Christian belief and practice. Obscured by this narrative are areas of dissatisfaction and anxiety which, lurking beneath the official public accounts of missionary triumph, questioned the integrity of conversion, the quality of the missionaries themselves, and the extent of England's 'civilisation' at home.

Missionary disappointments and anxieties of conversion

After the fanfare that accompanied the sailing of the *Duff* in 1796, disappointments among the missionaries ensured a subdued start to the mission. Despite sanitised accounts in the *Evangelical Magazine*, only one-third of the original 30 men stayed with the group. The men were ill prepared, with few linguistic skills and scant appreciation of indigenous customs beyond a Biblical expectation of gross immorality and the charms of native women – the latter contributing to the downfall of no small number amongst them.[76] George Vason, who separated from his missionary brethren in Tonga to take native wives and live the life of a chief, understood his backsliding in terms of personal weakness, the strength of temptation and the lack of preparation or support provided by the LMS.[77] Despite the sternness of the LMS directors when selecting missionaries for the expedition, the Board seemed to abdicate responsibility for the men during the early years of the mission. Even correspondence from the directors was infrequent. John Davies, a successful teacher, was in Tahiti for six years before receiving communication from London. At different times missionaries sought guidance and care from the Directors but their requests concerning salary, provisions and furlough were unheeded or overruled. Henry Bicknell, destitute on his return to England, had not worn shoes for eight years. Henry Nott, a bricklayer and Congregationalist from Birmingham, who was mid-way through a 30-year commitment to translating the Scriptures into Tahitian, was disappointed that when the LMS begrudgingly agreed to his return home for treatment for elephantiasis, he was instructed to pay for his passage.[78] The men were further criticised by the new group of missionaries to arrive in 1817, who were horrified to discover the conditions in which their elderly brethren were living and, rather than challenge the general patronising air (but less than parental concern) of the directors, called for a deputation to investigate a range of troubling issues.[79] The deputees recognised the gravity of the breech, claiming that had their arrival been delayed by six months, the two groups would have been in 'such a state of open war as would have hazarded the present efficient existence of the Mission'.[80]

The new missionaries were also perplexed by conversions of the islanders, which were not articulated in terms easily understood by them.[81] Questions about the depth and integrity of the faith of converts, usually expressed by missionaries in personal letters to each other or to the directors rather than in public reports,[82] became more frequent. William Henry, writing in February 1825, claimed that 'The best native teachers that any of these Windward or Leeward Islands can as yet produce are very defective, and little more than fit to clear away the rubbish in the places to which they are sent, and prepare the way for more effective labourers.' A letter from Blossom of September 1827 made a similar point:

> I cannot help feeling that there is very little real religion among the people. The brethren have had a meeting, and some of them are very desirous of taking new ground. It is not for me to say whether it be right or wrong. But we should not think it right in a farmer to take more ground when he has already more than he can cultivate and keep in good order. And I would defy any man to say that there is a station or congregation in the islands fit to be left to themselves.[83]

Orsmond, the most bitter and caustic of the 1817 group, put it more bluntly: 'Tahiti is the vortex of iniquity, the Sodom of the Pacific and grazing stock to the world, a thorn in the eyes of the just...'[84] As Bennet and Tyerman noted from Huahine with rather more generosity, while progress was good, a 'greater care and circumspection are probably necessary here in the admission of persons to the Lord's table, than in England'. Believers were 'often imperfect in either knowledge or practice. They are children of a larger growth.'[85]

If conversions themselves were unconvincing, there were some instances of outright resistance. Bennet and Tyerman noted in 1823 that while there had been fewer ex-communications than they had expected, some had recently taken place in Haweis Town for tattooing. This 'barbarous species of embroidery' was generally popular with 'headstrong young men' and was recognised by Bennet and Tyerman as 'a symbol of their disaffection with the better order of things, and a signal for revolt against the existing government'.[86] Tyerman wrote to Samuel Marsden from Huahine that 'Religion and Civilisation' were 'going hand in hand', but also reported on the 30–40 'profligate young men' on each island, who breached law and order, sold liquor and were antagonistic to the missionaries.[87] Rod Edmond has detailed further incidents of antagonism, including the wearing of Western dress in an inappropriate style, the collective refusal of women to uphold Williams' moral objection to their preparations of food for the wife of a chief about to give birth to a child by another man, and the baring of bottoms in an expression of resistance, on this occasion to the practice of tithing.[88]

Most perplexing and distressing for the missionaries was the behaviour of the island elites. From the early days of the mission, the missionaries to Tahiti had become intimately acquainted with the person, household and fortunes of Pomare II whom, following Cook, they believed were Tahitian royalty. Pomare is represented in public LMS accounts as fulfilling the missionary reconstruction of the 'heathen' masculine subject. Missionaries believed that, despite his tattooed hands, beard and pony-tailed long hair and continued indulgence in 'debasing habits' and dissipated pastimes, the six-foot tall king possessed 'more of a personal dignity than could be expected from one who had been so lately a rude and fierce barbarian.'[89] They learned from Nott that he spent his evenings teaching his attendants to read the Scriptures and was involved in translation work. Noted for his cruelty in the past, he was now subduing warring groups. Later meetings with Queen Taaroa Vahine confirmed that she too was 'a truly pious and intelligent woman'.[90] Adopting a model of cultural change as emanating outwards and downwards from the royal household, Bennet and Tyerman countered the belief that Pomare and Vahine were 'insignificant barbarians invested with a little brief authority.'[91] Like George III, whose influence on the public education system at home the missionaries relayed to Pomare, it was believed that the Tahitian royals could nurture the nation's progress. People everywhere, including kings, queens and chiefs from nearby islands, followed their example: 'the mighty moral change', Bennet wrote, 'commenced from the King himself.'[92] Along with the groundswell of Christian conversions in Tahiti and Eimeo and missionary extension to the islands of Huahine, Raiatea and Bora-bora, Pomare's conduct as a benign, nurturing, Christian patriarch supported the interpretation of the South Seas Mission, for a brief moment in the 1820s at least, as an unqualified story of success.

Bennet and Tyerman's confident public account of Pomare was very different from representations of him provided by other missionaries, and belied the concerns hinted at by the visitors themselves in their personal correspondence with the Directors. Missionaries were distressed by the king's apparent reluctance to break free from 'sinful habits' and doubted his true commitment to Christianity. Indeed, some habits could not even be talked about, including his relationship with a *mahu*, a transgender man, who lived with him.[93] Other sources confirm such beliefs: Russian navigator Baron von Bellinghausen, for example, witnessed Pomare sending secret notes to passing whalers, requesting rum and wine; Vahine asked for a bottle of rum for herself, complaining that her husband had consumed the last whole bottle.[94] LMS historian Richard Lovett argued in 1893 that Pomare was more similar to his father, Pomare I, described both as 'majestic' and 'a poor untaught heathen, under the dominion of a reprobate mind', than to civilised man. His mother, the Queen, had died in 1806 while apparently trying to bring on an abortion; she was known to have already killed numerous children, all conceived by 'common men'. Questioning the King's motivation for turning to Christianity, Lovett suggested that the combination of a general decline in idolatry, the role of missionaries and bounty hunters in assisting him to extend his rule, and the fact that missionaries came with gifts and other goods to barter, were of greater significance than spiritual motives. At his death in 1822, Pomare's friend, missionary W. P. Crook, wept with grief while also feeling that it might be 'a public benefit': 'the King's conduct', he wrote, 'has been the greatest check to the civilisation of the people.'[95]

Writing his history of the LMS in the harsher racial climate of the 1890s, Lovett criticised the missionaries' lack of awareness concerning 'outward observances' of religious practice which were not matched by a change of heart. 'Having been eye-witness of such astounding transformations', he wrote, they 'possibly did not allow sufficiently for the innate depravity of the human heart, and for the abiding demoralisation due to generations of heathenism.'[96] The period from 1825 was disappointing. After the death of Pomare II, hopes were pinned on his little son Teariitaria, who, as the four-year old Pomare III, became the first king to experience a Christian coronation. While he was a student at the missionary school at Eimeo, the young king died. The throne then passed to Aimata, Pomare's daughter by a former spouse who, in Lovett's words and reflecting later nineteenth-century emphasis on the hereditary nature of inferiority and moral failure, was influenced by the 'evil lives' of her mother and aunts and soon began 'to manifest many of the worst qualities of the vicious ancestry from which she sprang.'[97] For early nineteenth-century missionaries, however, Lovett's potentially biological approach to Tahitian capacities held no appeal. Polynesians, like themselves, were God's children and members of the same human family. But missionaries everywhere were beginning to question the length of time within which the mission might be expected to yield success.

The questions raised by the brethren in the South Pacific echoed those in other colonies and mission stations, as missionaries puzzled over why it was proving so hard to persuade people of the benefits of Christianity. As the refusal of Christianity could not suggest an inadequacy of the Biblical framework within which they operated, missionaries came to wonder, in their frustration, whether this occurrence was on account of native incapacity. In Australia and New Zealand the argument for 'fixed' cultural differences was a feature not only of settler discourse,[98] but was taken up by some missionaries, perhaps the most notable of whom was the adversary to Lancelot Threlkeld's plans for an Australian Aboriginal Mission, the Reverend Samuel Marsden. Champion of the 'civilisation-first' philosophy, Marsden maintained that the native people of Australia were as yet beyond the power of God's grace: 'The Aborigines are the most degraded of the human race', he wrote in 1819; '... the time is not yet arrived for them to receive the blessings of civilization and the knowledge of Christianity.'[99] Seven years later, he declared 'the civilization of the Blacks' to appear to him 'almost a hopeless task.'[100] In the Caribbean, before the poor and dwindling fortunes of the Caribbean islands in the immediate post-emancipation years had fuelled disillusionment with the missionary philanthropic paradigm, missionaries despaired for their hopes for the social and religious progress of freed slaves, as worshippers at missionary chapels declined in numbers and independent black preachers and Creole religious practitioners became more popular.[101] India also, acknowledged as the most difficult of mission fields where missionaries were up against sophisticated religious systems, was the source of great anxiety. While immensely popular at home – one in every two speakers at domestic anniversary meetings had been serving in India in the 1840s[102] – missionaries in India were failing to extend the appeal of Christianity beyond the Harijan class and children in Christian orphanages.[103] Richard Price has recently illuminated this issue in his account of the impact on the Reverend Henry Calderwood, LMS missionary to the Xhosa in the 1830s, of the refusal by the chief Maqoma to accept the Christian message. The realisation that he was facing a much more sophisticated culture than stories prior to his arrival had prepared him for saw a 'dislocation' of the missionary's own knowledge system.[104] Left in ignorance, and with no other way of framing Maqoma's persistent moral degeneracy, Calderwood began to renege on his evangelical commitment to racial equality, and construed Maqoma's 'refusal' to accept Christianity as an 'inability' to receive the word. As Price argues, 'humanitarianism imploded from within as it faced the colonial encounter.'[105] The gospel was not having the 'universal sway' that had been anticipated, but was being received in ways which were sometimes too complex for missionaries to comprehend.

Although the challenge to the humanitarian paradigm was in evidence across the globe during the 1820s and 1830s, it had little impact in England in these years. The vibrant missionary culture which continued in Sheffield throughout the 1840s is suggestive of the sustained power of a humanitarian analysis and of a missionary propaganda in which there were few mentions of failure and disillusionment.[106] Certainly there was evidence of a harsher language of cultural difference. The Wincobank sources, for example, discussed in Chapter 3, reveal Lizzie Rawson to be both shocked at the use of the word 'nigger' and amused at a newspaper report which, 'either by mistake, or for a jest', referred to George Thompson's friend Tagore (presumably Debendranath, the Bengali reformer) as 'the great Baboon', a play on 'Baboo'.[107] Campaigners for domestic reform, maybe echoing some of the writing of Cobbett and Carlyle, also more readily utilised pejorative terms.[108] But the destabilising of humanitarianism in the colonies had not reached the missionary public back home.

Indeed, the case in England against missionary humanitarianism was slim in these years. Historians tend to fall back on a small number of texts in order to chart the rise of biological racism, notably Carlyle's essay on the 'Negro Question' (1849) and Robert Knox's *Races of Man* (1850). But, as Peter Mandler convincingly argues, the 'civilisational approach' continued triumphant in England into the 1840s and 1850s, if not on mainland Europe.[109] Even when such ideas did begin to make their mark in England, they led to a mere adjustment to the time frame: for those cultures not destined for extinction,[110] the process of civilisation would take longer than had previously been hoped for or anticipated. In the words of Charles Dickens, a vociferous critic of the Niger Expedition, there was a 'great gulf' between the 'civilised European' and 'barbarous African', and to 'change the customs' even of civilised people was 'a most difficult and slow proceeding; but to do this by ignorant and savage races, is a work which, like the progressive changes of the globe itself, requires a stretch of years that dazzles in the looking at.'[111] Dickens' objection was to the naïve optimism exhibited by missionaries. But it reflected a view increasingly held by evangelicals themselves, certainly those embroiled in overseas missionary affairs. Back-tracking from the belief that 'the book of God could contain the world', in Zemka's words, it was increasingly recognised that 'incremental progress' characterised the way forward.[112]

'The associations awakened by their presence': England's civilisation

Montgomery's *Voyages and Travels* is a paean to missionary labour and to the transforming power of the Word. While the complexity of the ethnographic detail occasionally bursts beyond the biblical paradigm, with discussions of cultural practices which could not be marshalled to neatly support an evangelical interpretation,[113] the book remains a confident account of missionary success. *Voyages and Travels* is not, to use Edmond's description of William Ellis's *Polynesian Researches*, an 'alternation between science and sermon', between 'neutral description and vehement denunciation'[114]; it is all sermon, with ethnography utilised in its support. To appeal to a wider liberal public, however, the missionary narrative needed to make more formal connections with science and areas of social reform which fell outside of evangelical enthusiasm.

Missionaries were well aware of the value of artefacts which might be sent home as ethnographic, geological and natural history specimens. The LMS museum in London, opened directly following Pomare's rejection of idolatry, had become home to a range of missionary artefacts. Bennet and Tyerman draw attention to the 'great variety of merchandise' that this might include: on one occasion, men wishing 'to tempt us to barter' presented 'native cloth, pearl shells, fishing hooks (very ingenious and beautiful contrivances), lines, cordage made of various materials, mats, bags, nets, calabashes for water vessels ... umitis (large wooden dishes), penus (stone hammers), stools, spears, bows and arrows etc etc' in anticipation of an exchange for knives, forks, scissors and other imported goods.[115] While Bennet asked Montgomery and Hodgson to select pieces for themselves and their mutual friends as tokens of friendship and remembrance from crates sent to Sheffield, his intention was for the artefacts to be bestowed 'for the interests of Science'.[116] Montgomery, elected president of the Lit and Phil in 1824, committed some of Bennet's 'spoils of gospel' to the Society's Ethnographic collection in the newly opened museum.[117] Two boxes of 'Curiosities from Otaheite, consisting of War Instruments, Dresses, [and] Musical Instruments' were received by the Society in 1824. A further donation of geological specimens, collections of shells, birds (for the Natural History collection) and ethnographic material, including cloth, jewellery, domestic utensils, weapons of war and idols, was made to the museum in 1831, after Bennet's return to Britain.[118] At around the same time the museum acquired other donations, including a poem written in 'the ancient language of Ceylon' on the leaf of the Talipot tree, two casts of the heads of New Zealand chiefs, mother of pearl from Botany Bay and a stuffed lioness, two leopards and a tiger. In 1885, a local historian remembered visiting as a child the 'sombre apartment beneath the Music Hall' and seeing a stuffed fawn and tiger, a long case of minerals and fossils and the head of a New Zealander, with long black hair, behind the President's chair.[119]

Sujit Sivasundaram argues that the observational, collecting and categorising practices of missionaries constitute them as scientists. While in tension with elite and secular definitions of science, the religious view of nature was immensely popular, and was believed by many to provide an accurate assessment of the true state of society.[120] But missionaries also sought to engage the interest and support of men with a commitment to secular science. John Williams, whose scientific explorations (and death) associated him with Cook, but whose piety made him 'a better Cook for a religiously awakened public', enchanted English audiences with his lecture tours and *Memoirs* in the late 1830s. He believed that if he could 'induce men of rank and science, with the merchants and shipowners of Britain to ponder over its pages, they would no longer occupy neutral ground in the great contest with heathenism'.[121] Of course, the missionary 'contest' would also be stronger for the new source of support.

Displays of missionary artefacts which were part of secular collections placed greater emphasis on a progressive trajectory and the historical development from 'primitive' to 'civilised' societies than had original missionary museums. The national Lit and Phil membership, including men of science as well as medical men and other professionals, later originated taxonomies which pre-empted the organisation of museums of the later nineteenth century.[122] As Ludmilla Jordanova argues, the practice of display – the taxonomies involved, the process of comparing, contrasting and labelling specimens – is central to the categorisation through which narratives of human progress are made.[123] In contrast, the early organisation of artefacts by the LMS was less concerned with representing progressive social development than with illustrating the triumph of Christianity. Items were not categorised, but displayed together as a general representation of island life prior to the arrival of missionaries.[124] This appears to have been the case in the Sheffield Lit and Phil museum where, at the transitory moment of the 1840s, such artefacts were

> memorials of a state of society gone by in the South Sea Islands, where society had previously not changed a feature of its aspects for ages beyond the memory of man, having been apparently incapable either of improvement or degradation.[125]

Fixing the cultures of the South Seas in a timeless and static past, they served to elicit admiration for the missionary enterprises and the progressive civilised culture which had enabled exposure to the gospel and so inspired profound change. In the words of the 1842 *Report*, their value lay not in any intrinsic worth but in 'the associations awakened by their presence, in a Christian and civilised land'.[126]

The Lit and Phil museum saw the beginnings of the extension of the missionary audience beyond the established evangelical networks to the wider liberal public.[127] In the 1840s, this was a tentative development; until the incorporation of the collection into Sheffield's municipal museum in 1875, it provided a limited forum, as only members and their guests were admitted. Its role within the wider middle class was significant nonetheless. As Kate Hill argues, museums operated as 'an arena for the establishment and consolidation of cultural identity and values', allowing the middle class to 'demonstrate authority, stamp their own values onto culture'.[128] Such emphasis on Sheffield's and Britain's civilisation was supported, as Simon Gunn has argued, by the monumentalism and spectacle of other aspects of middle-class civic culture.[129] The new Botanical Gardens (1833), a site of pleasant recreation for the middle class and a civilising space in which the working man could promenade with his family, was also emblematic of the desire to collect, order, display and re-present aspects of the colonial world.[130] The General Cemetery (1836), inspired in design and architecture by the classical civilisation of ancient Greece, and home to Bennet's memorial, along with Norfolk Park (1847), the first public park, and the Free Library (1856), encouraged by the success of the Mechanics' and Apprentices' Library, consolidated the town's sense of its considerable progress on the ladder of civilisation.[131] James Montgomery's funeral in May 1854, the first in the town of the new-style civic funerals, and the subsequent erection of the bronze statue to 'The Christian Poet' in the General Cemetery in 1860, and the array of busts, halls and street names all committed to Montgomery's memory, contributed to Sheffield's new civic culture.[132]

As suggested by the construction of George Bennet's public memorial in 1842, empire and civilisation were part of the Victorian commitment to the municipal commemoration of its townspeople.[133] One of the 'cross-mappings' which placed empire within the urban experience,[134] the memorial is a symbol of civic pride and national virtue, depicting Christian England at the apex of a hierarchy of civilisation and missionary supporters as the architects of global improvement.

Conclusion

By the 1840s, missions were under assault from a number of directions. Challenges came from domestic reformers, who viewed overseas enthusiasm as a distraction from the condition of the English poor (see Chapter 5), and from advocates of the argument that native peoples did not have an innate capacity for improvement. Many missionaries were also frustrated and disillusioned by the lack of anticipated response to their cause. Their personal correspondence further reveals their own lapses of judgement and morality, antagonisms of class and authority between the Directors and those they had selected, and a catalogue of jealousies and petty resentments between men in the field.

But missionary culture remained vibrant in these years. Such conflict and evidence of disappointment was rarely glimpsed in the public representations of mission at home. The memoirs and public speeches, displays and memorials that became a staple of Victorian popular middle-class culture encapsulated an unproblematic view of the missionary enterprise: of missionary men and their wives bringing Christian belief and practice to 'heathen' peoples. They challenged the established discourse of noble savagery and newer arguments for the essential inferiority of 'primitive' peoples, emphasising instead the positive role of missionary intervention in countering savage depravity and hastening the progress of individual 'babes in Christ' and 'infant' cultures in the transition to civilised society. Missionary societies responded to the problem of the errant missionary by providing a better education and preparation for their volunteers. As disappointments such as that with Pomare multiplied throughout the missionary world, missionaries began to talk in terms of a longer chronology of change, seeing Christianisation over the course of years and generations, and thus establishing the English missionary in the long-term position as overseer of global reform. The movement continued to benefit from the energy of women and children, but it was its appeal to a wider liberal public that secured its longevity and blossoming into the civilising mission of the mid-century.

Ethnography, science and the emphasis on 'civilisation' attracted groups beyond the established missionary public, for whom the civilising mission was a key component of local civic pride and England's own status as a 'Christian and civilized land'.

Conclusions

The Civilising Mission and the English Middle Class has explored the role of global missionary philanthropy as a crucible for middle-class formation in the early decades of the nineteenth century. Beginning as an evangelical project in the 1790s, missionary philanthropy was made respectable by the Clapham Sect and popularised by a middle-class grassroots membership drawn from all Protestant denominations, to become a mass provincial movement in the 1810s and 1820s. The formation of missionary societies created new patterns of organisation and cultural networks through which a broad middle-class culture took shape. The shared missionary impulse enabled points of connection across social, political and denominational differences. Technologies for reform, especially domestic visitation and social investigation, enabled the construction of a new social sphere of cultural intervention. Missionary representations of 'heathen' subjects as children in need of parental guidance reinforced the belief in the advanced state of civilisation at home and the role of the missionary middle class as supervisors of global reform. Missionary philanthropy was integral to the claims of the middle class for greater power and influence at home on the basis of their collective identity as agents of global civilisation.

Middle-class men played a central role in establishing the structures of the philanthropic movement and promoting the voluntary society in a civic forum. Involvement in the home-based missionary movement prepared them for other offices of power and created a shared identity as progressive citizens. The global dimension to their work provided a wider canvas for working out strategies for social change and consolidated a sense of their importance as teachers, moral exemplars and leaders. The new 'social' sphere was not solely equated with a masculine public world, however, but was fundamentally shaped by the domestic sphere. Much missionary work with the poor – domestic reform, distribution of Bibles and canvassing for missionary donations – was undertaken by women. For them, missionary philanthropy did not represent an escape from an otherwise confining domestic life, but was integral to their domestic responsibilities. Missionary domesticity, ordained by the scriptures and reinforced by the Enlightenment association of domesticity and civilisation, was intimately bound up with the construction of Christian subjects and the creation of the Christian social body. Missionary women took responsibility for the education of children, domestic management, the instruction of servants and overseeing neighbourhood social relations. Their domestic role also accommodated a range of global concerns: the abolition of slavery, developments in the education of girls and attention to the poor treatment of women in 'heathen' nations across the globe. Missionary women helped to shape a new religious public which was integral to the collective identity of the evangelical middle class, and in so doing created for themselves an expansive and commodious social world.

The civilising mission was enabled by an unprecedented enlargement of 'the world' in the late eighteenth century, as voyages of discovery and colonialism provided access to hitherto remote or unknown geographical regions. This world – its people, their histories and their potential – was interpreted primarily through the Bible. This book has argued for a more sustained consideration of the popular theological understandings of the role of the missionary. The identification of the 'heathen' and development of a programme for their salvation was derived from the apostles, especially from the writing of St Paul. Images of husbandry, cultivation, sowing and reaping through which missionary work was represented had Biblical origins. Scriptural visions of Christian change were consolidated by Enlightenment

AS part of this?

theories of global civilisation and social progress which saw an emphasis on 'civilising' practices alongside Christian instruction.

Home and overseas missions were part of the same social movement in the 1790s to 1830s. Representing a dual focus which reached its heights in the work of abolitionists between 1824 and 1838, the two branches of the movement informed each other, sharing personnel and technologies for social progress and change, in addition to origins in evangelicalism and Enlightenment social theory. Various sites of mission were identified as comparable 'contact zones': the church and chapel, the school-room, Bible and missionary meeting, and especially 'heathen' and working-class home and family life. Missionary insistence upon the similar characteristics of 'heathenism' at home and overseas challenged the discourse of noble savagery and newer arguments for the essential inferiority of 'primitive' peoples. It emphasised instead the spiritual equality of all people and the positive role of missionary intervention in countering savage depravity and hastening the progress of individual 'babes in Christ' and 'infant' cultures to civilisation.

The missionary narrative of cultural change experienced a number of setbacks during the early nineteenth century. Firstly, there was the errant missionary, the brother who went astray, attracted by 'heathen' women or lifestyles more generally. This problem was addressed by the provision of a better education for volunteers, their recruitment from higher social groups and the standard employment of the missionary couple from the 1820s. Secondly, was the uneven reception of Christianity. As early as the 1820s, a new knowledge was emanating from the letters and reports of missionaries, which pointed to the slow pace of change, the unfamiliar appearance of many conversions, peoples' continued attachment to 'immoral' practices and anxieties of control as the translation of the Scriptures generated the possibility of interpretations beyond the direction of the missionaries. At first, this was confined to private correspondence between missionaries themselves and with the Board. For some missionaries, the multiplying disappointments and anxieties of conversion led to frustration and a feeling of humiliation. Unable to break beyond the paradigm which saw exposure to the Bible as a catalyst for change, however, missionaries usually channelled their confusion into an acceptance of a longer chronology for change, over years and generations and requiring ongoing European supervision. But such criticisms coincided with a growing anti-humanitarianism within the settler colonies which denied the possibility of civilisation and Christian reform to peoples who were designated both 'heathen' and 'savage'. This made space for the development of separate trajectories for different 'heathen' peoples, expressed most famously by Carlyle and Knox, and thus unexpectedly giving challenge to the missionary philanthropic paradigm and providing an opening for a more essentialist racism to enter the culture from the 1840s and 1850s.

The extent of the popularity of such arguments in England, however, warrants further investigation. On the one hand, historians have emphasised a shift away from humanitarianism. Catherine Hall has recently contrasted the impatience with the post-emancipation Caribbean, evident in Carlyle's 'Occasional discourse on the Negro question' (1849) and Knox's *Races of Man* (1850), with the abolitionist heyday of the late 1830s. Similarly, Susan Thorne sees in Dickens' parody of Mrs Jellyby (*Bleak House*, 1853), whose preoccupation with the Borrioboola-Gha mission on the banks of the Niger rendered her unable to take care of her own household, an assault on the overseas missionary movement and its foundation in humanitarian universalism (as well as the feminine and domestic character of the missionary movement at home). Racism is also in evidence in the resurfacing of 'extinction theories' during this period.[1]

On the other hand, while Porter contends that disillusionment was expressed in a reduction in numbers of volunteers to represent a low point in missionary work overseas,[2] the rich missionary culture in England in the 1840s appears largely untouched by the harsher approach to cultural difference. Conflict and evidence of disappointment was rarely glimpsed in the public representations of the overseas missionary movement. The memoirs and public speeches, the displays and memorials that became a staple of Victorian popular middle-class culture encapsulated instead an unproblematic view of the missionary enterprise: of missionary men and their wives bringing Christian belief and practice to heathen peoples. As suggested by the great interest generated by the publication of Harriet Beecher Stowe's *Uncle Tom's Cabin*, the humanitarian epoch continued well into the 1840s and 1850s.[3]

Of greater significance in challenging missionary philanthropy in the 1820s and 1830s was a renewed and singular focus on the domestic poor. Tory paternalists issued polemical anti-missionary statements as part of their wider critique of urban industrial society. Missionaries and their supporters were to them one more group who had abandoned the domestic poor to the New Poor Law and the factory system, and whose mistaken priorities were enabling the rise to power of profiteering manufacturers who had no concern for England's tradition, people or established civilisation. At the same time, the doctors, merchants, manufacturers and ministers who formed the Lit and Phils, Mechanics' Institutes, Statistical Societies and City Missions also focused on the reform of the working-class man, his family and environment. These institutions promoted secular as well as Biblical knowledge. They delivered their programmes through a largely male agency and were supportive of material and environmental (rather than solely moral) reform and, increasingly, state intervention. The new urban missionary movement of the 1830s and 1840s thus saw a blurring of the hitherto well-established double focus of missionary philanthropy on the 'heathen' at home and overseas. Again, arguments for biological difference, while occasionally present, did not predominate: while sometimes involving growing doubts about the veracity of overseas missions, their impetus was the urgency of the 'condition of England'. The 1840s thus saw a separation of the two branches of the missionary movement, as home and overseas were no longer automatically part of the same project.

The emphasis in the 1830s on the civilisation of working men through the provision of secular education became connected with a competing power base in civic elites. In Sheffield, the town which has formed the sustained focus for the local/global aspect of this study, abolition in 1833 saw great rejoicing.[4] But many of the men who had formed the vanguard of the early missionary philanthropic and abolitionist campaigns in the town were already aware that they were involved in a struggle for power with newly rising social and professional groups. For doctors and other professionals, empowered by a catalogue of reforms from the Repeal of the Test and Corporation Acts (1828) to municipal government (1835 onwards), and by their contributions to the cholera epidemic of 1832, neither abolition nor missionary philanthropy was central to their reform priorities. While they were often subscribers to overseas missionary societies and supporters of abolition, it was their wives and daughters who were the active participants at missionary society events. These men instead concentrated their energies on questions concerning the condition of the English nation: the response to Chartism, poverty, sanitation and education. Such developments had implications for the missionary philanthropic model which, while enjoying a continued humanitarian heyday within some urban elites, was in other towns under threat of becoming a feminised and family-based missionary culture.[5]

The emphasis of middle-class men on the secular improvement of the working class also had the potential to marginalise those women who had been a driving force in the popularisation of the early missionary movement. Yet, women's philanthropy again gained ground in the 1850s, as the intensification of the language of women's mission saw women turn towards the poor and distressed and, increasingly, children in new institutional settings: as Scripture readers and Biblewomen, visitors to workhouses and hospitals, teachers of evening classes and Sunday schools. This was in some ways a continuation of earlier evangelical female philanthropy, in its focus on home visiting and in the emphasis on social investigation, for example.[6] However, 'woman's mission' was increasingly embraced by the growing liberal women's movement and, taken up by single women campaigners keen to carve out areas of female employment, was used to contest 'separate spheres'. While feminists prioritised work 'at home', the colonies continued to be an important focus of interest. The Langham Place group, for example, was interested in female emigration to white settler colonies as sites of useful work for women.[7] The home colonisation movement from the 1840s promoted domesticity as the best means of settling colonies, sending working- and middle-class women to settler colonies such as Canada and Australia as domestic servants and governesses. White women within the colonies were now under the scrutinising gaze of the missionary movement.[8] While the 1820s and 1830s were formative decades in missions for single women, the 1860s saw independent women travelling in their numbers, enlisted by the newly formed ladies' boards of the national missionary societies.[9] As Antoinette Burton has shown, feminist interest in raising 'heathen' women, in India especially, was central to English women's articulation of demands for the extension of their own domestic, political and civil rights.[10]

Traditional missionary philanthropy was also affected by the inevitable passing of the mantle to a new generation. The 1830s and 1840s saw the deaths of anti-slavery stalwarts William Wilberforce, Hannah More, Thomas Fowell Buxton and Thomas Clarkson. William Carey died in 1834, followed by John Williams five years later and William Knibb in 1845. The Reverend Malthus and Thomas Chalmers, originators of Christian economics, died in these decades, as did many provincial female reformers, including Elizabeth Heyrick and Elizabeth Fry. In Sheffield, George Bennet and Rowland Hodgson died in 1837 and Samuel Roberts in 1848. James Montgomery lived beyond the mid-century, continuing to the very end of his life with his missionary tours and involvement in evangelical and secular educational projects.[11] Mary-Anne Rawson continued to combine temperance and educational activities with abolitionism – she was visited by both Frederick Douglass and William Lloyd Garrison in the 1860s and 1870s – and support for missions. She followed George Thompson's later involvement with anti-slavery in India and in the 1850s extended her activities to anti-Catholic work, providing hospitality to Alessandro Gavazzi and joining an increasing number of ladies who travelled to Italy to offer support to Protestant schools.[12]

By the 1840s, support in England for the overseas missionary movement was part of the mainstream culture. This represented a great change in fortunes from half a century earlier, when the promotion of missions was a pioneering activity undertaken by the most devout of middle-class evangelicals. The change was due to a number of factors, including the national dominance of a middle-class culture which had evangelical tenets at its centre, the increased status and respectability conferred upon religious Dissent, and the popularity of missionary domesticity among middle-class women. The feminine and domestic character of the movement further consolidated the popularity of the lower-middle-class missionary couple, who had replaced the artisan and lay preacher of the 1790s, and so enhanced the appeal of the missionary vocation within the middle class by the middle of the nineteenth century.[13] But it was the extension of its appeal to a wider public that secured the longevity of the movement and its capacity to blossom into the national civilising mission of the mid-century. The involvement of liberal men, attracted not by evangelicalism but by natural science, ethnography and the emphasis on 'civilisation', established a popularity beyond the usual missionary public, ensuring that the civilising mission became a key component of local civic pride and England's own status as a 'Christian and civilized land'.

The years between the runaway success of John Williams *Memoirs* in 1839 and the rapturous welcome given to David Livingstone in 1856 require more research to place them in the context of the broadening appeal of the civilising mission. Livingstone especially, returning to England after 15 years service in Bechuanaland, was an unlikely national hero, not least, as Tim Jeal has noted, because in all those years he made but one convert, who later lapsed. Kuruman, the site of the most publicised of all mission stations, was 'an arid under-populated village', with fewer than 40 communicants and a congregation of 350. He failed miserably as a husband and father, dragging his wife Mary (the daughter of Robert Moffat) and five young children on long and dangerous expeditions, which caused intense suffering and death. He may have crossed Africa in 1853–1856, but the value of his other geographical discoveries, including the government-funded expedition that he led to the Zambesi, are contested. Yet when he arrived in England in December 1856, Livingstone was fêted up and down the country. He received a gold medal from the Royal Geographical Society, was awarded the Freedom of major cities, an honorary doctorate from Oxford

University, and finally, a private audience with Queen Victoria. His *Missionary Travels and Researches in South Africa*, published in November 1857, sold 70,000 copies.[14] The public liked his message regarding commerce and civilisation and his commitment to natural science. They appreciated his insistence on the importance of a British presence in Africa for economic, scientific and spiritual reasons. While Livingstone occasionally questioned the success of native agents of Christian conversion and expressed doubts that a European presence in Africa was worthwhile, his emphasis was on the impossibility of Africa 'raising itself' without contact with 'superior races'.[15] He captured the attention of powerful men as well as ordinary middle-class families. His new brand of imperial masculinity achieved a particular significance in 1857, as his book received acclaim amidst the huge public response (resulting in a larger missionary intake of 1858) to the threat to British womanhood and middle-class domestic life evident in the Indian Rebellion.[16]

The missionary solution posed by Hannah More to the crises of the 1790s had consisted of small-scale projects, inspired by the Bible and managed by middle-class women and men. Missionary philanthropy was a crucible for middle-class formation, enabling the missionary middle class in England to assume a role as overseer of national reform and a position at the helm of global change. If missions had been seen in their early years as marginal and, at times, worrisome, they were by the 1820s becoming 'emblematic of national virtue'; by the 1840s and 1850s, widespread enthusiasm for the civilising mission reflected acceptance of Protestant narratives about 'chosen communities' within the English nation.[17] By 1850, the national civilising mission drew upon Biblical, commercial and secular civilising technologies, involved the wider English populace and was sustained from within popular middle class as well as evangelical culture. The cultural ambitions of the early-nineteenth-century middle class thus paved the way for the imperial ambitions of the nation in mid-nineteenth-century England, as the civilising mission was consolidated as a national project. Missionaries were now at the centre of the master narrative of imperial history and at the heart of the cultural life of the nation.

Notes

Introduction: the missionary movement, the local and the global

1. Kathryn Sutherland, 'Hannah More's counter-revolutionary feminism', in Kelvin Everest (ed.), *Revolution in Writing: British Literary Responses to the French Revolution* (Buckingham: Open University Press, 1991), p. 40.
2. Reverend Arthur Roberts (ed.), *Mendip Annals, or, A Narrative of the Charitable Labours of Hannah and Martha More in their Neighbourhood*, 3rd edition (London: James Nisbet, 1839 [1834]), p. 28.
3. Hannah More to Elizabeth Montagu, 10 October 1789, quoted in Anne Stott, *Hannah More: The First Victorian* (Oxford: Oxford University Press, 2003), p. 110.
4. Hannah More to Zachary Macaulay, January 1796, about the prosperity of the new school ('Which you remember we used to call "Botany Bay" '). A. Roberts (ed.), *Letters of Hannah More to Zachary Macaulay* (London: James Nisbet, 1860), p. 10.
5. Roberts (ed.), *Mendip Annals*, p. 43.
6. See also: Hannah More to William Wilberforce, 14 October 1795, in W. Roberts (ed.), *Memoirs of the Life and Correspondence of Mrs Hannah More* (London: Seeley and Burnside, 1839), p. 244; M. G. Jones, *Hannah More* (Cambridge: Cambridge University Press, 1952), p. 165.
7. Extract from an account of the Mendip Schools, Society for Bettering the Condition of the Poor, *The Reports of the Society for Bettering the Condition and Increasing the Comforts of the Poor*, 4th edition, vol. 1 (London, 1805), p. 297.
8. The Sierra Leone project, which originated in the search for an alternative destination for convicts following the 'closure' of America to such purposes, aimed to promote legitimate commerce and agriculture and to provide a solution to the 'problem' of London's Black poor. See Philip D. Curtin, *The Image of Africa. British Ideas and Action, 1780–1850*, vol. 1 (London: University of Wisconsin Press, 1964), pp. 95–102, 105–119 and 123–139; Stephen J. Braidwood, *Black Poor and White Philanthropists: London's Blacks and the Foundation of the Sierra Leone Settlement 1786–1791* (Liverpool: Liverpool University Press, 1994); Christopher Fyfe, 'Freed slave colonies in West Africa', in John Flint (ed.), *The Cambridge History of Africa,*

Volume 5, from c 1790 to c 1870 (Cambridge: Cambridge University Press, 1976), pp. 170–199.

9. Sutherland, 'Hannah More's counter-revolutionary feminism', pp. 54–61; Jones, *Hannah More*, p. 62. More's poem *Slavery* indicates she was well-acquainted with Enlightenment arguments concerning biological and cultural bases for human difference. *Slavery, A Poem* (London: T. Cadell, 1788), pp. 16–17.
10. Whereas the auxiliaries of the BMS, LMS and CMS followed the formation of the national societies, the formation of the Leeds-based Methodist Missionary Society (1813) stimulated the formal organisation of the WMMS in 1819.
11. Anne Summers, 'A home from home – women's philanthropic work in the nineteenth century', in Sandra Burman (ed.), *Fit Work for Women* (London: Croom Helm, 1979); F. K. Prochaska, *Women and Philanthropy in Nineteenth Century England* (Oxford: Clarendon Press, 1980).
12. This book is about middle-class formation. It is not my intention to downplay working-class evangelicalism but it is not my focus here.
13. For late-eighteenth-century revivalism, see David Bebbington, *Evangelicalism in Modern Britain: A History from the 1730s to the 1980s* (London: Unwin Hyman, 1989).
14. G. M. Ditchfield, 'English rational dissent and philanthropy, c.1760–c. 1810', in Hugh Cunningham and Joanna Innes (eds), *Charity, Philanthropy and Reform from the 1690s to 1850* (Basingstoke: Macmillan, 1998), pp. 193–207; Helen Plant, 'Gender and the Aristocracy of Dissent: A Comparative Study of the Beliefs, Status and Roles of Women in Quaker and Unitarian communities, 1770–1830, with Particular Reference to Yorkshire' (University of York: unpublished PhD thesis, 2000).
15. R. J. Morris, 'Voluntary societies and British urban elites, 1780–1850: an analysis', *The Historical Journal*, vol. 26, no. 1 (1983), 95–118; *Class, Sect and Party: The Making of the British Middle Class: Leeds 1820–1850* (Manchester: Manchester University Press, 1990).
16. Leonore Davidoff and Catherine Hall, *Family Fortunes: Men and Women of the English Middle Class, 1780–1850* (London: Hutchinson, 1987).
17. Davidoff and Hall argue that philanthropy enabled the extension of women's sphere, but underplay women's involvement in public societies. *Family Fortunes*, pp. 429–436.
18. Susan Thorne's point that overseas missions of the 1790s were promoted because of obstacles to work at home is important, but that they were a natural outcome of eighteenth-century shifts in theology and new access to heathen peoples should not be overlooked. See *Congregational Missions and the Making of an Imperial Culture in*

19th Century England (California: Stanford University Press, 1999), pp. 44–51.

19. The exceptions are: Thorne, *Congregational Missions*; David Turley, *The Culture of English Antislavery, 1780–1860* (London: Routledge, 1991); and 'British antislavery reassessed', in Arthur Burns and Joanna Innes (eds), *Rethinking the Age of Reform: Britain 1780–1850* (Cambridge: Cambridge University Press, 2003).
20. Denise Riley, *Am I That Name? Feminism and the Category of 'Women' in History* (Basingstoke: Macmillan, 1989); Mary Poovey, *Making a Social Body: British Cultural Formation 1830–1864* (London: Chicago University Press, 1995); Eileen Janes Yeo, *The Contest for Social Science: Relations and Representations of Gender and Class* (London: Rivers Oram Press, 1996).
21. Anne Summers, *Female Lives, Moral States: Women, Religion and Public Life in Britain 1800–1930* (Berks: Threshold Press, 2000); Catherine Hall, *Civilising Subjects, Metropole and Colony in the English Imagination 1830–1867* (Cambridge: Polity, 2002); M. J. D. Roberts, *Making English Morals. Voluntary Association and Moral Reform in England, 1787–1886* (Cambridge: Cambridge University Press, 2004).
22. Jurgen Habermas, *The Structural Transformation of the Public Sphere: An Inquiry into a Category of Bourgeois Society*, trns. by T. Burger and F. Lawrence (Oxford: Polity Press, 1989). For qualifications, see Craig Calhoun (ed.), *Habermas and the Public Sphere* (Cambridge: MIT Press, 1992); Jane Rendall, 'Women and the public sphere', *Gender & History*, vol. 11, no. 3 (November 1999), pp. 475–488.
23. For critiques of the over-privatisation of the domestic, see '"Our Several Spheres"; middle class women and the feminisms of early Victorian radical politics', in K. Gleadle and S. Richardson (eds) *Women in British Politics, 1760–1860: The Power of the Petticoat* (Basingstoke: Palgrave, 2000); Lawrence E. Klein, 'Gender and the public/private distinction in the eighteenth century: some questions about evidence and analytic procedure', *Eighteenth-Century Studies*, vol. 29, no. 1 (Fall 1995), pp. 97–109.
24. For 'missionary domesticity' see chapter three.
25. Hall, *Civilising Subjects*. See also Andrew Porter, *Religion versus Empire? British Protestant Missionaries and Overseas Expansion, 1700–1914* (Manchester: Manchester University Press, 2004).
26. For missions as a 'contact zone', see Mary Louise Pratt, *Imperial Eyes: Travel Writing and Transculturation* (New York: Routledge, 1992).
27. Peter Mandler, 'Poverty and charity in the nineteenth-century metropolis', *The Uses of Charity: The Poor on Relief in the Nineteenth-Century Metropolis* (Philadelphia: University of Pennsylvania Press, 1990), pp. 1–37.

28. Frederick Cooper and Ann Laura Stoler, 'Between metropole and colony: rethinking a research agenda', *Tensions of Empire: Colonial Cultures in a Bourgeois World* (London: University of California Press, 1997). For a recent contribution in this field, see Catherine Hall and Sonya O. Rose (eds), *At Home with the Empire: Metropolitan Culture and the Imperial World* (Cambridge: CUP, 2006).
29. For the sati campaigns, see Clare Midgley, 'From supporting missions to petitioning Parliament: English women and the evangelical campaign against "sati" (widow-burning) in India, 1813–1830', in Gleadle and Richardson (eds), *Women in British Politics*, pp. 74–92.
30. Prochaska, *Women and Philanthropy*, pp. 5, 11; R. H. Martin, *Evangelicals United: Ecumenical Stirrings in Pre-Victorian Britain, 1795–1830* (London: Scarecrow Press, 1983), p. 115. For a discussion of the complexity of charitable 'giving', see Colin Jones, 'Some recent trends in the history of charity', in M. Daunton, *Charity, Self-Interest and Welfare in the English Past* (London: UCL Press, 1996), pp. 51–63.
31. See Antoinette Burton, *Burdens of History: British Feminists, Indian Women, and Imperial Culture, 1865–1915* (Chapel Hill: University of North Carolina Press, 1994).
32. Valentine Cunningham. ' "God and nature intended you for a missionary's wife": Mary Hill, Jane Eyre and other missionary women', in Fiona Bowie, Deborah Kirkwood, and Shirley Ardener (eds), *Women and Missions: Past and Present. Anthropological and Historical Perceptions* (Oxford: Berg Publishers, 1993), p. 89. See also: Sean Gill, 'Heroines of missionary adventure: the portrayal of Victorian women missionaries in popular fiction and biography', in A. Hogan and A. Bradstock (eds), *Women of Faith in Victorian Culture. Reassessing the Angel in the House* (Basingstoke: Macmillan 1998), pp. 172–185; Judith Rowbotham, ' "Hear an Indian sister's plea": reporting the work of nineteenth century British female missionaries', *Women's Studies International Forum* vol. 21, no. 3 (1998), pp. 247–262; and 'Ministering angels, not ministers: women's involvement in the foreign missionary movement, c. 1860–1910', in Sue Morgan (ed.), *Women, Religion and Feminism in Britain 1750–1900* (Basingstoke: Palgrave, 2002), pp. 179–195; Stephen Maughan, 'Civic culture, women's foreign missions and the British imperial imagination, 1860–1914', in Frank Trentmann (ed.), *Paradoxes of Civil Society: New Perspectives on Modern German and British History* (Oxford: Berghahn Books, 2000). For an exception, see Clare Midgley, 'Can women be missionaries? Envisioning female agency in the early nineteenth-century British empire', *Journal of British Studies*, vol. 45, no. 2 (April 2006), pp. 335–358.

33. See Emma Raymond Pitman, *Heroines of the Mission Field* (London: Cassle and Co., 1880).
34. Adele Perry, 'Metropolitan knowledge, colonial practice, and indigenous womanhood: missions in nineteenth-century British Columbia', in Katie Pickles and Myra Rutherdale (eds), *Contact Zones: Aboriginal and Settler Women in Canada's Colonial Past* (Vancouver: UBC Press, 2005), p. 126. See also: Jane Haggis, 'Gendering colonialism or colonizing gender', *Women's Studies International Forum*, vol. 13 (1990), pp. 105–115; Margaret Jolly, 'Colonizing women: the maternal body and empire', in Sneja Gunew and Anna Yeatman (eds), *Feminism and the Politics of Difference* (NSW: Allen and Unwin, 1993), pp. 103–127; Myra Rutherdale, *Women and the White Man's God. Gender and Race in the Canadian Mission Field* (Vancouver: UBC Press 2002).
35. 'Reading Cook's voyages was the first thing that engaged my mind to think of missions'. Eustace Carey, *Memoir of William Carey* (London: Jackson and Walford, 1836), p. 18. See also: John Eimeo Ellis (ed.), *Life of William Ellis* (London: John Murray 1873), p. 8; Hugh R. Haweis, *Travel and Talk* (London, 1896), p. 194. For the popularity of Hawkesworth's *Account* (1773) of Cook's voyages, see Paul Kaufman, *Borrowings from the Bristol Library, 1773–1784: A Unique Record of Reading Vogues* (Charlottesville: Bibliographical Society of the University of Virginia, 1960).
36. See Alan Frost, 'The Pacific Ocean: The eighteenth century's "New World"', *Studies in Voltaire and the Eighteenth Century*, vol. 142 (1976), pp. 279–322; C. A. Bayly, *Imperial Meridian: The British Empire and the World, 1780–1830* (Harlow: Longman, 1989), pp. 1–15 and 75–216.
37. Peter Marshall and Glyndr Williams, *The Great Map of Mankind: Perceptions of New Worlds in the Age of Enlightenment* (Cambridge: Harvard University Press, 1982), pp. 45–61, 67–97, 128–154 and 187–226.
38. Porter, *Religion versus Empire?*
39. For a more complex account of the relationship between missions and imperialism, see Elizabeth Elbourne, *Blood Ground: Colonialism, Missions and the Contest for Christianity in the Cape Colony and Britain, 1799–1853* (Montreal and Kingston: McGill-Queen's University Press, 2002), pp. 12–13; Thorne, *Congregational Missions*, pp. 2–12; and Hall, *Civilising Subjects*.
40. Edward Said, *Orientalism* (London: RKP [1985], 1978); *Culture and Imperialism* (London: Chatto and Windus, 1993). For support and qualifications, see Pratt, *Imperial Eyes*.
41. Frantz Fanon, *The Wretched of the Earth* (Harmondsworth: Penguin, [1961], 1985), p. 32.

42. Mary Taylor Huber and Nancy C. Lutkehaus (eds), *Gendered Missions: Women and Men in Missionary Discourse and Practice* (Ann Arbor: University of Michigan Press, 1999), p. 7.
43. Bebbington, *Evangelicalism in Modern Britain*, pp. 16–17, 27–28, 60.
44. Jean and John Comaroff, *Of Revelation and Revolution: Christianity, Colonialism and Consciousness in South Africa* (London: University of Chicago Press, 1991), p. 310.
45. Comaroff, *Revelation and Revolution*. For more contemporary cultural usage of the conversion narrative, see Geoffrey White, *Identity through History: Living Stories in a Solomon Islands Society* (Cambridge: Cambridge University Press, 1991).
46. Jeffrey Cox, *Imperial Faultlines: Christianity and Colonial Power in India, 1818–1940* (California: Stanford University Press, 2002). See also Elizabeth Brusco and Laura F. Klein, *The Message in the Missionary: Local Interpretations of Religious Ideology and Missionary Personality* (Williamsburg: Studies in Third World Societies, no. 50, January 1994).
47. Elizabeth Elbourne and Robert Ross, 'Combating spiritual and social bondage: early missions in the Cape Colony', in Richard Elphick and Rodney Davenport (eds), *Christianity in South Africa* (Berkeley: University of California at Los Angeles Press, 1997), pp. 31–50. For the role of missionaries in protecting people against the ravages of colonialism, see Elbourne, *Blood Ground*, p. 15. For the prominent place of men and women who had been educated at mission schools in the struggle for decolonisation, see Kenelm Burridge, *In the Way: A Study of Christian Missionary Endeavours* (Vancouver: UBC, 1991), pp. 5, 22–23.
48. Elbourne, *Blood Ground*, p. 438.
49. Nicholas Thomas, 'Colonial conversions: difference, hierarchy and history in early twentieth-century evangelical propaganda', in Catherine Hall (ed.), *Cultures of Empire. Colonizers in Britain and the Empire in the Nineteenth and Twentieth Centuries* (Manchester: Manchester University Press, 2000), pp. 298–328, here p. 322. See also Thomas, *Colonialism's Culture. Anthropology, Travel and Government* (Cambridge: Polity Press, 1994).
50. Ann Laura Stoler, 'Cultivating bourgeois bodies and racial selves', in Hall (ed.), *Cultures of Empire*, pp. 87–119, here pp. 89, 95; also Stoler, 'Rethinking colonial categories: European communities and the boundaries of rule', *Comparative Studies in Society and History* 31 (1989), pp. 134–161.
51. Ivan Hannaford, *Race: The History of an Idea in the West* (Baltimore: Johns Hopkins University Press, 1996), especially chapter seven; George W. Stocking, *Victorian Anthropology* (New York: Free Press, 1987).

52. Hannaford, *Race: The History of an Idea* chapters 1 and 7; Nancy Stepan, *The Idea of 'Race' in Science: Great Britain 1800–1960* (London: Macmillan, 1982); Kenan Malik, *The Meaning of Race: Race, History and Culture in Western Society* (Basingstoke: Macmillan, 1996), chapters 2 and 8, especially p. 81. See also, for changing meanings of the term 'class', Raymond Williams, *Keywords* (London: Croom Helm, 1976), pp. 51–58; Stoler, *Race and the Education of Desire: Foucault's* History of Sexuality *and the Colonial order of Things* (Durham and London: Duke University Press, 1995), pp. 123–130.
53. Jones, *Hannah More*, pp. 161, 165; Jane and Ann Taylor, *Original Poems, for Infant Minds. By several young persons* (London: Darton and Harvey, 1805).
54. William Carey, *An Enquiry into the Obligation of Christians to use Means for the Conversion of the Heathens* (Leicester: Ann Ireland, 1792), pp. 63–64.
55. Thorne, *Congregational Missions*, p. 248.
56. While ostensibly concerned with 'primitive' cultures, such interpretations were also necessarily about 'home'. In the Scottish context, the endeavour to reconcile sophisticated commercial development with political subservience to England fuelled enquiry into the relationships between property and social development, self-interest and civilisation, and the competing claims of wealth and virtue. See Ronald L. Meek, *Social Science and the Ignoble Savage* (Cambridge: Cambridge University Press, 1976), pp. 125–130; Nicholas Phillipson, 'The Scottish Enlightenment', in Mikulas Teich and Roy Porter (eds), *The Enlightenment in National Context* (Cambridge: Cambridge University Press, 1981), pp. 19–40. For the origins in France of 'civilisation' as both a value judgement, that is, a sense of the superiority of some social groups over others on account of their *possessing culture,* and increasingly, a process, whereby societies *became* civilised, see Peter Burke (ed.), *A New Kind of History from the writings of Lucien Febvre* (Routledge and Kegan Paul, 1973), pp. 219–257; also Norbert Elias, *The Civilizing Process. The History of Manners* (Oxford: Basil Blackwell, [1939] 1978).
57. See: Jane Rendall, *The Origins of the Scottish Enlightenment 1707–1776* (Basingstoke: Macmillan, 1978), p. 145; Sylvana Tomaselli, 'The Enlightenment debate on women', *History Workshop Journal*, vol. 19 (1985), pp. 101–124.
58. For a discussion of Enlightenment interest in the Scottish Highlands, see Charles J. Withers, 'Geography, natural history and the eighteenth-century Enlightenment: putting the world in place', *History Workshop Journal*, vol. 39 (Spring 1995), pp. 137–163.
59. Marshall and Williams, *Great Map of Mankind*; Curtin, *The Image of Africa*. For the hierarchies of conversion and different perceptions of

'heathens' in Africa, India and Jamaica, see Hall, *Civilising Subjects*, pp. 303, 186–188, 301–309.

60. Brett Christophers, *Positioning the Missionary. John Booth Good and the Confluence of Cultures in British Columbia* (Vancouver: UBC Press, 1998), p. 30.
61. Brian Stanley argues that this is the most powerful point of convergence between the Enlightenment and the evangelical missionary movement. Brian Stanley, 'Christian missions and the Enlightenment: a re-evaluation', in Stanley (ed.), *Christian Missions and the Enlightenment* (Cambridge: William B. Eerdmans, 2001). See also Bebbington, *Evangelicalism in Modern Britain*.
62. For the debate about civilisation in Scotland, where the Scottish Missionary Society and Glasgow Missionary Society were both formed in 1796, see I. Douglas Maxwell, 'Civilization or Christianity? the Scottish debate on mission methods, 1750–1835', in Stanley (ed.), *Christian Missions and the Enlightenment*, pp. 123–140.
63. See: Stepan, *The Idea of Race in Science*; Stocking, *Victorian Anthropology*; Hall, *Civilising Subjects*.
64. Andrew Bank, 'Losing faith in the civilising mission: the premature decline of humanitarian liberalism at the Cape, 1840–60', in M. Daunton and R. Halpern (eds), *Empire and Others: British Encounters with Indigenous Peoples, 1600–1850* (London: UCL Press, 1999), pp. 364–383; Richard Price, 'Encounters of empire: the British, the Xhosa and the making of an imperial culture at the frontier and at home 1830–1870', pp. 22–23; and 'Bad education: how British humanitarians learnt racism in the empire, 1840–1860', unpublished papers, 2005; to be published in R. Price, *Empire and its Encounters: The British and the Xhosa Peoples in Nineteenth-century Africa* (Cambridge University Press, forthcoming, 2009).
65. Sue Zemka, *Victorian Testaments: The Bible, Christianity, and Literary Authority in early Nineteenth Century British Culture* (California: Stanford University Press 1997), p. 194; Anna Johnston, *Missionary Writing and Empire* (Cambridge: Cambridge University Press, 2003).
66. Andrew F. Walls, *The Missionary Movement in Christian History: Studies in the Transmission of Faith* (Edinburgh and Maryknoll: Orbis, 1996), p. xviii.
67. Burridge, *In the Way*, p. 72. See also Johannes van den Berg, *Constrained by Jesus' Love: An Inquiry into the Motives of the Missionary Awakening in Great Britain in the Period between 1698 and 1815* (Kampen: Kok, 1956).
68. See Chapter 1.
69. See Andrew Porter's criticism of Catherine Hall's reluctance to engage with theology. Porter, *Religion versus Empire?* p. 10. While

Porter reports the broad theological shifts which gave rise to popular support for Christian missions, greater discussion of Biblical justification would have been useful. Note also Sujit Sivasundaram's reluctance to explore Biblical origins of imagery of sowing, reaping and husbandry in his otherwise splendid study of 'missionaries of evangelical science'. Sivasundaram, *Nature and the Godly Empire: Science and Evangelical Mission in the Pacific, 1795–1850* (Cambridge: Cambridge University Press, 2005).

70. Jacqueline de Vries, 'Rediscovering Christianity after the post-modern turn', *Feminist Studies*, vol. 30, no. 4 (Winter 2004), pp. 135–155. For a stimulating discussion of the difficulty of engaging in discussions about belief in an age of post-modern scepticism, see Gauri Viswanathan, *Outside the Fold: Conversion, Modernity and Belief* (Princeton: Princeton University Press, 1998).
71. Niel Gunson, *Messengers of Grace: Evangelical Missionaries in the South Seas, 1797–1860* (Melbourne: Oxford University Press, 1978), chapter one; F. Stuart Piggin, *Making Evangelical Missionaries 1789–1858. The Social Background, Motives and Training of British Protestant Missionaries in India* (Oxford: Sutton Courtenay press, 1984), chapters one and five.
72. See Chapters 3 and 4.
73. Cox, *Imperial Faultlines*, p. 52; see also Zemka, *Victorian Testaments*, final chapter.
74. Stanley, 'Christian missions and the Enlightenment', p. 8.
75. Stanley , 'Christian missions and the Enlightenment', p. 9; Walls, 'Romans one and the missionary movement', *The Missionary Movement in Christian History*, pp. 55–67.
76. 'It was their supreme paradigmatic history, through which they recognised new situations and even their own actions. These missionaries, at the actual level of religious encounter, had virtually no missiology, no theory as to how mission should be done other than that provided by the Bible itself.' J. D. Y. Peel, 'For who hath despised the day of small things? Missionary narratives and historical anthropology', *Comparative Studies in Society and History*, vol. 37 (1995), pp. 581–607, here p. 595. See also T. O. Beidelman, *Colonial Evangelism: A Socio-historical study of an East African Mission at the Grassroots* (Bloomington: Indiana University Press, 1982).
77. Bosch argues that the Christian faith is intrinsically missionary, in that it holds to 'some great "unveiling" of ultimate truth believed to be of universal import'. The first expression of mission was the sending of Jesus Christ to man, the second, Jesus' ministry (to all). David J. Bosch, *Transforming Mission: Paradigm Shifts in Theology of*

Mission (Maryknoll, New York: Orbis Books, 1991), pp. 9, 56–122; Walls, *The Missionary Movement*, p. xviii.
78. See for example William Carey, *An Enquiry*, pp. 20–28.
79. Bosch, *Transforming Mission*, pp. 123–178, here pp. 172, 178; Walls, *The Missionary Movement*, pp. 57, 239–243. For a stimulating discussion of the influence of Paul on missionary practice, see Christophers, *Positioning the Missionary*, especially chapter two.
80. For this relationship, see Susan Thorne, 'Religion and empire at home', in Hall and Rose (eds), *At Home with the Empire*, pp. 143–165.
81. Elbourne, *Blood Ground*, pp. 26, 44, 56–59.
82. For the difficulties of the term 'post-colonial', see McLintock, *Imperial Leather*, pp. 1–17; Hall, *Cultures of Empire*, pp. 16–20.
83. R. S. Sugirtharajah, *Asian Biblical Hermeneutics and Postcolonialism. Contesting the Interpretations* (Maryknoll: Orbis, 1998); 'A Postcolonial exploration of collusion and construction in Biblical interpretation', Sugirtharajah (ed.), *The Postcolonial Bible* (Sheffield: Sheffield Academic Press, 1998), pp. 91–116; Fernando F. Segovia, 'Biblical criticism and postcolonial studies: towards a postcolonial optic', in Sugirtharajah (ed.), *The Postcolonial Bible*, pp. 49–90.
84. Anna Johnston, 'The book eaters: textuality, modernity, and the London Missionary Society', *Semeia* 88 (2001), pp. 13–40. See also Sugirtharajah's discussion of the dispute between Raja Ram Mohan Roy and missionary Joshua Marshman, 'A postcolonial exploration', p. 46.
85. Hall, *Civilising Subjects*; Morris, *Class, Sect and Party*; T. Koditschek, *Class Formation and Urban-Industrial Society: Bradford 1750–1850* (Cambridge: Cambridge University Press, 1990); Kate Hill, *Culture and Class in English Public Museums, 1850–1914* (Aldershot: Ashgate, 2005), pp. 27–28.
86. For example, see Elbourne, *Blood Ground*, on southern Africa; Thorne, *Congregational Missions*, on the LMS; and Hall, *Civilising Subjects*.
87. As Nicholas Thomas has argued, 'localised theories and historically specific accounts' give insight into the variety of colonising and counter-colonising tendencies. *Colonialism's Culture*, p. ix.
88. In this I follow Catherine Hall, *Civilising Subjects*, pp. 11–12.

1 'One blood': the 'Heathen' at home and overseas in late-eighteenth and early-nineteenth-century missions

1. See the Introduction to this volume for a fuller discussion of the historiography.
2. Meek, *Social Science and the Ignoble Savage*.

3. For Wesley in America, see H. D. Rack, *Reasonable Enthusiast: John Wesley and the Rise of Methodism* (London: Epworth Press, 1989), pp. 107–136. For American revivalism, see Susan O'Brien, 'A transatlantic community of saints: the Great Awakening and the first evangelical network, 1735–1755', *American Historical Review*, vol. 91 (1986), pp. 811–832; W. R. Ward, *The Protestant Evangelical Awakening* (Cambridge: Cambridge University Press, 1992); John Walsh, '"Methodism" and the origins of English-speaking Evangelicalism', in Mark A. Noll, David W. Bebbington and George A. Rawlyk (eds), *Evangelicalism: Comparative Studies of Popular Protestantism in North America, the British Isles, and Beyond 1700–1990* (Oxford: Oxford University Press, 1994), pp. 19–37. For George Whitefield in Georgia and New England, see Michael Crawford, *Seasons of Grace: Colonial New England's Revival Tradition in its British Context* (New York: Oxford University Press, 1991), pp. 151–156.
4. For the Methodist Revivals, see Rupert Davies, A. R. George and Gordon Rupp, *A History of the Methodist Church in Great Britain*, vol. 1 (London: Epworth Press, 1965), especially pp. 37–79, 115–144, 190–203; John Walsh, 'Religious societies: Methodist and Evangelical, 1738–1800', in W. J. Sheils and Diana Wood (eds), *Voluntary Religion* (Ecclesiastical History Society: Basil Blackwell, 1986), pp. 279–302; Michael Watts, *The Dissenters*, vol. 2 (Oxford: Clarendon Press, 1995), pp. 394–490; Bebbington, *Evangelicalism in Modern Britain*, pp. 20–74.
5. David Hempton, *The Religion of the People. Methodism and Popular Religion, c. 1750–1900* (London: Routledge, 1996).
6. Anthony Armstrong, *The Church of England, the Methodists and Society 1700–1850* (London: University of London Press, 1973), p. 93.
7. Mass expulsions frequently followed Wesley's visits, though such discipline was usually left in the hands of his appointed assistants. See Watts, *The Dissenters*, p. 404.
8. Some of the most salient texts include: E. P. Thompson, *The Making of the English Working Class* (Harmondsworth: Penguin, 1963), pp. 411–440; J. Obelkevich, *Religion and Rural Society: South Lindsey, 1825–1875* (Oxford: Clarendon Press, 1976); Deborah Valenze, *Prophetic Sons and Daughters. Female Preaching and Popular Religion n Industrial England* (Princeton: Princeton University Press, 1985); Robert Colls, *The Pitmen of the Northern Coalfield: Work, Culture and Protest, 1790–1850* (Manchester: Manchester University Press, 1987); W. R. Ward, *Faith and Faction* (London: Epworth Press, 1993).
9. Watts, *The Dissenters*, p. 410.
10. Armstrong, *The Church of England*, p. 89.

11. Armstrong, *The Church of England*, p. 92.
12. Wesley's oft-quoted statement that 'I look upon all the world as my parish' (Journal, 11 June 1739) referred less to a global mission than to a challenge to the boundaries of the Anglican parish. See Rack, *Reasonable Enthusiast*, p. 189. I am grateful to Edward Royle for this clarification.
13. While Coke gained Wesley's approval for his informal excursions to the West Indies, Wesley blocked his plans to travel to Asia in the 1780s. Coke finally embarked for Sri Lanka in 1813, but died on the way. See J. W. Etheridge, *The Life of Thomas Coke* (London 1860); G. Findlay and W. W. Holdsworth, *The History of the Wesleyan Methodist Missionary Society*, vols 1 and 2 (London: Epworth Press, 1921–22); N. Allen Birtwhistle, 'Methodist missions', in Rupert Davies, A. Raymond George and Gordon Rupp (eds), *A History of the Methodist Church in Great Britain*, vol. 3 (London: Epworth Press, 1983).
14. Thomas Coke, *Address to the Pious and Benevolent* (London, 1786).
15. Thomas Coke, *Account of the Rise, Progress, and Present State of the Methodist Missions* (London: Conference Office, 1804), pp. 6–7, 31, 35.
16. S. Piggin, 'Halevy revisited: the origins of the WMMS: an examination of Semmel's thesis', *Journal of Imperial and Commonwealth History*, vol. 9, no. 1 (1980), pp. 17–37; R. H. Martin, 'Missionary competition between evangelical dissenters and Wesleyan Methodists in the early nineteenth century', *Proceedings of the Wesley Historical Society*, vol. 42 (1979), pp. 81–86.
17. Michael Watts describes the eighteenth-century Baptists as representing 'a desire not to convert the world, but to separate from it', a reformulation of Isaac Watts' statement that 'We are a garden wall'd around/Chosen and made peculiar ground'. See Watts, *The Dissenters*, p. 439. Similarly, Tudur Jones describes Congregationals moving from the 'dignified shyness' of the eighteenth century to the 'militant assertiveness' of the nineteenth. R. Tudur Jones, *Congregationalism in England* (London: Independent Press, 1962), pp. 109, 162, 172. For the relationship between Methodism and Dissent, see Bebbington, *Evangelicalism in Modern Britain*; Watts, *The Dissenters*, pp. 443–444.
18. Andrew Fuller, *The Gospel of Christ Worthy of all Acceptation* (Northampton: T. Dicey, 1785).
19. A. C. Underwood, *A History of the English Baptists* (London: Baptist Union of Great Britain and Ireland, 1970 [1947]).
20. D. W. Lovegrove, *Established Church, Sectarian People: Itinerancy and the Transformation of English Dissent, 1780–1830* (Cambridge: Cambridge University Press, 1988). Carey, *An Enquiry into the*

Obligation of Christians to use Means for the Conversion of the Heathens in which the Religious State of the Different Nations of the World, the Success of former Undertakings, and the Practicability of Further Undertaking, are Considered (Leicester: Ann Ireland, 1792).

21. See George Smith, *The Life of William Carey, Shoemaker and Missionary* (London: J. M. Dent, 1878); Brian Stanley, *The History of the Baptist Missionary Society, 1792–1992* (Edinburgh: T. T. Clark, 1992).
22. Tudur Jones, *Congregationalism in England*; James Miall, *Congregationalism in Yorkshire* (London: John Snow and Co, 1868).
23. *Evangelical Magazine*, March 1796, p. 120; June 1797, pp. 253–233; June 1797, p. 255; November 1797, pp. 473–474; May 1800, pp. 215–217. Tudur Jones, *Congregationalism in England*, p. 175.
24. John Morison, *The Fathers and Founders of the London Missionary Society*, vols I and II (London: Fisher, Son and Co., 1844).
25. *Evangelical Magazine*, February 1799, pp. 33–34.
26. Watts, *The Dissenters*, pp. 450–461.
27. Bebbington, *Evangelicalism in Modern Britain*, pp. 63–65; Lovegrove, *Established Church, Sectarian People*, pp. 17–22.
28. Carey, *Enquiry*, preface. For an interesting discussion of what he calls the 'reactivation' of Matthew and the misrepresentation of the pattern of Paul's missionary tours, see Sugirtharajah, 'A postcolonial exploration'.
29. Carey, *Enquiry*, preface, pp. 7, 9, 25. For the importance to missionaries of St Paul, see Introduction.
30. Rowland Hill, *Glorious Displays of Gospel Grace*; and Thomas Haweis, *Sermons Before the Missionary Society. Sermon 1. The Apostolic Commission, preached at Spa Fields Chapel, September 22 1795* (London: T. Chapman, 1795). For the formation of the LMS, see Richard Lovett, *A History of London Missionary Society 1795–1895*, vol. 1 (London: Henry Froude, 1899); Morrison, *Fathers and Founders*; Norman Goodall, *A History of the London Missionary Society, 1795–1895* (London: Oxford University Press, 1954); Watts, *The Dissenters*, pp. 450–461.
31. Thomas Raffles, *Missions to the Heathen Vindicated from the Charge of Enthusiasm* (Liverpool: Sunday School Press, 1814), p. 32.
32. *Evangelical Magazine*, February 1799, pp. 33–34.
33. Carey, *An Enquiry*, pp. 13–14.
34. Porter, *Religion Versus Empire?*, pp. 63–64, 70.
35. Porter, *Religion Versus Empire?*, pp. 40–41.
36. Martin, *Evangelicals United*, pp. 39–60.
37. Porter, *Religion versus Empire?*, pp. 40–41.
38. Martin, *Evangelicals United*, pp. 43–44.

39. Martin, *Evangelicals United*, p. 44.
40. The national make-up of Wesleyan congregations between 1800 and 1837 included 62.7 per cent artisans and only 2.2 per cent manufacturers and merchants. See Gilbert, *Religion and Society in Industrial England*, pp. 3–22, 63.
41. Specifically, this refers to the failure to conform to the legal and constitutional strictures of the Established Church. David Hempton argues that Methodism posed the same threat to the Church of England as did the Corresponding Societies to the British State. Hempton, *The Religion of the People*, p. 8). See also W. R. Ward, 'The religion of the people and the problem of control, 1790–1830', *Studies in Church History*, vol. 8 (1972), 237–257; A. D. Gilbert, 'Methodism, Dissent and political stability in early industrial England', *Journal of Religious History*, vol. 10, no. 4 (1979), 381–399. For fears of irregularity generally, see W. R. Ward, *Religion and Society in England, 1790–1850* (London: B. T. Batsford, 1972); Jon Mee, *Dangerous Enthusiasm: William Blake and the Culture of Radicalism in the 1790s* (Oxford: Clarendon Press, 1992).
42. Ward, *Religion and Society*, pp. 12–16 and 40–43.
43. Martin, *Evangelicals United*, chapters 3 and 4. For the financial concerns of the WMMS meeting, see David Hempton, *Methodism and Politics in British Society, 1750–1850* (London: Harper Collins, 1987), p. 97.
44. See, for example, the 1803 Blagdon controversy, discussed in Stott, *Hannah More*, pp. 232–257.
45. See for example Thomas Barnard's criticism of the over-emphasis on overseas missions at the expense of the 'pagan' London poor, in *Fifteenth Report of the Society for Bettering the Condition and Increasing the Comforts of the Poor*, vol. III (1801), 131–132.
46. This is the case for the BMS and LMS; the WMMS recruited from a slightly less educated group, and the CMS from higher occupational groups. Changes are noticeable from the mid-century, whereby the numbers of recruits from manual occupations declined and a corresponding increase occurred in the numbers of clerks, schoolmasters, doctors, and, in the CMS, graduates. Gunson, *Messengers of Grace*; Sarah Potter, 'The making of missionaries in the nineteenth century: conversion and convention', *A Sociological Yearbook of Religion* (London: SCM Press, 1975), pp. 103–124.
47. Birtwhistle, 'Methodist missions', p. 1.
48. Gunson states that of the 108 LMS missionaries sent to the Pacific between 1795 and 1860, over 70 were ordained men, with 64 planning to be ordained. Gunson, *Messengers of Grace*, pp. 35–36. Only the CMS, more concerned with ecclesiastical authority

and anxious to assert its superior credentials, followed their disappointment with the uptake of missionary work by ordained men from within the British Isles by looking overseas to solicit the support of German Lutherans. See J. Pinnington, 'Church principles in the early years of the Church missionary society: the problem of the "German Missionaries"', *Journal of Theological Studies*, New Series, 20 (2) (1969), pp. 523–532; T. Thomas, 'Foreign missions and missionaries in Victorian Britain', in John Wolffe (ed.), *Religion in Victorian Britain, IV Culture and Empire* (Manchester: Manchester University Press, 1997), p. 105; Walls, *The Missionary Movement*, pp. 164–165.

49. Lady Knutsford, *Life and Letters of Zachary Macaulay* (London 1900), pp. 116–125, here 122.
50. L. Colley, *Britons: Forging the Nation, 1707–1837* (London: Yale University Press, 1992); Roberts, *Making Morals*, pp. 65–88.
51. Ford K. Brown, *Fathers of the Victorians: The Age of Wilberforce* (Cambridge: Cambridge University Press, 1961); Ernest M. Howse, *Saints in Politics: The 'Clapham Sect' and the Growth of Freedom* (London: George Allen and Unwin, 1953).
52. Michael J. Turner, 'The limits of abolition: government, Saints and the "African Question", c. 1780–1820', *English Historical Review* (April 1997), pp. 319–357.
53. Howse, *Saints in Politics*, pp. 23–24.
54. Maurice Quinlan, *Victorian Prelude: A History of English Manners 1700–1830* (New York: Colombia University Press, 1941); Howse, *Saints in Politics*; Joanna Innes, 'Politics and morals: the reformation of manners movement in later eighteenth century England', in E. Hellmuth (ed.), *The Transformation of Political Culture: England and Germany in the late Eighteenth Century* (Oxford: Oxford University Press, 1990), pp. 57–118.
55. More was already a practicing Christian whose observance had become increasingly strict and 'Methodistical' since the late 1770s. Stott, *Hannah More*, pp. 80, 85; Anne Mellor, *Mothers of the Nation: Women's Political Writing in England 1780–1830* (Bloomington: Indiana University Press, 2000), pp. 13–38, 46–51.
56. Hannah More, *Slavery, A Poem* (London: J. Cadell 1788).
57. Hannah More, *Thoughts on the Importance of the Manners of the Great to General Society*, 7th edition (London: T. Cadell, 1789), pp. 1, 116. Both this and *An Estimate of the Religion of the Fashionable World* (London: T. Cadell, 1790) were popular: according to Howse, the former went through seven editions in a few months, while the second had five editions in two years. See Howse, *Saints in Politics*, p. 100; Roberts, *Memoirs of the Life of Mrs Hannah More*, p. 169. See also Wilberforce, *A Practical View of the Prevailing Religious System of Professed Christians in the Higher and Middle Classes of this*

Country Contrasted with Real Christianity (London: T. Cadell, Jun. and W. Davies, 1797), in which he urged the middle and upper classes to understand and act upon their duty to lead by example.

58. Roberts (ed.), *Mendip Annals*, pp. 12–13.
59. 'They learn of weekdays such coarse material as may fit them for servants', More wrote to John Bowdler, in order to assuage his fears concerning their potentially subversive nature. 'I allow of no writing... Principles, not opinions, are what I labour to give them'. Quoted in Robert Hole, *Pulpits, Politics and Public Order in England 1760–1832* (Cambridge: Cambridge University Press, 1989), p. 138.
60. Roberts, *Mendip Annals*; Jones, *Hannah More*, p. 107; Yeo, *The Contest for Social Science*, pp. 10–15. See Dorice Williams Elliott's useful discussion of More and the gift relationship in Williams, *The Angel out of the House. Philanthropy and Gender in Nineteenth-Century England* (London: University of Virginia, 2002), pp. 54–80.
61. Roberts, *Mendip Annals*, p. 133.
62. Stott, *Hannah More*, p. 117. For tensions of class and gender in More's evangelicalism, see Beth Kowaleski-Wallace, *Their Fathers' Daughters: Hannah More, Maria Edgeworth, and Patriarchal Complicity,* (Oxford: Oxford University Press, 1991), chapter 3.
63. See Introduction, pp. 1–2.
64. Roberts, *Mendip Annals*, p. 28. See Kathryn Sutherland, 'Hannah More's counter-revolutionary feminism', in Kelvin Everest (ed.), *Revolution in Writing: British Literary Responses to the French Revolution* (Buckingham: Open University Press, 1991), p. 40.
65. Roberts, *Mendip Annals*, p. 34.
66. Roberts, *Memoirs*, p. 183.
67. Roberts, *Memoirs*, p. 183; Roberts (ed.), *Mendip Annals*, p. 78.
68. Roberts, *Memoirs*, p. 290.
69. Roberts, *Mendip Annals*, p. 39.
70. Hannah More, *Village Politics* (1793), in Marilyn Butler (ed.), *Burke, Paine, Godwin and the Revolution Controversy* (Cambridge: Cambridge University Press, 1984), pp. 179–184.
71. For the spread of Painite doctrines and the loyalist backlash, see Robert Hole, 'British counter-revolutionary propaganda in the 1790s', in Colin Jones (ed.), *Britain and Revolutionary France: Conflict, Subversion and Propaganda* (University of Exeter: Exeter Studies in History, 1983), pp. 53–69; H. T. Dickinson, 'Popular Conservatism and Militant Loyalism, 1789–1815', in H. T. Dickinson (ed.), *Britain and the French Revolution 1789–1815* (Basingstoke: Macmillan, 1989), pp. 103–126; Robert Hole, *Pulpits, Politics and Public Order*; also Hole, 'English sermons and tracts as media of debate', in Mark Philp, (ed.), *The French Revolution and British Popular Politics* (Cambridge: Cambridge University Press, 1991), pp. 18–37.

72. Gertrude Himmelfarb, *The Idea of Poverty: England in the Early Industrial Age* (London: Faber and Faber, 1984), pp. 42–63; Gregory Claeys, *Machinery, Money and the Millenium* (Oxford: Polity, 1987); I. Hont and M. Ignatieff, 'Needs and Justice in the *Wealth of Nations*: an introductory essay' in Hont and Ignatieff (eds), *Wealth and Virtue: the Shaping of Political Economy in the Scottish Enlightenment* (Cambridge: Cambridge University Press, 1983), pp. 1–44; Mitchell Dean, *The Constitution of Poverty: Toward a Genealogy of Liberal Governance* (London: Routledge, 1991); Deborah Valenze, 'Charity, Custom and Humanity: Changing Attitudes towards the Poor in Eightenth-Century England', in Jane Garnett and Colin Matthew (eds), *Revival and Religion since 1700: Essays for John Walsh* (London: Hambledon Press, 1993), pp. 59–78.
73. The Cheap Repository produced three tracts a month from 1795, selling 3000 copies between 3 March and 18 April 1795, rising to 700,000 by July 1795, and over two million by March 1796. See Richard Altick, *The English Common Reader: A Social History of the Mass Reading Public 1800–1900* (Chicago: University of Chicago Press, 1957), p. 75.
74. 'The Story of Simple Sally...', *The Works of Hannah More...in Eleven Volumes* (London: T. Cadell, 1830), vol. 5; 'Black Giles the Poacher', vol. 4, pp. 115–147; 'Tawny Rachel; or, the Fortune-teller: with some Account of Dreams, Omens, and Conjurors', vol. 4, pp. 148–163.
75. Betty Brown the St. Giles's Orange Girl: with some account of Mrs Sponge, the money lender', *Works*, vol. 4, pp. 115–147, 148–163, 99–114.
76. For the Cheap Repository Tracts, see Sutherland, 'Hannah More's counter-revolutionary feminism'; Susan Pedersen, 'Hannah More Meets Simple Simon: Tracts, Chapbooks, and Popular Culture in Late Eighteenth-Century England', *Journal of British Studies*, 25 (1986), pp. 84–113; Olivia Smith, *The Politics of Language, 1791–1819* (Oxford: Clarendon Press, 1985), pp. 68–109, esp. 91–96; Mitzi Myers, 'Hannah More's Tracts for the Times. Social Fiction and Female Ideology', in Mary Anne Schofield and Cecelia Macheski (eds), *Fetter'd or Free? British Women Novelists, 1670–1815* (London: Ohio University Press, 1986), pp. 264–284.
77. See Jones, *Hannah More*, p. 139; Hannah More to Zachary Macaulay, 1796, quoted in Howse, *Saints in Politics*, p. 103. For chapbooks and popular literacy, see Pedersen, 'Hannah More Meets Simple Simon'; Victor Neuburg, *The Penny Histories: A Study of Chapbooks for Young Readers over Two Centuries* (London: Oxford University Press, 1968) and *Popular Literature* (London: Woburn Press, 1977).

78. Mellor cites a variety of commentators suggesting that a rendition of 'The Riot, or, Half a Loaf is Better than No Bread', stopped riots at opposite ends of England. See *Mothers of the Nation*, p. 15. See also R. K. Webb, *The British Working Class Reader, 1790–1848* (London: Allen and Unwin, 1955), p. 43; Ivana Kovacevic, *Fact Into Fiction* (Leicester: Leicester University Press, 1975), pp. 149–52. A London pickpocket interviewed by Mayhew told him that tracts were used for lighting pipes: 'Tracts won't fill your belly. Tracts is no good, except to a person that has a home; at the lodging houses they're laughed at.' See P. Hollis, *The Pauper Press: A Study of Working-Class Radicalism in the 1830s* (Oxford: Oxford University Press, 1970), p. 42.
79. Pedersen, 'Hannah More meets Simple Simon', p. 110. An 1834 edition of *The Works of Hannah More* was subtitled: 'containing stories for persons in the middle ranks' (London: H. Fisher, R. Fisher and P. Jackson, 1834). For the popularity of The Lancashire Collier Girl, see Kovacevic, *Fact into Fiction*, p. 152.
80. 'Mr Fantom; or, The History of the New-Fashioned Philosopher, and his Man William', *Works*, vol. 3, pp. 1–43, here pp. 41, 7. As Hole has argued, More was here contributing to an established theological debate, supporting the critique by evangelicals and non-evangelicals within the Church of the idea of human perfectibility as promoted by members of rational dissent. For members of the established Church, man was a necessarily fallen creature, unable through his necessary imperfection to provide a perfect system of government – a fact borne out by the French experience: Hole, 'English sermons and tracts as media of debate', p. 36; and *Pulpits, Politics and Public Order*, pp. 97–173, especially pp. 142–143 and 158–159.
81. More, *Works*, vol. 1 (London: H. Fisher, R. Fisher and P. Jackson, 1834), pp. 37–40.
82. Sutherland, 'Hannah More's counter-revolutionary feminism'.
83. For women's complex relationship to Enlightenment thought, see Jane Rendall, *The Origins of Modern Feminism: Women in Britain, France and the United States, 1780–1860* (Basingstoke: Macmillan, 1985), Chapter 1; Jane Rendall, 'Virtue and Commerce: Women in the making of Adam Smith's political economy', in Ellen Kennedy and Susan Mendus (eds.), *Women in Western Civilisation: Kant to Nietzsche* (Brighton: Harvester Wheatsheaf, 1987), pp. 44–77; Jane Rendall, (ed.), Introduction to *William Alexander's History of Women* (Bristol: Thoemmes Press, [1777] 1994); S. Tomaselli, 'The Enlightenment debate on women'; and 'Reflections on the history of the science of woman', *History of Science*, vol. 29 (1991), pp. 185–205; K. Sutherland, 'Adam Smith's Master Narrative: Women and

the *Wealth of Nations*', S. Copley and K. Sutherland (ed), *Adam Smith's Wealth of Nations. New Interdisciplinary Essays* (Manchester: Manchester University Press, 1995), pp. 97–121.

84. The family was referred to by Scottish writers as 'the little society', with the family understood as the first form of social organisation, the safeguard of virtue and responsible for the moral community. See J. Dwyer, *Virtuous Discourse: Sensibility and Community in Late Eighteenth Century Scotland* (Edinburgh: John Donald, 1987), Chapter 4. See also: K. Gleadle '"Opinions deliver'd in Conversation": Conversation, politics and gender in the late eighteenth century', J. Harris (ed.), *Civil Society in History* (Oxford: Oxford University Press, 2003); J. Rendall, 'Women and the public sphere', *Gender & History*, vol. 11, no. 3 (November 1999), pp. 475–488.
85. *The Works of Hannah More*, vol. 3, pp. 273–292; vol. 3, pp. 293–310; vol. 4, pp. 42–73.
86. Elisabeth Schussler Fiorenza, 'Women in the New Testament', *New Catholic World* (Nov–Dec 1976), pp. 256–260. See also: E. Schussler Fiorenza, '"You are not to be called Father": early Christian history in a feminist perspective', *Discipleship of Equals: A Critical Feminist Ekklesialogy of Liberation* (New York: Crossroads, 1993), pp. 151–179; *In Memory of Her: A Feminist Theological Reconstruction of Christian Origins* (London: SCM, 1983).
87. Schussler Fiorenza, 'Women in the New Testament', p. 259.
88. See Fiorenza, 'Women in the New Testament', p. 260; *In Memory of Her*, pp. 168–184. See also Gerd Theissen, *The Social setting of Pauline Christianity. Essays on Corinth*, trns by John H. Schutz (Philadelphia: Fortress Press, 1982), pp. 36, 88, 89–90, 91–94.
89. 1 Corinithians 14, 33–35; Ephesians 5, 21–30.
90. Theissen, *The Social setting of Pauline Christianity*, pp. 15, 37, 107. See also Theissen's discussion of the veiling of women and its implications for men: Gerd Theissen, *Psychological Aspects of Pauline Christianity*, trns John P Galvin (Edinburgh: Fortress Press, 1987), pp. 158–175.
91. Fiorenza, *Discipleship of Equals*, p. 178. See also D. Balch, *"Let Wives be Submissive…" the domestic code in 1 Peter* (Chico, CA: Scholars Press, 1981).
92. Hannah More, *An Essay on the Character and Practical Writings of Saint Paul*, 4th edition, vol. I (London: T. Cadell and W. Davies, 1815), pp. 65–66.
93. More, *Saint Paul*, vol. I, pp. 65–66.
94. Hannah More, 'The white slave trade' (1805), in Fiona Robertson (ed.), *Women's Writing 1778–1838: An Anthology* (Oxford: Oxford University Press, 2001), pp. 157–162, p. 158.

95. The Corpus Christianum refers to the Christian body, or the community of Christians. See van den Berg, *Constrained by Jesus' Love.*
96. More, *Saint Paul*, vol. II, pp. 342–348.
97. More, *Saint Paul*, vol. I, pp. 1–2, 8–9.
98. Hannah More, *Strictures on the Modern System of Female Education*, vol. I (Dublin: D. Wogan, 1799), p. 4.
99. Hannah More, *Hints Towards forming the Character of a Young Princess*, in 2 vols (London: T. Cadell and W. Davies, 1805), pp. 33, 57, 300, 381.
100. Mellor, *Mothers of the Nation*, pp. 13–38.
101. Christine L. Kruegar, *The Reader's Repentance: Women Preachers, Women Writers and Nineteenth-Century Social Discourse* (Chicago: University of Chicago Press, 1992).
102. For the distribution of the tracts outside of England, see Jones, *Hannah More*, pp. 144–145.
103. Yeo, *The Contest for Social Science*, pp. 28–29. For the SBCP see also Donna Andrew, *Philanthropy and Police: London Charity in the Eighteenth Century* (Princeton: Princeton University Press, 1989), pp. 174–177 and 163–196. For the monitorial system, see Brian Simon, *Studies in the History of Education 1780–1870* (London: Lawrence and Wishart, 1960), pp. 17–163. The phrase 'narrow utilitarianism' is Simon's, p. 70. For Bentham, see Dean, *The Constitution of Poverty*, pp. 88–96, 137–155, here p. 93. Malthus also draws upon travel narratives and histories of civilisation to refer to the vagaries of population in cultures 'at the lowest stage of human society'. See Randi Davenport, 'Thomas Malthus and maternal bodies politic: gender, race and empire', *Women's History Review*, vol. 4, no. 4 (1995), pp. 415–439; M. Godelier, 'Malthus and ethnography', in J Dupaquier, A Fauvre-Chamoux, E Grebenik (eds), *Malthus Past and Present* (London: Academic Press, 1983).
104. See Catherine Hall, 'White visions, Black lives: the free villages of Jamaica', *History Workshop Journal*, vol. 36 (Autumn 1993), pp. 100–132; and chapter 4 in this volume.
105. Gunson, *Messengers of Grace*, pp. 181–194; E. Daniel Potts, *British Baptist Missionaries in India, 1793–1837: A History of Serampore and its Missions* (Cambridge: Cambridge University Press, 1967), pp. 139–188. In India at least, early emphasis on the negative aspects of Hinduism and Islam soon gave way to a focus on the more positive and beneficial characteristics of Christianity.
106. For many missionaries, the debate as to whether civilisation should precede or succeed conversion was discussed more in terms of whether or not artisans, with no experience as preachers, should

be included as part of the party. See Gunson, *Messengers of Grace*, pp. 267–279; Bosch, *Transforming Mission*, p. 296.

107. David M. Thompson, *Denominationalism and Dissent, 1795–1835: A Question of Identity* (London: Friends of Dr. Williams Library, 1985). As Bebbington has claimed, 'the line between those who had undergone the [conversion] experience and those who had not was the sharpest in the world. It marked the boundary between a Christian and a pagan'. Bebbington, *Evangelicalism in Modern Britain*, p. 5. Bebbington's phrase, the 'evangelical consensus', is most (and perhaps only) applicable to the missionary aspect of the revival.
108. Roberts, *Making Morals*, p. 121.

2 Charity begun at home: missionary philanthropy and the new middle class in Sheffield

1. See Davidoff and Hall, *Family Fortunes*; John Tosh, *A Man's Place: Masculinity and the Middle-Class Home in Victorian England* (London: Yale University Press 1999).
2. Morris, 'Voluntary societies'; and *Class, Sect and Party*, p. 5. For the especial importance of associational networks for Dissenters, see Davidoff and Hall, *Family Fortunes*.
3. Women's involvement scarcely merits a mention in a number of accounts of middle-class formation. See Morris, *Class, Sect and Party*; Koditschek, *Class Formation*; M. Rose, 'Culture, philanthropy and the Manchester middle classes', in Alan Kidd and K. W. Roberts (eds), *City, Class and Culture: Studies of Cultural Production and Social Policy in Victorian Manchester* (Manchester: Manchester University Press, 1985); Simon Gunn, *The Public Culture of the Victorian Middle Class: Ritual and Authority in the English Industrial City, 1840–1914* (Manchester: Manchester University Press, 2000). Even Davidoff and Hall downplay women's membership of philanthropic societies prior to the anti-slavery heyday of the 1830s and 1840s. *Family Fortunes*, pp. 108–148. See Simon Morgan's critique: '"A sort of land debatable": Female influence, civic virtue and middle-class identity, c. 1830–1860', *Women's History Review*, vol. 13, no. 2 (2004), pp. 183–210; and Morgan, *A Victorian Woman's Place: Public Culture in the Nineteenth Century* (London: I.B. Tauris, 2007).
4. Martin, *Evangelicals United*, p. 115. For the traditional exposition of this view, see Prochaska, *Women and Philanthropy*, pp. 5, 11.
5. For the beginnings of a reassessment of the significance of women's philanthropy, see Summers, *Female Lives, Moral States*; and Sarah Richardson, 'Women, Philanthropy and Politics in early

C19th Britain', (unpublished paper, 2003); Sarah Richardson, *The Political Worlds of Middle-Class Women in Nineteenth Century Britain* (forthcoming, Routledge 2008).

6. Mary Walton, *Sheffield, its Story and its Achievements* (Otley: Amethyst Press, 1948), p. 158; William Odom, *Hallamshire Worthies* (Sheffield: J. W. Northend Press, 1926), pp. 22–23, 77, 87 and 99–101; R. E. Leader, *Reminiscences of Old Sheffield: Its Streets and its People* (Sheffield: Leader and Sons, 1876), pp. 300–310; *Sheffield in the Eighteenth Century* (Sheffield: Leng, 1905), p. 79; John Holland and James Everett, *Memoirs of the Life and Writing of James Montgomery, Vols 1–7* (London: Longman, Brown, Green and Longmans, 1855–66), vol. 3, pp. 44, 47, 68, 93, 108 and 117 and vol. 2 (frontspiece) for a picture of the 'four friends'. See also: Samuel Roberts, 'The Four Friends: a fable for young people', in Roberts, *The Blind Man and his Son* (London: Taylor and Hessey, 1816); *Autobiography and Select Remains of the late Samuel Roberts* (London: Longman, Brown, Green and Longmans, 1849); 'Memoir of the late George Bennet Esq., of Sheffield', *Evangelical Magazine and Missionary Chronicle* (February 1842), pp. 53–62.
7. *SI*, 24 April 1810.
8. *SI*, 30 January 1810, 6 February 1810, 13 February 1810, 20 February 1810, 3 April 1810, 9 April 1811.
9. *SI*, 30 December 1812, 8 December 1812; *The Tenth Report of the Auxiliary Bible Society for Sheffield and the Vicinity* (Sheffield: Todd, 1820); Holland and Everett, *Memoirs*, vol. 2, p. 306; Alexander B. Bell, *Peeps into the Past, being Passages from the Diary of Thomas Asline Ward*, (Sheffield: Leng and Co., 1909), p. 167.
10. Holland and Everett, *Memoirs*, vol. 3, pp. 12, 43 and 93; *SI*, 4 February 1812, 2 March 1813, 15 June 1813, 16 May 1815, 27 May 1815, 19 March 1816, 25 March 1817, 1 April 1817; *Reports of the Sheffield Sunday School Union*, (Sheffield: J. Montgomery, 1813–1817); *First Annual Report of the Committee of the Methodist Sunday School for Poor Children* (Sheffield: J. Montgomery 1816); James Montgomery, *A Retrospect of the Origins, Proceedings and Effects of the Sheffield Sunday School Union* (Sheffield: J. Montgomery, 1824); John Holland, *Memorials of the Founders of the First Methodist Sunday Schools in Sheffield* (Sheffield: Harrison, 1870); H. G. Roberts, *Red Hill Sunday School Centenary* (Sheffield: J. W. Northend, n.d.), pp. 5–29. See also John Salt, 'Early Sheffield Sunday schools and their educational importance', *Transactions of the Hunter Archaeological Society*, vol. 9, no. 3 (1966), pp. 179–184.
11. *SI*, 5 October 1813, 15 February 1814, 21 June 1814, 18 April 1815, 18 May 1815, 7 May 1816, 18 March 1817, 1 April 1817, 3 May

1817, 13 May 1817, 31 March 1818; Holland and Everett, *Memoirs*, vol. 3, pp. 44, 47, 68, 93 and 117.

12. For example, Montgomery, Ward and Bennet shared positions in the Aged Female Society for many years, while Roberts and Montgomery organised and attended the Society for Superseding the Necessity for Climbing Boys annual Easter Monday Dinner for the boys from 1807 into the 1840s. *Reports of the Female Friendly Society*, 1815 (Sheffield: J. Montgomery); 1817 (Sheffield: J. Montgomery and M. Smith); 1819 (Sheffield: J. Montgomery); 1826 (Sheffield: J. Blackwell); and 1827 (Sheffield: J. Blackwell); Holland and Everett, *Memoirs*, vol. 2, pp. 306–307; vol. 3, pp. 150, 221–222, 355–356; vol. 4, p. 256; vol. 5, pp. 33–34. Montgomery and Ward continued to share the writing of the Annual Reports and presided over the annual meeting of the Bible Society and Montgomery and Hodgson continued to undertake their annual autumn Bible Society tours, during which they addressed the members of societies around the country into the 1830s. Holland and Everett, *Memoirs*, vol. 4, pp. 50–62 and vol. 6, pp. 23–24.
13. James Montgomery gave the opening speech of the Literary and Philosophical Society in December 1822. See: *SI*, 7 October 1823, 23 December 1823, 30 December 1823. He was vice-president in 1823, following Ward's vice-presidency of 1822, and both men continued to lecture for the Society. Ward was a central figure in opening the Mechanics' Library. *Sheffield Independent*, 5 January 1828, 3 January 1829 and 26 December 1829. All except Bennet (who was in the South Pacific at the time) were involved in the Anti-Slavery Society (1824).
14. *The Reports of the Society for Bettering the Condition and Increasing the Comforts of the Poor*, 4th edition, vol. 1 (London, 1805), pp. 118–136 (SBCP hereafter); Sir Thomas Bernard, *Pleasure and Pain, 1780–1818* (London, 1930).
15. The Society wanted to 'deal with facts', to gain useful and practical information derived from EXPERIENCE, and stated briefly and plainly.' From an account of the opening meeting in December 1796, SBCP, *Reports*, p. 391; Appendix, p. 3.
16. Wilberforce, Shute Barrington and Barnard belonged to the Proclamation Society. See J. B. Baker, *The Life of Sir Thomas Bernard Baronet* (London, 1819); David Owen, *English Philanthropy, 1660–1960* (London: Oxford University Press, 1965), p. 105; Roberts, *Making English Morals*, pp. 63–65.
17. Reverend Thomas Malthus, *An Essay on the Principle of Population, as it affects the Future Improvement of Society* (London: J. Johnson, 1803).

18. Malthus, Works, III, p. 533, quoted in M. O. Grenby, '"Real Charity Makes Distinctions": schooling the charitable impulse in early British children's literature', *British Journal of Eighteenth-Century Studies*, 27 (2002), pp. 185–202, here pp. 196–197. For Malthusianism as 'moral discipline', see Hilton, *The Age of Atonement: The Influence of Evangelicalism on Social and Economic Thought, 1795–1865* (Oxford: Clarendon Press, 1988); Dean, *The Constitution of Poverty*, pp. 88–96, 137–155. See also Patricia James, *Population Malthus: His Life and Times* (London: RKP, 1979), pp. 109, 222.
19. *SI*, 18 May 1804; *Eleventh Annual Report of the Sheffield Society for Bettering the Condition of the Poor* (Sheffield: J. Montogmery, 1814), p. 2.
20. *SI*, 18 May 1804, 31 May 1804.
21. Colley, *Britons*, pp. 283–319.
22. E. P. Thompson uncovered evidence of secret societies and oath-taking in the town. Thompson, *The Making of the English Working Class*, pp. 163–167, 516–521.
23. Reverend T. Alexander Seed, *Norfolk Street Wesleyan Chapel, Sheffield* (London: Jarrold and Sons, n.d.), p. 63.
24. James Montgomery, 'An ode to the volunteers of Britain on the prospect of invasion' (1804). The first imprisonment was for the circulation of a ballad in commemoration of the Fall of the Bastille. The poem was not his own and had been printed before the war (by Joseph Gales, his radical predecessor at the *Sheffield Register*). His critical reportage of the role of Colonel Althorpe in the dispersal of a riot which had been started when soldiers opened fire on demonstrators, killing two and injuring many others, saw his return to gaol the following year.
25. See Dennis Smith, *Conflict and Compromise: Class Formation in English Society 1830–1914* (London: Routledge, 1982), pp. 31, 52–53; Caroline O. Reid, 'Middle-class values and working-class culture in nineteenth-century Sheffield: the pursuit of respectability', in Sidney Pollard and Colin Holmes (eds), *Essays in the Economic and Social History of South Yorkshire* (Sheffield: South Yorkshire County Council, 1976), pp. 275–295.
26. Sidney Pollard, *A History of Labour in Sheffield*, (Liverpool: Liverpool University Press, 1959), pp. 50–77; G. I. H. Lloyd, *The Cutlery Trades: An Historical essay in the Economics of Small-Scale Production* (London: Longmans, Green and Co., 1913), pp. 171–208.
27. Smith, *Conflict and Compromise*, p. 34.
28. *Sketchley's Sheffield Directory* (Bristol 1777); J. Robinson, *A Directory of Sheffield* (Sheffield: J. Montgomery, 1797); Leader, *Sheffield in the Eighteenth Century*; R. E. Leader, *The Early Sheffield Banks* (London:

Blades, East and Blades, 1917); Walton, *Sheffield, Its Story and its Achievements*, pp. 124–142; Sarah E. Joynes, 'The Sheffield library 1771–1907', *Library History: Journal of the Library History Group of the Library Association*, vol. 2, no. 3 (Spring 1971), pp. 91–116; E. D. Mackerness, *Somewhere Further North: A History of Music in Sheffield* (Sheffield: J. W. Northend, 1974), pp. 10–20; Donald Read, *Press and People, 1790–1850: Opinion in Three English Cities* (London: Edward Arnold, 1961), p. 14.

29. E. R. Wickham, *Church and People in an Industrial City* (London: Lutterworth Press, 1957), p. 57; James Everett, *Historical Sketches of Wesleyan Methodism in Sheffield and the Vicinity* (Sheffield: James Montgomery, 1823).
30. Holland and Everett, *Memoirs*, vol. 3, pp. 44, 47, 68, 93 and 117.
31. Roberts, *Autobiography and Select Remains*, pp. 14–15.
32. As nationally, Sheffield Methodism had a profound effect on local Independent congregations, though these represented a wealthier constituency. Miall, *Congregationalism in Yorkshire,* pp. 164–167; *A Brief History of Queen Street Congregational Chapel* (Sheffield: Pawson and Brailsford, 1933); Wickham, *Church and People,* Appendix V (a); Clyde Binfield, 'Religion in Sheffield', in Clyde Binfield, Richard Childs, Roger Harper, David Hey, David Martin, Geoffrey Tweedale (eds), *The History of Sheffield, 1843–1993*, vol. II: Society (Sheffield: Sheffield Academic Press, 1993), pp. 405–409.
33. The combined Methodist congregations formed the largest group of worshippers in Sheffield in the 1851 Census. The Anglican Church did not significantly increase its congregations until the second half of the century, although Thomas Sutton, Vicar of Sheffield from 1805, ensured the evangelical sympathies of all incoming clergy, including those appointed to the four new churches built under the 1818 Million Act. Wickham, *Church and People*, pp. 41–106.
34. Walton, *Sheffield, its Story and its Achievements*; p. 158; Odom, *Hallamshire Worthies*, pp. 22–23, 77, 87, 99–101; Leader, *Reminiscences of Old Sheffield,* pp. 300–310; Leader, *Sheffield in the Eighteenth Century*, p. 79.
35. *SI*, 9 August 1814.
36. *SI*, 14 February 1809, 28 January 1812, 11 May 1813, 18 May 1813, 21 June 1814, 28 June 1814, 27 September 1814, 9 August 1814, 23 May 1815. While some, including T. A. Ward, were irritated by the Anglicans' presumption in labelling themselves 'national', educationalists in Sheffield tended to emphasise the similarities between the two approaches. *SI*, 18 May 1813; W. H. G. Armytage, 'Education in Sheffield, 1603–1955', *Sheffield and its Region*, (Sheffield: Sheffield Association for the Advancement of Social

Science, 1956); Malcolm Mercer, *Schooling the Poorer Child: Elementary Education in Sheffield 1560–1902* (Sheffield: Sheffield Academic Press, 1996), pp. 70–71.

37. *Ninth Report of the Sheffield Lancasterian School for Boys in Sheffield* (Sheffield: J. Montgomery, 1818).
38. *SI*, 28 May 1816.
39. James Montgomery, *The West Indies, and other Poems*, 4th edition (London: Longman, Hurst, Rees, Orme and Brown, 1814), pp. 1–79. For a comment of the sources, see *The Poetical Works of James Montgomery, Collected by Himself, in Four Volumes*, vol. 1 (London: Longman, Brown, Green and Longman, 1841), pp. 61, 133 and 154–158.
40. James Montgomery, *Greenland and other Poems*, 2nd edition (London: Longman, Rees, Orme and Brown, 1819), pp. 1–146, here p. vi. For missionary writing of the 1820s, see: 'A theme for a poet' (1814), *Poetical Works* (1855–1856), vol. 3, pp. 200–204; 'Abdallah and Sabat' (1821), vol. 3, pp. 164–170; 'A voyage around the world' (1826), vol. 3, pp. 117–126; 'Perils by the Heathen', vol. 3, pp. 359–362; 'To my friend George Bennet of Sheffield', vol. 4, pp. 184–187; 'A Cry from South Africa' (1828), vol. 4, pp. 181–183; Jonathan Edwards, *Life of David Brainerd, Missionary to the American Indians,* Introductory Essay by James Montgomery (Glasgow: William Collins, 1829), pp. iv–xlx; 'A spirit of the living God' (1823), *Hymns for Anti-Slavery Meetings* (London: Jackson and Walford, 1833); 'For a Juvenile Missionary Meeting', 'Garden thoughts for a missionary meeting in a garden', 'On the Jubilee of the LMS', 'All nations shall serve him', 'Jubilee Anniversary of the BMS', James Montgomery, *Original Hymns* (proof copy, Sheffield Archives, SLPS 48), pp. 263, 265, 267, 269, 275, 281. 'Angels from the realms of glory' (1816) and 'Hail to the Lord's anointed' (1822), *The Methodist Hymn Book* (London: Methodist Publishing House, 1933), pp. 119 and 245.
41. *SI*, 2 February 1804, 9 February 1804, 21 March 1805, 20 January 1806, 12 December 1809, 24 April 1810, 1 February 1812, 13 April 1813, 11 May 1813, 4 January 1814, 24 January 1815.
42. See also: Odom, *Hallamshire Worthies;* Henry Hunt Piper, 'A Sermon…on the occasion of the death of Samuel Shore . . . ' (London: R. Hunter, 1829); Jabez Bunting, *Memoirs of the late Thomas Holy Esq. of Sheffield* (London: James Nicholls, 1832); Sarah Biller, *Memoir of the late Hannah Kilham* (London: Darton and Harvey, 1837); Henry Longden, *The Life of Henry Longden,* (London: Wesleyan Conference office 1865 [1813]); William Hudson, *The Life of John Holland of Sheffield Park* (London: Longmans, Green and Co., 1874); Thomas Best, *Memoranda of the late*

Ann Harrison (Sheffield: George Ridge, 1860); *Daniel Doncaster and Sons, Sheffield 1788–1928* (Sheffield: William Townsend, 1928); M. H. F. Chaytor, *The Wilsons of Sharrow. The Snuff-Makers of Sheffield* (Sheffield, 1962).

43. Davidoff and Hall, *Family Fortunes*, p. 416.
44. The Municipal Corporations Act of 1835 was resisted in Sheffield until 1843. Roberts, Hodgson and Ward were all town trustees. Ward was Master Cutler in 1816, a town collector from 1825, founder member and president of Sheffield Political Union and defeated election candidate in 1832, and West Riding magistrate from 1836. See Derek Fraser, *Power and Authority in the Victorian City* (Oxford: Blackwell, 1979), pp. 139–148; Richard J. Childs, 'Sheffield before 1843', Binfield et al. (eds), *The History of Sheffield*, vol. 1, pp. 7–24.
45. See Seed, *Norfolk Street Wesleyan Chapel, Sheffield* (London: Jarrold and Sons, n.d.), pp. 111–117; Holland and Everett, *Memoirs*, vol. 7, p. 215; Odom, *Hallamshire Worthies*, pp. 101, 87, 77.
46. See Bell, *An Analysis of the Experiment in Education, made at Egmore, near Madras*, 3rd edition (London: Cadell and Davies, 1807 [1797]). Bell had previously run a Sunday school in Swanage, Dorset.
47. Joseph Lancaster, *The British System of Education: being a Complete Epitome of the Improvements and Inventions Practised at the Royal Free Schools, Borough Road, Southwark* (London: Longman and Co, 1810); and *Address of the Committee of the Institute for Promoting the British System for the Education of the Labouring and Manufacturing Classes of Society of Every Religious Persuasion...* (London: J. Lancaster, 1813), pp. 3–5.
48. For Lancaster, Bible learning was appropriate for all denominations and could involve various ministers; in his view, 'the substance of Christianity is the same in all'. Joseph Lancaster, *Outline of a Plan for Educating Ten Thousand Poor Children* (London 1806). See Simon, *Studies in the History of Education*, pp 129–136 and 148–152.
49. The SBCP and School of Industry paved the way for acceptance of Bell's and Lancaster's ideas. *SI*, 17 November 1807; 18 August 1818. For Lancaster's visit, see the *SI*, 14 February 1809.
50. *SI*, 27 September 1814 and 3 January 1815. Sir Thomas Bernard, 'Extract from an Account of the Free School for Boys at Sheffield' (1812), Sheffield Local Studies Library, Local Pamphlets, vol. 87, no. 5, pp. 173–184; G. J. Eltringham, 'The Lancasterian schools in Sheffield', *Transactions of the Hunter Archaeological Society*, vol. 5 (1943), pp. 147–152.
51. Lancaster, *The British System of Education*.
52. Richard Johnson, 'Notes on the schooling of the English working class', in Roger Dale, Geoff Esland and Madeleine MacDonald

(eds), *Schooling and Capitalism. A Sociological Reader* (London: RKP and the Open University Press, 1976), pp. 44–54.

53. Simon, *Studies in the History of Education*, pp 129–136 and 148–152; Alan Richardson, *Literature, Education and Romanticism: Reading as Social Practice 1780–1832* (Cambridge: Cambridge University Press, 1994), pp. 91–103.
54. Quoted in Mercer, *Schooling the Poorer Child*, p. 69. Visiting the Borough Road school in 1799, philanthropist William Allen was overwhelmed by the image of children transformed to 'the most perfect order, and training to habits of subordination and usefulness, and learning the great truths of the gospel from the Bible'. Quoted in Harold M. Silver, *The Concept of Popular Education: A Study of Ideas and Social Movements in the Early Nineteenth Century* (London: MacGibbon and Kee, 1965), p. 26.
55. *SI*, 21 June 1814, 28 June 1814; *Reports of the Sunday School Union*; *Seventh Annual Report of the Sheffield and District National Society* (Sheffield: J. Montgomery, 1822).
56. Sheffield Methodist Sunday School, *First Annual Report of the Committee of the Methodist Sunday School for Poor Children of All Denominations in Sheffield and its Vicinity* (Sheffield: J. Montgomery, 1816), p. 1.
57. Sheffield Sunday School Union, *Second Report of the Sheffield Sunday School Union* (Sheffield: J. Montgomery, 1814), pp. 4–5.
58. *SI*, 21 June 1814. Mather was the father of Dr Robert Cotton Mather, an oriental linguist and missionary in India for nearly 40 years. See Leader, *Reminiscences*, pp. 236–237.
59. Quoted in Mercer, *Schooling the Poorer Child*, p. 69.
60. Sheffield Lancasterian School, *Fifth Annual Report of the Sheffield Girls' Lancasterian School* (1820), pp. 3–4.
61. Lancasterian School for Boys, *Ninth Annual Report* (1818), p. 8. See Carl F. Kaestle, '"Between the Scylla of brutal ignorance and the Charybdis of a literary education": elite attitudes towards mass schooling in early industrial England and America', in Lawrence Stone (ed.), *Schooling and Society: Studies in the History of Education* (Baltimore and London: Johns Hopkins University Press, 1976), pp. 177–191.
62. Sheffield Sunday School Union, *First Report of the Sheffield Sunday School Union* (1813), p. 30.
63. James Montgomery, *An Address to Uninstructed Youth* (Sheffield: James Montgomery, 1821).
64. Sheffield, *Eighth Report of the Sheffield Lancasterian School for Boys* (Sheffield: William Todd, 1817), pp. 2 and 13. For 'youthful delinquency', see successive reports.

65. *Reports of the Sunday School Union in Sheffield* (Sheffield: James Montgomery, 1813–1824), here 1813, p. 11 and 1814, p. 22. *The Life of a Sunday Scholar. Memoirs of Henry Crookes of Sheffield* (Sheffield: Montgomery and Smith, 1817). The young Isaac Ironside, future Chartist leader of Sheffield council, thanked the school 'for the favours I have received'. *Fifteenth Annual Report of the Sheffield Lancasterian School for Boys* (1824), p. 1. See also Sheffield Lancasterian School for Boys, *Annual Reports* (1823 and 1825). For 'heathen' masculinity, see Callum Brown, *The Death of Christian Britain: Understanding Secularisation 1800–2000* (London: Routledge, 2001).
66. *Sixth Annual Report of the Sheffield Girls' Lancasterian School* (1821), p. 4. For domesticity and girls' education, see Meg Gomersall, *Working-Class Girls in Nineteenth-Century England: Life, Work and Schooling* (New York: St. Martin's Press, 1997); June Purvis, *Hard Lessons: The Lives and Education of Working-Class Women in Nineteenth-Century England* (Cambridge: Polity Press, 1989).
67. *Sixteenth Annual Report of the Sheffield Lancasterian School for Boys* (1825), pp. 1, 4.
68. *Fifth Annual Report of the Trustees of the Sheffield National District Society* (1820); Smith, *Conflict and Compromise*, pp. 119–126; Thomas Laqueur, 'Working-class demand and the growth of English Elementary Education, 1750–1850', in Stone (ed.), *Schooling and Society*, pp. 192–205.
69. Lancasterian School for Boys, *Fifth Annual Report* (1814), p. 7; *Ninth Annual Report* (1818), pp. 2–3. See Joyce Goodman, 'Languages of female colonial authority: the educational network of the ladies' committee of the British and foreign school society, 1813–1837', *Compare*, vol. 30, no. 1 (2000), pp. 7–19.
70. Lucy Aikin to William Ellery Channing, 1841, quoted in Williams, *The Angel out of the House*, p. 54.
71. See 'An Account of the Society', from a letter of 17 December 1796, SBCP *Reports* (1805), p. 39.
72. To reflect this, Howsam suggests a reformulation of the name to 'the (Women's) British and (Men's) Foreign Bible Society', Leslie Howsam, *Cheap Bibles: Nineteenth-Century Publishing and the British and Foreign Bible Society* (Cambridge: Cambridge University Press, 1991), p. 60.
73. *SI*, 17 November 1807, 18 August 1818.
74. 'Society for Bettering the Condition of the Poor at Clapham', SBCP *Reports* (1805), pp. 335–353.
75. *SI*, 18 May 1804, 31 May 1804. See also: 'Extract from an Account of the Ladies' Society for the Education and Employment of

the Female Poor' (London, April 1804); Prochaska, *Women and Philanthropy*, p. 24.
76. Kilham, 'Extract from an Account of the Sheffield Society for Bettering the Condition of the Poor' (Sheffield: J. Montgomery, 1813); Zemka, *Victorian Testaments*, p. 192.
77. Hannah Kilham, 'Extract'; Biller, *Memoir of the Late Hannah Kilham*, pp. 116, 205; Sheffield SBCP, *Eleventh Annual Report* (Sheffield: J. Montgomery, 1814), p. 2. For the hardship of 1817, see *SI*, 14 January 1817 and 7 October 1817.
78. Sheffield SBCP, *Tenth Annual Report* (1813), p. 2.
79. This was an amalgam of previous societies, including the Annuity Society for the Benefit of Widows and Aged Persons (1805) and the Female Merciful Society (1807).
80. Letter from George Bennet, 'A Townsman', on Female Friendly Societies, *SI*, 24 October 1810; Sheffield Female Friendly Society, *Seventh Annual Report* (Sheffield: J. Montgomery, 1817), pp. 3–4; *Ninth Annual Report of the Female Friendly Society for the Relief of Widows and Single Women, above Sixty-Five Years of Age* (Sheffield: J. Montgomery, 1819); 'History of Widow Hancock', *Twenty-First Annual Report of the Female Friendly Society for the Relief of Widows and Single Women, above Sixty-Five Years of Age* (Sheffield: Blackwell, 1831).
81. Sheffield SBCP, *Eleventh Report* (1814), p. 3.
82. Biller, *Memoir of the late Hannah Kilham*, p. 116; Hannah Kilham, *Family Maxims* (Sheffield: Bentham and Ray, 1817).
83. *SI*, 27 July 1819.
84. Margaret Howitt (ed.), *Mary Howitt, An Autobiography*, vol. 1, (London: William Isbister, 1889), p. 86.
85. Sheffield SBCP, *Fifteenth Report* (1801), p. 189; *SI*, 14 January 1817. Dorothy Thompson aptly refers to this practice as 'charitable surveillance'. See 'Women, work and politics in nineteenth-century England: the problem of authority', in Jane Rendall (ed.), *Equal or Different: Women's Politics, 1800–1914* (Oxford: Basil Blackwell, 1987), pp. 57–81, here p. 73; also Yeo, *The Contest for Social Science*, pp. 28–29.
86. Sheffield SBCP, *Twentieth Annual Report* (Sheffield: J. Montgomery, 1824), p. 4. See also the *Fifth Annual Report of the Female Friendly Society for the Relief of Aged Women* (Sheffield: J. Montgomery, 1815), p. 6.
87. Mora Dickson, *The Powerful Bond* (London: Dennis Dobson, 1980), p. 124.
88. Biller, *Memoir of the late Hannah Kilham*, p. 114.
89. Sheffield SBCP, *Tenth Annual Report* (1813), p. 2, *Eleventh Annual Report* (1814), p. 2, *Fourteenth Annual Report* (1817), pp. 7–8.

90. Sheffield SBCP, *Eighteenth Annual Report* (1821), p. 7.
91. Morris, *Class, Sect and Party*, pp. 184–189; Zemka, *Victorian Testaments*, p. 194.
92. See Peter Mandler, 'Poverty and charity in the nineteenth-century metropolis: an introduction', in Peter Mandler (ed.), *The Uses of Charity: The Poor on Relief in the Nineteenth-Century Metropolis* (Philadelphia: University of Pennsylvania Press, 1990), pp. 1–37, here pp. 1–2, 7–8. For a stimulating discussion of power and official and unofficial stories, see James C. Scott, *Domination and the Arts of Resistance: Hidden Transcripts* (New Haven and London: Yale University Press, 1990).
93. See, for example, the Sheffield SBCP, *Twenty-First Report* (1824), p. 4.
94. Alan Kidd, 'Philanthropy and the "Social History Paradigm"', *Social History*, vol. 21, no. 2 (May 1996), pp. 180–192, here p. 187.
95. Homi Bhabha's concept of 'mimicry' – of colonial peoples being 'almost the same, but not quite' like their colonisers – is also appropriate for understanding philanthropic relationships. H. Bhabha, *The Location of Culture* (London: Routledge, 1994), pp. 85–92.
96. Sheffield Female Friendly Society, *Ninth Report*, p. 6.
97. Charles S. Dudley, *An Analysis of the System of the Bible Society throughout its Various Parts* (London: BFBS, 1821); Sir Thomas Bernard, 'Extract from an Account of the Juvenile Bible Society at Sheffield' (1814), Sheffield Local Studies Library, Local Pamphlets, vol. 87, no. 7.
98. *SI*, 24 August 1819.
99. *SI*, 2 February 1819. See also *The Third Annual Report of the Ladies' Branch of the Liverpool Auxiliary Bible Society* (Liverpool, 1819), pp. 3–4, 11–20.
100. Dudley, *Analysis*, p. 372. Such reorganisation was sometimes made essential, as in Liverpool in 1817, by 'the great inefficiency of the men'.
101. Dudley, *Analysis*, pp. 536, 403, 413. See also Martin, *Evangelicals United*, pp. 92–94, for impact on church attendance.
102. Quoted in Dudley, *Analysis*, p. 349.
103. Quoted in Howsam, *Cheap Bibles*, p. 50; Dudley, *Analysis*, p. 214.
104. Dudley, *Analysis*, pp. 349, 411, 410.
105. *SI*, 3 January 1815.
106. *SI*, 3 August 1813, 17 August 1813, 5 October 1813, 9 November 1813, 16 November 1813, 30 November 1813. For Basil Woodd's successful tour of Yorkshire, see Stanley, 'Home Support

for Overseas Missions in early Victorian England, c. 1838–1873' (University of Cambridge: unpublished PhD thesis, 1979), p. 264.

107. See Dudley, *Analysis*, p. 410. For the 'reflex principle', see Stanley, 'Home Support for Overseas Missions', p. 264.
108. Richard Watson, quoted in F. S. Piggin, 'Halévy Revisited: the origins of the Wesleyan Methodist Missionary Society: an examination of Semmel's thesis', *Journal of Imperial and Commonwealth History*, vol. 9, no. 1 (1980), 17–37, 30.
109. In Sheffield in 1819, female societies affiliated to chapels or based in areas of the town raised a combined total of £158 1s 0d, rather more than the men, with their sum of £116 5s 9d. *Sixth Report of the Auxiliary Missionary Society for the West Riding of Yorkshire* (Sheffield: James Montgomery, 1819), appendix. See also: *Twelfth Annual Report of the Wesleyan Methodist Auxiliary Missionary Society for the Sheffield District* (Sheffield: Blackwell, 1827), *Thirteenth Annual Report of the Wesleyan Methodist Auxiliary Missionary Society for the Sheffield District* (1827), *Report of the Church Missionary Association for Sheffield and the Neighbourhood* (Sheffield: James Montgomery 1842). For the missionary anniversaries, see Stanley, 'Home Support for Overseas Missions', pp. 272–275.
110. See Howsam, *Cheap Bibles*, chapter two; also Thomas Rock, moving a resolution on Penny Associations at a Birmingham meeting in 1815, claimed it was women's 'domestic habits and affectionate minds' which 'form[ed] them in a peculiar manner to assist us in these weekly societies.' Reverend TT Biddulph, *The Duty of Communicating the Bread of Life to the Heathen World, Considered in a Sermon* (Birmingham: Thos Knott, 1815), p. 91; *The Third Report of the General Committee of the Methodist Auxiliary Missionary Society* (Nottingham: Shorrock and Son, 1819), p. 8.
111. For unhappiness with Dudley and 'his women', see Martin, *Evangelicals United*, pp. 114–116.
112. See Amanda Vickery's argument that the controversy over separate spheres in the 1830s indicates that 'many women were seen to be active outside the home rather than proof that they were so confined.' Vickery, 'Golden age to separate spheres? A review of the categories and chronology of English women's history', *The Historical Journal*, vol. 36, no. 2 (1993), pp. 383–414, 400.
113. See Anne Summers' useful discussion of the continued separation of the male secular and state-financed 'public' and the religious and voluntary public to which women were admitted. *Female Lives, Moral States*, p. 17.
114. Quoted in Dudley, *Analysis*, pp. 359, 349, 351.

3 Missionary domesticity and 'woman's sphere': the Reads of Wincobank Hall

1. For the evangelical family, see Davidoff and Hall, *Family Fortunes*, pp. 108–118, 169–192; Tosh, *A Man's Place*, pp. 27–50.
2. Davidoff and Hall, *Family Fortunes*. Christopher Tolley, *Domestic Biography: The Legacy of Evangelicalism in Four Nineteenth-Century Families* (Oxford: Oxford University Press, 1997).
3. Gleadle, 'Our several spheres'; and '"The Age of Physiological Reformers": rethinking gender and domesticity in the age of reform', in Innes and Burns (eds), *Rethinking the Age of Reform*; Elizabeth Langland, 'Women's writing and the domestic sphere', in Joanne Shattock (ed.), *Women and Literature in Britain 1800–1900* (Cambridge: Cambridge University Press, 2001), pp. 119–141; Zoe Laidlaw, '"Aunt Anna's Report": the Buxton Women and the Aborigines Select Committee, 1835–37', *Journal of Commonwealth and Imperial History*, vol. 32, no. 2 (April 2004), pp. 1–28. See also: Eleanor Gordon and Gwyneth Nair, *Public Lives: Women, Family and Society in Victorian Britain* (New Haven: Yale University Press, 2003).
4. See for example, Hall, *Civilising Subjects*.
5. See Burton, *Burdens of History*; Thorne, *Congregational Missions*; Rhonda Semple, *Missionary Women: Gender, Professionalism and the Victorian Idea of Christian Mission* (Woodbridge: the Boydell Press, 2003).
6. Prochaska, *Women and Philanthropy*, p. 76.
7. Dudley, *Analysis of the System of the Bible Society*, pp. 73–94.
8. A seventh child, Julia (1818–1819), died in infancy. While the presence of Edmund offers some opportunity to compare the socialisation of girls and boys within evangelical families, there is considerably less extant material relating to him. With his birth coming so many years after those of his sisters, it is impossible to judge what is precisely gendered and what is merely the product of a more established method or relaxed style of parenting.
9. For Rotherham College, see Holland and Everett, *Memoirs*, vol. 3, pp. 74–82.
10. R. E. Wilson, *Two Hundred Precious Metal Years: A History of the Sheffield Smelting Company Ltd, 1760–1960* (London: Ernest Benn, 1960); Philip Robinson, *The Smiths of Chesterfield: A History of the Griffin Foundry, Brampton 1775–1833* (Chesterfield: Thomas Brayshaw, 1957), pp. 1–18 and 45–52.
11. Binfield, 'Religion in Sheffield', in Binfield et al., *The History of Sheffield*, vol. II, pp. 405–409; Holland and Everett, *Memoirs*, vol. 3, pp. 74–82.

12. Joseph Read had supported the rebuilding of Zion Chapel through subscription, and he and Elizabeth worked alongside Maurice Phillips, the Classical Tutor at Rotherham College and first settled minister at Zion Chapel, in promoting the Sunday school. Elizabeth Read's Diaries (Mary-Anne Rawson Papers, HJ Wilson Collection, Sheffield City Archives, MAR/HJW hereafter, MD 6042); Letters from Catherine Read to Eliza Read, September 1813 (MAR/HJW MD 5694) and Joseph Smith to Joseph Read, 1 May 1814 (MAR/HJW MD 6403); P. G. S. Hopwood, 'The gates of Zion: the story of a Church' (unpublished, n.d.), pp. 30–60.
13. Mary-Anne Rawson, 'Memorials of James Montgomery', James Montgomery Collection, Sheffield University.
14. Elizabeth Read to Mary-Anne Read, 8 February 1817, 22 March 1820 and 21 April 1821 (MAR/HJW MD 6043); see also Account Book for Wincobank, 1817–1822 (MAR/HJW MD 5702).
15. For evangelical constructions of father- and motherhood, see Davidoff and Hall, *Family Fortunes*, pp. 329–335; John Tosh, *A Man's Place*.
16. Standish Meacham, *Henry Thornton of Clapham, 1760*–1815, cited by Doreen M. Rosman, *Evangelicals and Culture* (London: Croom Helm, 1984) p. 9.
17. Rosman, *Evangelicals and Culture*, pp. 68–80; Watts, *The Dissenters*, vol. 2, pp. 634–646.
18. For 'religious terrorism' in England, see Rosman, *Evangelicals and Culture*, p. 101; Paul Sangster, *Pity My Simplicity: The Evangelical Revival and the Religious Education of Children, 1738–1800* (London: Epworth Press, 1963), pp. 31–39 and 75–81.
19. This view is supported by Tolley's discussion of the Clapham Sect. *Domestic Biography*, pp. 11–41.
20. Nancy F. Cott, 'Notes toward an interpretation of antebellum childrearing', *The Psychohistory Review*, vol. 4, no. 4 (1978), pp. 4–20, here p. 5. See also: J. H. Plumb, 'The new world of children in eighteenth century England', *Past and Present*, vol. 67 (May 1975), pp. 64–95; Davidoff and Hall, *Family Fortunes*, pp. 343–348.
21. Smith letters (MAR/HJW MD 6038i); Elizabeth Read's Diaries (MAR/HJW MD 6042).
22. Elizabeth Read's Diaries, 1804–1806, 1813–1814 (MAR/HJW MD 6042); letters from Elizabeth Read to Mary-Anne Read, 8 February 1817; Eliza Read to Mary-Anne Read, 19 June 1815; Elizabeth Read to Mary-Anne Read, 8 February 1817, 12 April 1817 (MAR/HJW MD 6043).
23. Elizabeth Read to Eliza Read, 4 April 1819, 8 August 1819 (MAR/HJW MD 6043).

24. Elizabeth Read to Mary-Anne Read, 22 November 1819. See also: Elizabeth Read to Mary-Anne Read, 17 August 1813, 21 November 1813, 21 June 1819, 22 March 1820; Elizabeth Read to Eliza Read, 4 April 1820; Elizabeth Read to Edmund Read, 23 February 1830 (MAR/HJW MD 6043).
25. Elizabeth Read to Mary-Anne Read, 21 November 1813 (MAR/HJW MD 6043).
26. Elizabeth Read to Edmund Read, 10 November 1823 (MAR/HJW MD 5697).
27. For the importance of benevolence in child-rearing, see Davidoff and Hall, *Family Fortunes*, pp. 329–256; Sangster, *Pity My Simplicity*, p. 79; Prochaska, *Women and Philanthropy*, pp. 73–94: Grenby, 'Real Charity Makes Distinctions'.
28. *Evangelical Magazine*, July 1812, pp. 140–141.
29. *Evangelical Magazine*, June 1800, December 1800, August 1802, June 1805, December 1807, Supplement, September 1810, December 1813.
30. *Evangelical Magazine* (Supplement, September 1810).
31. William Buchan, M. D., *Domestic Medicine* (London: T. Cadell and W. Davies [1769] 1803); *Advice to Mothers, on the Subject of their Own Health; and on the Means of Promoting the Health, Strength, and Beauty, of their Offspring* (London: T. Cadell and W. Davies, 1803).
32. Hannah More, *Coelebs in Search of a Wife* (1809), went through 12 editions in the first year of publication. See Robert A. Colby, *Fiction with a Purpose: Major and Minor Nineteenth-Century Novels* (Bloomington: Indiana University Press, 1967), p. 80. See also Ann Martin Taylor, *Practical Hints to Young Females on the Duties of a Wife, a Mother and a Mistress of a Young Family*, 3rd edition (London: Taylor and Hessey, 1815).
33. Ebenezer Elliott, 'The Ranter', *The Splendid Village: Corn Law Rhymes, and other Poems* (Sheffield: J. Pearce, 1833), pp. 144–156, here p. 144. While the move reflected their growing affluence, the family retained and regularly returned to the house near the works at Royds Mill. For the movement between industrial areas and the suburbs, see Davidoff and Hall, *Family Fortunes*, pp. 364–369.
34. Account Book for Wincobank, 1817–1822; George Bennet to Joseph Read, 4 October 1817 (MAR/HJW MD 5690).
35. See Mary V. Jackson, *Engines of Instruction, Mischief and Magic. Children's Literature in England from its beginnings to 1839* (Lincoln: University of Nebraska, 1989), p. 111; Kristin Drotner, *English Children and their Magazines, 1751–1945* (London: Yale University Press, 1988), pp. 24–27.

36. The 'Wincobank Remembrancer', July 1819, September 1819; the 'Wincobank Repository', August 1819. Other extant editions from this period include the 'Family Miscellany', August and December 1816; the 'Family Repository', April 1819, March 1820 (MAR/HJW MD 5703).
37. The 'Wincobank Remembrancer', July 1819 and November 1819; 'A Walk in the Country', 'Family Repository', April 1819 (MAR/HJW MD 5703).
38. Elizabeth's brother William Smith penned the admonishing response: 'I think your Mama cannot feel altogether contented when she considers that her eldest daughter is giving her presence to that Worship which she herself does not judge it expedient to countenance. Do not smile, Mary Ann[*sic*]; you know these are not smiling subjects – but still may I enquire if you do not think that the Church people have some good qualities in their Composition? If not, do be on your guard.' (MAR/HJW MD 6038i).
39. Dinah Ball, *The Missionary Society, A Dialogue* (Sheffield: James Montgomery, n.d.).
40. For attacks on the imaginative and fantastical (and the Frenchified) see the monthly instalments (between 1802 and 1806) of Mrs Trimmer, *The Guardian of Education: A Periodical Work, Vols 1–5* (London: J. Hatchard, 1802).
41. Grenby, 'Real Charity Makes Distinctions'.
42. See M. Nancy Cutt, *Mrs Sherwood and her Books for Children* (Oxford: Oxford University Press, 1974); Cutt, *Ministering Angels. A Study of Evangelical Writing for Children* (Herts: Five Owls press, 1979); Lynne Vallone, *Disciplines of Virtue. Girls' Culture in the Eighteenth and Nineteenth Centuries* (London: Yale University Press, 1995), pp. 69–105.
43. Mary-Anne's 'Missionary Atlas', 1819 (MAR/HJW MD 5708a); George Bennet to Catherine Read, 21 April 1820 (MAR/HJW MD 5690).
44. Sarah Read, 'Journal of a voyage from Gravesend to Madeira, May 1819–April 1822' (MAR/HJW MD 5695).
45. Letters from George Bennet to Edmund Read, November 1822, 24 April 1826; George Bennet to Mrs Read, April 1824 (MAR/HJW MD5690).
46. George Bennet to Joseph Read, 27 April 1826 (MAR/HJW MD5690).
47. Sarah Read, untitled (MAR/HJW MD 5695).
48. Apart from the occasional letter from Elizabeth cajoling her seemingly reluctant young son into collecting for missions, there is

little evidence concerning his extra-curricular activities. On one occasion she promised him a gift of a book in return for some anti-slavery verse; his first verse ended with the lines: 'Not more then half do reach the native land,/ And they so weak that they can hardly stand'. There is no evidence of any further poetic contribution from Edmund. Edmund Read to Elizabeth Read, no date (MAR/HJW MD 5697).

49. Sarah Read, 'A Tale of Woe' and 'The Recaptured Negro', 1820s (MAR/HJW MD 5695).
50. Their attendance at the consecration of an Anglican church points to emerging differences of denominational loyalty, most notable in Sarah's and Emily's decision to attend Ecclesfield Parish church, where the family bought a pew in 1823. There is little reference to family controversy concerning these events, although Sarah and Emily expressed some anxiety about their mother's response to their Anglican sympathies. It may be that these were successfully negotiated by missionary identities. Certainly when, in the 1840s, Catherine lamented Mary-Anne's developing interest in the Plymouth Brethren, Mrs Read was unperturbed, assuming that her elder daughter's involvement with a forthcoming teetotal festival would divert her attention. See: Sarah Read to Eliza Read, 25 October 1827 (MAR/HJW MD 5695); Mrs Read to Eliza Wilson, 11 December 1837; Catherine Read to Mary-Anne Rawson, November 20 1841 (MAR/HJW MD 5694).
51. The 'Wincobank Gazette', 14 August 1826 (MAR/HJW 5703).
52. Rosman has described English evangelicalism as 'a federation of country houses... (and) godly families'. Rosman, *Evangelicals and Culture*, p. 14.
53. See, for example, Catherine Read to Mary-Anne Rawson, 22 September 1831 (MAR/HJW MD 5694).
54. Mary-Anne Rawson, 'Treasury of Pen and Pencil Memorials of Absent Friends, 1824–1828' (unpublished, JM/SU).
55. *A Short History of the Upper Wincobank Chapel* (Sheffield: Ward, 1908), p. 6 (H. J. Wilson Collection).
56. William Rawson died from tuberculosis shortly after Sarah in 1829. Mary-Anne stayed at Wincobank for the remainder of her life, except for a period at the time of Joseph Read's bankruptcy and subsequent death in 1836–1837, when the family was forced to sell the house and to return to The Mills. Mary-Anne was able to buy back the house in 1837. See Crisis Letters (MAR/HJW MD 5692).
57. See Clare Midgley, *Women against Slavery: The British Campaigns, 1780–1870* (London: Routledge, 1992).
58. For women and the anti-apprenticeship campaign, see Midgley, *Women Against Slavery*, pp. 117–118.

59. Letters from Sophia Sturge to Mary-Anne Rawson, including extracts of letters from Baptist missionaries, 1838, n. d. (Mary-Anne Rawson papers, John Rylands Library, Manchester (MAR/JR hereafter) Eng Ms 741 113a–c). For the free villages in Jamaica, see Catherine Hall, 'White visions, Black lives: the free villages of Jamaica', *History Workshop Journal*, vol. 36 (Autumn 1993), pp. 100–132. Mary-Anne would have been well-acquainted with an earlier African experiment in 'free villages' which involved fellow Sheffield missionary Hannah Kilham in the mid-1820s. Alison Twells, '"Let us begin well at home": class, ethnicity and Christian motherhood in the writing of Hannah Kilham', in Eileen Janes Yeo (ed.), *Radical Femininity: Women's Self-Representation in the Public Sphere* (Manchester: Manchester University Press, 1998); and Chapter 4 in this volume.
60. Rawson, 1845 Circular (MAR/HJW MD 5699).
61. Eliza married William Wilson, a widowed cotton factory owner. For philanthropic activities in Nottingham, see Catherine Read to Mrs Read, September 1831; Catherine Read to Mary-Anne Rawson, September 1831; Catherine Read to Mr Read, 24 October 1831; Catherine Read to Mrs Read, September 1834 (MAR/HJW MD 5694); Emily Read to Joseph Read, 11 November 1832 (MAR/HJW MD 5696); Mrs Read to Edmund Read, 13 October 1838 (MAR/HJW 5697). Also: Sarah's Weekly Budget and Radford Gazette for 1837–1840 (MAR/HJW MD 5709.).
62. Mary-Anne Rawson, Journal, 1842 (MAR/HJW MD 5704); Elizabeth Read's Diary, 1844–1850, (MAR/HJW MD 6042). When Mrs Read visited in the autumn of 1847 for the opening of the new chapel by John Angell James, she was thrilled at the network her daughter had helped to construct. Elizabeth Read's Diary, 1844–1850 (MAR/HJW MD 6042).
63. Lizzie Rawson to Mary Wilson, 12 January 1838, February 1838, December 1839, 17 August 1843. (MAR/HJW MD 5698). Only Elizabeth Rawson's side of the correspondence survives.
64. Lizzie Rawson to Mary Wilson, 7 January 1841, 11 January 1843, 12 February 1845, 4 February 1848, 10 February 1848 (MAR/HJW MD 5698). See also George Thompson to Elizabeth Rawson, October 1847, June 1849 (MAR/HJW MD 5693). George Thompson (1804–1878), son of a Wesleyan bank clerk from Liverpool, was a radical abolitionist and member of the Agency Committee. According to C. Duncan Rice, Thompson was 'a superlative orator with somewhat vulgar good looks' who inspired an especially intense following among women. *The Scots Abolitionists, 1833–1861* (Baton Rouge: Louisiana State University Press, 1981), p. 55.

65. Lizzie Rawson to Mary Wilson, n.d., 12 January 1838, 26 July 1843, 17 August 1843, 16 November 1843, May 1844, 2 March 1848, 17 May 1848, 13 April 1849 (MAR/HJW MD 5698).
66. See: Wincobank Total Abstinence Society, printed sheet, 1840; Elizabeth Rawson to Mary Eliza Wilson, 12 January 1838, 17 April 1841, 31 May 1842, 17 April 1843, 17 August 1843, 16 November 1843, 31 May 1844, June 1848, 10 February 1848 and 7 March 1848 (MAR/HJW MD 5698).
67. Quoted in Norma Taylor, 'The Life of Mary-Anne Rawson' (Sheffield University: unpublished BA dissertation, 1972), p. 12.
68. Taylor, 'The Life of Mary-Anne Rawson'.
69. Ann Gilbert, 'For the Parents', (MAR/HJW MD 6041).
70. Account Book for Wincobank, 1817–1822; Sarah Read to Elizabeth Read, n. d. (MAR/HJW MD 5695); Elizabeth Read to Mary-Anne Read, 11 February 1828; Eliza Wilson to Mary-Anne Rawson, 22 July 1830 (MAR/HJW MD 6045); Catherine Read to Mary-Anne Rawson, December 1845 (MAR/HJW MD 5694).
71. Lizzie Rawson to Mary Wilson, 17 August 1843 (MAR/HJW MD 5698). R. E. Wilson, 'The Story of Wincobank School and Chapel' (unpublished, 1955); Joyce Goodman, 'Women and the Management of the Education of Working-Class Girls 1800–61', (University of Manchester, unpublished PhD thesis, 1992). For the education of working-class girls, see Gomersall, *Working-Class Girls in Nineteenth-Century England.*
72. See Mary-Anne Rawson, 'Memorials of James Montgomery'.
73. Sheffield Ladies' Anti-Slavery Society, *Report of the Sheffield Ladies' Anti-Slavery Society* (Sheffield: J. Blackwell, 1827), p. 10. See also *Report of the Sheffield Ladies' Anti-Slavery Society* (1830). See Midgley, *Women against Slavery*, pp. 107–108.
74. *Report of the Sheffield Ladies' Anti-Slavery Society* (1827), pp. 10–11. William Wilberforce, writing to Macaulay, had claimed that 'for ladies to meet, to publish, to go from house to house stirring up petitions' was unsuited to the female character 'as delineated in Scripture.' Robert Isaac and Samuel Wilberforce, *The Life of William Wilberforce by His Sons*, vol. v (London 1838), pp. 264–265, quoted in Kenneth Corfield, 'Elizabeth Heyrick: radical Quaker', in Gail Malmgreen (ed.), *Religion in the Lives of English Women, 1760–1930* (London: John Murray, 1986), pp. 41–67, here p. 64.
75. *Report of the Sheffield Ladies' Anti-Slavery Society* (1830), p. 14.
76. See also various contributions to James Montgomery (ed.), 'The Negro's Album of the Sheffield Anti-Slavery Society' unpublished, 1828 (JM/SU) and Mary-Anne Rawson, *The Bow in the Cloud; Or, the Negro's Memorial* (London: Jackson and Walford, 1834).

For civilisation, abolitionism and feminism, see Clare Midgley, 'Anti-slavery and the roots of "imperial feminism"', in Midgley (ed.), *Gender and Imperialism* (Manchester: Manchester University Press, 1998), pp. 161–179.

77. *Appeal to the Christian Women of Sheffield from the Association for the Universal Abolition of Slavery* (Sheffield: R. Leader, 1837), p. 13. The *Appeal* formed the basis of a small pamphlet, of which 1000 copies were distributed, and the ladies' petition of 25,000 signatures. See Sheffield Ladies' Association for the Universal Abolition of Slavery, *Report of the Sheffield Ladies' Association for the Universal Abolition of Slavery* (Sheffield: R. Leader, 1839).
78. *Appeal to the Christian Women of Sheffield from the Association for the Universal Abolition of Slavery* (1837), pp. 9, 11.
79. 'Resolutions of the Ladies' Committee of the Universal Abolition Society, 13 March 1838', and letter from Mary-Anne Rawson to the Men's Committee (n.d.) (MAR/JR 743/62–63).
80. Midgley, *Women against Slavery*, p. 116.
81. Rawson, 'Memorials of James Montgomery'.
82. Quoted in Midgley, *Women against Slavery*, p. 165. Rawson reflected dispassionately on the incident on the occasion of William Lloyd Garrison's fleeting visit to her home at Wincobank Hall in 1877, recalling that Garrison, her 'great hero', had been 'vexed at the women not being allowed to speak, and Mr Sturge with him for wishing it.' William Lloyd Garrison to H. J. Wilson, July 1877; Mary-Anne Rawson to Henry Joseph and Charlotte Wilson, July 1877 (MAR/HJW MD 5693). See Kathryn Kish Sklar, '"Women who speak for an entire nation": American and British women at the World Anti-slavery Convention, London, 1840', *Pacific Historical Review* (1990), pp. 453–499.
83. Sarah Stickney Ellis, *The Women of England, Their Social Duties, and Domestic Habits* (London: Fisher, Son and Co, 1839); *The Daughters of England, Their Position in Society, Character and Responsibilities* (London: Fisher, Son and Co, 1842); *The Wives of England, Their Relative Duties, Domestic Influence and Social Obligations* (London: Fisher, Son and Co, 1843); and *The Mothers of England, Their Influence and Responsibility* (London: Fisher, Son and Co, 1843).
84. Josiah Gilbert (ed.), *Autobiography and other Memorials of Mrs Gilbert* (London: Henry S. King, 1874), pp. 185–188.
85. Gilbert (ed.), *Autobiography and other Memorials*.
86. Prochaska, *Women and Philanthropy*, p. 5.
87. In co-operation with her sister Jane, she had written *Original Poems, for Infant Minds* (1805), including 'Twinkle, Twinkle, little star' and 'My Mother', followed by *Hymns for Infant Minds*

(London: T. Conder, 1810). See J. Gilbert (ed.), *Autobiography and other Memorials*, pp. 59, 162, 282, 295–297, 304–305, 322.

88. The petition was signed by 15,000 local women, and 5000-plus men. Ann Taylor Gilbert to Mary-Anne Rawson, 10 May 1833, (MAR/JR), quoted in Midgley, *Women against Slavery*, p. 69; Ann Gilbert to Mary-Anne Rawson, 9 April 1838, (MAR/HJW MD 2019).
89. Letter to Anne Knight, 1849, Gilbert (ed.), *Autobiography and other Memorials*, pp. 185–188.
90. Ann Taylor Gilbert, *A Biographical Sketch of the Rev. Joseph Gilbert* (London: Jackson and Walford, 1853), pp. 48, 55–56.
91. Christina Duff Stewart (ed.), *Ann Taylor Gilbert's Album* (New York and London: Garland, 1978), pp. 69, 125, 159, 141, 269, 277, 549, 564, 568, 579.
92. Ann Gilbert to Mary-Anne Rawson, 9 April 1838.
93. Gilbert, *Autobiography and other Memorials*, pp. 185–188.
94. Rawson, 'Memorials of James Montgomery'.
95. Holland and Everett, *Memoirs*; Rawson, 'Memorials of James Montgomery'; E. D. Mackerness, 'Mary-Anne Rawson and the memorials of James Montgomery', *Transactions of the Hunter Archaeological Society*, vol. 8 (1962), pp. 218–228.
96. Rawson's uncle and father provided bail following his imprisonment in York Castle for 'libel' in 1796. See Mackerness, 'Mary-Anne Rawson and the memorials'.
97. Rawson, 'Memorials of James Montgomery'.
98. Rawson's use of this 'private' memoir to contest contemporary biographies and to highlight aspects of her own life is of interest in terms of women's strategies for self-representation and public writing. Despite indications in earlier drafts that she intended to publish the 'Memoirs', they remained unpublished, the final version beginning with the disclaimer that the volume was not a biography but was written principally for the 'amusement' of herself and her daughter Elizabeth. Whether the process that led to this decision involved a reluctant acknowledgement that she could not compete with Holland's tomes, or was simply a matter of confidence (she had taken a lot of persuasion to publish *The Bow in the Cloud* in 1832), is impossible to know. The result was that Mary-Anne Rawson failed to make public her belief in the profoundly social nature of the missionary family. For a critique of the easy assumption that the failure to publish resulted from anxieties, see Helen Rogers, 'In the name of the father: political biographies by radical daughters', in David Amigoni (ed.), *Life Writing and Victorian Culture*, (Aldershot: Ashgate, 2006), pp. 202–227.
99. Mary-Anne Rawson to Henry Joseph Wilson, 3 December 1845 (MAR/HJW MD 6044). For H. J. Wilson, see Mosa Anderson,

H. J. Wilson, Fighter for Freedom (London: James Clarke and Co., 1953) and W. S. Fowler, *A Study in Radicalism and Dissent: The Life and Times of Henry Joseph Wilson 1833–1914* (London: Epworth Press, 1961).

100. Edmund Read to Mary Eliza Wilson, 19 December 1843 (MAR/HJW MD 5697).
101. See *Sheffield Mercury*, 3 December 1842.

4 'Bringing about the world's restoration': missionary women and the creation of a global Christian community

1. Jemima Thompson, *Memoirs of British Female Missionaries: With a Survey of the Condition of Women in Heathen Countries and also A Preliminary Essay on the Importance of Female Agency in Evangelizing Pagan Nations* (London: William Smith, 1841).
2. Cunningham, '"God and nature intended you for a missionary's wife"', p. 89. See my Introduction for further discussion of this issue.
3. Emma Pitman, *Heroines of the Mission Field* (London: Cassle and Co., 1880) and *Female Missionaries in Eastern Lands* (London: S. W. Partridge, 1895); Priscilla Chapman, *Hindoo Female Education* (London: Seeley and Burnside, 1839?); John Telford, *Women in the Mission Field. Glimpses of Christian Women Among the Heathen* (London: C. H. Kelly, 1895).
4. Thompson, *Memoirs of British Female Missionaries*, pp. 68–69; Clough, Margaret M., *Extracts* (London: J. Mason, 1829).
5. See for example: Alison Twells, '"So distant and wild a scene": Hannah Kilham's writing from West Africa, 1822–1832', *Women's History Review*, vol. 4, no. 3, pp. 301–318; Hilary M. Carey, 'Companions in the wilderness? Missionary wives in colonial Australia, 1788–1900', *Journal of Religious History*, vol. 19, no. 2 (December 1995), pp. 226–248; Tanya Fitzgerald, 'Cartographies of friendship: mapping missionary women's educational networks in Aoteara/New Zealand 1823–40', *History of Education*, vol. 32, no. 5 (2003), pp. 513–527; Midgley, 'Can women be missionaries?'
6. Biller (ed.), *Memoir of the late Hannah Kilham*; Clare Balfour, *A Sketch of the Life of Hannah Kilham* (London: W. and F. G. Cash, 1854); Pitman, *Heroines of the Mission Field*; Dickson, *The Powerful Bond*.
7. P. E. H. Hair, *The Early Study of Nigerian Languages* (Cambridge: Cambridge University Press, 1967), quoted in Ormerod Greenwood, 'Hannah Kilham's Plan', reprinted from *The Sierra Leone Bulletin of Religion*, vol. 4, part 1 (1962) p. 73; A. Werner, 'English

Contributions to the Study of African Languages', *Journal of the Royal African Society*, vol. 29, no. 117 (October 1930), p. 78.

8. For the language of maternalism and the colonial reform of familial relationships, see Haggis, 'Gendering colonialism or colonizing gender'; and 'Good wives and mothers' or 'dedicated workers'? Contradictions of domesticity in the 'mission of sisterhood', Travancore, south India', in Kalpana Ram and Margaret Jolly (eds), *Maternities and Modernities. Colonial and Postcolonial Experiences in Asia and the Pacific* (Cambridge: Cambridge University Press, 1998), pp. 81–113; Margaret Jolly, ' "To save the girls for brighter and better lives." Presbyterian Missions and Women in the South of Vanuatu, 1848–1870', *Journal of Pacific History*, vol. 26, no. 1 (1991), pp. 27–48; and 'Colonizing women: the maternal body and empire'.
9. See Susan Thorne, 'Missionary-imperial feminism', in Taylor Huber and Lutkehaus (eds), *Gendered Missions*, pp. 39–65.
10. 'Considerations and Regulations Respecting Missionaries in Connection with the Missionary Society', London, February 1811, George Mundy's Candidates Papers, SOAS, CWM/LMS Archive, Candidates Papers 1796–1899, Box 12.
11. Fears for safety did occasionally mitigate against this policy. Following the departure from Tahiti for New South Wales of three missionary couples in 1798 due to anxieties about the safety of the wives, the Board declared that new missions were initially to 'consist of single brethren *only*' until their security be ascertained. 'Letter of Instructions from the Directors of the Missionary Society to Captain Robson, of the Missionary Ship, Duff', *Evangelical Magazine*, January 1799.
12. Thomas Middleditch, *The Youthful Female Missionary: A Memoir of Mary Ann Hutchins, Baptist Missionary, Savanna-la-Mar, Jamaica; and Daughter of the Rev. T. Middleditch, of Ipswich; Compiled Chiefly from her own Correspondence, by her Father* (London: Wrightman, Hamilton Adams and Co., 1840), p. 31
13. *The Youthful Female Missionary*, p. 60.
14. *The Youthful Female Missionary*, pp. 4, 61–63, 167.
15. For would-be missionary wives seeking husbands in early nineteenth-century America, see Patricia Grimshaw, *Paths of Duty: American Missionary Wives in Nineteenth Century Hawaii* (Honolulu: University of Hawaii Press, 1989).
16. Thompson, *Memoirs of Female Missionaries*, pp. 36, 12, 68–69.
17. Eliza Ann Foster, *Memoirs of Mrs. Eliza Ann Foster: Wife of H. B. Foster, Wesleyan Missionary, Jamaica. Compiled from her Diary and Correspondence. By her Husband* (London: John Mason, 1844), pp. 22, 64, 78, 84, 98, 118, 127, 238.

18. It is notoriously difficult to find the names of missionary wives; their husbands usually referred to them (in writing) as 'Mrs'.
19. J. Williams, *Euthanasia: A Funeral Sermon for Mrs Williams, With a Memoir* (London: S. T. Williams, 1852), pp. 66–67. See also *Memoirs of Female Labourers in the Missionary Cause*, introduction by Reverend Richard Hill (London: Binns and Goodwin, 1839).
20. Letter from John Williams, *Euthanasia*, pp. 61–62.
21. Ellis, William, *Memoir of Mary M. Ellis, Wife of the Rev. William Ellis, Missionary to the South Seas, and Foreign Secretary of the London Missionary Society* (London: Fisher, Son and Co., 1835).
22. Williams, *Euthanasia*, p. 60.
23. See Alison Twells, 'Missionary "fathers" and Wayward "sons": British missionaries in the South Pacific, 1797–1840', in Trev Lynn Broughton and Helen Rogers (eds), *Gender and Fatherhood in the Nineteenth Century* (Basingstoke: Palgrave, 2007), pp. 153–164. For the Henry family, see Niel Gunson, 'The deviations of a missionary family: the Henrys of Tahiti', in J. W. Davidson and Deryck Scarr, *Pacific Island Portraits* (Canberra: Australian National University Press, 1970), pp. 31–54.
24. Gunson, *Messengers of Grace*, pp. 111–121, 132–136.
25. *Missionary Register*, 1827, p. 130; see also 1828, p. 131.
26. Niel Gunson, 'John Williams and his Ship: the Bourgeois Aspirations of a Missionary Family', in D. P. Crook (ed.), *Questioning the Past: A Selection of Papers in History and Government* (Brisbane: University of Queensland Press, 1972), pp. 73–95.
27. See Chapter 6.
28. Lancelot Threlkeld to the LMS, 29 September 1818 (SOAS CWM/LMS Box 2).
29. See letters and journals throughout the 1820s. For example, George Bennet to Orsmond, 15 March 1824; Orsmond, 24 July, 19 August and 28 August 1829 (Box 10, Folder 1, Jacket C). See also Gunson, 'The deviations of a missionary family'.
30. For the significance of missionary domesticity in challenges to the civilising mission in the 1840s, see Elizabeth Elbourne, 'Domesticity and dispossession: the ideology of 'home' and the British construction of the 'primitive' from the eighteenth to the early nineteenth century', in W. Woodward, P. Hayes and G. Minkley (eds), *Deep Histories: Gender and Colonialism in Southern Africa* (Amsterdam: Rodopi, 2002).
31. For Sheffield as a centre of the Methodist revival, see Wickham, *Church and People in an Industrial City*. The New Connexion (1796), known as the 'Tom Paine Methodists', had pressed for greater popular involvement in the government of the Methodist Society; its members were subsequently expelled. See Bernard

Semmel, *The Methodist Revolution* (London: Heinemann, 1974), pp. 113–124.

32. Hannah Kilham, *Scripture Selections on Attributes of the Divine Being…Designed Chiefly for the Instruction of Young Persons* (Sheffield: William Todd, 1813); *Questions on the Principles of the Christian Religion to be answered from the Scriptures Adapted for Schools and for Private Instruction* (Sheffield: Bentham, 1817); *Family Maxims*.
33. Elizabeth Isichei, *Victorian Quakers* (Oxford: Oxford University Press, 1970); Plant, 'Gender and the aristocracy of Dissent'.
34. Kilham was inspired by William Allen's sponsorship of four West African youths who attended Joseph Lancaster's Borough Road school from 1811 to 1814 before returning home as missionaries. See Greenwood, 'Hannah Kilham's Plan', p. 11.
35. Greenwood, *Quaker Encounters, Vines on the Mountain*, vol. 2 (York: William Sessions, 1977), p. 98.
36. Singleton (1770–1832) ran a boarding school in Broomhall, Sheffield, and had also been a member of the Methodist New Connexion prior to joining the Friends. There was much disapproval of his ministry from Friends who disliked his missionary tendencies. He eventually left the Society in 1824. William Singleton, *The Result of Seven Years Mission among Friends of Balby Monthly Meeting* (Sheffield: H. A. Bacon, 1823).
37. WMMS, Missionary Notices (London) Vol. IV, p. 359 (SOAS, CWM/Methodist Missionary Archive).
38. Plant, 'Gender and the aristocracy of Dissent'.
39. Hannah Kilham was a member of the committee. See G. Bartle, 'The role of the ladies' committee in the affairs of the BFSS', *Journal of Educational Administration and History*, vol. 27, no. 1 (1995), pp. 51–61; Goodman, 'Languages of female colonial authority'.
40. As Howard wrote in *The Yorkshireman* in 1833: 'While other Christians have been rough-hammering the heathen abroad, and thus making converts *in their way*, it has been *our* proper business, to be filing and polishing those who were already of the household of faith.' *The Yorkshireman: A Religious and Literary Journal, by a Friend* (Pontefract, March 1833), no. xi, p. 274. It was not until 1866 that the first official Quaker missionary, Rachel Metcalfe, left for India. Isichei, *Victorian Quakers*, p. 13.
41. Howard talked of the 'frigid indifference' that Kilham's proposals received from the Friends. *The Yorkshireman* (March 1833), p. 274.
42. Anon, *Address to Friends, on a Proposal made by a Member of our Society to Instruct some African Negroes, with a View to the Future Translation of the Scriptures, or some Portions of them, in the Languages of Africa* (1820, Library of the Religious Society of Friends).

43. For the developing tradition of Quaker women as authoritative educators, see Goodman, 'Languages of female colonial authority'.
44. Sandanee and Mahmadee both spoke the language now known in Senegal as Jolof and in the Gambia as Wolof; Sandanee also spoke Mandingo. Kilham variously refers to Wolof as Wolof, Waloof and Jaloof. For discussion of the Wolof and Mandingo peoples, see Harry A. Gailey, *A History of the Gambia* (London: RKP, 1964), pp. 10–13.
45. See John D. Crosfield, 'Richard Smith and his journal', *Journal of the Friends' Historical Society*, vol. 14, no. 3 (1917), p. 110; William Singleton, *Report of the Committee Managing a Fund Raised by some Friends, for the Purpose of Promoting African Instruction; with an Account of a Visit to the Gambia and Sierra Leone* (London: Darton and Harvey, 1822) (Library of the Religious Society of Friends); Alison Twells, '"A State of Infancy": West Africa and Britsh missionaries in the 1820s', *Wasafiri*, no. 23 (Spring 1996), pp. 19–25.
46. The BILS emerged in August 1822 out of the Ladies' Committee for Contributing Clothing towards the Relief of the Distressed. See 'Notice', 23 August 1822; 'Resolution on the formation of the British and Irish Ladies' Society for Improving the Condition and Promoting the Industry and Welfare of the Female Peasantry in Ireland'; 'Report of the Committee for the Relief of the Distressed Districts in Ireland... on the 7th of May 1822' (1823), p. 5 (Irish Relief Fund papers, London Guildhall Library, MS 7466, IRF hereafter). See also Helen Hatton, '"The Largest Amount of Good": Quaker Relief in Ireland' (University of Toronto: unpublished PhD thesis, 1988).
47. *Report of the Committee of the Society for Improving the Condition and Increasing the Comforts of the Irish Peasantry* (London: F. Marshall, 1823), p. 22.
48. These were, primarily, the Hibernian Bible Society (1806), Hibernian School Society (1806), Baptist Society for Ireland (1814), Irish Evangelical Society (1814), Irish branch of the Religious Tract and Book Society (1816), Irish Society for Promoting the Education of the Native Irish through the Medium of their own Language (1818), Scripture Readers Society (1822) and the Ladies' Hibernian Female School Society (1824). As Maria Luddy has shown, membership was overwhelmingly female: in 1816 women made for 82 per cent of the subscribers to the Dublin Female Association, an auxiliary to the Irish Evangelical Society and LMS, founded in 1814. Luddy, *Women and Philanthropy in Nineteenth-Century Ireland,* (Cambridge: Cambridge University Press, 1995) p. 55.
49. Luddy, *Women and Philanthropy in Ireland*, pp. 181–182, 186.

50. Report on the formation of the Ladies' Hibernian Female School Society, 2 July 1823; letter from P. Besnard to H. Kilham, 21 July 1823 (IRF/MS 7466).
51. Biller, *Memoir of Hannah Kilham,* p. 149.
52. See Luddy, *Women and Philanthropy in Ireland,* pp. 68, 74, 21–22, 181–185.
53. Biller, *Memoir of Hannah Kilham,* pp. 37, 159–160, 262–263; Maria Luddy, personal correspondence, 10 May 2004. See also David Hempton and Myrtle Hill, *Evangelical Protestantism in Ulster Society 1740–1890* (London: Routledge, 1992), pp. 47–61, 81–128; D. Cairns and S. Richards, *Writing Ireland: Colonialism, Nationalism and Culture* (Manchester: Manchester University Press, 1989).
54. Dickson, *The Powerful Bond,* p.134.
55. See Kidd, 'Philanthropy and the "Social History Paradigm"'.
56. *Report of the Committee of the Society for Improving the Condition and Increasing the Comforts of the Irish Peasantry, May 1823* (London: F. Marshall, 1823).
57. British and Irish Ladies' Society for Improving the Condition and Promoting the Industry and Welfare of the Female Peasantry in Ireland, *First Report* (London, 1823–1828), vol. 1, pp. 8, 26.
58. Biller, *Memoir of Hannah Kilham.* For English representations of the Irish, see Cairns and Richards, *Writing Ireland.*
59. Kilham, 'Thoughts for the House', reprinted in the British and Irish Ladies' Society (BILS) *Fourth Report* (1826).
60. BILS, *First Report,* p. 26.
61. Report on the Formation of the Ladies Hibernian Female School Society, London 2 July 1823. See also reports of 22 August 1823; 14 January 1824 (IRF/MS 7466).
62. BILS, *Fifth Report,* appendix.
63. BILS, *Second Report,* pp. 28, 32. For the structure of missionary reports, see Natasha Erlank, '"Civilising the African": The Scottish Mission to the Xhosa, 1821–64', in B. Stanley (ed.), *Christian Missions and the Enlightenment* (London: Curzon Press, 2001), pp. 141–168.
64. BILS, *Fifth Report,* p. 5.
65. Biller, *Memoir of Hannah Kilham,* p. 150.
66. BILS, *First Report,* pp. 39–40.
67. BILS, *First Report,* p. 48.
68. Jane Haggis has elaborated this point in her discussion of missionary women in Travancore, south India. '"Good wives" or "dedicated workers"'?
69. BILS, *First Report,* p. 46.
70. Balfour, *A Sketch of the Life of Hannah Kilham,* pp. 29–30.
71. Biller, *Memoir of Hannah Kilham,* pp. 240 and 190.

72. Biller, *Memoir of Hannah Kilham*, p. 183.
73. 'Alcaide' and 'Alikali' are both derived from the Arabic, El Kadi, 'the judge'. Christopher Fyfe, *A History Of Sierra Leone* (London: Oxford University Press, 1962), p. 125.
74. Biller, *Memoir of Hannah Kilham*, pp. 184–185. Note echoes of William Singleton's meeting with King of Combo, who expressed a profound indifference to the missionary agenda, evident in his half-hearted attempt at regal clothing, and his preference to nurse an infant and perform Islamic prayers than to receive the party of Englishmen. Singleton, *Account of a Visit to the Gambia and Sierra Leone*, pp. 47–48.
75. *Missionary Register* (July 1824), p. 297.
76. Biller, *Memoir of Hannah Kilham*, pp. 184–185. For respectability and house building in southern Africa, see Robert Ross, *Status and Respectability in the Cape Colony: A Tragedy of Manners* (Cambridge: Cambridge University Press, 1999), pp. 78–85.
77. Biller, *Memoir of Hannah Kilham*, pp. 178–179.
78. Bathurst, which developed from the British settlement established as a point from which to defeat the slave trade, is now known as Banjul, the capital of the Gambia. Gailey, *A History of the Gambia*.
79. Biller, *Memoir of Hannah Kilham*, pp. 299, 241.
80. *Missionary Register* (1824), p. 224. For accounts of polygamy and the low status of women, see *Missionary Register* (July 1824), pp. 224, 297, 301.
81. *Missionary Register* (July 1824), p. 299.
82. *Missionary Register* (September 1824), p. 397.
83. *Missionary Register* (June 1822), p. 245.
84. *Missionary Register* (September 1824), pp. 394–395, 397; (July 1824), p. 299.
85. *Missionary Register* (September 1824), p. 395.
86. Hannah Kilham to William Allen, 8 March 1824, *Second Report of the Committee on African Instruction* (London: Darton and Harvey, 1824), Appendix, p. 4.
87. Biller, *Memoir of Hannah Kilham*, pp. 221–222.
88. *Missionary Register* (September 1824), pp. 394–395.
89. Kilham, *The Claims of West Africa*, p. 1.
90. Africa was seen, in Philip Curtin's words, 'as it might be... a tabula rasa, ready and waiting for the utopian inscription.' Curtin, *The Image of Africa*, p. vi and p. 116. See also: Fyfe, *A History Of Sierra Leone*, pp. 14–57; Fyfe, 'Freed slave colonies in West Africa', in John Flint (ed.), *The Cambridge History of Africa, Volume 5, from c 1790 to c 1870* (Cambridge: Cambridge University Press, 1976), pp. 170–199; John Peterson, 'The Enlightenment and the founding of Freetown: an interpretation of Sierra

Leone history', C. Fyfe and E. Jones (eds), *Freetown: A Symposium* (Freetown: Sierra Leone University Press, 1968); John Peterson, *Province of Freedom: A History of Sierra Leone 1787–1870* (London: Faber and Faber, 1969); Turner, 'The limits of abolition'; Walls, 'Black Europeans – White Africans, Some missionary motives in West Africa', *The Missionary Movement in Christian History*, pp. 102–110.

91. Bringing with them their own preachers, they were said to have marched ashore singing a hymn of Isaac Watts. Andrew F. Walls, 'The evangelical revival, the missionary movement, and Africa', in M. Noll, D. Bebbington and G. Rawlyk (eds), *Evangelicalism* (Oxford: Oxford University Press, 1994), pp. 310–330; see also Walls, 'A Christian Experiment: The Early Sierra Leone Colony', in G. J. Cumming (ed.), *The Mission of the Church and the Propagation of the Faith*, Studies in Church History (Cambridge: Cambridge University Press, 1970), pp. 107–130; Charles Pelham Groves, *The Planting of Christianity in Africa, Vol I: to 1840* (London: Lutterworth Press, 1964).
92. The Methodists, LMS and Glasgow Missionary Society had sent men in 1797, mostly, with the exception of Henry Brunton, with unhappy outcomes. Fyfe, 'Freed slave colonies'; Erlank, 'Civilising the African'. For Bickersteth's account of Sierra Leone, see the *Missionary Register*, February 1817, pp. 50–57; March 1817, pp. 98–112; April 1817, pp. 159–170; May 1817, pp. 206–212; June 1817, pp. 241–252.
93. Fyfe, 'Freed slave colonies', pp. 181–183.
94. See Walls, 'A Christian experiment'; D. Bruce Hindmarsh, 'Patterns of conversion in early evangelical history and overseas mission experience', in Stanley (ed.), *Christian Missions and the Enlightenment*, pp. 71–98.
95. Kilham, Hannah, *Ta-Re Waloof, Ta-re boo Juk-a: First Lessons in Jaloof* (Coventry: George Stockwell, 1820); *African Lessons: Wolof and English* (London: William Phillips, 1823).
96. Kilham, *Scriptures Selections* (1813); *Questions on the Principles of the Christian Religion* (1817); *Family Maxims* (1817). See also 'Proposed system of school instruction', *Missionary Register* (July 1824), pp. 301–303. The process of reducing African languages to written form was itself seen as civilising. See Howard, *The Yorkshireman* (1832), p. 163.
97. M. G. Jones, *The Charity School Movement. A Study of Puritanism in Action* (London: Frank Cass, 1964).
98. Elizabeth Rowntree to John Rowntree, 4 September 1828, John S. Rowntree (ed.), *The Family Memoir of Joseph Rowntree* (Birmingham, 1868). For Carey, see George Smith, *The Life of William Carey* (London: J. M. Dent, 1878).
99. *Missionary Register* (December 1817), pp. 527–528.

100. Hannah Kilham, *Specimens of African Languages spoken in the Colony of Sierra Leone* (Printed for the Society of Friends Committee for the Promotion of African Instruction, 1828).
101. Hannah Kilham, *Report of a Recent Visit to Sierra Leone* (London: Darton and Harvey, 1828).
102. *Missionary Register*, July 1824, p. 300; July 1830, p. 314; 1831 pp. 308, 375.
103. Threlkeld to George Burder and William Alers Hankey, January 1826, in Niel Gunson, *Australian Reminiscences and Papers of Lancelot E. Threlkeld, Missionary to the Aborigines 1824–1859*, vol. II (Canberra: Australian Institute of Aboriginal Studies, 1974), p. 198.
104. Kilham, *Report of a Recent Visit to Sierra Leone*, p. 7. This was reproduced in the *Missionary Register* (June 1828), pp. 280–286. For Kilham's criticism of missionary attempts 'to force the English language upon the people, despising their own as not worth cultivation', see Kilham to Joseph Rowntree, July 1829 (Library of the Religious Society of Friends).
105. Biller, *Memoir of Hannah Kilham*, p. 207.
106. Hannah Kilham, *The Claims of West Africa to Christian Instruction, through the native languages* (London: Darton and Harvey, 1830), pp. 28, 6.
107. See Singleton, *Account of a Visit to the Gambia and Sierra Leone*, p. 51.
108. John Morgan's Journal, April–October 1823 (WMMS Archive, John Rylands Library, Manchester); John Morgan, *Reminiscences of the Founding of a Christian Mission on the Gambia* (London: Wesleyan Mission House, 1864), pp. 65–68; WMMS, Missionary Notices, vol. III, 1821–1822, pp. 150–151; vol. IV, pp. 247–259. Morgan provides a fascinating account of the abortive WMMS attempt to preach in the strongly Muslim town of Mandinari due to the general 'invincible obstinacy' and argumentativeness of Muslims. *Reminiscences*, pp. 46, 74–75. See also Martha Th. Frederiks, 'Methodists and Muslims in the Gambia: a Case Study', paper given at MMS conference, 'From World Parish to World Church', Sarum College, Birmingham, 2003, p. 2 (copy available from MMS History Project).
109. *Missionary Register*, (July 1830), p. 310.
110. *Extracts from the Letters of Hannah Kilham from Sierra Leone* (Lindfield: C.Greene, 1831), pp. 8–9.
111. See Elbourne, *Blood Ground*, pp. 174, 187–188. See also Elbourne and Ross, 'Combating Spiritual and Social Bondage'.
112. Johnston, 'The book eaters'.
113. They should not be like the CMS, 'so much above the catechists', Biller, *Memoir of Hannah Kilham*, pp. 401, 471.
114. Letters from Hannah Kilham to the Committee of the Friends for Anti-slavery Concerns, 12 April 1830, 2 September 1830 (Library of the Religious Society of Friends).

115. *Missionary Register* (July 1831), p. 310. Examples like this can be found in any edition of this magazine. For the premature impact of disillusioned humanitarianism on missionaries at the Cape, see Price, *Missionary Encounters*.
116. Kilham, *The Claims of West Africa*, p. 9. For Sandanee and Mahmadee, see Twells, 'A State of Infancy'.
117. Kilham, *Report on a Recent Visit to Sierra Leone*, p. 19.
118. Biller, *Memoir of Hannah Kilham*, p. 440.
119. Kilham, *The Claims of West Africa*, p. 8; Biller, *Memoir of Hannah Kilham*, pp. 389, 467.
120. Biller, *Memoir of Hannah Kilham*, p. 286. Catherine Hall has suggested that the 'free villages' of the Caribbean in the 1830s represented ideal societies, 'a dream of a more ordered England', *White, Male and Middle Class: Explorations in Feminism and History* (Cambridge: Polity Press, 1992), p. 243.
121. For St Giles see Donald Lewis, *Lighten Their Darkness: The Evangelical Mission to Working-Class London, 1828–1860* (Westpoint: Greenwood Press, 1986), pp. 35–38. Kilham was involved with the founding of the (Chalmers-inspired) St Giles Committee in 1826.
122. Biller, *Memoir of Hannah Kilham*, pp. 294–295, 279.
123. Biller, *Memoir of Hannah Kilham*, pp. 283–4, 294.
124. Biller, *Memoir of Hannah Kilham*, p. 308; Kilham, *The Claims of West Africa*, p. 7.
125. Peter Williams, ' "The missing link": the recruitment of female missionaries in some English evangelical missionary societies in the nineteenth century', in Bowie, et al. (ed.) *Women and Missions*; Semple, *Missionary Women*.
126. Society for Promoting Female Education in China, India and the East, *Female Agency among the Heathen, as recorded in the History and Correspondence of the Society for Promoting Female Education in the East* (London: Edward Suter, 1850).
127. Thompson, 'The importance of female agency', *Memoirs*, pp. ix, xliii.

5 Trembling Philanthropists? missionary philanthropy under pressure

1. 'Indian missions', *Edinburgh* Review, vol. 12 (April 1808), p. 179; Piggin, *Making Evangelical Missionaries*, pp. 29, 64.
2. For the late-eighteenth-century campaign, see K. H. Strange, *The Climbing Boys: A Study of Sweeps' Apprentices, 1773–1875* (London: Allison and Busby, 1982).
3. *SI*, 25 August 1807, 25 April 1808.

4. *SI*, 11 October 1804; Samuel Roberts, *The Chimney-Sweepers' Boy: A Poem* (Sheffield: J. Montgomery, 1807); and *Tales of the Poor; or, Infant Sufferings* (Sheffield: J. Montgomery, 1813).
5. *SI*, 7 January 1812. See also: *SI*, 25 August 1807, 29 March 1808, 25 April 1808, 28 March 1809, 30 October 1809, 24 April 1810, 21 January 1812, 12 April 1814, 21 May 1815, 21 November 1815, 21 May 1816, 17 December 1816, 1 April 1817, 13 May 1817, 7 April 1818, 8 February 1820, 9 April 1822, 14 September 1824.
6. Samuel Roberts, *Chimney Sweepers' Boys: A Petition to Parliament* (Sheffield: Montgomery and Smith, 1817), See also letter to the *Iris* describing evidence from Sheffield, 5 May 1817.
7. For discussion of the argument that the distance between adults and children increases as civilisation progresses, see Hugh Cunningham, *Children and Childhood in Western Society since 1500* (London: Longman, 1995), p. 5. See also Ludmilla Jordanova, 'Conceptualizing childhood in the eighteenth century: the problem of child labour', *British Journal of Eighteenth Century Studies*, vol. 10 (1987), pp. 189–199.
8. *Observations on the Use of Machinery in the Manufactories of Great Britain Proving it to be the Cause of the Present Stagnation of Trade; and of the Distress Now Prevailing amongst the Industrious Classes of the People, With Remarks on Climbing Boys, and the Treatment of Children Employed in Cotton Manufactories: and on the Rev Malthus's Plan for Preventing the Poor from Intermarrying*, By a Mechanic (London, 1817), p. 13.
9. Charles Lamb, quoted in Cunningham, *Children and Childhood*, p. 60.
10. Samuel Roberts, 'Address', *Chimney Sweepers' Boys*, pp. 10–11.
11. *Chimney Sweeping Described, with a View to the Emancipation of Climbing Boys, by a Chimney Sweeper* (London: S. Bagster, 1816), p. 3.
12. The Moravian mission to Greenland was the subject of James Montgomery's 1819 poem, *Greenland and other Poems*.
13. Roberts, 'Address', *Chimney Sweepers' Boys* (1817), pp. 14, 18.
14. This had been successively postponed and finally 'laughed down' in the Lords by Lord Lauderdale. Lauderdale later lost a grandson in a fire, seen by evangelicals to be poignant and by Samuel Roberts as 'retributive justice'. Strange, *The Climbing Boys*, p. 57, and Roberts, *An Address to British Females of every Rank and Station on the Employment of Climbing Boys in Sweeping Chimnies* (Sheffield: Whitaker and Co, 1834), p. 20.
15. Roberts, Samuel, 'On the employment of climbing boys', in James Montgomery (ed.), *The Chimney Sweepers' Friend and Climbing Boys'*

Album, part I (London: Longman and Co., 1824), pp. 250–252, 262–267, 277–287, 300.

16. *SI*, 15 July 1823, reprinted in Montgomery, *The Chimney Sweepers' Friend*, p. 103.
17. Roberts, *An Address to British Females*, p. 17.
18. Roberts, *A Cry from the Chimnies; or, an Integral Part of the Total Abolition of Slavery Throughout the World* (London: Longman, Orme, Brown, Green and Longman, 1837), pp. 10, 22, 29–30.
19. William Cobbett, *Rural Rides*, vol. 1 (London: J. M. Dent, 1953), pp. 296–297 [October 1825]; *Political Register*, 29 May 1830.
20. Roberts, *A Cry from the Chimnies*, p. 30.
21. William Wilberforce to Samuel Roberts, 31 October 1827 (Sheffield City Archives, Letters to Samuel Roberts of Park Grange, Sheffield (SCA/SR hereafter), Bundle 2, 470). See also: Wilberforce to Roberts, 5 December 1811, 5 May 1814, 11 June 1817, 31 October 1817, 22 February 1819, 23 March 1819, 21 April 1819, 23 August 1824, 30 November 1825 (SCA/SR, bundles 1 and 2).
22. For the growth of 'Christian economics', see Hilton, *The Age of Atonement*, especially chapters 2 and 3.
23. Wilbeforce to Roberts, 18 April 1822, 8 October 1822 (SCA/SR, 2/33 and 2/34).
24. Stewart T. Brown, *Thomas Chalmers and the Godly Commonwealth in Scotland* (Oxford: Oxford University Press, 1982), pp. 135, 144.
25. Thomas Chalmers, *The Christian and Civic Economy of Large Towns* (1826), quoted in J. F. McCaffrey, 'Thomas Chalmers and social change', *The Scottish Historical Review*, vol. 60 (1981), pp. 32–60, 44.
26. R. A. Cage and O. A. Checkland, 'Thomas Chalmers and Urban Poverty: the St. John's Parish experiment in Glasgow, 1819–1837', *Philosophical Journal*, vol. 8 (1976), 37–56. For his influence in high places, see William Hanna, *Memoirs of the Life and Writings of Thomas Chalmers*, 4 vols (Edinburgh: Constable, 1849–1852). For Malthus and Chalmers, 'my ablest and best ally', see Brown, *Thomas Chalmers and the Godly Commonwealth*, p. 16; also McCaffrey, 'Thomas Chalmers and social change'; and 'The life of Thomas Chalmers' in A. C. Cheyne (ed.), *The Practical and the Pious* (Edinburgh: St. Andrew's Press, 1985), pp. 31–64.
27. See my Chapter 2. Rack also makes point that 'English precedents existed before Chalmers's work commenced.' H. D. Rack, 'Domestic visitation: a chapter in early nineteenth century evangelism', *Journal of Ecclesiastical History*, vol. xxiv, no. 4 (October 1973), pp. 357–376, 360.

28. R. A. Solway, *Prelates and People: Ecclesiastical Social Thought in England 1783–1852* (London: RKP, 1969), p. 93.
29. Samuel Roberts, *Chartism! Its Cause and Cure. Addressed to the Clergy and Others of Sheffield and Ecclesall* (Sheffield: Whitaker, 1839), p. 5.
30. See Boyd Hilton, 'The role of providence in evangelical social thought' in Derek Beales and Geoffrey Best (eds), *History, Society and the Churches. Essays in Honour of Owen Chadwick* (Cambridge: Cambridge University Press, 1985).
31. According to David Roberts, 'Few phrases were cited more often in the Parliament and the press of the 1840s than the dictum "property has its duties as well as its rights"'. D. Roberts, *Paternalism in Early Victorian England* (London: Croom Helm, 1979), p. 32. For clergy who believed that the Poor Laws themselves were undermining traditional relationships, see Solway, *Prelates and People*, p. 152; A. M. C. Waterman, 'The ideological alliance of political economy and Christian theology 1798–1833', *Journal of Ecclesiastical History*, vol. 34 (April 1983), pp. 231–44, here 242.
32. Samuel Roberts, *England's Glory; or, the Good Old Poor Laws, Addressed to the Working Classes of Sheffield* (Sheffield: Whitaker, 1836), p. 6.
33. Roberts, *England's Glory*, p. 9. See also his denunciation of the aims of the guardians in *The Anti-Bastille. An Address to the Inhabitants of the Ecclesall Bierlow Union* (Sheffield: Whitaker 1841), p. 4.
34. Samuel Roberts, *A Solemn Appeal to Ministers of the Gospel of Every Denomination, on the Subject of the Poor Laws* (Sheffield: Whitaker 1837), p. 9.
35. Samuel Roberts, *Mary Wilden, a Victim of the New Poor Law, or the Malthusian and Marcusian System Exposed* (London: Whittaker and Co., 1839), p. v; *The Anti-Bastille*, pp. 3, 9; *A Solemn Appeal*, p. 9; *England's Glory*, pp. 33, 39; *God's Vengeance for the National Violation of His Laws by the Enactment of the New Poor Law* (Sheffield: Whitaker, 1846). For earlier denunciation of activities of doctors, see *The Lecturers Lectured and the Dissectors Dissected* (Sheffield: A. Whitaker, 1834).
36. Roberts, *Chartism!*, p. 5; *England's Glory*, pp. 17, 54.
37. Roberts, *A Mill-Stone for the Necks of the Child-destroyers* (Sheffield: Saxton and Chalmer 1833), pp. 11–12, 20–21.
38. Roberts, *A Cry from the Chimnies*, p. 27. See also *A Mill-stone*, p. 16.
39. Roberts, *A Mill-stone*, p. 12.
40. Roberts, *The Anti-Bastille*, pp. 5–6.
41. For the extent of its support, see Hilton, 'The role of providence in evangelical social thought', p. 218; also: Peter Mandler, 'Tories and paupers: Christian political economy and the making of the New Poor Law', *The Historical Journal*, vol. 33, no. 1 (1990),

pp. 81–103; 83; Nigel Scotland, *The Life and work of John Bird Sumner, Evangelical Archbishop* (Herefordshire: Gracewing books, 1995); Solway, *Prelates and People*.

42. Samuel Roberts had initially 'stood alone' on the issue of immediatism among the men of Sheffield. Roberts, *Autobiography and Select Remains*, p. 3.
43. Cecil Driver, *Tory Radical: The Life of Richard Oastler* (Oxford: Oxford University Press, 1946), p. 50.
44. Driver, *Tory Radical*, pp. 19–20.
45. Oastler, 'Yorkshire slavery', *Leeds Mercury*, 16 October 1830 and 'Humanity against tyranny' (sixth letter), quoted in Driver, *Tory Radical*, pp. 42–44, 104. For the 'melodramatic mode', see Elaine Hadley, *Melodramatic Tactics: Theatricalized Dissent in the English Marketplace, 1800–1885* (California: Stanford University Press, 1995), p. 3.
46. For objections to the model of freedom implicit in the abolitionist campaign, see Catherine Gallagher, *The Industrial Reformation of English Fiction: Social Discourse and Narrative Form, 1832–1867* (Chicago: University of Chicago Press, 1985), pp. 22–25; R. Q. Gray, *The Factory Question and Industrial England, 1830–1860* (Cambridge: Cambridge University Press, 1996).
47. Oastler, 1831, quoted in Driver, *Tory Radical*, p. 120.
48. Samuel Roberts, *England's Passing Bell* (London: Benjamin Steill; and Sheffield: Whitaker, 1834), p. 11; *The Pauper's Advocate, A Cry from the Brink of the Grave against the New Poor Law* (London: Sherwood and Co.; Sheffield: Whitaker, 1841), p. 13.
49. Roberts, *Paternalism in Early Victorian England*, pp. 149–153.
50. Roberts, *Chartism!*, p. 4. See also *A Mill-stone*, p. 11; and *A Dry Crust of the Ecclesall Bierlow Pauper Bread* (Sheffield: Whitaker and Co., 1843).
51. Roberts, *A Mill-stone*, frontispiece; *England's Glory*, p. 10, frontispiece; *England's Passing Bell*; *Mary Wilden*, frontispiece; *The Pauper's Advocate*. See also Roberts, *The Wickedness of the New Poor Law, addressed to Serious Christians of all denominations, with an appeal to the clergy* (Sheffield: Whitaker, 1839); and *The Bone-Gnawing System, addressed to Michael Hunter Esq., the Deputy Chairman of the Sheffield Board of Guardians* (Sheffield: William Ford, 1845).
52. Eileen Yeo, 'Christianity in Chartist struggle 1838–1842', *Past & Present*, no. 91 (1981), pp. 109–139; and 'Chartist religious belief and the theology of liberation', in James Obelkevich, Lyndal Roper and Raphael Samuel (eds), *Disciplines of Faith: Studies in Religion, Politics and Patriarchy* (1987), pp. 410–421. See also Michael S. Edwards, *Purge this Realm: the Life of Joseph Rayner Stephens* (London: Epworth Press, 1994).

53. Gray, *The Factory Question*, p. 50.
54. Cobbett, *Rural Rides*.
55. Seymour Drescher, 'Cart whip and billy roller: antislavery and reform symbolism in industrializing Britain', *Journal of Social History*, vol. 15 (1981), pp. 3–24, and David Turley, *The Culture of English Antislavery, 1780–1860* (London: Routledge, 1991), chapter 4.
56. Quoted by Yeo, *The Contest for Social Science*, p. 35.
57. Claeys, *Machinery, Money and the Millenium*, pp. xxii–xxvii; Noel W. Thompson, *The People's Science: The popular political economy of exploitation and crisis, 1816–1834* (Cambridge: Cambridge University Press, 1984).
58. Samuel Roberts, *Wisdom, Its Nature and Effects, portrayed in a letter to the Reverend Thomas Allin on the Subject of the Sheffield Mechanics' Institute* (Sheffield: George Ridge, 1833), p. 14.
59. Roberts, *England's Crisis; A Letter to the Members of the Sheffield Mechanics' Institute and the Workmen in General* (Sheffield: Ridge, 1832), p. 7. See also Samuel Roberts, *Corn Law Prose* (Sheffield: Whitaker, 1834).
60. Roberts, *Paternalism in Early Victorian England*, pp. 72, 44. For Tories who were led towards state interventionism, for whom the state could fulfil a paternal duty as a 'Universal Parent', see J. Douglas Holladay, '19th Century Evangelical Activism from private charity to state intervention, 1830–50', *Historical Magazine of the Protestant Episcopalian Church*, vol. 1 (1982), pp. 53–79, here pp. 64–65.
61. See Chapter 3, p. 100.
62. Samuel Roberts to Mary-Anne Rawson, 20 April 1839 (MAR/HJW MD 5693).
63. Roberts, *Wisdom, its Nature and Effects*, p. 14. See also *England's Crisis*. It was from such a critique that the Church of England Instruction Society was formed in 1839. George Calvert Holland, *Vital Statistics of Sheffield* (London: Robert Tyas, 1843), p. 231.
64. Roberts, *The Lecturers Lectured*, p. 7.
65. Roberts, 'To the editors of the Sheffield Iris', *SI*, 7 September 1839.
66. James Montgomery, *An Essay on the Phrenology of the Hindoos and Negroes* (London: E. Lloyd and Co., 1827). For phrenology in Sheffield, see: *SI*, 31 August 1824, 25 January, 8 February 1825. For the enthusiasm surrounding Spurzheim's visit and lecture series, see *Sheffield Independent*, 3, 10, 31 January 1829. See also Ian Inkster, 'A phase in middle-class culture: phrenology in Sheffield, 1824–1850', in *Transactions of the Hunter Archaeological Society*, vol. 10, pt. 4 (1977), pp. 273–277.
67. Dr George Murray Paterson, 'On the phrenology of Hindostan', *Transactions of the Phrenological Society* (Edinburgh, 1824). Cited in

Crispin Bates, 'Race, Caste and Tribe in Central India: The Early Origins of Indian Anthropometry', Edinburgh Papers in South Asian Studies No. 3 (University of Edinburgh Centre for South Asian Studies, 1995), pp. 1–35, 3.

68. *SI*, 31 August 1824, 28 January and 4 February 1825.
69. Montgomery, *Phrenology of the Hindoos and Negroes*, pp. 12–13.
70. For Sandanee's dream and his subsequent lapse, see Twells, '"A State of Infancy"'.
71. Montgomery, *Phrenology of the Hindoos and Negroes*, pp. 26, 30–31.
72. Corden Thompson, 'On the Phrenology of the Hindoos and Negroes, showing, that the actual character of nations, as well as of individuals, may be modified by moral, political, and other circumstances, in direct contradiction to their cerebral developments', *An Essay on the Phrenology of the Hindoos and Negroes, by James Montgomery. Together with Strictures thereon by Corden Thompson* (London: E. Lloyd and Co., 1827).
73. Roger Cooter, *The Cultural Meaning of Popular Science: Phrenology and the Organization of Consent in Mid-Nineteenth Century Britain* (Cambridge: Cambridge University Press, 1984), pp. 114–117, here p. 114.
74. Cooter, *The Cultural Meaning of Popular Science*, pp. 67–98; Arnold Thackray, 'Natural knowledge in a cultural context: the Manchester model', *American Historical Review*, vol. 79 (1974), pp. 672–709; Ian Inkster, 'The social context of an educational movement: a revisionist approach to the English Mechanics' Institutes, 1820–1850', in Inkster (ed.), *Scientific Culture and Urbanisation in Industrialising Britain* (Aldershot: Ashgate, 1997).
75. Hilary Marland, *Medicine and Society in Wakefield and Huddersfield 1780–1850* (Cambridge: Cambridge University Press, 1989).
76. Ian Inkster, 'Marginal men: aspects of the social role of the medical community in Sheffield 1790–1850', in John Woodward and David Richards (eds), *Health Care and Popular Medicine in Nineteenth Century England. Essays in the Social History of Medicine* (New York: Holmes and Meier, 1977), pp. 128–163.
77. Robert Gray, 'Medical men, industrial labour and the State in Britain, 1830–50', *Social History*, vol. 16, no. 1 (January 1991), pp. 19–43.
78. See for example G. C. Holland, *Inquiry into the Condition of the Cutlery Trade* (February 1842) and *Diseases of the Lungs from Mechanical Causes; and Inquiries into the Condition of the Artisans Exposed to the Inhalation of Dust* (London [printed], 1843).
79. For the incidence of overlap between members of the Literary and Philosophical Society, the Mechanics' and Apprentices' Library

and the Mechanics' Institute, see Caroline O. Reid, 'Middle-Class Values and Working-Class Culture in Nineteenth-Century Sheffield' (University of Sheffield: Unpublished PhD thesis, 1976), chapter 19. For the statistical movement, see Michael J. Cullen, *The Statistical Movement in Early Victorian Britain: The Foundations of Empirical Social Research* (Brighton: Harvester Press, 1975), pp. 105–117.

80. *SI*, 30 December 1823. See also letter from William Atkins in the *Fourteenth Annual Report of the Sheffield Lancasterian School for Boys* (Sheffield: J. Montgomery, 1823), pp. 3–4; *SI*, 30 August 1823.
81. George Calvert Holland, *Essay on Education, founded on Phrenological Principles* (London: Longman, Rees, Orme, Brown and Green, 1828).
82. See Steven Shapin and Barry Barnes, 'Science, nature and control: interpreting Mechanics' Institutes', *Social Studies of Science*, vol. 7 (1977), 31–74, especially pp. 46–47.
83. Henry Brougham, *Practical Observations upon the Education of the People, Addressed to the Working Classes and their Employers* (Manchester: Archibald Prentice, 1825), pp. 3, 13, 9.
84. Quoted in Shapin and Barnes, 'Science, Nature and Control', p. 58.
85. *SI*, 23 December 1823, 20 December 1823, 6 January 1824, 9 March 1824; Sheffield Mechanics' and Apprentices' Library (Sheffield: Bacon, 1824).
86. Thomas Allin, *Mechanics' Institutes defended on Christian Principles* (Sheffield: T. M. Scott, 1833), p. 10; Sheffield Mechanics' Institute, *Annual Report* (Sheffield: R Leader, 1833), pp. 6, 11–12, 14. See also 'The Utility of Mechanics' Institutes', *SI*, 9 October 1832.
87. 'Report read at the Annual Meeting, 4 November 1833', *Sheffield Mechanics' Institute Minute Book 1832–1836*, vol. I. See also: *Rules of the Sheffield Mechanics' Institution* (Sheffield: Joseph Hawksworth Bramley, 1833); *Rules of the Sheffield Mechanics' Institute as Altered and Amended* (Sheffield: T. Scott, 1834, 1835, 1836); *SI*, 5 June 1838; *Sheffield Mercury*, 6 and 13 July 1839; 'Minutes of the Sheffield Mechanics' Institute', vol. 2, 5 November 1839; *Annual Reports* (Sheffield: E. Smith, 1832 and R. Leader, 1839).
88. *Annual Reports of the Sheffield Mechanics' Institute* (T. Scott, 1834, 1836; J. Pearce, 1835; Saxton and Chaloner, 1837; William Saxton, 1838; R. Leader, 1839; and E. Smith, 1842). See also: John Salt, 'The creation of the Sheffield Mechanics' Institute – social pressures and educational advance in an industrial town', *Vocational Aspects*, vol. 18, no. 40 (Summer 1966), pp. 143–150; Ian Inkster, 'Science and the Mechanics' Institutes, 1820–1850: the case of Sheffield', *Annals of Science*, vol. 32 (1975), pp. 451–474.

89. Charles Favel, *The Value and Importance of Mechanics' Institutions* (Sheffield: Robert Leader, 1836), p. 7; Allin, 'Mechanics' Institutions defended on Christian Principles', pp. 13–14.
90. See Edward Royle, 'Mechanics' Institutes and the Working Classes, 1840–1860', *Historical Journal*, vol. 14 (1971), pp. 305–321; Louis James, *Fiction for the Working Man, 1830–1850: A Study of the Literature Produced for the Working Classes in Early Victorian Urban England* (London: Oxford University Press, 1963); R. Johnson, '"Really Useful Knowledge": radical education and working-class culture, 1790–1848', in J. Clarke, C. Critcher, and R. Johnson (eds) *Working-Class Culture: studies in history and theory* (London: Hutchinson, 1979), pp. 75–102. For the Sheffield Institute, see John Salt, 'The Sheffield Hall of Science', *Vocational Aspect*, vol. 12, no. 25 (1960), pp. 133–138; and 'Isaac Ironside 1808–1870: The motives of a radical educationalist', *British Journal of Educational Studies*, vol. 19 (1971), pp. 183–201.
91. For Mechanics' Institutes nationally, see Mabel Tylecote, *The Mechanics' Institutes of Lancashire and Yorkshire before 1851* (Manchester: Manchester University Press, 1957); J. F. C. Harrison, *Learning and Living, 1790–1960: A Study in the History of the English Adult Education Movement* (London: RKP, 1961), pp. 57–89; Thomas Kelly, *A History of Adult Education in Great Britain* (Liverpool: Liverpool University Press, 1962), pp. 112–133; Silver, *The Concept of Popular Education*, pp. 210–226.
92. See *Annual Reports*, 1833–1842; Minutes, vol. II, 20 January 1840, 14 October 1842, 4 November 1844; Paul Rodgers, *A Lecture on the Origin, Progress and Results of the Sheffield Mechanics' Institution* (Sheffield: J. H. Greaves, 1840), p. 25; Favel, *The Value and Importance of Mechanics' Institutions;* Arnold Knight, *On the Causes which have Contributed to Produce a Greater Degree of Intemperance in the Habits of the People of England than Prevails on the Continent* (Sheffield: R. Leader, 1836).
93. See *Sheffield and Rotherham Independent*, 21 May 1842, 28 May 1842, 5 November 1842; *The Second Annual Report of the Sheffield Town Mission* (Sheffield: Ingham and Co., 1843).
94. See John Seed, 'Unitarianism, political economy and the antinomies of liberal culture in Manchester, 1830–50', *Social History*, vol. 7, no. 1 (January 1982), pp. 1–25; David Turley, 'The Anglo-American Unitarian connection and urban poverty', in Hugh Cunningham and Joanna Innes (eds), *Charity, Philanthropy and Reform from the 1690s to 1850* (Basingstoke: Macmillan, 1998), pp. 228–242. See also David Steers, 'The origin and development of the domestic mission movement especially in Liverpool and

Manchester', *Transactions of the Unitarian Historical Society*, vol. 21, no. 2 (April 1996), pp. 79–103.

95. See Lewis, *Lighten their Darkness*.
96. *The Fifth Annual Report of the Manchester and Salford Town Mission* (Manchester: Simpson and Gillett, 1842), p. 8.
97. *The First Annual Report of the Society for the Promotion of the Religious Instruction of the Poor in Liverpool and the North, or the Liverpool Christian Instruction Society* (Liverpool: D. Marples, 1830). See also: Leeds Town Mission, *First Annual Report* (Leeds: Edward Baines and Sons, 1838), p. 5; *Second Annual Report* (Leeds: Edward Baines and Sons, 1839), p. 2; Manchester and Salford Town Mission, *The First Annual Report of the Manchester and Salford Town Mission* (Manchester: Wm Simpson, 1838).
98. Leeds Town Mission, *Second Annual Report* (1839), p. 2; Manchester and Salford Town Mission, *First Annual Report* (1838), frontispiece.
99. Liverpool Christian Instruction Society, *First Annual Report* (Liverpool: D. Marples, 1830); *Second Annual Report* (Liverpool: D. Marples, 1831), pp. 12–22.
100. Manchester and Salford Town Mission, *First Annual Report*; *Fourth Annual Report*, pp. 1–4. For future visits planned to the Race Course, to Hackney Coachmen, Boatmen and Carters, p. 9.
101. Manchester and Salford Town Mission, *First Annual Report*, pp. 10–11.
102. See Manchester and Salford Town Mission, *Fourth Annual Report*, p. 10.
103. Liverpool Christian Instruction Society, *First Annual Report*, pp. 22–23, 26, 31. Manchester and Salford Town Mission, *First Annual Report*, pp. 13–26; *Third Annual Report* (Manchester: Wm Simpson, 1840), pp. 11–32; *Fourth Annual Report* (Manchester: Wm Simpson, 1841), pp. 10–36; *Fifth Annual Report* (Manchester: Simpson and Gillett, 1842), pp. 11–28; *Sixth Annual Report* (Manchester: Joseph Gillett, 1843), pp. 9–28; *Seventh Annual Report* (Manchester: Ellerby and Cheetham, 1844), pp. 9–28; *Eighth Annual Report* (Manchester: Joseph Gillett, 1845), pp. 9–28; *Ninth Annual Report* (Manchester: Joseph Gillett 1846), pp. 11–28; *Tenth Annual Report* (Manchester: Gillett and Moore, 1847), pp. 19–31. Also Liverpool Christian Instruction Society, *Third Annual Report* (1832), *Fourth Annual Report* (1833), *Fifth Annual Report* (1834), *Sixth Annual Report* (1835), *Seventh Annual Report* (1836), *The Eighth Report of the Liverpool Town Mission, formerly called the Liverpool Christian Instruction Society* (1837), Liverpool Town Mission, *Ninth Annual Report* (1838). See also *Sheffield and Rotherham Independent*, 28 May 1842.

104. See for example Leeds Town Mission, *Second Report* (1838), p. 33; Manchester and Salford Town Mission, *First Annual Report*, p. 9; *Seventh Annual Report*, pp. 5–6; *Eighth Annual Report*, p. 7.
105. Lewis, *Lighten their Darkness*, p. 121.
106. Lewis argues that from 1836, it was recognised that women were needed to work among 'women of bad character' and that women were 'employed' by City Missions prior to Ellen Ranyard's Biblewomen (1857), but were not paid. *Lighten their Darkness*, p. 221.
107. Such as in Manchester in 1837, where missionaries exclaimed at the 'heathenism' of the local poor and reiterated the importance of a domestic focus: 'And this in Manchester! The heathens at a distance very properly engage our attention, but surely heathens at home should not be neglected.' Manchester and Salford Town Mission, *First Annual Report*, pp. 10–11. See also *Sheffield and Rotherham Independent*, 5 November 1842.
108. Holland, *Vital Statistics*, p. 146.
109. For similar developments in Birmingham in the 1840s and 1850s, see Hall, *Civilising Subjects*, pp. 370–373.
110. Holland, *Vital Statistics of Sheffield*, pp. 224–225, 227.
111. For limited instances, see Liverpool Town Mission, *Ninth Report*, p. 8; Manchester and Salford Town Mission, *First Annual Report*, p. 11; 'Social and Physical Influences of the Mission', *Manchester City Missionary Magazine*, February 1848 (Manchester: Ellerby and Sons, 1848), pp. 11–12.
112. Lewis, *Lighten their Darkness*, pp. 124–126.
113. Quoted in J. Drummond and C. B. Upton, *The Life and Letters of James Martineau* I (London: James Nisbet and Co., 1902), p. 89. See also: Cullen, *The Statistical Movement*, p. 110; Anne Holt, *A Ministry to the Poor, being the History of the Liverpool Domestic Mission Society, 1836–1936* (Liverpool: Henry Young and Sons, Ltd, 1936), pp. 16, 38–39, 41; Margaret Simey, *Charitable Effort in Liverpool* (Liverpool: Liverpool University Press), p. 35; Records of the Liverpool Domestic Mission Society, Annual Reports from 1837 (Liverpool Record Office).
114. Seed, 'Unitarianism, political economy and the antinomies of liberal culture', p. 13.
115. Manchester Ministry to the Poor, *Fifth Report* (Manchester: Forrest and Fogg, 1839), pp. 19, 22–23.
116. Manchester Ministry to the Poor, *Fourth Report* (Manchester: Forrest and Fogg, 1837), pp. 14–15; *Fifth Report* (1839), pp. 12, 34–35; *Sixth Report* (Manchester: Thomas Forrest, 1840), pp. 29–30; *Seventh Report* (Manchester: Thomas Forrest, 1841), pp. 13–14, 44, also pp. 12–13; *Eighth Report* (Manchester: Thomas Forrest, 1842)

p. 17. See also the comparable conclusions of G. C. Holland, *An Inquiry into the Moral, Social, and Intellectual Condition of the Industrious Classes* (London: Longman, Orme, Brown, Green and Longman, 1839), pp. vii, 10, 34, 69, 140–143, chapters xi–xvii and *Vital Statistics of Sheffield* (1842). As Edward Royle has suggested, it is instructive to note that Ashworth was not a member of the well-heeled Cross Street congregation, but was a Rossendale handloom weaver and, with Buckland, a (Cookite) Methodist Unitarian. (Personal correspondence, February 2006). For the 'Cookites' see H. McLachlan, *Methodist Unitarian Movement* (1919); and D. A. Gowland, *Methodist Secessions* (1979).

117. Rawson, 'Memorials of James Montgomery.'
118. See for example, Holland and Everett, *Memoirs*, vol. vi, pp. 134–146; *Sheffield Mercury*, 8 October 1842.

6 'A Christian and civilized land': the English missionary public and the South Pacific

1. Stanley, 'Home Support for Overseas Missions', chapter one.
2. Potter, 'The making of missionaries in the nineteenth century', p. 111.
3. J. A. James quoted in Piggin, *Making Evangelical Missionaries*, p. 115.
4. The South Pacific refers to an area covering 49,000 square miles, including Tahiti in the West, through the Cook and Society Islands to the Marquesas in the East and the Sandwich Islands in the North.
5. James Montgomery (ed.), *Journal of Voyages and Travels by the Reverend Daniel Tyerman and George Bennet, Esquire, deputed from the London Missionary Society to Visit their Various Stations in the South Seas, China, India etc, Between the Years 1821 and 1829*, 2 vols (London: Frederick Westley and A. H. Davis, 1831).
6. See Hall, 'The nation within and without', C. Hall, K. McLelland and J. Rendall (eds), *Defining the Victorian Nation: Class, Race, Gender and the Reform Act of 1867* (Cambridge: Cambridge University Press, 2000), pp. 195–197; and *Civilising Subjects*, pp. 338–433.
7. *SI*, 26 November 1842.
8. Robert Moffat, quoted in Thorne, *Congregational Missions*, p. 64.
9. Prochaska, *Women and Philanthropy*, pp. 82–92. See also *Evangelical Magazine*, xx, n.s. (May 1842), p. 247; *The Children's Missionary Meeting in Exeter Hall, on Easter Tuesday, 1842* (London: John Snow, 1842), p. 4.
10. This marked the beginning of a shift by which, by the end of the century, women and children raised roughly 70 per cent of

the income of missionary societies. Prochaska, *Women and Philanthropy*, pp. 82–83. See also, for example, *Early Religion*; or, *A Memoir of Sophia F. Hoare* (Birmingham: J. Groome 1855?); Reverend T. Scott, *Memoir of Mary Scott* (Birmingham: 1855?); Mary Ann Barber, *Missionary Tales, for Little Listeners* (London: J. Nisbet and Co., 1840); *Missionary Stick Gatherers: an Address to the Members of the Juvenile Missionary Associations* (London 1854).

11. Sheffield Church Missionary Association, *The Report of the Church Missionary Association for Sheffield and the Neighbourhood* (Sheffield: Ridge and Jackson, 1842).
12. See for example *SRI*, 2 April 1842, 14 May 1842, 15 October 1842, 23 October 1842, 12 November 1842, 1 April 1843, 8 April 1843, 22 April 1843, 20 May 1843, 20 April 1844, 18 April 1846.
13. *SRI*, 2 April 1842.
14. *SRI*, 15 October 1842, 22 October 1842.
15. *SRI*, 12 November 1842.
16. See for example *SRI*, 18 April 1846, 16 May 1846, 23 May 1846, 22 May 1847. The lady subscribers to the Sheffield CMS were supporting a missionary in India. CMS *Report* (1842).
17. For Williams' death, see Gavan Daws, *A Dream of Islands: Voyages of Self-Discovery in the South Seas* (London: W. W. Norton, 1980), pp. 66–68; Rod Edmond, *Representing the South Pacific: Colonial Discourse from Cook to Gauguin* (Cambridge: Cambridge University Press, 1997), p. 118.
18. See the *Evangelical Magazine*, January 1800, pp. 3–14, 33–35; July 1800, pp. 2895–2896; May 1801, pp. 188–189; July 1802, p. 286; May 1803, pp. 214–220; February 1804, pp. 231, 278, 378; March 1804, pp. 231, 278, 378; March 1808, pp. 137–138; August 1808, p. 354; January 1810, p. 34; December 1813, pp. 473–477; February 1814, p. 174; April 1814, pp. 157–159; July 1814, p. 294; December 1814, p. 499; October 1816, pp. 36, 284, 321; 403, 408, 450; January 1817, pp. 75–76; January 1818, pp. 81–85; Supplement, April 1818, pp. 173–174; December 1818, pp. 572–573; Supplement 1819, pp. 40, 119, 349, 522; August 1821, pp. 349–352.
19. His father, Pomare I, who died in 1803, had been identified as a 'royal' by James Cook. While not kings, the Pomares were powerful men who ruled over the entire island; father and son, were, moreover, pitted against one another in rivalry. Michael Cathcart, Tom Griffiths, Lee Watts, Vivian Anceschi, Greg Houghton and David Goodman (eds), *Mission to the South Seas: The Voyage of the Duff, 1796–1799* (Melbourne: University of Melbourne 1990), p. 57.
20. See Kerry Howe, *Where the Waves Fall: A New South Seas Islands History from First Settlement to Colonial Rule* (Sydney & London: George Allen & Unwin, 1984), pp. 125–151.

21. Lovett, *History of the LMS*, pp. 202–203.
22. George Bennet to James Montgomery, 16 February 1830, 5 June 1830, 3 August 1830, 19 October 1830, April 1833, 19 May 1833, 23 October 1833 (Sheffield City Archives, Sheffield Literary and Philosophical Society, correspondence of James Montgomery (SCA/SLPS hereafter) 36–400, 824, 844, 853, 859, 977, 985, 1000.)
23. Alan Frost, 'The Pacific Ocean: the eighteenth century's "New World"'.
24. D. Charlton, *New Images of the Natural in France* (Cambridge: Cambridge University Press, 1984), p. 124; Dorinda Outram, *The Enlightenment* (Cambridge: Cambridge University Press, 1995), pp. 63–79.
25. John Gascoigne, *Joseph Banks and the English Enlightenment: Useful Knowledge and Polite Culture* (Cambridge: Cambridge University Press, 1994), pp. 149–156 and 172–176.
26. Rendall (ed.), *William Alexander's History of Women.*
27. Gascoigne, *Joseph Banks and the English Enlightenment*, pp. 119–183; Hans Aarsleff, *The Study of Language in England 1780–1860* (London: Athlone Press, 1983), pp. 115–161; Meek, *Social Science and the Ignoble Savage*; Stocking, *Victorian Anthropology*, pp. 8–45.
28. For the 'noble savage', see Bernard Smith, *European Vision and the South Pacific 1768–1850* (London: Oxford University Press, 1960), pp. 8–95. For anti-primitivism, see Nicholas Thomas, 'Liberty and licence; the Forsters' account of New Zealand sociality', in Chloe Chard and Helen Langdon (eds), *Transports: Travel, Pleasure and Imaginative Geography, 1600–1830* (New Haven: Yale University Press, 1996), pp. 243–262.
29. Daws, *A Dream of Islands*, pp. 11–12; Marshall and Williams, *The Great Map of Mankind*, pp. 258–298; Alan Morehead, *The Fatal Impact: An Account of the Invasion of the South Pacific, 1767–1840* (London: Hamish Hamilton, 1966), pp. 72–75.
30. See Introduction, note 35.
31. Thomas Haweis, *Sermon Preached at the Spa Fields Chapel*, 22 September 1795, in *Sermons Preached in London, at the formation of the Missionary Society, September 22, 23, 24 1795* (London: T. Chapman, 1795), pp. 12–13.
32. See for example his epic poems, *The West Indies, and other Poems* (London: Longman, Hurst, Rees, Orme and Brown, 1809) and *Greenland and other Poems* (London: Longman, Rees, Orme and Brown, 1819).
33. *SI*, 4 January 1814, 21 June 1814, 21 November 1815.
34. George Bennet to James Montgomery, 26 September 1823, (SCA/SLPS, James Montgomery Correspondence).
35. *SI*, 14 November 1820 and 6 March 1821.

36. Daniel Tyerman to Rowland Hill, 3 October 1823 (SOAS CWM/LMS, Box 10 (2)). Tyerman (1772–1828), a clergyman from the Isle of Wight, died in Madagascar on the journey home.
37. George Bennet to Rowland Hodgson, 14 January 1822; to James Montgomery, 22 January 1822 and 17 April 1823; to Edmund Read, 14 November 1822; to Catherine and Eliza Read, 30 September 1823; to Elizabeth Read, 29 September 1823, 13 April 1824; to 'my dear friend' (Joseph Read), 30 September 1823 (MAR/HJW MD 5690). For missionary involvement in the coronation ceremony, see Montgomery, *Voyages and Travels*, vol. 2, p. 90.
38. *SI*, 30 November 1824, 24 May 1825; 'Farewell to Tahiti', George Bennet to Elizabeth Read, 13 April 1824 (MAR/HJW MD 5690).
39. *SI*, 10 May 1826.
40. *Evangelical Magazine*, July 1812, pp. 140–141; Joseph Gilbert, 'Address to Sunday School children', *Evangelical Magazine*, May 1814.
41. Josiah Conder, 'The star in the east', Montgomery, *Voyages and Travels*, vol. 1, p. xvi.
42. Montgomery, *Voyages and Travels*, vol. 1, pp. 204, 519; also pp. 147, 172–173, 201–202, 310 and 335–357; vol. 2, pp. 5 and 515.
43. Montgomery, *Voyages and Travels*, vol. 1, p. 85; also pp. 74, 96, 113, 124, 163–164, 181, 265, 277, 285, 458 and 529.
44. Montgomery, *Voyages and Travels*, vol. 1, pp. 71–72, 172–173, 542. For explanations of infanticide, see vol. 1, p. 196.
45. Montgomery, *Voyages and Travels*, vol. 2, p. 5.
46. Montgomery, *Voyages and Travels*, vol. 1, pp. 221, 301, 132 and 218.
47. Montgomery, *Voyages and Travels*, vol. 1, pp. 66, 70 and 145, 512; vol. 2, p. 4. An exchange between Christian Tahitian women who accompanied Bennet and Tyerman to the Sandwich Islands, and Hawaiian women wearing little clothing, reveals the significance of dress to Christian conceptions of womanhood: 'we will not acknowledge you as women', threatened the Tahitians, 'if you do not dress more decently.' *Voyages and Travels*, vol. I, pp. 370–373. For 'bodywork' as part of a more general attempt to construct 'free individuals' and introduce European commodities, see Jean and John Comaroff, *Ethnography and the Historical Imagination* (Oxford: Westview Press, 1992), p. 41; Jean Comaroff, 'The empire's old clothes', in D. Howe (ed.), *Cross-Cultural Consumption: Global Markets, Local Realities* (London: Routledge, 1996), pp. 19–38.
48. Montgomery, *Voyages and Travels*, vol. 1, p. 512; vol. 2, p. 4.
49. Montgomery, *Voyages and Travels*, vol. 1, pp. 76–77, 332 and 463.
50. For the example of Queen Tarouarii on the birth of her daughter, see Montgomery, *Voyages and Travels*, vol. 1, p. 358.

51. Montgomery, *Voyages and Travels*, vol. 2, p. 293.
52. Montgomery, *Voyages and Travels*, vol. 1, p. 204; also vol. 1, p. 143 and vol. 2, p. 5. For evidence concerning missionaries' relationships with native women, and cruelty to their wives, see Gunson, *Messengers of Grace*, pp. 154–157.
53. Montgomery, *Voyages and Travels*, vol. 1, pp. 94, 348, 533; also p. 147. For discussion of a code of laws, courts of justice, trials and punishment, see pp. 91–92, 179–180, 520, 547.
54. Montgomery, *Voyages and Travels*, vol. 1, pp. 132, 245.
55. Montgomery, *Voyages and Travels*, vol. 1, pp. 172–173.
56. Lovett, *History of the London Missionary Society*, p. 292.
57. Montgomery, *Voyages and Travels*, vol. 1, pp. 335, 555.
58. Quoted in Morehead, *The Fatal Impact*, p. 87. Bennet, who was unimpressed upon meeting Kotzebue in March 1824, made notes in the margins of the LMS copy of the *Voyage round the World*: 'false', 'what ignorance', 'what horrid lies'. See also Bennet to Montgomery, 23 December 1830 (SCA/SLPS 36–1522).
59. Montgomery, *Voyages and Travels*, Introduction; see also vol. 1, pp. 437–438. For a fuller engagement with Kotzebue's argument see William Ellis, *A Vindication of the South Seas Missions from the Misrepresentation of Otto von Kotzebue, Captain in the Russian Navy*, (London: Frederick Westley and A. H. Davis, 1831).
60. *SI*, 13 and 20 July 1824.
61. See *The Poetical Works of James Montgomery, Collected by Himself* (London: Longman, Brown, Green and Longman, 1855–1856), especially vols 3 and 4.
62. Ellis, *A Vindication of the South Seas Missions*, p. 161; John Eimeo Ellis, *Life of William Ellis, Missionary to the South Seas and to Madagascar* (London: John Murray, 1873), pp. 125 and 134–135; George Bennet to James Montgomery, 16 March 1831, George Bennet to William Ellis, 23 December 1830 (SA/SLPS 36).
63. Ellis, *A Vindication of the South Seas Missions*, p. 4.
64. See Andrew F. Walls, 'The nineteenth-century missionary as scholar' and 'Humane learning and the missionary movement', *The Missionary Movement in Christian History: Studies in Transmission of Faith* (Maryknoll: Orbis, 1996), pp. 187–198, 199–210.
65. Montgomery, *Voyages and Travels*, vol. 1, pp. 380–383, 412, 419, 422.
66. Montgomery, *Voyages and Travels*, vol. 1, pp. 392, 412–413 and 469–471.
67. Montgomery, *Voyages and Travels*, vol. 2, p. 411; vol. 1, pp. 451, 453, 417.
68. Montgomery, *Voyages and Travels*, vol. 2, pp. 133–136.

69. Daniel Tyerman and George Bennet to George Burder, Sydney, NSW, 12 November 1824 (SOAS CWM/LMS Box 10); Montgomery, *Voyages and Travels*, vol. 2, pp. 130, 174, 141–182, 148.
70. Daniel Tyerman to George Burder, 8 February 1825 (SOAS CWM/LMS Box 10).
71. For the establishment of the mission at Reid's Mistake, see (SOAS CWM/LMS Box 10 and Australia Box 2). For Threlkeld, his stormy relationship with the LMS and his work among aboriginal Australians, see Gunson (ed.), *Australian Reminiscences*.
72. Montgomery, *Voyages and Travels*, vol. 2, p. 143; also 148–150; George Bennet to James Montgomery, 25 December 1824 (SCA/SLPS 36–528).
73. George Bennet and Daniel Tyerman to Governor Brisbane, 11 October 1824 (SOAS CWM/LMS Box 10).
74. George Bennet and Daniel Tyerman to Lancelot Threlkeld, 24 February 1824; George Bennet and Daniel Tyerman to George Burder, 8 December 1825 (SOAS CWM/LMS Box 10); Threlkeld to the LMS, 10 August 1826 (SOAS, CWM/LMS, Australia Box 2).
75. Montgomery, *Voyages and Travels*, vol. 2, p. 167.
76. For the various murders, marriages to native women and abandonments of the first mission, see Niel Gunson, *Messengers of Grace*, pp. 152–157; Cathcart et al., *Mission to the South Seas*.
77. See Twells, 'Missionary "fathers" and Wayward "sons" in the South Pacific, 1797–1825', in Trev Broughton and Helen Rogers (eds), *Gender and Fatherhood in the Nineteenth Century* (Basingstoke: Palgrave, 2007), pp. 153–164.
78. Gunson, *Messengers of Grace*, pp. 40, 114–120, 239–241; Daniel Tyerman to Samuel Marsden, 26 October 1822, 13 November 1822, (SOAS CWM/LMS Box 10); John Davies, *History of the Tahitian Mission 1799–1830*, C. W. Newbury (ed.) (Hakluyt Society and Cambridge University Press, 1961).
79. See Chapter 4, p. 122.
80. Gunson, *Messengers of Grace*, p. 123.
81. For William Ellis's puzzlement at the lack of emotion attendant at conversion, see Gunson, *Messengers of Grace*, p. 223.
82. For discussion of the complexities of letters home and the differences between the formal reports and informal correspondence, see Edmond, *Representing the South Pacific*, pp. 98–129.
83. Lovett, *History of the LMS*, pp. 292–294.
84. Edmond, *Representing the South Pacific*, p. 121.
85. Daniel Tyerman, Report from Huahine, 1822; Report from Eimeo, 1821–1822, August 1821 (SOAS CWM/LMS Box 10). Christian peoples of the Pacific often underwent two conversions, firstly

'from heathenism to Christianity as a system', and later, undergoing a 'faith experience leading to a positive assurance of a new birth.' Alan R. Tippett, quoted in D. Bruce Hindmarsh, 'Patterns of conversion in early evangelical history and overseas mission experience', Stanley (ed.), *Christian Missions and the Enlightenment*, p. 92.

86. Daniel Tyerman, Report, Oct. 1823 (SOAS CWM/LMS Box 10); Montgomery, *Voyages and Travels*, vol. 1, pp. 219, 239. For tattooing, see Harriet Guest, 'Curiously marked: tattooing, masculinity and nationality in eighteenth century British perceptions of the South Pacific', in John Barrell (ed.), *Painting and the Politics of Culture: New Essays in British Art, 1700–1850* (Oxford: Clarendon Press, 1992), pp. 101–134.
87. Daniel Tyerman to Samuel Marsden, 26 October 1822, (SOAS CWM/LMS Box 10).
88. Edmond, *Representing the Pacific*, pp. 124–126.
89. Montgomery, *Voyages and Travels*, vol. 1, p. 102. See C. Hall, 'William Knibb and the constitution of the new black subject', in Daunton and Halpern (eds), *Empire and Others*.
90. Montgomery, *Voyages and Travels*, vol. 1, pp. 66, 79, 75, 81, 102, 200.
91. Montgomery, *Voyages and Travels*, vol. 1, p. 209.
92. Montgomery, *Voyages and Travels*, vol. 1, p. 85.
93. Daniel Tyerman and George Bennet, Haweis Town, Papara, Tahiti, 3 November 1823, (SOAS CWM/LMS Box 10); Montgomery, *Voyages and Travels*, vol. 1, p. 102. See Daws, *A Dream of Islands*, p. 36; Rigby, 'A Sea of Islands: Tropes of Travel and Adventure in the Pacific' (University of Kent: unpublished PhD thesis, 1995), chapter five.
94. Quoted in Morehead, *The Fatal Impact*, p. 85. Morehead also quotes the example of Charles Darwin, who wrote of an occasion when out walking in the mountains with two Tahitian guides in 1835: 'I took with me a flask of spirits which they could not resolve to refuse; but as often as they drank a little, they put their fingers before their mouths and uttered the word, "missionary" ', p. 87.
95. Lovett, *History of the London Missionary Society*, vol. 1, pp. 181, 186, 228–230.
96. Lovett, *History of the London Missionary Society*, vol. 1, p. 290.
97. Lovett, *History of the London Missionary Society*, vol. 1, pp. 291–292. For Aimata, see ' "Think of me as a woman": Queen Pomare of Tahiti and Anglo-French imperial conquest in the 1840s Pacific', *Gender & History*, vol. 18, no. 1 (April 2006), pp. 108–129.
98. Alan Lester, 'British settler discourse and the circuits of Empire', *History Workshop Journal*, vol. 54 (2002), pp. 24–48.

99. Quoted in John Harris, *One Blood: 200 Years of Aboriginal Encounter with Christianity: A Story of Hope* (Sutherland: Albatross Books, 1990), p. 24.
100. Samuel Marsden, 'Report to Archdeacon Scott on the Aborigines of New South Wales', 2 December 1826, quoted in Gunson, *Australian Reminiscences*, pp. 347–349.
101. W. A. Green, 'Was British emancipation a success? The abolitionist perspective', in David Richardson (ed.), *Abolition and its Aftermath* (London: Frank Cass, 1985), pp. 183–303, here pp. 192–193. See also Catherine Hall's discussion of myalism, *Civilising Subjects*, pp. 151–156.
102. Brian Stanley, 'Christian responses to the Indian mutiny of 1857', *The Church and War: Studies in Church History* 20 (1983), pp. 277–289, p. 278.
103. G. A. Oddie, *Social Protest in India: British Protestant Missionaries and Social Reform, 1850–1900* (New Delhi: Manohar 1978), p. 9; Porter, *Religion versus Empire*, p. 164.
104. Richard Price, 'Encounters of Empire: the British, the Xhosa and the Making of an Imperial Culture at the Frontier and at Home 1830–1870' (unpublished paper, 2005), pp. 22–23.
105. Price, 'Encounters of Empire', p. 7; and 'Bad Education: How British Humanitarians Learnt Racism in the Empire, 1840–1860' (unpublished paper, March 2005). See also Bank, 'Losing faith in the civilizing mission'.
106. Price, 'Encounters', pp. 30–31, p. 35. See also Hall, *Civilising Subjects*, for the harsher attitudes of Dawson and that 'the Birmingham missionary public remained focused on "the heathen" ', p. 370.
107. Lizzie Rawson to Mary Wilson, 7 January 1841, 26 July 1843 (MAR/HJW MD 5698).
108. See chapter five.
109. Peter Mandler, 'The problem with cultural history', *Cultural and Social History*, vol. 1, 1 (2004), pp. 94–117; and ' "Race" and "Nation" in mid-Victorian thought', in S. Collini, R. Whatmore and R. Young, *History, Religion and Culture: British Intellectual History 1780–1950* (Cambridge: Cambridge University Press, 2000), p. 232.
110. See Patrick Brantlinger, *Dark Vanishings: Discourse on the Extinction of Primitive Races, 1800–1930* (Ithaca: Cornell University Press, 2003).
111. Charles Dickens, 'The Niger expedition', *Miscellaneous Papers*, vol. 1 (London: Chapman and Hall, 1848).
112. Zemka, *Victorian Testaments*, p. 223.
113. See discussion of women, chapter four.
114. Edmond, *Representing the South Pacific*, p. 107.

115. Quoted in 'George Bennet' (Sheffield City Museums: printed booklet, n.d.), p. 5.
116. Bennet had assumed that a selection would be made for the museum at Rotherham College, unaware that during 1823 science in Sheffield had become best represented by the newly-formed Literary and Philosophical Society. Letters from George Bennet to James Montgomery, 10 August 1823, 26 January 1824, 17 May 1824 (MAR/HJW MD 5690).
117. Montgomery, *Voyages and Travels*, vol. 1, p. 85, vol. 2, p. 527; see also George Bennet and Daniel Tyerman to John Arundell, 21 May 1823 and 29 September 1823 (SOAS CWM/LMS, Box 10). Other material was sent to the Lit and Phil museums at Leeds, Whitby and Saffron Waldon. George Bennet to James Montgomery, 15 May 1826 (SCA/SLPS); George Bennet to John Arundell, 21 May 1823 and 29 September 1823 (SOAS CWM/LMS, Box 10); Edward Mcoy to James Montgomery, 9 April 1824 (SCA/SLPS 36–460); 10 May 1824 (MAR/HJW MD 5690).
118. Some of these artefacts remain in Sheffield City Museums today. Others formed part of a collection deposited in the British Museum in 1871. Other Bennet material is in the Cambridge University Museum of Archaeology and Anthropology, acquired in 1891 from Sheffield Museum. Bennet material from Leeds, Sheffield and Saffron Waldon was acquired for the Hooper Collection; most of this has now gone to the Tahiti Museum. See Sheffield City Museums, 'George Bennet' (printed pamphlet, n.d.).
119. Sheffield Literary and Philosophical Society, *Annual Reports* (Sheffield: William Todd, 1825), p. 11; (Sheffield: J. Blackwell, 1826), pp. 12–13; (Sheffield: George Ridge, 1827), p. 11; (Sheffield: George Ridge, 1832), p. 5; (Sheffield: Robert Leader, 1833); (Sheffield: Leader and Sons, 1886), p. 25.
120. Sivasundaram, *Nature and the Godly Empire*.
121. Ebenezer Prout, *Memoirs of the life of the Rev. John Williams*, p. 454, quoted in Sivasundaram, *Nature and the Godly Empire*, pp. 120–121.
122. Brian Durrans, 'The future of the other: changing cultures on display in ethnographic museums', Robert Lumley (ed.), *The Museum Time-Machine: Putting Cultures on Display* (London: Routledge, 1988), pp. 144 and 169.
123. Ludmilla Jordanova, 'Objects of knowledge: a historical perspective on museums', in Peter Vergo (ed.), *The New Museology* (London: Reaktion Books Ltd, 1989), pp. 22–40, here p. 32; also Susan M. Pearce, *Museums, Objects and Collections: A Cultural Study* (Leicester: Leicester University Press, 1992).
124. Sivasundaram, *Nature and the Godly Empire*, pp. 181–185.

125. Sheffield Literary and Philosophical Society, *Annual Report of the Sheffield Literary and Philosophical Society* (Sheffield: George Ridge, 1841).
126. Sheffield Literary and Philosophical Society, *Annual Report of the Sheffield Literary and Philosophical Society* (Sheffield: George Ridge, 1842).
127. See endnotes 11–16 in this chapter for reports of the popularity of missionary culture in 1840s Sheffield.
128. Hill, *Culture and Class in English Public Museums*, pp. 36–37.
129. Gunn, *The Public Culture of the Victorian Middle Class*, p. 163.
130. On the importance of parks and gardens for civilising the poor, see for example, Knight, *On the Causes which have Contributed to Produce a Greater Degree of Intemperance*.
131. Binfield, et al. (eds), *The History of Sheffield, 1843–1993, Vol II: Society*, pp. 3–4, 20.
132. For the extent of participation, the interdenominational character of the event and the gendered nature of middle-class public culture, see *The Death of James Montgomery, Esq., with a Sketch of his life, and an account of his public funeral* (Sheffield: Leader, 1854).
133. See Gunn, *The Public Culture of the Victorian Middle Class*, chapter seven.
134. Felix Driver and David Gilbert, *Imperial Cities: Landscape, Display and Identity* (Manchester: Manchester University Press, 1999), p. 3.

Conclusions

1. See Stepan, *The Idea of Race in Science*; Christine Bolt, *Victorian Attitudes to Race* (London: Routledge & Kegan Paul, 1971); Hall, *Civilising Subjects*, pp. 357–354, 275–280; Thorne, *Congregational Missions and the Making of an Imperial Culture*, pp. 90–91; Brantlinger, *Dark Vanishings*. Interestingly, for the argument that racism came home from the colonies (see chapter six), Robert Knox was a surgeon at the Cape to British military forces between 1817 and 1821. Bank, 'Losing Faith in the civilising mission', p. 380.
2. Porter, *Religion Versus Empire?* pp. 163–164.
3. See Lorimer, *Colour, Class and the Victorians*, pp. 82–86.
4. *Sheffield Mercury*, 2 August 1834; *SI*, 5 August 1834. By the time of the abolition of apprenticeship in 1838, however, the emphasis was less on celebrations than on Maynooth, Daniel O'Connell and Chartism. *Sheffield Mercury*, 4 August 1838; *SI*, 7 August 1838.
5. See Hall, *Civilising Subjects*; Thorne, *Congregational Missions*, chapter four.
6. Yeo, *Contest for Social Science*, chapter five; Helen Rogers, *Women and the People: Authority, Authorship and the Radical Tradition in*

Nineteenth-Century England (Aldershot: Ashgate, 2000), chapter five.

7. A. J. Hammerton, *Emigrant Gentlewomen: Genteel Poverty and Female Emigration, 1830–1914* (London: Croom Helm, 1979).
8. See Brett Christophers' discussion of domesticity in relation to missions in British Columbia. *Positioning the Missionary*, chapter three, especially pp. 50–59.
9. See Rhonda Semple, *Missionary Women.*
10. Antoinette Burton, *Burdens of History.*
11. Holland and Everett, *Memoirs of James Montgomery, Vols 5–7*; Bell, *Peeps into the Past.*
12. Mary-Anne Rawson's diaries (MAR/HJW MD 5706); letters from Alessandro Gavazzi to Mary-Anne Rawson, May 1859 and 27 September 1865 (MD 5700). See also poems on Gavazzi at Wincobank, and extract from *SRI*, 2 July 1853 (MD 5700). For this particular mother and daughter, travel to southern Europe was also about health: Lizzie had tuberculosis, from which she was to die in 1862.
13. Williams, Peter 'The missing link'; and Potter, 'The making of missionaries in the nineteenth century'.
14. Tim Jeal, *Livingstone* (London: Heinemann, 1973), pp. 1–3, 39, 163. See also Price, 'Encounters of empire', p. 31.
15. Porter, *Religion Versus Empire?*, pp. 163–164; Livingstone quoted in Jeal, *Livingstone*, pp. 146, 124.
16. Jeal, *Livingstone*, p. 3. For female missionaries after 1857, see Geraldine H. Forbes, 'In search of the pure heathen': missionary women in nineteenth century India', *Economic and Political Weekly*, vol. 21, pt. 17 (1986), pp. 2–8. For Livingstone's significance, see also M. Oliphant, 'The missionary explorer', *Blackwood's Magazine*, vol. 83 (April 1858), pp. 385–401. I am grateful to Anna Afanassieva for this reference and discussion of Livingstone's popularity (personal correspondence, January 2006). See also John MacKenzie, 'Heroic myths of empire', in John MacKenzie (ed.), *Popular Imperialism and the Military 1850–1950* (Manchester: Manchester University Press, 1992), pp. 109–138.
17. Elbourne, *Blood Ground*, pp. 26, 44, 56–59.

Bibliography

Manuscript collections

Sheffield City Archives

Mary Anne Rawson Collection, H. J. Wilson Papers
James Montgomery Letters and Papers
Samuel Roberts Letters

Sheffield University Library

James Montgomery Manuscripts
Mary Anne Rawson, 'Memorials of James Montgomery, consisting of portraits, letters with explanatory notes, personal recollections, and notices of some of his friends' (1857).

John Rylands Library, Manchester

Mary Anne Rawson Papers
Methodist Missionary Archive

SOAS Library

Council for World Mission/London Missionary Society Archive

Birmingham University Library

Church Missionary Society Archive

Library of the Religious Society of Friends

Richard Smith's Journal
Reports of the African Instruction Committee
London Guildhall Library, Manuscript Collection Irish Relief Fund Papers, 1822–1843

Newspapers and periodicals

The Amulet
Baptist Magazine
Cobbett's Political Register
The Evangelical Magazine
The Missionary Register
Sheffield Iris
Sheffield Mercury
Sheffield and Rotherham Independent
The Yorkshireman: A Religious and Literary Journal, by a Friend

Books, articles, pamphlets and speeches published before 1940

A Short History of the Upper Wincobank Chapel (Sheffield: Ward, 1908).

African Instruction Committee, *Circular to Subscribers of the Committee for African Instruction* (1820).

African Instruction Committee, *Report of the Committee Managing a Fund Raised by Some Friends, for the Purpose of Promoting African Instruction: With an Account of a Visit to the Gambia and Sierra Leone* (London: Darton and Harvey, 1822, 1823–1825).

——, *Circular from the Committee on African Instruction to the Subscribers* (London: Darton and Harvey, 1825).

Allin, Thomas, *Mechanics' Institutions Defended on Christian Principles. A Lecture Delivered on the Opening of the Sheffield Mechanics' Institute on the 14th January 1833* (Sheffield: T. Scott, 1833).

Anon., *Address to Friends, on a Proposal made by a Member of our Society to Instruct Some African Negroes, with a View to the Future Translation of the Scriptures, or Some Portions of Them, in the Languages of Africa* (1820).

An Appeal of the Friends of the Negro to the British People on Behalf of the Slaves in their Colonies (Sheffield: J. Blackwell, 1830).

Appeal to the Christian Women of Sheffield from the Association for the Universal Abolition of Slavery (Sheffield: R. Leader, 1837).

Balfour, Clara Lucas, *A Sketch of the Life of Hannah Kilham* (London: W. and F. G. Cash, 1854).

Ball, Dinah, *The Missionary Society, A Dialogue* (Sheffield: James Montgomery, n.d.).

Barber, Mary Ann, *Missionary Tales, for Little Listeners* (London: J. Nisbet and Co. 1840).

Bell, Alexander B. (ed.), *Peeps into the Past, Being Passages from the Diary of Thomas Asline Ward* (Sheffield: Leng and Co., 1909).

Bell, Andrew, *An Analysis of the Experiment in Education, Made at Egmore, Near Madras* in 1797, 3rd edition (London: Cadell and Davies, 1807 [1797]).

Benson, Jane, *From the Lune to the Neva, Sixty Years Ago* (London: Samuel Harris, 1879).

Bernard, Sir Thomas, 'Extract from an Account of the Free School for Boys at Sheffield, 1812' (Sheffield Local Studies Library: Local Pamphlets, vol. 87, no. 5).

——, 'Extract from an Account of the Juvenile Bible Society at Sheffield, 1814' (Sheffield Local Studies Library: Local Pamphlets, vol. 87, no. 7).

Bernard Baker, J. (ed.), *Pleasure and Pain, 1780–1818* (London: John Murray, 1930).

Best, Thomas, *Memoranda of the Late Ann Harrison* (Sheffield: George Ridge, 1860).

Beverley, R. M., *A Speech on Negro Apprenticeship, Delivered in the Cutler's Hall, Sheffield, on Monday Evening, February 12 1838* (London: Simpkin, Marshall and Co., 1838).
Biddulph, Rev. TT., *The Duty of Communicating the Bread of Life to the Heathen World, Considered in a Sermon* (Birmingham: Thos Knott, 1815).
Biller, Sarah (ed.), *Memoir of the Late Hannah Kilham* (London: Darton and Harvey, 1837).
Blackwell, John, *The Sheffield Directory and Guide* (Sheffield: J. Blackwell, 1828).
Blackwell, John, *Life of Alexander Kilham* (London: R. Groombridge, 1838).
Boden, Reverend James, *Religion and Loyalty United: A Discourse Addressed to the Congregation Assembling in Queen Street Chapel, Sheffield, October 25 1809* (Sheffield: J. Montgomery, 1809).
Boys' Charity School, *Sheffield, Bi-Centenary, 1706–1906. History of the Institution* (Sheffield: Loxley Brothers, 1905).
Bridgeford, John et al., *To the Members of the Sheffield Mechanics' Library and the Inhabitants of the Town generally* (Sheffield: Scott, 1832).
British and Irish Ladies' Society, *Reports of the British and Irish Ladies' Society*, 5 vols (1823–1828).
Brougham, H., *Practical Observations upon the Education of the People, Addressed to the Working Classes and their Employers* (Manchester: Archibald Prentice, 1825).
Bunting, Jabez, *Memoir of the Late Thomas Holy Esq of Sheffield* (London: James Nicholls, 1832).
Buzacott, Aaron, *Mission Life in the Islands of the Pacific* (London: John Snow, 1866).
Carey, William, *An Enquiry into the Obligation of Christians to use Means for the Conversion of the Heathens in which the Religious State of the Different Nations of the World, the Success of Former Undertakings, and the Practicability of Further Undertaking, are Considered* (Leicester: Ann Ireland, 1792).
Carlyle, Thomas, 'Occasional Discourse on the Negro Question', *Fraser's Magazine*, vol. 40 (December 1849).
Catalogue of Books of the Sheffield Mechanics' and Apprentices' Library (Sheffield: T. Scott, 1845).
Chapman, Priscilla, *Hindoo Female Education* (London: Seeley and Burnside, 1839).
Chimney Sweeping Described, with a View to the Emancipation of Climbing Boys, by a Chimney Sweeper (London: S. Bagster, 1816).
Clough, Margaret M., *Extracts from the Journal and Correspondence of the Late Mrs M. M. Clough, Wife of the Rev. Benjamin Clough, Missionary in Ceylon.* (London: J. Mason, 1829).
Cobbett, William, *Rural Rides*, vol. 1 (London: Dent, 1912 [1825]).

Coke, Thomas, *Address to the Pious and Benevolent, Proposing an Annual Subscription for the Support of Missionaries in the Highlands and Adjacent Islands of Scotland, the Isles of Jersey, Guernsey and Newfoundland, the West Indies, and the Provinces of Nova Scotia and Quebec* (London, 1786).

——, *Account of the Rise, Progress, and Present State of the Methodist Missions* (London: Conference Office, 1804).

Cotterill, Thomas, *A Speech Delivered at the First Anniversary of the Church Missionary Association in Sheffield* (1817).

Crothers, Hamilton, *The Methodist New Connexion 1797–1897: A Centenary Review* (Sheffield: Sheffield Independent Press, 1897).

Dickens, Charles, 'The Niger expedition', *Miscellaneous Papers*, vol. 1 (London: Chapman and Hall, 1848).

——, *Bleak House* (Basingstoke: Macmillan, 1987 [1853]).

Dudley, Charles S., *An Analysis of the System of the Bible Society Throughout its Various Parts. Including a Sketch of the Origin and Results of Auxiliary and Branch Societies and Bible Associations with Hints for their Better Regulation* (London: BFBS, 1821).

Edwards, Jonathan, *Life of David Brainerd, Missionary to the American Indians*, with an introduction by James Montgomery (Glasgow: Collins, 1828).

Elliott, Ebenezer, 'The Ranter', *The Splendid Village: Corn Law Rhymes; and other Poems* (Sheffield: J. Pearce, 1833), pp. 144–156.

Ellis, John Eimeo (ed.), *Life of William Ellis* (London: John Murray, 1873).

Ellis, Samuel, *Novel-Reading Intellectually and Morally Injurious* (Sheffield: T. Scott, 1845).

——, *Life, Times and Character of James Montgomery* (London: Jackson, Walford and Hodder, 1864).

Ellis, Sarah Stickney, *The Women of England, Their Social Duties, and Domestic Habits* (London: Fisher, Son and Co., 1839).

——, *The Daughters of England, Their Position in Society, Character and Responsibilities* (London: Fisher, Son and Co., 1842).

——, *The Wives of England, Their Relative Duties, Domestic Influence and Social Obligations* (London: Fisher, Son and Co., 1843).

——, *The Mothers of England, Their Influence and Responsibility* (London: Fisher, Son and Co., 1843).

Ellis, William, *Narrative of a Tour Through Hawaii, or Owhyee; with Observations on the Natural History of the Sandwich Islands and Remarks on the Manners, Customs, Traditions, History and Language of their Inhabitants*, 2nd edition (London: H. Fisher, Son and P. Jackson, 1827).

——, *Polynesian Researches, During a Residence of Nearly Eight Years in the Society and Sandwich Islands* (London: H. Fisher, Son and P. Jackson, 1831).

——, *A Vindication of the South Seas Missions from the Misrepresentation of Otto von Kotzebue, Captain in the Russian Navy* (London: Frederick Westley and A. H. Davis, 1831).

—— (ed.), *The Missionary; or, Christian's New Year's Gift* (London: Seeley and Sons, 1832).

——, *Memoir of Mary M. Ellis, Wife of the Rev. William Ellis, Missionary to the South Seas, and Foreign Secretary of the London Missionary Society* (London: Fisher, Son and Co., 1835).

Everett, James, *Historical Sketches of Wesleyan Methodism in Sheffield and the Vicinity* (Sheffield: James Montgomery, 1823).

Favel, Charles, *The Value and Importance of Mechanics' Institutions. An Address, Delivered on Monday Evening, the 29th of May, 1836, before the Managers, Teachers, Members and Friends of the Sheffield Mechanics' Institution* (Sheffield: R. Leader, 1836).

Foster, Eliza Ann, *Memoirs of Mrs. Eliza Ann Foster: Wife of H.B. Foster, Wesleyan Missionary, Jamaica. Compiled from her Diary and Correspondence. By her Husband* (London: John Mason, 1844).

Fuller, Andrew, *The Gospel of Christ Worthy of all Acceptation: or the Obligations of Men Fully to Credit, and Cordially to Approve, Whatever God Makes Known* (Northampton: T. Dicey, 1785).

Gaskell, Elizabeth, *Mary Barton. A Tale of Manchester Life* (Harmondsworth: Penguin, 1994 [1848]).

——, *North and South* (Harmondsworth: Penguin, 1994 [1854–1855]).

Gilbert, Ann Taylor, *Original Anniversary Hymns, Adapted to the Public Services of Sunday Schools and Sunday School Unions* (London: B.J. Holdsworth, 1827).

——, *Biographical Sketch of the Rev. Joseph Gilbert, by his Widow. With Recollections of the Discourses of his Closing Years, from Notes at the Time, by One of his Sons* (London: Jackson and Walford, 1853).

Gilbert, Ann Taylor ('A Rustic Rambler') and R. M. Beverley, Esq, *Letters on the Subject of Dr Knight's Lecture* (Sheffield: R. Leader, 1836).

Gilbert, Joseph, *Christian Benevolence; a Sermon Preached at Sheffield, June 7 1813, before the Teachers and Superintendents of the Sunday School Union; to which is Annexed an Address to the Children* (Sheffield: J. Montgomery, 1813).

Gilbert, Josiah (ed.), *Autobiography and other Memorials of Mrs Gilbert* (London: Henry S. King, 1874).

Greg, W. R., 'Mary Barton', *Edinburgh Review*, April 1849.

Hanna, William, *Memoirs of the Life and Writings of Thomas Chalmers*, 4 vols (Edinburgh: Constable, 1849–1852).

Hanway, Jonas, *The State of Master Chimney Sweepers and their Journeymen; Particularly of Distressed Boys, Apprentices* (London, 1779).

——, *A Sentimental History of Chimney Sweepers, in London and Westminster. Shewing the Necessity of Putting them under Regulations, to Prevent the Grossest Inhumanity to the Climbing Boys. With a Letter to a London Clergyman on Sunday Schools Calculated for the Preservation of the Children of the Poor* (London, 1785).

Haweis, Thomas, *Sermons before the Missionary Society. Sermon 1. The Apostolic Commission, Preached at Spa Fields Chapel, September 22 1795* (London: T. Chapman, 1795).

Haylock, W., *A Brief History of Queen Street Congregational Chapel* (Sheffield: Pawson and Brailsford, 1933).

Highfield, George, *Christian Zeal: A Sermon Preached at the Methodist Chapel in Sheffield, May 30 1814, before the Teachers and Superintendents of the Sunday School Union; to which is Annexed an Address to the Children . . .* (Sheffield: J. Montgomery, 1814).

Hole, Charles, *The Early History of the Church Missionary Society for Africa and the East to the End of AD 1814* (London: Church Missionary Society, 1896).

Holland, George Calvert, *Essay on Education, Founded on Phrenological Principles* (London: Longman, Rees, Orme, Brown and Green, 1828).

——, *An Inquiry into the Moral, Social and Intellectual Condition of the Industrious Classes of Sheffield* (London: Longman, Orme, Brown, Green and Longman, 1839).

——, *Unoccupied Houses; or, what Evidence do they Afford of Existing Distress, Read before the Literary and Philosophical Society, 5 November 1841* (Sheffield: Ridge and Jackson, 1841).

——, *Inquiry into the Condition of the Cutlery Trade: Being a Paper Read before Members of the Literary and Philosophical Society of Sheffield* (February 1842).

——, *The Mortality, Sufferings, and Diseases of Grinders 1844–1848*, 3 vols (London 1841; Sheffield: Ridge and Jackson, 1842).

——, *Vital Statistics of Sheffield* (London: Robert Tyas, 1843).

——, *Diseases of the Lungs from Mechanical Causes; and Inquiries into the Condition of the Artisans Exposed to the Inhalation of Dust* (London [printed], 1843).

Holland, John, *Memorials of the Founders of the First Methodist Sunday School in Sheffield: being a Paper Read at the Annual Social Tea Meeting of the Red Hill Sunday School, December 28th 1869* (Sheffield: Harrison, 1870).

Holland, John and Everett, James, *Memoirs of the Life and Writing of James Montgomery, Vols* 1–7 (London: Longman, Brown, Green and Longmans, 1855–1856).

Holt, Anne, *A Ministry to the Poor, being the History of the Liverpool Domestic Mission Society, 1836–1936* (Liverpool: Henry Young and Sons, Ltd, 1936).

Howitt, Margaret (ed.), *Mary Howitt, An Autobiography*, vol. 1 (London: William Isbister, 1889).

Hudson, William, *The Life of John Holland of Sheffield Park* (London: Longmans, Green and Co., 1874).

Kay, James Philips, *The Moral and Physical Condition of the Working Classes Employed in the Cotton Manufactories in Manchester* (London: Cass, 1970 [1832]).
Kilham, Hannah, 'Extract from an Account of the Sheffield Society for Bettering the Condition of the Poor, 1812' (Sheffield Local Studies Library: Local Pamphlets vol. 87, no. 6).
——, *Scripture Selections on Attributes of the Divine being . . . Designed Chiefly for the Instruction of Young Persons* (Sheffield: W. Todd, 1813).
——, *Questions on the Principles of the Christian Religion to be Answered from the Scriptures, Adapted for Schools and for Private Instruction* (Sheffield: Bentham and Ray, 1817).
——, *Family Maxims* (Sheffield: Bentham and Ray, 1817).
——, *Ta-Re Waloof, Ta-re boo Juk-a: First Lessons in Jaloof* (Coventry: George Stockwell, 1820).
——, *African Lessons: Wolof and English* (London: William Phillips, 1823).
——, *Report of a Recent Visit to Sierra Leone, to the Committee for African Instruction, and other Friends Concerned in Promoting its Object* (Lindfield: C. Greene, 1828).
——, *Specimens of African Languages Spoken in the Colony of Sierra Leone* (Printed for the Society of Friends Committee for the Promotion of African Instruction, 1828).
——, *The Claims of West Africa to Christian Instruction, Through the Native Languages* (London: Darton and Harvey, 1830).
——, *Report of a Recent Visit to Sierra Leone. Being Extracts from Recent Letters* (Linfield: G. Greene, 1831).
King, J. W., *James Montgomery: A Memoir, Political and Poetical* (London: Partridge and Co., 1858).
Kirk, John, *James Montgomery* (London: Hamilton, Adams and Co., 1861).
Knight, Arnold, *On the Causes which have Contributed to Produce a Greater Degree of Intemperance in the Habits of the People of England than Prevails on the Continent* (Sheffield: R. Leader, 1836).
Knight, Helen C., *Life of James Montgomery* (Boston: Gould and Lincoln, 1857).
Knutsford, Lady, *Life and Letters of Zachary Macaulay* (London: E. Arnold, 1900).
Kotzebue, Otto von, *A Voyage of Discovery into the South Sea and Beering's Straits, for the Purpose of Exploring a North-East Passage, Undertaken in the Years 1815–1818*, 3 vols (London: Longman, Hurst, Rees, Orme and Brown, 1821).
Ladies' Society for the Education and Employment of the Female Poor, *Extract from an Account of the Ladies' Society for the Education and Employment of the Female Poor* (London, April 1804).

Lancaster, Joseph, *Outline of a Plan for Educating Ten Thousand Poor Children, by Establishing Schools in Country Towns and Villages; and for Uniting Works of Industry with Useful Knowledge* (London 1806).

——, *The British System of Education: Being a Complete Epitome of the Improvements and Inventions Practised at the Royal Free Schools, Borough Road, Southwark* (London: Longman and Co., 1810).

——, *Address of the Committee of the Institute for Promoting the British System for the Education of the Labouring and Manufacturing Classes of Society of Every Religious Persuasion...* (London: J. Lancaster, 1813).

Larom, Charles, *Townhead: The History of the Baptist Chapel Assembling in Townhead Street, Sheffield* (Sheffield: Leader and Sons, 1870).

Leader, John D., *1797–1897: Sheffield General Infirmary* (Sheffield: Infirmary Board, 1927).

Leader, R. E., *Reminiscences of Old Sheffield: Its Streets and its People* (Sheffield: Leader and Sons, 1876).

——, *Sheffield in the Eighteenth Century* (Sheffield: W. C. Leng, 1905).

Leeds Town Mission, *Reports* (Leeds: Edward Baines and Sons, 1839–1840).

Lewis, N. B., 'The abolitionist movement in Sheffield, 1822–1833', reprinted from *Bulletin of the John Rylands Library*, vol. 18, no. 2 (July 1934).

Lister, Edward, *A Sketch of the life, Labours and Character of George Bennet, Founder of the Sheffield Sunday School Union* (Sheffield: J. Morton, 1863).

Liverpool Christian Instruction Society, *Reports*.

Liverpool Town Mission, *Reports of the Liverpool Town Mission, formerly called the Liverpool Christian Instruction Society* (1837–1839).

Liverpool Domestic Mission Society, *Reports* from 1837.

Livesey, John, *Mechanics' Churches: A Letter to Sir Robert Peel on Church Extension in the Populous Towns and Manufacturing Districts* (Sheffield: Pearce, 1840).

Livingstone, David, *Missionary Travels and Researches in South Africa* (London: John Murray, 1857).

Lloyd, G. I. H., *The Cutlery Trades: An Historical Essay in the Economics of Small-Scale Production* (Longman: Longmans, Green and Co., 1913).

Longden, Henry, *The Life of Henry Longden, Compiled from his own Memoirs, from his Diary and his Letters* (London: Wesleyan Conference Office 1865 [1813]).

Lovett, Richard, *The History of the London Missionary Society 1795–1895*, vol.1 (London: Henry Froude, 1899).

Luke, Jemima, *Early Years of My Life* (London: Hodder and Stoughton, 1900).

Malthus, Reverend Thomas, *An Essay on the Principle of Population, as it Affects the Future Improvement of Society; with Remarks on the Speculations of W. Godwin, M. Condorcet and other Writers* (London: J. Johnson, 1803).

Manchester Ministry to the Poor, *Reports of the Manchester Ministry to the Poor* (1834–1850).

Manchester and Salford Town Mission, *Reports of the Manchester and Salford Town Mission* (1838–1847).

Manning, J. E., *A History of Upper Chapel, Sheffield* (Sheffield: Independent Press, 1900).

Marrat, Jabez, *James Montgomery: Christian Poet and Philanthropist* (London: Wesleyan Conference Office, 1879).

Miall, J. G., *Congregationalism in Yorkshire: A Chapter of Modern Church History* (London: John Snow, 1868).

Middleditch, Thomas, *The Youthful Female Missionary: A Memoir of Mary Ann Hutchins, Wife of the Rev. John Hutchins, Baptist Missionary, Savanna-la-Mar, Jamaica; and Daughter of the Rev. T. Middleditch, of Ipswich; Compiled Chiefly from her own Correspondence, by her Father* (London: Wrightman, Hamilton Adams and Co., 1840).

Montgomery, James, *The Trial of James Montgomery for Libel on the War by Reprinting and Republishing a Song Originally Printed and Published Long before the War begun: at Doncaster Sessions, January 22 1795* (Sheffield: J. Montgomery, 1795).

——, *The West Indies, and other Poems*, 4th edition (London: Longman, Hurst, Rees, Orme and Brown, 1814).

——, *The Abolition of the Slave Trade, a Poem in Four Parts* (London: R. Bowyer, 1814).

——, *Greenland and other Poems*, 2nd edition (London: Longman, Rees, Orme and Browne, 1819).

——, *An Address to Uninstructed Youth, in the Town and Neighbourhood of Sheffield* (Sheffield: James Montgomery, 1821).

——(ed.), *The Chimney-Sweeper's Friend and Climbing Boys Album* (London: Longman, 1824).

——, *A Retrospect of the Origins, Proceedings and Effects of the Sheffield Sunday School Union* (Sheffield: J. Montgomery, 1824).

——, 'On the Phrenology of the Hindoos and Negroes, showing, that the actual character of nations, as well as of individuals, may be modified by moral, political, and other circumstances, in direct contradiction to their cerebral developments', *An Essay on the Phrenology of the Hindoos and Negroes, by James Montgomery. Together with Strictures Thereon by Corden Thompson* (London: E. Lloyd and Co., 1827).

——, *The Pelican Island and other Poems* (London: Longman et al., 1828).

——, Introductory Essay to Jonathan Edwards, *Life of David Brainerd, Missionary to the American Indians* (Glasgow: William Collins, 1829 [1749]).

——, 'Sandanee's Dream', *The Amulet* (1829).

——, *A Word for the Slave*, with *A Cry from Africa* (Sheffield: J. Blackwell, 1830).

—— (ed.), *Journal of Voyages and Travels by the Reverend Daniel Tyerman and George Bennet, Esquire, deputed from the London Missionary Society to Visit their Various Stations in the South Seas, China, India etc, Between the Years 1821 and 1829*, 2 vols (London: Frederick Westley and A. H. Davis, 1831).

——, 'A spirit of the living God' (1823), *Hymns for Anti-Slavery Meetings* (London: Jackson and Walford, 1833).

——(ed.), *Voyages and Travels Round the World, by the Reverend Daniel Tyerman and George Bennet, Esquire, Deputed from the London Missionary Society to Visit their Various Stations on the South Sea Islands, Australia, China, India, Madagascar and South Africa Between the years 1821 and 1829, Compiled from Original Documents by James Montgomery*, 2nd edition, corrected (London: John Snow, 1840).

——, *Original Hymns for Public, Private and Social Devotion* (London: Longman, Brown et al, 1853).

——, *The Poetical Works of James Montgomery, Collected by Himself, in Four Volumes* (London: Longman, Brown, Green and Longman, 1855–1856).

——, 'Angels from the Realms of Glory' (1816) and 'Hail to the Lord's Anointed' (1822), *The Methodist Hymn Book* (London: Methodist Publishing House, 1933), pp. 119 and 245.

——, 'Memoir of the late George Bennet Esq of Sheffield', *The Evangelical Magazine and Missionary Chronicle* (February 1842), pp. 53–62.

Morgan, John, *Reminiscences of the Founding of a Christian Mission on the Gambia* (London: Wesleyan Mission House, 1864).

More, Hannah, *Slavery, A Poem* (London: T. Cadell, 1788).

——, *Thoughts on the Importance of the Manners of the Great to General Society*, 7th edition (London: T. Cadell, 1789).

——, *An Estimate of the Religion of the Fashionable World* (London: T. Cadell, 1790).

——, *Village Politics. Addressed to all the Mechanics, Journeymen, and Day Labourers, in Great Britain. By Will Chip, a Country Carpenter* (1793).

—— *Strictures on the Modern System of Female Education. With a View of the Principles and Conduct Prevalent Among Women of Rank and Fortune* (Dublin: D. Wogan, 1799).

——, *Hints Towards Forming the Character of a Young Princess*, 2 vols (London: T. Cadell and W. Davies, 1805).

——, *Coelebs in Search of a Wife*, 2 vols (London: T. Cadell and W. Davies, 1809).

——, *An Essay on the Character and Practical Writings of Saint Paul*, 2 vols, 4th edtion (London: T. Cadell and W. Davies, 1815).

More, Hannah, *The Works of Hannah More, A New Edition, with Additions and Corrections, in Eleven Volumes* (London: T. Cadell, 1830).

Morrison, John, *The Fathers and Founders of the London Missionary Society* (London: Fisher and Son, 1844).

Observations on the Use of Machinery in the Manufactories of Great Britain; Proving it to be the Cause of the Present Stagnation of Trade; and of the Distress Now Prevailing Amongst the Industrious Classes of the People, with Remarks on Climbing Boys, and the Treatment of Children Employed in Cotton Manufactories: and on the Rev Malthus's Plan for Preventing the Poor from Intermarrying, By a Mechanic (London, 1817).

Odom, William, *Hallamshire Worthies. Characteristics and Work of Notable Sheffield Men and Women* (Sheffield: J. W. Northend, 1926).

Orange, Reverend James, *Life of the late George Vason of Nottingham. One of the Troop of Missionaries first Sent to the South Sea Islands by the London Missionary Society in the Ship Duff.* (London: John Snow, 1840).

Parker, John, *A Statement of the Population of the Town of Sheffield* (Sheffield: R. Leader, 1830).

Piggott, S. (ed.), *An Authentic Narrative of Four Years' Residence at Tongataboo, One of the Friendly Islands, in the South Seas, by [George Vason], Who Went Thither in the Duff, under Captain Wilson, in 1796* (London: Longman, Hurst, Rees, Orme, 1810).

Pitman, Emma Raymond, *Heroines of the Mission Field* (London: Cassle and Co., 1880).

——, *Missionary Heroines in Eastern Lands: Woman's Work in Mission Fields* (London: S. W. Partridge, 1895).

Porter, W. S., *Sheffield Royal Infirmary* (Oldham: J Allan Hanson and Son Ltd, 1922).

——, *Sheffield Literary and Philosophical Society: A Centenary Retrospect, 1822–1922* (Sheffield: J. W. Northend, 1922).

Proceedings of a Public Meeting for the Purpose of Establishing a Literary and Philosophical Society in Sheffield, held at the Cutler's Hall, on Thursday December 12 1822 (Sheffield: J. Montgomery, 1822).

Raffles, Reverend Thomas, *Missions to the Heathen Vindicated from the Charge of Enthusiasm. A Sermon Delivered at the Tabernacle, Moorfields, before the Missionary Society, May 11 1814* (Liverpool: Sunday School Press, 1814).

Ramsay, Thomas, *A Picture of Sheffield; or an Historical and Descriptive View of the Town of Sheffield* (Sheffield: George Ridge, 1824).

Rawson, Mary Anne, *The Bow in the Cloud; or, the Negro's Memorial* (London: Jackson and Walford, 1834).

——, *The Thompson Normal School, Jamaica* (Sheffield: Leader, 1845).

Red Hill Wesleyan Methodist Sunday School Rules (Sheffield: J. Montgomery 1815).

Religious Tract Society, *Child's Companion, or, Sunday Scholar's Reward* (1824).

Roberts, Reverend Arthur (ed.), *Mendip Annals, or, A Narrative of the Charitable Labours of Hannah and Martha More in their Neighbourhood. Being the Journal of Martha More*, 3rd edition (London: James Nisbet, 1839 [1834]).

—— (ed.), *Letters of Hannah More to Zachary Macaulay, Esq. Containing Notices of Lord Macaulay's Youth* (London: James Nisbet, 1860).

Roberts, H. G., *Red Hill Sunday School Centenary* (Sheffield: J. W. Northend, n.d.).

Roberts, Samuel, *The Chimney-Sweepers' Boy: A Poem* (Sheffield: J. Montgomery, 1807).

——, *Tales of the Poor; or, Infant Sufferings* (Sheffield: J. Montgomery, 1813).

——, 'The Four Friends: a fable for young people', in Roberts (ed.), *The Blind Man and His Son* (London: Taylor and Hessey, 1816).

——, *Chimney Sweepers' Boys: The Resolutions and Petition to Parliament, Respecting Children Employed by Chimney Sweepers as Climbing Boys, Agreed upon at a Public Meeting of the Inhabitants of Sheffield, Held at the Cutler's Hall, on April 16 1817* (Sheffield: J. Montgomery and M. Smith, 1817).

——, 'On the employment of climbing boys', in James Montgomery (ed.), *The Chimney Sweepers' Friend and Climbing Boys' Album* (London: Longman and Co., 1824).

——, *The Negro's Friend* (Sheffield: Blackwell, 1826).

——, *Tocsin the Second; or, the Vital and Immediate Abolition of Slavery* (Sheffield: Blackwell, 1827).

——, *A Layman Volunteer* (Sheffield: Blackwell, 1828).

——, *England's Crisis; A Letter to the Members of the Sheffield Mechanics' Institute and the Workmen in General* (Sheffield: Ridge, 1832).

——, *A Mill-Stone for the Necks of the Child-destroyers. A Letter Addressed to Lord Viscount Morpeth* (Sheffield: Saxton and Chalmer 1833).

——, *Omnipotence; as Exemplified in the Abolition of Slavery* (Sheffield: Saxton and Chaloner, 1833).

——, *Wisdom, Its Nature and Effects, Portrayed in a Letter to the Reverend Thomas Allin on the Subject of the Sheffield Mechanics' Institute* (Sheffield: George Ridge, 1833).

——, *An Address to British Females of Every Rank and Station on the Employment of Climbing Boys in Sweeping Chimnies* (Sheffield: Whitaker and Co., 1834).

——, *The Lecturers Lectured and the Dissectors Dissected. Addressed to the Gentlemen Styling Themselves 'the Lecturers of the Sheffield School of Anatomy and Medicine'* (Sheffield: A. Whitaker, 1834).

——, *England's Passing Bell, or the Obsequies of National Holiness, Liberty and Honour; Humbly Addressed to the King, as the Guardian of the*

Religious and Political Rights of the Poor (London: Benjamin Steill; and Sheffield: Whitaker, 1834).
——, *Corn Law Prose: Containing The Old Sow and Her Litter of Piglets: Look before you Leap: and a Letter to the Author of 'Thoughts on the Corn-Laws'* (Sheffield: Whitaker, 1834).
——, *England's Glory; or, the Good Old Poor Laws, Addressed to the Working Classes of Sheffield* (Sheffield: Whitaker, 1836).
——, *A Cry from the Chimnies; or, an Integral Part of the Total Abolition of Slavery Throughout the World* (London: Longman, Orme, Brown, Green and Longman, 1837).
——, *A Solemn Appeal to Ministers of the Gospel of Every Denomination, on the Subject of the Poor Laws* (Sheffield: Whitaker 1837).
——, *Chartism! Its Cause and Cure. Addressed to the Clergy and Others of Sheffield and Ecclesall* (Sheffield: Whitaker, 1839).
——, *Mary Wilden, a Victim of the New Poor Law, or the Malthusian and Marcusian System Exposed* (London: Whittaker and Co., 1839).
——, *The Wickedness of the New Poor Law, Addressed to Serious Christians of all Denominations, with an Appeal to the Clergy* (Sheffield: Whitaker, 1839).
——, *The Pauper's Advocate, A Cry from the Brink of the Grave Against the New Poor Law* (London: Sherwood and Co.; Sheffield: Whitaker, 1841).
——, *The Anti-Bastille. An Address to the Inhabitants of the Ecclesall Bierlow Union* (Sheffield: Whitaker 1841).
——, *The Voice of an Octogenarian, Denouncing Wickedness in High Places. Addressed to Sir Robert Peel* (Sheffield: Whitaker, 1842).
——, *A Dry Crust of the Ecclesall Bierlow Pauper Bread, for the Building Committee of the Sheffield Guardians of the Poor* (Sheffield: Whitaker and Co., 1843).
——, *The Bone-Gnawing System, Addressed to Michael Hunter Esq, the Deputy Chairman of the Sheffield Board of Guardians* (Sheffield: William Ford, 1845).
——, *God's Vengeance for the National Violation of his Laws by the Enactment of the New Poor Law Displayed in the Infliction of War, Pestilence and Famine, and the Almost Universal Spreading of Villainy and every Species of Wickedness Throughout the Whole of the United Kingdom* (Sheffield: Whitaker, 1846).
——, *Autobiography and Select Remains of the Late Samuel Roberts* (London: Longman, 1849).
Roberts, W., *Memoirs of the Life and Correspondence of Mrs Hannah More* (London: Seeley and Burnside, 1839).
Robinson, J., *A Directory of Sheffield* (Sheffield: J. Montgomery, 1797).
Rodgers, Paul, *A Lecture on the Origin, Progress and Results of the Sheffield Mechanics' Institution; Delivered in Surrey Street Chapel, May 25 1840* (Sheffield: J. H. Greaves, 1840).

Rowntree, John S. (ed.), *The Family Memoir of Joseph Rowntree* (Birmingham: privately printed, 1868).
Seed, Alexander, *Norfolk Street Wesleyan Chapel, Sheffield* (London: Jarrold and Sons, n.d.).
Seeley, B., *Memoirs of the Life and Writings of Michael Sadler* (London, 1842).
Sheffield Bible Society, *The Sixth Report of the Bible Society for Sheffield and its Vicinity* (Sheffield: J. Montgomery, 1816).
——, *The Tenth Report of the Bible Society for Sheffield and the Vicinity* (Sheffield: W. Todd, 1820).
Sheffield Charity School for Poor Boys, *A List of the Annual Subscribers to the Charity School for Poor Boys in Sheffield* (Sheffield: W. Ward, 1788 and 1794; J. Gales, 1790; J. Northall, 1795 and 1797; T. Pierson, 1796 and 1800; J. Montgomery, 1798).
Sheffield Charity School for Poor Girls, *A List of the Benefactors and Annual Subscribers to the Charity School for Poor Girls in Sheffield* (Sheffield: J. Gales, 1788–1790; W. Ward, 1792–1794; J. Northall, 1795; T. Pierson, 1796 and 1798; James Montgomery, 1797).
Sheffield Church Missionary Association, *The Report of the Church Missionary Association for Sheffield and the Neighbourhood* (Sheffield: Ridge and Jackson, 1842).
——, *The Church Missionary Society's Jubilee. Our Duty in Respect of Missions to the Heathen*; by the Reverend Thomas Best (Sheffield: Ridge and Jackson, 1848).
Sheffield Female Friendly Society, *Reports of the Female Friendly Society for the Relief of Aged Women* (Sheffield: J. Montgomery, 1815, 1816, 1817).
Sheffield Ladies' Anti-Slavery Society, *Reports of the Sheffield Ladies' Anti-Slavery Society* (Sheffield: J. Blackwell, 1826, 1827, 1828, 1830).
Sheffield Ladies' Association for the Universal Abolition of Slavery, *Ladies' Petition* (Sheffield: Leader, 1838).
——, *Report of the Sheffield Ladies' Association for the Universal Abolition of Slavery* (Sheffield: R. Leader, 1839).
Sheffield Lancasterian School, *Reports of the Sheffield Girls' Lancasterian School* (Sheffield: W. Todd, 1817; J. Montgomery, 1818, 1820–1822, 1824, 1824–1825; J. Blackwell, 1826).
——, *Reports of the Lancasterian School for Boys in Sheffield* (Sheffield: J. Montgomery, 1815–1816, 1818, 1820, 1824; W. Todd, 1817, 1823; J. Blackwell, 1825; J. and H. Todd, 1826).
Sheffield Literary and Philosophical Society, *Reports of the Sheffield Literary and Philosophical Society* (Sheffield: William Todd, 1825; J. Blackwell, 1826; George Ridge, 1827, 1832, 1841; Robert Leader, 1833; Leader and Sons, 1886).
Sheffield Mechanics' Institute, *Reports of the Sheffield Mechanics' Institute* (Sheffield: R. Leader, 1833; T. Scott, 1834, 1836, 1839; J. Pearce, 1835; Saxton and Chaloner, 1837; William Saxton, 1838; E. Smith, 1842).

——, *Rules of the Sheffield Mechanics' Institution* (Sheffield: Joseph Hawksworth Bramley, 1833); *Rules of the Sheffield Mechanics' Institute as altered and amended* (Sheffield: T. Scott, 1834, 1835, 1836).

——, *Report of a Soiree Held by the Members of the Sheffield Mechanics' Institution and the Mechanics' Library in Honour of Sir Arnold Jas. Knight M. D.* (Sheffield: R. Leader, 1843).

Sheffield Methodist Sunday School, *First Annual Report of the Committee of the Methodist Sunday School for Poor Children of All Denominations in Sheffield and its Vicinity* (Sheffield: J. Montgomery, 1816).

Sheffield School of Industry, *Some Account of the Institution and Management of the School of Industry, in Sheffield, for Poor Girls* (Sheffield: James Montgomery, 1790).

Sheffield Society for Bettering the Condition of the Poor. *Reports of the Society for Bettering the Condition of the Poor* (Sheffield: J. Montgomery, 1812–1822, 1824–1826).

Sheffield Sunday School Union, *Reports of the Sheffield Sunday School Union* (Sheffield: J. Montgomery, 1813–1817).

Sherwood, Mary Martha, *The History of Susan Gray* (London: R. Ogle, 1812).

——, *The Ayah and the Lady* (Dublin: R. Napper, 1816).

——, *The Indian Pilgrim* (Wellington, Salop: F. Houlston and Son, 1818).

Singleton, William, *Report of the Committee Managing a Fund Raised by some Friends, for the Purpose of promoting African Instruction; with an Account of a Visit to the Gambia and Sierra Leone* (London: Darton and Harvey, 1822).

——, *The Result of Seven Years' Mission Among Friends of Balby Monthly Meeting* (Sheffield: H. A. Bacon, 1823).

Smith, George, *The Life of William Carey* (London: J. M. Dent, 1878).

Society for Bettering the Condition of the Poor, *Fifteenth Report of the Society for Bettering the Condition and Increasing the Comforts of the Poor*, vol. III (London, 1801).

——, *The Reports of the Society for Bettering the Condition and Increasing the Comforts of the Poor*, vol. 1, 4th edition (London, 1805).

Society for the Promotion of the Religious Instruction of the Poor in Liverpool, *Reports of the Society for the Promotion of the Religious Instruction of the Poor in Liverpool and the North, or the Liverpool Christian Instruction Society* (Liverpool, 1830–1836).

The Life of a Sunday Scholar. Memoirs of Henry Crookes of Sheffield, Read at the Quarterly Meeting of the Red Hill Methodist Sunday School Teachers, October 1817 (Sheffield: Montgomery and Smith, 1817).

Smith, Thomas, *Speech Delivered at the Twelfth Annual Meeting of the Sheffield Auxiliary Bible Society, Held in the National School Room, Carver Street, on Friday October 22 1822* (Sheffield Local Studies Library: Local Pamphlets, vol. 157, no. 6).

Society for Promoting Female Education in China, India and the East, *Female Agency among the Heathen, as Recorded in the History and Correspondence of the Society for Promoting Female Education in the East* (London: Edward Suter, 1850).

Stock, Eugene, *A History of the Church Missionary Society. Its Environment, its Men and its Work*, vol. 1 (London: Church Missionary Society, 1899).

Street, Christopher J., *T. A. Ward and Upper Chapel, Sheffield: The Sunday School Centenary Volume* (Sheffield: Upper Chapel Bookstall, 1910).

Symons, Jelinger, *Report on the Trades of Sheffield and the Moral and Physical Condition of Young Persons Employed in Them*, Royal Commission of Enquiry into the Employment of Children in Trades and Manufactures not under the Factory Act (Sheffield: Leader, 1843).

Taylor, Ann and Jane, *Original Poems, for Infant Minds* (London: Darton and Harvey, 1805).

——, *Hymns for Infant Minds* (London: T. Conder, 1810).

Taylor, Ann Martin, *Practical Hints to Young Females on the Duties of a Wife, a Mother and a Mistress of a Young Family*, 3rd edition (London: Taylor and Hessey, 1815).

Taylor, Ann Martin (Mrs. Taylor of Ongar), *Maternal Solicitude for a Daughter's Best Interests* (London: Taylor and Hessey, 1815).

Taylor, Ann, and Taylor, Jane, *Correspondence between a Mother and Her Daughter at School* (London: Taylor and Hessey, 1817).

Telford, John, *Women in the Mission Field. Glimpses of Christian Women Among the Heathen* (London: C. H. Kelly, 1895).

The Anti-Slavery Album: Selections in Verse from Cowper, Hannah More, Montgomery, Pringle and Others (London: Howlett and Brimmer, 1828).

The West Indian Slave's Address to his Inhuman Oppressors and the English Public (Sheffield: Hopkinson, 1830).

Thompson, Corden, 'Strictures on Mr Montgomery's essay on the phrenology of the Hindoos and Negroes', in *An Essay on the Phrenology of the Hindoos and Negroes, by James Montgomery. Together with Strictures Thereon by Corden Thompson* (London: E. Lloyd and Co., 1827).

Thompson, Jemima, *Memoirs of British Female Missionaries: With a Survey of the Condition of Women in Heathen Countries. And Also A Preliminary Essay on the Importance of Female Agency in Evangelizing Pagan Nations* (London: William Smith, 1841).

Trimmer, Mrs., *The Guardian of Education, A Periodical Work; Consisting of a Practical Essay on Christian Education, founded Immediately on the Scriptures, and the Sacred Offices of the Church of England; Memoirs of Modern Philosophers, and Extracts from their Writing; Extracts from Sermons and other Books Relating to Religious Education; and a Copious Examination of Modern Systems of Education, Children's Books, and Books for Young Persons*, vol. 1 (London: J. Hatchard, 1802).

Wilberforce, William, *A Practical View of the Prevailing Religious System of Professed Christians in the Higher and Middle Classes of this Country Contrasted with Real Christianity* (London: T. Cadell Jun. and W. Davies, 1797).

Williams, John, *A Narrative of the Missionary Enterprises in the South Sea Islands* (London: John Snow, 1837).

——, *Euthanasia: A funeral Sermon for Mrs Williams, With a Memoir. By her Son* (London: S. T. Williams, 1852).

Winterbottom, Thomas, *An Account of the Native Africans in the Neighbourhood of Sierra Leone: To Which Is Added an Account of the Present State of Medicine Among Them* (London: Frank Cass, 1969 [1803]).

Select bibliography: books and articles published after 1940

Aarsleff, Hans, *The Study of Language in England 1780–1860* (London: Athlone Press, 1983).

Ajayi, J. F. Ade and Oloruntimehin, B. O., 'West Africa in the anti-slave trade era', in John E. Flint (ed.), *The Cambridge History of Africa*, Vol. 5 from c. 1790 to c. 1870 (Cambridge: Cambridge University Press, 1976), pp. 200–221.

Altick, Richard, *The English Common Reader: A Social History of the Mass Reading Public, 1800–1900* (Chicago: University of Chicago Press, 1957).

Amos, Valerie and Parmar, Pratibha, 'Challenging Imperial Feminism', *Feminist Review*, no. 17 (Autumn 1984), pp. 3–19.

Anderson, Mosa, *H.J. Wilson, Fighter for Freedom* (London: James Clarke and Co., 1953).

Andrew, Donna, *Philanthropy and Police: London Charity in the Eighteenth Century* (Princeton: Princeton University Press, 1989).

Anstey, Roger, *The Atlantic Slave Trade and British Abolitionists, 1760–1810* (Atlantic Highlands: Humanities Press, 1975).

Armstrong, Anthony, *The Church of England, the Methodists and Society, 1700–1850* (London: University of London Press, 1973).

Armytage, W. H. G., 'The editorial experience of Joseph Gales, 1786–1794', *The North Carolina Historical Review*, vol. 28, no. 3 (July 1951), pp. 332–361.

Balch, David, *'Let Wives be Submissive…' the Domestic Code in 1 Peter* (Chico, CA: Scholars Press, 1981).

Bank, Andrew, 'Losing faith in the civilizing mission: the premature decline of humanitarian liberalism at the Cape, 1840–60', in M. Daunton and R. Halpern (eds), *Empire and Others. British Encounters with Indigenous Peoples, 1600–1850* (London: UCL Press, 1999), pp. 364–383.

Bartle, G., 'The role of the ladies' committee in the affairs of the BFSS', *Journal of Educational Administration and History*, vol. 27, no. 1 (1995), pp. 51–61.

——, 'The role of the BFSS in elementary education in India and the East Indies 1813–1875', *History of Education*, vol. 23, no. 1 (1995), pp. 17–33.

Bates, Crispin, 'Race, caste and tribe in Central India: the early origins of Indian anthropometry', Edinburgh Papers in South Asian Studies, no. 3 (University of Edinburgh Centre for South Asian Studies, 1995), pp. 1–35.

Bayly, C. A., *Imperial Meridian: The British Empire and the World, 1780–1830* (Harlow: Longman, 1989).

Bebbington, David, *Evangelicalism in Modern Britain: A History from the 1730s to the 1980s* (London: Unwin Hyman, 1989).

Beidelman, T.O., *Colonial Evangelism: A Socio-Historical Study of an East African Mission at the Grassroots* (Bloomington: Indiana University Press, 1982).

Bennett, Tony, *The Birth of the Museum: History, Theory, Politics* (London: Routledge, 1995).

Bhabha, Homi, *The Location of Culture* (London: Routledge, 1994).

Billington, Louis and Billington, Rosamund, ' "A burning zeal for righteousness": women in the British anti-slavery movement, 1820–1860', in Jane Rendall (ed.), *Equal or Different: Women's Politics in Britain, 1800–1914* (Basingstoke: Macmillan, 1985), pp. 82–111.

Binfield, Clyde, *So Down to Prayers: Studies in English Nonconformity* (London: J. M. Dent, 1977).

Binfield, C., Childs, R., Harper, R., Hey, D., Martin, D. and Tweedale, G. (eds), *The History of Sheffield, 1843–1993, Vol 2: Society* (Sheffield: Sheffield Academic Press, 1993).

Binney, Judith, *The Legacy of Guilt. A Life of Thomas Kendall* (Auckland: Oxford University Press, 1968).

Birtwhistle, N. Allen, 'Methodist Missions', in Rupert Davies, A. Raymond George and Gordon Rupp (eds), *A History of the Methodist Church in Great Britain*, vol. 3 (London: Epworth Press, 1983).

Bolt, Christine, *Victorian Attitudes to Race* (London: RKP, 1971).

—— and Drescher, Seymour (eds), *Anti-Slavery, Religion and Reform: Essays in Memory of Roger Anstey* (Folkstone: William Dawson, 1980).

Bosch, David J., *Transforming Mission: Paradigm Shifts in Theology of Mission* (New York: Maryknoll, 1993).

Bradley, James, *Religion, Revolution and English Radicalism: Nonconformity in Eighteenth-Century Politics and Society* (Cambridge: Cambridge University Press, 1990).

Braidwood, Stephen J., *Black Poor and White Philanthropists: London's Blacks and the Foundation of the Sierra Leone Settlement, 1786–1791* (Liverpool: Liverpool University Press, 1994).

Brantlinger, Patrick, *Dark Vanishings: Discourse on the Extinction of Primitive Races, 1800–1930* (Ithaca: Cornell University Press, 2003).
——, 'Victorians and Africans: The genealogy of the myth of the dark continent', in Gates, Henry Louis Jr. (ed.), *'Race', Writing and Difference* (Chicago: University of Chicago Press, 1986), pp. 185–222.
Brewer, John, 'This, that and the other: public, social and private in the seventeenth and eighteenth centuries', in Dario Castiglione and Lesley Sharpe (eds), *Shifting the Boundaries: Transformation of the Languages of Public and Private in the Eighteenth Century* (Exeter: University of Exeter Press, 1995), pp. 1–21.
Bristow, Edward J., *Vice and Vigilance: Purity Movements in Britain since 1700* (Dublin: Gill and Macmillan, 1977).
Brown, Callum, *The Death of Christian Britain: Understanding Secularisation 1800–2000* (London: Routledge, 2001).
Brown, Ford K., *Fathers of the Victorians: the Age of Wilberforce* (Cambridge: Cambridge University Press, 1961).
Brown, Stewart T., *Thomas Chalmers and the Godly Commonwealth in Scotland* (Oxford: Oxford University Press, 1982).
Brusco, Elizabeth and Klein, Laura F., *The Message in the Missionary: Local Interpretations of Religious Ideology and Missionary Personality* (Williamsburg: Studies in Third World Societies, no. 50, January 1994).
Bryson, Gladys, *Man and Society: The Scottish Inquiry of the Eighteenth Century* (New York: Augustus M. Kelley 1968 [1945]).
Bullock, Frederick W., *Voluntary Religious Societies, 1520–1799* (St Leonard's-on-Sea: Budd and Gillatt, 1963).
Burridge, Kenelm, *In the Way: A Study of Christian Missionary Endeavours* (Vancouver: UBC, 1991).
Burton, Antoinette, *Burdens of History: British Feminists, Indian Women and Imperial Culture, 1865–1915* (Chapel Hill: University of North Carolina Press, 1994).
——, 'Rules of thumb: British history and "imperial culture" in nineteenth- and twentieth-century Britain', *Women's History Review*, vol. 3, no. 4 (1994), pp. 483–500.
Cage, R. A. and Checkland, O. A., 'Thomas Chalmers and Urban Poverty: the St. John's Parish Experiment in Glasgow, 1819–1837', *Philosophical Journal*, vol. 8 (1976), pp. 37–56.
Cairns, David, and Richards, Shaun, *Writing Ireland: Colonialism, Nationalism and Culture* (Manchester: Manchester University Press, 1988).
Calhoun, Craig (ed.), *Habermas and the Public Sphere* (Cambridge: MIT Press, 1992).
Callaway, Helen, *Gender, Culture and Empire: European Women in Colonial Nigeria* (London: Macmillan, 1987).
Campbell, I. C., 'Polynesian perceptions of Europeans in the eighteenth and nineteenth centuries', *Pacific Studies*, vol. 5, no. 2, 1982, pp. 64–80.

——, *Island Kingdom. Tonga Ancient and Modern* (Christchurch: Canterbury University Press, 1992).

Carey, Hilary M., 'Companions in the Wilderness? Missionary Wives in Colonial Australia, 1788–1900', *Journal of Religious History*, vol. 19, no. 2 (December 1995), pp. 226–248.

Cathcart, Michael, Tom Griffiths, Lee Watts, Vivian Anceschi, Greg Houghton and David Goodman (eds), *Mission to the South Seas: The Voyage of the Duff, 1796–1799* (Melbourne: University of Melbourne Press, 1990).

Chapple, J. A. V. and Pollard, Arthur, *The Letters of Mrs Gaskell* (Manchester: Mandolin 1997 [1966]).

Charlton, D., *New Images of the Natural in France* (Cambridge: Cambridge University Press, 1984).

Chaudhuri, Nupur and Stroebel, Margaret (eds), *Western Women and Imperialism: Complicity and Resistance* (Bloomington: Indiana University Press, 1992).

Chitnis, Anand, *The Scottish Enlightenment: A Social History* (London: Croom Helm, 1976).

Christophers, Brett, *Positioning the Missionary: John Booth Good and the Confluence of Cultures in British Columbia* (Vancouver: UBC Press, 1998).

Church, Leslie F., *The Early Methodist People* (London: Epworth Press, 1948).

——, *More About the Early Methodist People* (London: Epworth Press, 1949).

Claeys, Gregory, 'The French Revolution debate and British political thought', *History of Political Thought*, vol. 11, no. 1 (Spring 1990), pp. 59–80.

——, *Machinery, Money and the Millenium* (Cambridge: Polity, 1987).

Colby, Robert A., *Fiction with a Purpose: Major and Minor Nineteenth-Century Novels* (Bloomington: Indiana University Press, 1967).

Colley, Linda, *Britons: Forging the Nation 1707–1837* (London: Pimlico, 1992).

——, *Captives: Britain, Empire and the World, 1600–1850* (London: Pimlico, 2002).

Collingwood, Jeremy and Mary, *Hannah More* (Oxford: Lion Publishing, 1990).

Comaroff, Jean, 'The Empire's old clothes', in D. Howe (ed.), *Cross-cultural Consumption: Global markets, local realities* (London: Routledge, 1996), pp. 19–38.

—— and John, *Of Revelation and Revolution: Christianity, Colonialism and Consciousness in South Africa* (London: University of Chicago Press, 1991).

——, *Ethnography and the Historical Imagination* (Oxford: Westview Press, 1992).

Coombes, Annie E., *Reinventing Africa: Museums, Material Culture and Popular Imagination* (London: Yale University Press, 1994).
Cooper, Frederick and Stoler, Ann Laura (eds), *Tensions of Empire: Colonial Cultures in a Bourgeois World* (London: University of California Press, 1997).
Cooter, Roger, *The Cultural Meaning of Popular Science: Phrenology and the Organisation of Consent in Nineteenth Century Britain* (Cambridge: Cambridge University Press, 1984).
Corfield, Kenneth, 'Elizabeth Heyrick: radical Quaker', in Gail Malmgreen (ed.), *Religion in the Lives of English Women, 1760–1930* (London: Croom Helm, 1986), pp. 41–67.
Cott, Nancy F., 'Notes toward an interpretation of antebellum childrearing', *The Psychohistory Review*, vol. 4, no. 4 (1978), pp. 4–20.
Cox, Jeffrey, *Imperial Faultlines: Christianity and Colonial Power in India, 1818–1940* (California: Stanford University Press, 2002).
Crawford, Michael, *Seasons of Grace: Colonial New England's Revival Tradition in its British Context* (New York: Oxford University Press, 1991).
Crosfield, D., 'Richard Smith and his Journal', *Journal of the Friends' Historical Society*, vol. 14, no. 3 (1917), pp. 110–116.
Cullen, Michael J., *The Statistical Movement in Early Victorian Britain: The Foundations of Empirical Social Research* (Brighton: Harvester Press, 1975).
Cunningham, Hugh, *Children and Childhood in Western Society since 1500* (London: Longman, 1995).
Cunningham, Valentine. ' "God and nature intended you for a missionary's wife": Mary Hill, Jane Eyre and other missionary women', in Fiona Bowie, Deborah Kirkwood and Shirley Ardener (eds), *Women and Missions: Past and Present. Anthropological and Historical Perceptions* (Oxford: Berg Publishers, 1993).
Currie, Robert, *Methodism Divided: A Study in the Sociology of Ecumenicalism* (London: Faber, 1968).
Curtin, Philip D., *The Image of Africa: British Ideas and Action, 1780–1850*, 2 vols (Madison: University of Wisconsin Press, 1964).
Cutt, M. Nancy, *Mrs Sherwood and her Books for Children* (Oxford: Oxford University Press, 1974).
——, *Ministering Angels. A Study of Evangelical Writing for Children* (Herts: Five Owls Press, 1979).
Davies, John, *History of the Tahitian Mission 1799–1830*, C. W. Newbury (ed.) (Hakluyt Society and Cambridge University Press, 1961).
Davidoff, Leonore and Hall, Catherine, *Family Fortunes: Men and Women of the English Middle Class, 1780–1850* (London: Hutchinson, 1987).
Davies, Rupert and Rupp, Gordon, *A History of the Methodist Church in Great Britain*, vol. 1 (London: Epworth Press, 1965).

Davies, R., Raymond, George A. and Rupp, G., *A History of the Methodist Church in Great Britain*, vol. 3 (London: Epworth Press, 1983).

Daws, Gavan, *A Dream of Islands: Voyages of Self-Discovery in the South Seas* (London: W. W. Norton, 1980).

de Vries, Jacqueline, 'Rediscovering Christianity after the Postmodern Turn', *Feminist Studies*, vol. 30, no. 4 (Winter 2004), pp. 135–155.

Dean, Mitchell, *The Constitution of Poverty: Toward a Genealogy of Liberal Governance* (London: Routledge, 1991).

Dening, Greg, *Beach Crossings. Voyaging Across Time, Cultures and Self* (Philadelphia: University pf Pennsylvania Press, 2004).

Dickson, Mora, *The Powerful Bond* (London: Dennis Dobson, 1980).

Ditchfield, G. M., 'English Rational Dissent and Philanthropy, c.1760–c. 1810', in Hugh Cunningham and Joanna Innes (eds), *Charity, Philanthropy and Reform from the 1690s to 1850* (Basingstoke: Macmillan, 1998), pp. 193–207.

Drescher, Seymour, 'Cart Whip and Billy Roller: antislavery and reform symbolism in industrializing Britain', *Journal of Social History*, vol. 15 (1981), pp. 3–24.

Driver, Cecil, *Tory Radical: The Life of Richard Oastler* (Oxford: Oxford University Press, 1946).

Drotner, Kristin, *English Children and their Magazines, 1751–1945* (London: Yale University Press, 1988).

Drummond, J. and Upton, C. B., *The Life and Letters of James Martineau I* (London: James Nisbet and Co., 1902).

Durrans, Brian, 'The future of the other: changing cultures on display in ethnographic museums', in Robert Lumley (ed.), *The Museum Time-Machine: Putting Cultures on Display* (London: Routledge, 1988).

Dwyer, J. *Virtuous Discourse: Sensibility and Community in Late Eighteenth Century Scotland* (Edinburgh: John Donald, 1987).

Earle, Peter, *The Making of the English Middle Class: Business, Society and Family Life in London, 1660–1730* (London: Methuen, 1989).

Edmond, Rod, *Representing the South Pacific: Colonial Discourse from Cook to Gauguin* (Cambridge: Cambridge University Press, 1997).

Edwards, Michael S., *Purge this Realm: The Life of Joseph Rayner Stephens* (London: Epworth Press, 1994).

Elbourne, Elizabeth, *Blood Ground: Colonialism, Missions and the Contest for Christianity in the Cape Colony and Britain, 1799–1853* (Montreal and Kingston: McGill-Queen's University Press, 2002).

——, 'Domesticity and dispossession: the ideology of "Home" and the British construction of the "Primitive" from the eighteenth to the early nineteenth century', in W. Woodward, P. Hayes and G Minkley (eds), *Deep Histories: Gender and Colonialism in Southern Africa* (Amsterdam: Rodopi, 2002).

—— and Ross, Robert. 'Combating spiritual and social bondage: early missions in the Cape Colony', in Richard Elphink and Rodney Davonport (eds), *Christianity in South Africa* (Berkeley: University of California, 1997), pp. 31–50.
Eley, Geoff, 'Re-thinking the political: social history and political culture in eighteenth and nineteenth century Britain', *Archiv fur Sozialgeschichte*, vol. 21 (1981), pp. 427–457.
Elias, Norbert, *The Civilizing Process: The History of Manners* (Oxford: Basil Blackwell 1978 [1939]).
Elliott, Dorice Williams, *The Angel out of the House: Philanthropy and Gender in Nineteenth-Century England* (London: University of Virginia, 2002).
Eltringham, G. J., 'The Lancasterian Schools in Sheffield', *Transactions of the Hunter Archaeological Society*, vol. 5 (1943), pp. 147–152.
Erlank, Natasha, '"Civilising the African": The Scottish mission to the Xhosa, 1821–64', in B. Stanley (ed.), *Christian Missions and the Enlightenment* (Cambridge: William B. Erdmans, 2001), pp. 141–168.
Fanon, Frantz, *The Wretched of the Earth*, trns by Constance Farrington (Harmondsworth: Penguin, 1976 [1961]).
Fast, Hildegard, '"In at one ear and out at the other": African response to the Wesleyan message in Xhosaland 1825–35', *Journal of Religion in Africa*, vol. 23, no. 2 (1993), pp. 147–174.
Febvre, Lucien, '*Civilisation*: evolution of a word and a group of ideas', in Peter Burke (ed.), *A New Kind of History from the Writings of Febvre* (London: RKP, 1973), pp. 219–257.
Ferguson, Moira, *Subject to Others: British Women Writers and Colonial Slavery, 1670–1834* (London: Routledge, 1992).
—— (ed.), *The Hart Sisters: Early African Caribbean Writers, Evangelicals and Radicals* (London: University of Nebraska Press, 1993).
Findlay, G. G. and Holdsworth, W. W., *The History of the Wesleyan Methodist Missionary Society*, vols 1 and 2 (London: Epworth Press, 1921–1922).
Fiorenza, Elisabeth Schussler, 'Women in the New Testament', *New Catholic World* (November–December 1976), pp. 256–260.
——, *In Memory of Her: A Feminist Theological Reconstruction of Christian Origins* (London: SCM, 1983).
——, *Discipleship of Equals: A Critical Feminist Ekklesialogy of Liberation* (New York: Crossroads, 1993), pp. 151–179.
Fitzgerald, Tanya, 'Jumping the fences: Maori women's resistance to missionary schooling in northern New Zealand, 1823–1835', *Pedagogica Historica*, vol. 37, no. 1 (2001), pp. 175–192.
——, 'Fences, boundaries and imagined communities: re-thinking the construction of early mission schools and communities in New Zealand, 1823–1830', *History of Education Review*, vol. 30, no. 2 (2001), pp. 14–25.

——, 'Cartographies of friendship: mapping missionary women's educational networks in Aotearoa/New Zealand 1823-40', *History of Education*, vol. 32, no. 5 (2003), pp. 513–527.

——, 'Creating a disciplined society: CMS women and the re-making of Nga Puhi women, 1823–35', *History of Education Review*, vol. 32, no. 1 (2003), pp. 84–98.

Fladeland, Betty, '"Our cause being one and the same": Abolitionists and Chartism', in J. Walvin (ed.), *Slavery and British Society* (London: Macmillan, 1982).

Forbes, Geraldine, 'In search of the "pure" heathen', *Economic and Political Weekly*, vol. 21, no. 17 (1986), WS 2–8.

Fowler, W. S., *A Study in Radicalism and Dissent: The Life and Times of Henry Joseph Wilson, 1833–1914* (London: Epworth Press, 1961).

Fraser, Derek, *Power and Authority in the Victorian City* (Oxford: Basil Blackwell, 1979).

Frost, Alan, 'The Pacific Ocean: the eighteenth century's "New World"', *Studies in Voltaire and the Eighteenth Century*, vol. 142 (1976), pp. 279–322.

Fyfe, Christopher, *A History Of Sierra Leone* (London: Oxford University Press, 1962).

——, 'Freed slave colonies in West Africa', in John Flint (ed.), *The Cambridge History of Africa, volume 5, from c. 1790 to c. 1870* (Cambridge: Cambridge University Press, 1976), pp. 170–199.

Gallagher, Catherine, *The Industrial Reformation of English Fiction: Social Discourse and Narrative Form, 1832–1867* (Chicago: University of Chicago Press, 1985).

Gascoigne, John, *Joseph Banks and the English Enlightenment: Useful Knowledge and Polite Culture* (Cambridge: Cambridge University Press, 1994).

Gates, Henry Louis Jr., *'Race', Writing and Difference* (Chicago: University of Chicago Press, 1986).

Gilbert, Alan D., *Religion and Society in Industrial England: Church, Chapel and Social Change 1740–1914* (London: Longman, 1976).

——, 'Religion and political stability in early industrial England', in P. O'Brien and R. Quinault (eds), *The Industrial Revolution and British Society* (Cambridge: Cambridge University Press, 1993), pp. 79–99.

Gilley, Sheridan and Sheils, W. J., *A History of Religion in Britain* (Oxford: Basil Blackwell, 1994).

Gill, Sean, 'Heroines of missionary adventure: the portrayal of Victorian women missionaries in popular fiction and biography', in A. Hogan and A. Bradstock (eds), *Women of Faith in Victorian Culture: Reassessing the Angel in the House* (Basingstoke: Macmillan 1998), pp. 172–185.

Gleadle, Kathryn, '"Opinions deliver'd in Conversation": conversation, politics and gender in the late eighteenth century', in J. Harris (ed.), *Civil Society in History* (Oxford: Oxford University Press, 2003), pp. 61–78.

——, '"Our several spheres": middle-class women and the feminisms of early Victorian radical politics', in Kathryn Gleadle and Sarah Richardson (eds), *Women in British Politics: The Power of the Petticoat* (Basingstoke: Macmillan, 2000), pp. 134–152.

——, '"The Age of Physiological Reformers": rethinking gender and domesticity in the age of reform', in Joanna Innes and Arthur Burns (eds), *Rethinking the Age of Reform: Britain 1780–1850* (Cambridge: Cambridge University Press, 2003), pp. 200–219.

Goldstrom, J. M., 'The content of education and the socialization of the working-class child 1830–1860', in Phillip McCann (ed.), *Popular Education and Socialization in the Nineteenth Century* (London: Methuen, 1977), pp. 94–107.

Gomersall, Meg, *Working-Class Girls in Nineteenth-Century England: Life, Work and Schooling* (New York: St. Martin's, 1997).

Goodall, Norman, *A History of the London Missionary Society, 1795–1895* (London: Oxford University Press, 1954).

Goodlad, Lauren M. E., '"Making the Working Man Like Me": charity, pastorship, and middle-class identity in nineteenth-century Britain; Thomas Chalmers and James Phillips Kay', *Victorian Studies*, vol. 43, no. 4 (Summer 2001), pp. 591–617.

Goodman, Joyce, 'Languages of female colonial authority: the educational network of the Ladies' Committee of the British and Foreign School Society, 1813–1837', *Compare*, vol. 30, no. 1 (2000), pp. 7–19.

——, '"At the centre of a circle whose circumference spans all nations": the Ladies' Committee of the British and Foreign School Society, 1813–1837', in S. Morgan (ed.), *Religion and Feminism in Modern Britain, 1750–1950*, (Basingstoke: Palgrave, 2002), pp. 53–69.

Gordon, Eleanor and Nair, Gwyneth. *Public Lives: Women, Family and Society in Victorian Britain* (New Haven: Yale University Press, 2003).

Gray, J. M., *A History of the Gambia* (Cambridge: Cambridge University Press, 1940).

Gray, Robert, 'Medical men, industrial labour and the state in Britain, 1830–50', *Social History*, vol. 16, no. 1 (January 1991), pp. 19–43.

——, *The Factory Question and Industrial England, 1830–1860* (Cambridge: Cambridge University Press, 1996).

Green, W. A., 'Was British emancipation a success? The abolitionist perspective', in David Richardson (ed.), *Abolition and its Aftermath* (London: Frank Cass, 1985), pp. 183–202.

Greenwood, Ormerod, 'Hannah Kilham's Plan', *The Sierra Leone Bulletin of Religion*, vol. 4, pt. 1 (1962), pp. 11–20.

——, *Quaker Encounters: Vines on the Mountain*, vol. 2 (York: William Sessions, 1977).
Grenby, M. O., '"Real charity makes distinctions": schooling the charitable impulse in early British children's literature', *British Journal of Eighteenth-Century Studies*, vol. 27 (2002), pp. 185–202.
Grimshaw, Patricia, *Paths of Duty: American Missionary Wives in Nineteenth Century Hawaii* (Honolulu: University of Hawaii Press, 1989).
Groves, Charles Pelham, *The Planting of Christianity in Africa, Vol I: to 1848* (London: Lutterworth Press, [1948] 1964).
Guest, Harriet, 'Curiously marked: tattooing, masculinity and nationality in eighteenth-century British perceptions of the South Pacific', in John Barrell (ed.), *Painting and the Politics of Culture: New Essays in British Art, 1700–1850* (Oxford: Clarendon Press, 1992), pp. 101–134.
Gunn, Simon, *The Public Culture of the Victorian Middle Class: Ritual and Authority in the English Industrial City, 1840–1914* (Manchester: Manchester University Press, 2000).
Gunson, Niel, 'John Williams and his ship: the bourgeois aspirations of a missionary family', in D. P. Crook (ed.), *Questioning the Past: A Selection of Papers in History and Government* (Brisbane: University of Queensland Press, 1972), pp. 73–95.
——, *Australian Reminiscences and Papers of Lancelot E. Threlkeld, Missionary to the Aborigines 1824–1859*, 2 vols (Canberra: Australian Institute of Aboriginal Studies, 1974).
——, *Messengers of Grace: Evangelical Missionaries in the South Seas, 1797–1860* (Melbourne: Oxford University Press, 1978).
—— (ed.), *The Changing Pacific. Essays in Honour of H. E. Maude* (Oxford: Oxford University Press, 1978).
Habermas, Jurgen, *The Structural Transformation of the Public Sphere: An Inquiry into a Category of Bourgeois Society*, trns by Thomas Burger and Frederick Lawrence (Cambridge: Polity Press, 1989).
Hadley, Elaine, *Melodramatic Tactics: Theatricalized Dissent in the English Marketplace, 1800–1885* (California: Stanford University Press, 1995).
Haggis, Jane, 'Gendering colonialism or colonizing gender', *Women's Studies International Forum*, vol. 13 (1990), pp. 105–115.
Haggis, Jane, '"Good wives and mothers" or "dedicated workers"? Contradictions of domesticity in the "mission of sisterhood", Travancore, South India', in Kalpana Ram and Margaret Jolly (eds), *Maternities and Modernities: Colonial and Postcolonial Experiences in Asia and the Pacific* (Cambridge: Cambridge University Press, 1998), pp. 81–113.
Hair, P. E. H., *The Early Study of Nigerian Languages* (Cambridge: Cambridge University Press, 1967).
Hall, Catherine, *White, Male and Middle Class: Explorations in Feminism and History* (Cambridge: Polity Press, 1992).

——, ' "From Greenland's Icy Mountain . . . to Africa's Golden Sand": ethnicity, race and nation in mid-nineteenth century England', *Gender & History*, vol. 5, no. 2 (Summer 1993), pp. 212–230.
——, 'White visions, Black lives: the free villages of Jamaica', *History Workshop Journal*, vol. 36 (Autumn 1993), pp. 100–132.
——, 'William Knibb and the constitution of the new black subject', in M. Daunton and R. Halpern (eds), *Empire and Others: British Encounters with Indigenous Peoples, 1600–1850* (London: UCL Press, 1999), pp. 303–324.
——, *Cultures of Empire: A Reader. Colonizers in Britain and the Empire in the Nineteenth and Twentieth Centuries* (Manchester: Manchester University Press, 2000).
——, *Civilising Subjects: Metropole and Colony in the English Imagination, 1830–1867* (Cambridge: Polity Press, 2002).
——, and Rose, Sonya, *At Home with the Empire: Metropolitan Culture and the Imperial World* (Cambridge: CUP, 2006).
Hall, Stuart, 'The West and the rest: discourse and power', in Stuart Hall and Bram Gieben (eds), *Formations of Modernity* (Cambridge: Polity Press in association with the Open University, 1992).
——, 'The multi-cultural question', in Barnor Hesse (ed.), *Un/Settled Multiculturalisms. Diasporas, Entanglements, Disruptions* (London: Zed Books, 2001), pp. 209–241.
Hannaford, Ivan, *Race: The History of an Idea in the West* (Baltimore: Johns Hopkins University Press, 1996).
Harris, John, *One Blood: 200 Years of Aboriginal Encounter with Christianity: A Story of Hope* (Sutherland: Albatross Books, 1990).
Harrison, Brian, *Drink and the Victorians: The Temperance Question in England, 1815–1872* (London: Faber and Faber, 1971).
Harrison, J. F. C., *Learning and Living, 1790–1960: A Study in the History of the English Adult Education Movement* (London: RKP, 1961).
Hempton, David, *Methodism and Politics in British Society, 1750–1850* (London: Harper Collins, 1987).
——, *The Religion of the People: Methodism and Popular Religion, c. 1750–1900* (London: Routledge 1996).
—— and Hill, Myrtle, *Evangelical Protestantism in Ulster Society 1740–1890* (London: Routledge, 1992).
Hewitt, Martin, *The Emergence of Social Stability in the Industrial City: Manchester, 1832–1867* (Aldershot: Ashgate, 1995).
——, 'The travails of domestic visiting: Manchester, 1830–70', *Historical Research*, vol. 71, no. 175 (1998), pp. 196–227.
Hill, Kate, *Culture and Class in English Public Museums, 1850–1914* (Aldershot: Ashgate, 2005).
Hilton, Boyd, *The Age of Atonement: The Influence of Evangelicalism on Social and Economic Thought, 1795–1865* (Oxford: Clarendon Press, 1988).

Himmelfarb, Gertrude, *The Idea of Poverty: England in the Early Industrial Age* (London: Faber and Faber, 1984).
Hindmarsh, D. Bruce, 'Patterns of conversion in early evangelical history and overseas mission experience', in B. Stanley (ed.), *Christian Missions and the Enlightenment* (Cambridge: William B. Erdmans, 2001), pp. 71–98.
Hole, Robert, *Pulpits, Politics and Public Order in England 1760–1832* (Cambridge: Cambridge University Press, 1989).
——, 'English sermons and tracts as media of debate', in Mark Philp (ed.), *The French Revolution and British Popular Politics* (Cambridge: Cambridge University Press, 1991), pp. 18–37.
Holladay, J. Douglas, '19th Century evangelical activism: from private charity to state intervention, 1830–50', *Historical Magazine of the Protestant Episcopalian Church*, vol. 1 (1982), pp. 53–79.
Hollis, Patricia, *Pressure from Without in Early Victorian England* (London: Edward Arnold, 1974).
——, 'Anti-slavery and British working-class radicalism in the years of reform', in Christine Bolt and Seymour Drescher (eds), *Anti-Slavery, Religion and Reform: Essays in Memory of Roger Anstey* (Folkstone: William Dawson, 1980), pp. 294–315.
Holt, Istvan and Ignatieff, Michael, (eds), *Wealth and Virtue: The Shaping of Political Economy in the Scottish Enlightenment* (Cambridge: Cambridge University Press, 1983).
Hopkins, Mary Alden, *Hannah More and her Circle* (New York: Longman, Greens and Co, 1947).
Howe, Kerry, 'The fate of the "savage" in Pacific historiography', *New Zealand Journal of History*, vol. 11 (1977), pp. 137–154.
——, *Where the Waves Fall: A New South Seas Islands History from First Settlement to Colonial Rule* (Sydney and London: George Allen & Unwin, 1984).
Howsam, Leslie, *Cheap Bibles: Nineteenth Century Publishing and the British and Foreign Bible Society* (Cambridge: Cambridge University Press, 1991).
Howse, Ernest M., *Saints in Politics: The 'Clapham Sect' and the Growth of Freedom* (London: George Allen and Unwin, 1953).
Huber, Mary Taylor and Lutkehaus, Nancy C. (eds), *Gendered Missions: Women and Men in Missionary Discourse and Practice* (Ann Arbor: University of Michigan Press, 1999).
Inkster, Ian, 'Science and the Mechanics' Institutes, 1820–1850: the case of Sheffield', *Annals of Science*, vol. 32 (1975), pp. 451–474.
——, 'Marginal men: aspects of the social role of the medical community in Sheffield 1790–1850', in John Woodward and David Richards (eds), *Health Care and Popular Medicine in Nineteenth Century England: Essays in the Social History of Medicine* (New York: Holmes and Meier, 1977), pp. 128–163.

——, 'A phase in middle class culture: phrenology in Sheffield, 1824–1850', *Transactions of the Hunter Archaeological Society*, vol. 10, no. 4 (1977), pp. 273–279.

——, 'Aspects of the history of science and science culture in Britain, 1780–1850', in Ian Inkster and Jack Morrell (eds), *Metropolis and Province: Science in British Culture, 1780–1850* (London: Hutchinson, 1983).

——, 'The social context of an educational movement: a revisionist approach to the English Mechanics' Institutes, 1820–1850', in Inkster (ed.), *Scientific Culture and Urbanisation in Industrialising Britain* (Aldershot: Ashgate, 1997).

Innes, Joanna, 'Politics and morals: the Reformation of Manners movement in later eighteenth-century England', in E. Hellmuth (ed.), *The Transformation of Political Culture: England and Germany in the late Eighteenth Century* (Oxford: Oxford University Press, 1990), pp. 57–118.

Isichei, Elizabeth, *Victorian Quakers* (London: Oxford University Press, 1970).

Jackson, Mary V., *Engines of Instruction, Mischief and Magic. Children's Literature in England from its Beginnings to 1839* (Lincoln: University of Nebraska, 1989).

James, Louis, *Fiction for the Working Man, 1830–1850: A Study of Literature Produced for the Working Classes in Early Victorian Urban England* (London: Oxford University Press, 1963).

James, Patricia, *Population Malthus: His Life and Times* (London: RKP, 1979).

Johnson, Richard, 'Notes on the schooling of the English working class', in Roger Dale, Geoff Esland and Madeleine MacDonald (eds), *Schooling and Capitalism: A Sociological Reader* (London: RKP and the Open University Press, 1976), pp. 44–54.

Johnson, Richard, '"Really useful knowledge": radical education and working-class culture', in J. Clarke, C. Crichter and R. Johnson (eds), *Working-Class Culture: Studies in History and Theory* (London: Hutchinson, 1979), pp. 75–102.

Johnston, Anna, 'The book eaters: textuality, modernity, and the London Missionary Society', *Semeia*, vol. 88 (2001), pp. 13–40.

——, *Missionary Writing and Empire* (Cambridge: Cambridge University Press, 2003).

Jolly, Margaret, '"To save the girls for brighter and better lives": Presbyterian missions and women in the South of Vanuatu, 1848–1870', *Journal of Pacific History*, vol. 26, no. 1 (1991), pp. 27–48.

——, 'Colonizing women: the maternal body and empire', in Sneja Gunew and Anna Yeatman (eds), *Feminism and the Politics of Difference* (NSW: Allen and Unwin, 1993), pp. 103–127.

Jones, Colin, *Britain and Revolutionary France: conflict, subversion and propaganda* (University of Exeter: Exeter Studies in History, 1983).

——, 'Some recent trends in the history of charity', in M. Daunton (ed.), *Charity, Self-Interest and Welfare in the English Past* (London: UCL Press, 1996), pp. 51–63.

Jones, M. G., *Hannah More* (Cambridge: Cambridge University Press, 1952).

——., *The Charity School Movement: A Study of Puritanism in Action* (London: Frank Cass, 1964).

Jones, R. Tudur, *Congregationalism in England* (London: Independent Press, 1962).

Jordan, Winthrop, 'First impressions: initial English confrontations', in Charles Husband (ed.), *'Race' in Britain: Continuity and Change* (London: Hutchinson, 1992), pp. 42–58.

Jordanova, Ludmilla, 'Conceptualizing childhood in the eighteenth century: the problem of child labour', *British Journal of Eighteenth Century Studies*, vol. 10 (1987), pp. 189–199.

——, 'Objects of knowledge: a historical perspective on museums', in Peter Vergo (ed.), *The New Museology* (London: Reaktion Books Ltd, 1989), pp. 22–40.

Joynes, Sarah E., 'The Sheffield Library 1771–1907', *Library History: Journal of the Library History Group of the Library Association*, vol. 2, no. 3 (Spring 1971), pp. 91–116.

Kaestle, Carl F., '"Between the Scylla of brutal ignorance and the Charybdis of a literary education": elite attitudes towards mass schooling in early industrial England and America', in Lawrence Stone (ed.), *Schooling and Society: Studies in the History of Education* (Baltimore and London: Johns Hopkins University Press, 1976), pp. 177–191.

Kaufman, Paul, *Borrowings from the Bristol Library, 1773–1784: A Unique Record of Reading Vogues* (Charlottesville: Bibliographical Society of the University of Virginia, 1960).

Kelly, Gary, *Women, Writing and Revolution, 1790–1827* (Oxford: Clarendon Press, 1993).

Kelly, Thomas, *A History of Adult Education in Great Britain* (Liverpool: Liverpool University Press, 1962).

Kennon, Donald R., '"An Apple of Discord": the Woman Question at the World's Anti-Slavery Convention of 1840', *Slavery and Abolition*, vol. 5, no. 3 (December 1984), pp. 244–266.

Kidd, Alan, 'Philanthropy and the "Social History paradigm"', *Social History*, vol. 21, no. 2 (May 1996), pp. 180–192.

Klein, Lawrence E., 'Gender and the public/private distinction in the eighteenth century: some questions about evidence and analytic procedure', *Eighteenth-Century Studies*, vol. 29, no. 1 (Fall 1995), pp. 97–109.

Koditschek, Theodore, *Class Formation and Urban-Industrial Society, Bradford 1750–1850* (Cambridge University Press, 1990).

Kovacevic, Ivana, *Fact Into Fiction* (Leicester: Leicester University Press, 1975).

Kruegar, Christine L., *The Reader's Repentance: Women Preachers, Women Writers and Nineteenth-Century Social Discourse* (Chicago: University of Chicago Press, 1992).

Laqueur, Thomas, *Religion and Respectability: Sunday Schools and Working Class Culture, 1780–1850* (New Haven: Yale University Press, 1976).

——, 'Working-class demand and the growth of English elementary education, 1750–1850', in L. Stone, (ed.), *Schooling and Society: Studies in the History of Education* (Baltimore and London: Johns Hopkins University Press, 1976).

——, 'Bodies, details and the humanitarian narrative', in Lynn Hunt (ed.), *The New Cultural History* (London: University of California Press, 1989), pp. 176–204.

Laidlaw, Zoe, '"Aunt Anna's Report": the Buxton Women and the Aborigines Select Committee, 1835–37', *Journal of Commonwealth and Imperial History*, vol. 32, no. 2 (April 2004), pp. 1–28.

Langland, Elizabeth, 'Women's writing and the domestic sphere', in Joanne Shattock (ed.), *Women and Literature in Britain 1800–1900* (Cambridge: Cambridge University Press, 2001), pp. 119–141.

Latukefu, Sione, *Church and State in Tonga: the Wesleyan Methodist Missionaries and Political Development 1822–1875* (Canberra: Australian National University Press, 1974).

Lester, Alan, 'British settler discourse and the circuits of empire', *History Workshop Journal*, vol. 54 (2002), pp. 24–48.

Lewis, Donald, *Lighten their Darkness: The Evangelical Mission to London, 1828–1860* (Connecticut: Grenwood Press, 1986).

Lewis, Donald M., '"Lights in Dark Places": women evangelists in early Victorian Britain, 1838–1857', in W. J. Sheils and Diana Wood (eds), *Women in the Church. Studies in Church History*, vol. 27 (1990), pp. 415–427.

Lorimer, Douglas A., *Colour, Class and the Victorians* (Leicester: Leicester University Press, 1978).

Lovegrove, D. W., *Established Church, Sectarian People: Itinerancy and the Transformation of English Dissent, 1780–1830* (Cambridge: Cambridge University Press, 1988).

Lovett, Richard, *History of the London Missionary Society, 1795–1895*, vol. 1 (London: Henry Froude, 1899).

Luddy, Maria, *Women and Philanthropy in Nineteenth-Century Ireland* (Cambridge: Cambridge University Press, 1995).

MacKenzie, John M., *Imperialism and Popular Culture* (Manchester: Manchester University Press, 1986).

——, 'Heroic myths of empire', in MacKenzie (ed.), *Popular Imperialism and the Military 1850–1950* (Manchester: Manchester University Press, 1992), pp. 109–138.

Mackerness, E. D., 'Mary-Anne Rawson and the memorials of James Montgomery', *Transactions of the Hunter Archaeological Society*, vol. 8 (1962), pp. 218–228.

Malmgreen, Gail (ed.), *Religion in the Lives of English Women, 1760–1930* (London: Croom Helm, 1986).

Mandler, Peter, 'Poverty and charity in the nineteenth-century metropolis: an introduction', in Peter Mandler (ed.), *The Uses of Charity: The Poor on Relief in the Nineteenth-Century Metropolis* (Philadelphia: University of Pennsylvania Press, 1990), pp. 1–37.

——, 'Tories and Paupers: Christian political economy and the making of the New Poor Law', *The Historical Journal*, vol. 33, no. 1 (1990), pp. 81–103.

——, '"Race" and "Nation" in mid-Victorian thought', in S. Collini, R. Whatmore and B. Young (eds), *History, Religion and Culture: British Intellectual History 1780–1950* (Cambridge: Cambridge University Press, 2000).

——, 'The problem with cultural history', *Cultural and Social History*, vol. 1, no. 1 (2004), pp. 94–117.

Mangan, J. A. and Walvin, James (eds), *Manliness and Morality* (Manchester: Manchester University Press, 1987).

Mani, Lata, *Contentious Traditions: The Debate on Sati in Colonial India* (Berkeley: University of California Press, 1998).

Marland, Hilary, *Medicine and Society in Wakefield and Huddersfield 1780–1850* (Cambridge: Cambridge University Press, 1989).

Marshall, P. J. and Williams, Glyndwr, *The Great Map of Mankind: British Perceptions of the World in the Age of Enlightenment* (London: J. M. Dent and Sons Ltd., 1982).

Martin, Roger H., 'Missionary competition between evangelical dissenters and Wesleyan Methodists in the early nineteenth century', *Proceedings of the Wesley Historical Society*, vol. 42 (1979), pp. 81–86.

——, *Evangelicals United: Ecumenical Stirrings in Pre-Victorian Britain, 1795–1830* (London: Scarecrow Press, 1983).

Maughan, Stephen S., 'Civic culture, women's foreign missions and the British imperial imagination, 1860–1914', in Frank Trentmann (ed.), *Paradoxes of Civil Society: New Perspectives on Modern German and British History* (Oxford: Berghahn Books, 2000).

McCaffrey, J. F., 'Thomas Chalmers and social change', *The Scottish Historical Review*, vol. 60 (1981), pp. 32–60.

——, 'The life of Thomas Chalmers', in A. C. Cheyne (ed.), *The Practical and the Pious* (Edinburgh: St. Andrew's Press, 1985), pp. 31–64.

McLintock, Anne, *Imperial Leather: Race, Gender and Sexuality in the Colonial Contest* (London: Routledge, 1995).

Mee, John, *Dangerous Enthusiasm: William Blake and the Culture of Radicalism in the 1790s* (Oxford: Clarendon Press, 1992).

Meek, Ronald L., *Social Science and the Ignoble Savage* (Cambridge: Cambridge University Press, 1976).

Mellor, Anne, *Mothers of the Nation: Women's Political Writing in England 1780–1830* (Bloomington: Indiana University Press, 2000).

Mercer, Malcolm, *Schooling the Poorer Child: Elementary Education in Sheffield, 1560–1902* (Sheffield: Sheffield Academic Press, 1996).

Midgley, Clare, *Women Against Slavery: The British Campaigns, 1780–1870* (London: Routledge, 1992).

——, 'Anti-Slavery and Feminism in nineteenth-century Britain', *Gender & History*, vol. 5, no. 3 (Autumn 1993), pp. 343–362.

——, 'Slave sugar boycotts, female activism and the domestic base of British anti-slavery culture', *Slavery and Abolition*, vol. 17, no. 3 (1996), pp. 137–162.

——, 'Anti-slavery and the roots of "imperial feminism" ', in C. Midgley (ed.), *Gender and Imperialism* (Manchester: Manchester University Press, 1998), pp. 161–179.

——, 'From supporting missions to petitioning Parliament: English women and the evangelical campaign against "sati" (widow-burning) in India, 1813–1830', in K. Gleadle and S. Richardson (eds), *Women in British Politics* (Basingstoke: Macmillan, 2000), pp. 74–92.

——, 'Can women be missionaries? Envisioning female agency in the early nineteenth-century British empire', *Journal of British Studies*, vol. 45, no. 2 (April 2006), pp. 335–358.

Morgan, Simon J., ' "A sort of land debatable": female influence, civic virtue and middle-class identity, c. 1830–1860', *Women's History Review*, vol. 13, no. 2 (2004), pp. 183–210.

——, *A Victorian Woman's Place: Public Culture in the Nineteenth Century* (London: IB Tauris, 2007).

Morris, Robert J., 'Voluntary societies and British urban elites, 1780–1850: an analysis', *The Historical Journal*, vol. 26, no. 1 (1983), pp. 95–118.

——, *Class, Sect and Party: The Making of the British Middle Class, Leeds 1820–1850* (Manchester: Manchester University Press, 1990).

Myers, Mitzi, 'Hannah More's tracts for the times: social fiction and female ideology', in Mary Anne Schofield and Cecelia Macheski (eds), *Fetter'd or Free? British Women Novelists, 1670–1815* (London: Ohio University Press, 1986), pp. 264–284.

Nair, Janaki, 'Uncovering the Zenana: visions of Indian womanhood in Englishwomen's writing 1813–1940', *Journal of Women's History*, vol. 2, no. 1 (Spring 1990), pp. 8–34.

Neuburg, Victor, *Popular Literature* (London: Woburn Press, 1977).

O'Brien, Susan, 'A transatlantic community of Saints: The Great Awakening and the first evangelical network, 1735–1755', *American Historical Review*, vol. 91 (1986), pp. 811–832.

Obelkevich, James, *Religion and Rural Society: South Lindsey* (Oxford: Clarendon Press, 1976).

——, Roper, L., and Samuel, R., *Disciplines of Faith: Studies in Religion, Politics and Patriarchy* (London: RKP, 1987).

Oddie, G. A., *Social Protest in India: British Protestant Missionaries and Social Reform, 1850–1900* (New Delhi: Manohar, 1978).

Oliver, W. H., *Prophets and Millenialists: The Uses of Biblical Prophecy in England from the 1790s to the 1840s* (Oxford: Oxford University Press, 1978).

Outram, Dorinda, *The Enlightenment* (Cambridge: Cambridge University Press, 1995).

Owen, David, *English Philanthropy 1660–1960* (London: Oxford University Press, 1965).

Owens, J. M. R., *Prophets in the Wilderness: The Wesleyan Mission to New Zealand, 1819–27* (Oxford: Oxford University Press, 1974).

Paton, Diana, 'Decency, dependency and the lash: gender and the British debate over slave emancipation 1830–34', *Slavery and Abolition*, vol. 17, no. 3 (December 1996), pp. 163–184.

Pearce, Susan M., *Museums, Objects and Collections: A Cultural Study* (Leicester: Leicester University Press, 1992).

Peel, J. D. Y., 'For who hath despised the day of small things? Missionary narratives and historical anthropology', *Comparative Studies in Society and History*, vol. 37 (1995), pp. 581–607.

Pedersen, Susan, 'Hannah More meets Simple Simon: tracts, chapbooks, and popular culture in late eighteenth-century England', *Journal of British Studies*, vol. 25 (1986), pp. 84–113.

Perry, Adele, 'Metropolitan knowledge, colonial practice, and indigenous womanhood: missions in nineteenth-century British Columbia', in Katie Pickles and Myra Rutherdale (eds), *Contact Zones: Aboriginal and Settler Women in Canada's Colonial Past* (Vancouver: UBC Press, 2005).

Piggin, Stuart, 'Sectarianism versus Ecumenism: the impact on British Churches of the missionary movement to India, c. 1800–1860', *Journal of Ecclesiastical History*, vol. 27, no. 4 (October 1976), pp. 387–402.

—— 'Halevy revisited: the origins of the WMMS: an examination of Semmel's thesis', *Journal of Imperial and Commonwealth History*, vol. 9, no. 1 (1980), pp. 17–37.
——, *Making Evangelical Missionaries, 1789–1858: The Social Background, Motives, and Training of the British Protestant Missionaries* (Oxford: Sutton Courtney Press, 1984).
Pinches, Sylvia, 'Women as objects and agents of charity in eighteenth century Birmingham', in R. Lane and P. Sweet (eds), *Women and Urban Life in Eighteenth Century England* (Aldershot: Ashgate, 2003).
Pinnington, J., 'Church principles in the early years of the Church Missionary Society: the problem of the "German missionaries" ', *Journal of Theological Studies*, New Series, vol. 20, no. 21 (1969), pp. 523–532.
Plant, Helen, ' "Subjective Testimonies": women Quaker ministers and spiritual authority in England, 1750–1825', *Gender and History*, vol. 15, no. 2 (August 2003), pp. 296–318.
Plumb, J. H., 'The new world of children in eighteenth-century England', *Past and Present*, no. 67 (May 1975), pp. 64–95.
Pollard, Sydney, *A History of Labour in Sheffield* (Liverpool: Liverpool University Press, 1959).
Poovey, Mary, *Making a Social Body: British Cultural Formation, 1830–1864* (London: University of Chicago Press, 1995).
Porter, Andrew, 'Religion, missionary enthusiasm and empire', in Andrew Porter (ed.), *The Oxford History of the British Empire, vol. 3: The Nineteenth Century* (Oxford: Oxford University, 1999), pp. 222–246.
——, *Religion Versus Empire? British Protestant Missionaries and Overseas Expansion, 1700–1914* (Manchester: Manchester University Press, 2004).
Potter, S. C., 'The making of missionaries in the nineteenth century: conversion and convention', *A Sociological Yearbook of Religion in Britain* (London: SCM Press, 1975), pp. 103–124.
Potts, E. D., *British Baptist Missionaries in India, 1793–1837: The History of Serampore and its Mission* (Cambridge: Cambridge University Press, 1967).
Poynter, J. R., *Society and Pauperism: English Ideas on Poor Relief, 1795–1834* (London: RKP, 1969).
Pratt, Mary Louise, *Imperial Eyes: Travel Writing and Transculturation* (London: Routledge, 1992).
Price, Richard, *The British and the Xhosa Peoples in Nineteenth-Century Africa* (Cambridge: Cambridge University Press, forthcoming, 2009).
Prochaska, Frank K., *Women and Philanthropy in Nineteenth-Century England* (Oxford: Clarendon Press, 1980).
Purvis, June, *Hard Lessons: The Lives and Education of Working-Class Women in Nineteenth-Century England* (Cambridge: Polity Press, 1989).

Quinlan, Maurice, *Victorian Prelude: A History of English Manners 1700–1830* (New York: Colombia University Press, 1941).

Rack, H. D., 'Domestic visitation: a chapter in early nineteenth-century evangelism', *Journal of Ecclesiastical History*, vol. 24, no. 4 (October 1973), 357–376.

——, *Reasonable Enthusiast: John Wesley and the Rise of Methodism* (London: Epworth Press, 1989).

Ramsden, Eric, *Marsden and the Missions: Prelude to Waitangi* (Sydney: Angus and Robertson, 1936).

Read, Donald, *Press and People, 1790–1850: Opinion in Three English Cities* (London: Edward Arnold, 1961).

——, *The English Provinces 1760–1960: A Study in Influence* (London: Edward Arnold, 1964).

Reid, Caroline O., 'Middle-class values and working-class culture in nineteenth-century Sheffield: the pursuit of respectability', in Sidney Pollard and Colin Holmes (eds), *Essays in the Economic and Social History of South Yorkshire* (Sheffield: South Yorkshire County Council, 1976), pp. 275–295.

——, 'Temperance, teetotalism and local culture: the early temperance movement in Sheffield', *Northern History*, vol. 13 (1977), pp. 248–264.

Rendall, Jane, 'Scottish orientalism: from Robertson to James Mill', *The Historical Journal*, vol. 25, no. 1 (1982), pp. 43–69.

——, *The Origins of Modern Feminism* (Basingstoke: Macmillan, 1985).

——, 'Virtue and Commerce: women in the making of Adam Smith's political economy', in Ellen Kennedy and Susan Mendus (eds), *Women in Western Civilisation: Kant to Nietzsche* (Brighton: Harvester Wheatsheaf, 1987), pp. 44–77.

——, 'Nineteenth-century feminism and the separation of the spheres; reflections on the public/private dichotomy', in Tayo Andreasen, Annette Borchost, Drude Dahlerup, Hanne Rimmen Nielsen and Eva Louis (eds), *Moving On: New Perspectives on the Women's Movement* (Aarhus: Aarhus University Press, 1991), pp. 17–37.

——(ed.), Introduction to *William Alexander's History of Women from the Earliest Antiquity to the Present Time* (Bristol: Thoemmes Press, 1994 [1777]).

——, ' "The Grand Causes which combine to carry men forward": Wollstonecraft, History and Revolution', *Women's Writing: the Elizabethan to Victorian Period*, vol. 4, no. 2 (1997), pp. 155–172.

——. 'Women and the public sphere', *Gender & History*, vol. 11, no. 3 (November 1999), pp. 475–488.

Rice, C. Duncan, *The Scots Abolitionists, 1833–1861* (Baton Rouge: Louisana State University Press, 1981).

Richardson, Alan, *Literature, Education and Romanticism: Reading as Social Practice 1780–1832* (Cambridge: Cambridge University Press, 1994).

Roach, John. 'The Sheffield community and public work, 1790–1914', *Yorkshire Archaeological Journal*, vol. 77 (2005), pp. 225–240.
Roberts, M. J. D., *Making English Morals: Voluntary Association and Moral Reform in England, 1787–1886* (Cambridge: Cambridge University Press, 2004).
Robinson, Philip, *The Smiths of Chesterfield: A History of the Griffin Foundry, Brampton 1775–1833* (Chesterfield: Thomas Brayshaw, 1957).
Robson, A. P., *On Higher than Commercial Grounds: The Factory Controversy, 1830–1853* (London and New York: Garland, 1985).
Rogers, Helen, 'In the name of the father: political biographies by radical daughters', in David Amigoni (ed.), *Life Writing and Victorian Culture* (Aldershot: Ashgate, 2006), pp. 202–227.
——, *Women and the People: Authority, Authorship and the Radical Tradition in Nineteenth-Century England* (Aldershot: Ashgate, 2000).
Roper, Michael and Tosh, John, (eds), *Manful Assertions: Masculinities in Britain since 1800* (London: Routledge, 1991).
Rose, M. E., 'Culture, philanthropy and the Manchester middle classes', in Alan Kidd and K. W. Roberts (eds), *City, Class and Culture: Studies of Cultural Production and Social Policy in Victorian Manchester* (Manchester: Manchester University Press, 1985).
Rosman, Doreen M., *Evangelicals and Culture* (London: Croom Helm, 1984).
Ross, Robert, *Status and Respectability in the Cape Colony: A Tragedy of Manners* (Cambridge: Cambridge University Press, 1999).
Rowbotham, Judith, 'Ministering Angels, not Ministers: women's involvement in the foreign missionary movement, c. 1860–1910', in S. Morgan (ed.), *Women, Religion and Feminism in Britain 1750–1900* (Basingstoke: Palgrave, 2002), pp. 179–195.
Royle, Edward, 'Mechanics' Institutes and the working classes, 1840–1860', *Historical Journal*, vol. 14 (1971), pp. 305–321.
Rutherdale, Myra, *Women and the White Man's God: Gender and Race in the Canadian Mission Field* (Vancouver: UBC Press 2002).
Sahlins, Marshall, *How "natives" Think About Captain Cook, for Example* (Chicago: University of Chicago Press, 1995).
Said, Edward W., *Orientalism* (Harmondsworth: Penguin, 1978).
——, *Culture and Imperialism* (London: Vintage, 1993).
Salt, John, 'The Sheffield Hall of Science', *Vocational Aspect*, vol. 12, no. 25 (1960), pp. 133–138.
——, 'The creation of the Sheffield Mechanics' Institute: social pressures and educational advance in an industrial town', *Vocational Aspect*, vol. 18, no. 40 (Summer 1966), pp. 143–150.
——, 'Early Sheffield Sunday Schools and their educational importance', *Transactions of the Hunter Archaeological Society*, vol. 9, no. 3 (1966), pp. 179–184.

—— 'Isaac Ironside 1808–1870: the motives of a radical educationalist', *British Journal of Educational Studies*, vol. 19 (1971), pp. 183–201.

Samson, Jane, *Imperial Benevolence: Making British Authority in the Pacific Islands* (Honolulu: University of Hawaii Press, 1998).

——, 'Ethnology and Theology: nineteenth-century mission dilemmas', in B. Stanley (ed.), *Christian Missions and the Enlightenment* (Grand Rapids: William B. Eerdmans and Curzon Press, 2001), pp. 99–122.

Sangari, K. and Vaid, S., *Recasting Women: Essays in Indian Colonial History* (New Brunswick: Rutgers University Press, 1990).

Sangster, Paul, *Pity My Simplicity: The Evangelical Revival and the Religious Education of Children, 1738–1800* (London: Epworth Press, 1963).

Sanneh, Lamin, *West African Christianity: The Religious Impact* (London: C. Hurst, 1983).

Scotland, Nigel, *The Life and Work of John Bird Sumner, Evangelical Archbishop* (Herefordshire: Gracewing books, 1995).

Seed, John, 'Unitarianism, political economy and the antinomies of liberal culture in Manchester, 1830–1850', *Social History*, vol. 7, no. 1 (1982), pp. 1–25.

——, 'Gentleman dissenters: the social and political meanings of Rational Dissent in the 1770s and 1780s', *The Historical Journal*, vol. 28, no. 2 (1985), pp. 299–325.

——, 'Theologies of power: unitarianism and the social relations of religious discourse, 1800–50', in R. J. Morris (ed.), *Class, Power and Social Structure in British Nineteenth-Century Towns* (Leicester: Leicester University Press, 1986), pp. 107–156.

—— 'From "middling sort" to middle class in late eighteenth- and early nineteenth-century England', in M. L. Bush (ed.), *Social Orders and Social Classes in Europe Since 1500: Studies in Social Stratification* (London: Longman 1992), pp. 114–135.

Segovia, Fernando F., 'Biblical criticism and postcolonial studies: towards a postcolonial optic', in R. S. Sugirtharajah (ed.), *The Postcolonial Bible* (Sheffield Academic Press, 1998), pp. 49–90.

Semmel, Bernard, *The Methodist Revolution* (London: Heineman, 1974).

Semple, Rhonda, *Missionary Women: Gender, Professionalism and the Victorian Idea of Christian Mission* (Woodbridge: the Boydell Press, 2003).

Shapin, Steven and Barnes, Barry, 'Science, nature and control: interpreting Mechanics' Institutes', in Roger Dale, Geoff Esland and Madeleine MacDonald (eds), *Schooling and Capitalism: A Sociological Reader* (London: RKP and the Open University Press, 1976), pp. 55–65.

Shiman, Lilian Lewis, *Crusade Against Drink in Victorian England* (New York: St. Martin's Press, 1988).

Silver, Harold M., *The Concept of Popular Education: A Study of Ideas and Social Movements in the Early Nineteenth Century* (London: MacGibbon and Kee, 1965).

Simey, Margaret, *Charitable Effort in Liverpool in the Nineteenth Century* (Liverpool: Liverpool University Press, 1951).

Simon, Brian, *Studies in the History of Education 1780–1870* (London: Lawrence and Wishart, 1960).

Sivasundaram, Sujit, *Nature and the Godly Empire: Science and Evangelical Mission in the Pacific, 1795–1850* (Cambridge: Cambridge University Press, 2005).

Sklar, Kathryn Kish, '"Women Who Speak for an Entire Nation": American and British women at the World Anti-Slavery Convention, London, 1840', *Pacific Historical Review* (1990), pp. 453–499.

Smail, John, *The Origins of Middle-Class Culture: Halifax, Yorkshire, 1660–1780* (London: Cornell University Press, 1994).

Smith, Bernard, *European Vision and the South Pacific 1768–1850* (London: Oxford University Press, 1960).

Smith, Dennis, *Conflict and Compromise: Class Formation in English Society 1830–1914* (London: Routledge, 1982).

Smith, Olivia, *The Politics of Language, 1791–1819* (Oxford: Clarendon Press, 1985).

Solway, R. A., *Prelates and People: Ecclesiastical Social Thought in England 1783–1852* (London: RKP, 1969).

Spadafora, David, *The Idea of Progress in Eighteenth-Century Britain* (London: Yale University Press, 1990).

Spivak, Gayatri Chakravorty, *In Other Worlds: Essays in Cultural Politics* (London: Routledge, 1988).

——, 'Can the Subaltern Speak?', in Cary Nelson and Larry Grossberg (eds), *Marxism and the Interpretation of Culture* (Urbana: University of Illinois Press, 1988), pp. 271–313.

Stanley, Brian, 'Christian responses to the Indian Mutiny of 1857', *The Church and War: Studies in Church History*, vol. 20 (1983), pp. 277–289.

——, *The Bible and the Flag: Protestant Missions and British Imperialism in the Nineteenth and Twentieth Centuries* (Leicester: Apollos, 1990).

——, *The History of the Baptist Missionary Society 1792–1992* (Edinburgh: T. T. Clark, 1992).

——, 'Christian missions and the Enlightenment: a re-evaluation', in Brain Stanley (ed.), *Christian Missions and the Enlightenment* (Cambridge: William B. Eerdmans, 2001).

Stepan, Nancy, *The Idea of Race in Science: Great Britain, 1800–1960* (London: Macmillan, 1982).

Stevenson, John, *Artisans and Democrats: Sheffield in the French Revolution, 1789–1897* (Sheffield, 1989).

Stewart, Christina Duff (ed.), *Ann Taylor Gilbert's Album* (New York and London: Garland, 1978).

Stock, Eugene, *History of the Church Missionary Society*, vol. 1 (London: Church Missionary Society, 1899).

Stocking, George W. Jr., *Victorian Anthropology* (New York: The Free Press, 1987).

Stoler, Ann Laura, 'Rethinking colonial categories: European communities and the boundaries of rule', *Comparative Studies in Society and History*, vol. 31 (1989), pp. 134–161.

——, 'Cultivating bourgeois bodies and racial selves', in C. Hall (ed.), *Cultures of Empire. Colonizers in Britain and the Empire in the Nineteenth and Twentieth Centuries* (Manchester: Manchester University Press, 2000), pp. 87–119.

Stott, Anne, *Hannah More: The First Victorian* (Oxford: Oxford University Press, 2003).

Strange, K. H., *The Climbing Boys: A Study of Sweeps' Apprentices, 1773–1875* (London: Allison and Busby, 1982).

Sugirtharajah, R. S., *Asian Biblical Hermeneutics and Postcolonialism: Contesting the Interpretations.* (Maryknoll: Orbis, 1998).

—— *The Postcolonial Bible* (Sheffield: Sheffield Academic Press, 1998).

Summers, Anne, 'A home from home – women's philanthropic work in the nineteenth century', in Sandra Burman (ed.), *Fit Work for Women* (London: Croom Helm, 1979).

——, *Female Lives, Moral States: Women, Religion and Public Life in Britain 1800–1930* (Berks: Threshold Press, 2000).

Sutherland, Kathryn, 'Hannah More's counter-revolutionary feminism', in Kelvin Everest (ed.), *Revolution in Writing: British Literary Responses to the French Revolution* (Buckingham: Open University Press, 1991), pp. 27–63.

——, 'Adam Smith's master narrative: women and the *Wealth of Nations*', S. Copley and K. Sutherland (ed.), *Adam Smith's Wealth of Nations. New Interdisciplinary Essays* (Manchester: Manchester University Press, 1995), pp. 97–121.

Teich, Mikulas and Porter, Roy, *The Enlightenment in National Context* (Cambridge: Cambridge University Press, 1981).

Temperley, Howard, *British Anti-Slavery, 1832–1870* (London: Longman, 1972).

Thackray, Arnold, 'Natural knowledge in a cultural context: the Manchester Model', *American Historical Review*, vol. 79 (1974), pp. 672–709.

Theissen, Gerd, *The Social Setting of Pauline Christianity: Essays on Corinth,* trns by John H. Schutz (Philadelphia: Fortress Press, 1982).

Thomas, Nicholas, *Entangled Objects: Exchange, Material Culture and Colonialism in the Pacific* (London: Harvard University Press, 1991).

Thomas, Nicholas, *Colonialism's Culture: Anthropology, Travel and Government* (Cambridge: Polity Press, 1994).

——, 'Colonial conversions: difference, hierarchy and history in early twentieth-century evangelical propaganda', in Catherine Hall (ed.),

Cultures of Empire. Colonizers in Britain and the Empire in the Nineteenth and Twentieth Centuries (Manchester: Manchester University Press, 2000), pp. 298–328.

Thompson, David M., *Denominationalism and Dissent, 1795–1948: A Question of Identity* (London: Friends of Dr. Williams Library, 1985).

Thompson, Dorothy, 'Women, work and politics in nineteenth-century England: the problem of authority', in Jane Rendall (ed.), *Equal or Different: Women's Politics, 1800–1914* (Oxford: Basil Blackwell, 1987), pp. 57–81.

Thompson, Noel W., *The People's Science: The Popular Political Economy of Exploitation and Crisis, 1816–34* (Cambridge: Cambridge University Press, 1984).

Thorne, Susan, *Congregational Missions and the Making of an Imperial Culture in 19th Century England* (California: Stanford University Press, 1999).

——, 'Missionary-Imperial Feminism', in M. Taylor Huber and Nancy C. Lutkehaus (eds), *Gendered Missions: Women and Men in Missionary Discourse and Practice* (Ann Arbor: University of Michigan Press, 1999), pp. 39–65.

Tolley, Christopher, *Domestic Biography: The Legacy of Evangelicalism in Four Nineteenth-Century Families* (Oxford: Oxford University Press, 1997).

Tomaselli, Sylvana, 'The Enlightenment debate on women', *History Workshop Journal*, vol. 19 (1985), pp. 101–124.

Tosh, John, 'Authority and nurture in middle-class fatherhood: the case of early and Mid-Victorian England', *Gender & History*, vol. 8, no. 1 (April 1996), pp. 48–64.

——, *A Man's Place: Masculinity and the Middle-Class Home in Victorian England* (London: Yale University Press 1999).

——, *Manliness and Masculinities in Nineteenth-Century England* (London: Longman, 2004).

Turley, David, *The Culture of English Anti-Slavery 1780–1860* (London: Routledge, 1991).

——. 'British antislavery reassessed', A. Burns and J. Innes (eds), *Rethinking the Age of Reform: Britain 1780–1850* (Cambridge: Cambridge University Press, 2003).

Turner, Mary, *Slaves and Missionaries: The Disintegration of Jamaican Slave Society, 1787–1834* (Urbana: University Of Illinois Press, 1982), pp. 182–199.

Turner, Michael J., 'The limits of abolition: government, Saints and the "African Question", c. 1780–1820', *English Historical Review* (April 1997), pp. 319–357.

Twells, Alison, '"A State of Infancy": West Africa and British missionaries in the 1820s', *Wasafiri*, no. 23 (Spring 1996), pp. 19–25.
——, '"So distant and wild a scene": Hannah Kilham's writing from West Africa, 1822–1832', *Women's History Review*, vol. 4, no. 3 (1995), pp. 301–318.
——, '"Let us begin well at home": class, ethnicity and Christian motherhood in the writing of Hannah Kilham', in Eileen Janes Yeo (ed.), *Radical Femininity: Women's Self-Representation in the Public Sphere* (Manchester: Manchester University Press, 1998), pp. 25–51.
——, '"Happy English Children": class, ethnicity and the making of missionary women in the early nineteenth century', *Women's Studies International Forum*, vol. 21, no. 3 (1980), pp. 235–245.
——, 'Missionary "fathers" and wayward "sons": British missionaries in the South Pacific, 1797–1840', in Trev Lynn Broughton and Helen Rogers (eds), *Gender and Fatherhood in the Nineteenth Century* (Basingstoke: Palgrave, 2007), pp. 153–164.
——, 'Missionary domesticity, global reform and "woman's sphere" in early nineteenth-century England', *Gender and History*, Vol. 18, no. 2 (2006), pp. 266–284.
Tylecote, Mabel, *The Mechanics' Institutes of Lancashire and Yorkshire before 1851* (Manchester: Manchester University Press, 1957).
Tyrrell, Alex, '"Woman's Mission" and Pressure Group Politics in Britain 1825–60', *Bulletin of the John Rylands Library*, vol. 63 (1980), pp. 194–230.
Underwood, A. C., *A History of the English Baptists* (London: Baptist Union of Great Britain and Ireland, 1970 [1947]).
Valenze, Deborah M., *Prophetic Sons and Daughters: Female Preaching and Popular Religion in Industrial England* (Princeton: Princeton University Press, 1985).
——. 'Charity, custom and humanity: changing attitudes towards the poor in eighteenth-century England', in Jane Garnett and Colin Matthew (eds), *Revival and Religion since 1700: Essays for John Walsh* (London: Hambledon Press, 1993), pp. 59–78.
Vallone, Lynne, *Disciplines of Virtue: Girls' Culture in the Eighteenth and Nineteenth Centuries* (London: Yale University Press, 1995).
Van den Berg, Johannes, *Constrained by Jesus' Love: An Inquiry into the Motives of the Missionary Awakening in Great Britain in the Period between 1698 and 1815* (Kampen: Kok, 1956).
Vickery, Amanda, 'Golden age to separate spheres? A review of the categories and chronology of English women's history', *The Historical Journal*, vol. 36, no. 2 (June 1993), pp. 383–414.
Viswanathan, Guari, *Outside the Fold: Conversion, Modernity and Belief* (Princeton: Princeton University Press, 1998).

Wahrman, Dror, *Imagining the Middle Class: The Political Representation of Class in Britain, c. 1780–1840* (Cambridge: Cambridge University Press, 1995).

Walker, Pamela J., *Pulling the Devil's Kingdom Down: The Salvation Army in Victorian Britain* (Berkley: University of California Press, 2001).

Walls, Andrew F., 'A Christian experiment: the early Sierra Leone colony', in G. J. Cumming (ed.), *The Mission of the Church and the Propagation of the Faith*, Studies in Church History (Cambridge: Cambridge University Press, 1970), pp. 107–130.

—— 'The Evangelical revival, the missionary movement, and Africa', in Mark A. Noll, David W. Bebbington and George A Rawlyk (eds), *Evangelicalism: Comparative Studies of Popular Protestantism in North America, the British Isles, and Beyond 1700–1990* (Oxford: Oxford University Press, 1994), pp. 310–330.

——, *The Missionary Movement in Christian History: Studies in the Transmission of Faith* (Edinburgh and Maryknoll: Orbis, 1996).

Walsh, J. D., 'Methodism at the end of the Eighteenth Century', in A. Davies, G. Rupp, *A History of the Methodist Church in Great Britain*, vol. 1 (London: Epworth Press, 1966), pp. 277–315.

Walsh, John, 'Religious societies: Methodist and Evangelical, 1738–1800', in W. J. Sheils and Diana Wood (eds), *Voluntary Religion* (Oxford: Blackwell, 1986), pp. 279–302.

——, ' "Methodism" and the origins of English-speaking Evangelicalism', in Mark A. Noll, David W. Bebbington and George A. Rawlyk (eds), *Evangelicalism: Comparative Studies of Popular Protestantism in North America, the British Isles, and Beyond 1700–1990* (Oxford: Oxford University Press, 1994), pp. 19–37.

Walton, Mary, *Sheffield: Its Story and its Achievements* (Otley: Amethyst Press, 1948).

Ward, W. R., *Religion and Society in England, 1790–1850* (London: B. T. Batsford, 1972).

—— 'The religion of the people and the problem of control, 1790–1830', *Studies in Church History*, 8, 1972, pp. 237–257.

——, *The Protestant Evangelical Awakening* (Cambridge: Cambridge University Press, 1992).

——, *Faith and Faction* (London: Epworth Press, 1993).

Ware, Vron, *Beyond the Pale: White Women, Racism and History* (London: Verso, 1992).

Waterman, A. M. C. 'The ideological alliance of political economy and Christian theology 1798–1833', *Journal of Ecclesiastical History*, vol. 34 (April 1983), pp. 231–244.

Watts, Michael, *The Dissenters*, vols 1 and 2 (Oxford: Clarendon Press, 1977, 1995).

Wearmouth, Robert F., *Methodism and the Common People of the Eighteenth Century* (London: Epworth Press, 1945).

Webb, R. K., *The British Working Class Reader, 1790–1848* (London: Allen and Unwin, 1955).

Werner, A., 'English contributions to the study of African languages', *Journal of the Royal African Society*, vol. 29, no. 117 (October 1930), pp. 509–528.

White, Geoffrey, *Identity Through History: Living Stories in a Solomon Islands Society* (Cambridge: Cambridge University Press, 1991).

Wickham, E. R., *Church and People in an Industrial City* (London: Lutterworth Press, 1957).

Williams, C. P., '"Not quite gentlemen": an examination of 'middling class' Protestant missionaries from Britain 1850–1900', *Journal of Ecclesiastical History*, vol. 31, no. 3 (1980), pp. 301–315.

Williams, Peter, '"The missing link": the recruitment of female missionaries in some English evangelical missionary societies in the nineteenth century', in Fiona Bowie, Deborah Kirkwood and Shirley Ardener (eds), *Women and Missions: Past and Present. Anthropological and Historical Perceptions* (Oxford: Berg Publishers, 1993), pp. 43–69.

Williams, C. Peter, 'British religion and the wider world: mission and empire, 1800–1940', in Sheridan Gilley and W. J. Sheils (eds), *A History of Religion in Britain: Practice and Belief from Pre-Roman Times to the Present* (Cambridge: Basil Blackwell, 1994), pp. 381–485.

Wilson, Kathleen, *The Island Race. Englishness, Empire and Gender in the Eighteenth Century* (London: Routledge, 2003).

Wilson, R. E., *Two Hundred Precious Metal Years: A History of the Sheffield Smelting Company Ltd, 1760–1960* (London: Ernest Benn, 1960).

Winch, Donald, *Riches and Poverty: An Intellectual History of Political Economy 1750–1834* (Cambridge: Cambridge University Press, 1996).

Yeo, Eileen, 'Christianity in Chartist Struggle 1838–1842', *Past & Present*, no. 91, (1981), pp. 109–139.

——, 'Chartist religious belief and the theology of liberation', in James Obelkevich, Lyndal Roper and Raphael Samuel (eds), *Disciplines of Faith: Studies in Religion, Politics and Patriarchy* (London: Routledge, 1987).

Yeo, Eileen Janes, *The Contest for Social Science: Relations and Representations of Gender and Class* (London: Rivers Oram Press, 1996).

——, *Radical Femininity: Women's Self-Representation in the Public Sphere* (Manchester: Manchester University Press, forthcoming 1998).

Young, Robert, *Colonial Desire. Hybridity in Theory, Culture and Race* (London and New York: Routledge, 1995).

Zemka, Sue, *Victorian Testaments: The Bible, Christianity, and Literary Authority in Early Nineteenth Century British Culture* (California: Stanford University Press 1997).

Unpublished work

Baxter, John, 'Origin of the Social War: A History of the Economic, Political and Cultural Struggles of Working People in South Yorkshire, 1750–1850' (University of Sheffield: unpublished PhD thesis, 1976).

Beutner, Harvey Fremont, 'With Fraternal Feeling Fired: the Life and Works of James Montgomery' (Northwestern University: unpublished PhD dissertation, 1967).

Frederiks, Martha Th., 'Methodists and Muslims in the Gambia: a Case Study' (unpublished paper, 2003).

Goodman, Joyce, 'Women and the Management of the Education of Working-Class Girls 1800–18961' (Manchester University: unpublished PhD thesis, 1992).

Hatton, Helen, '"The Largest Amount of Good": Quaker Relief in Ireland' (University of Toronto: unpublished PhD thesis, 1988).

Hawksworth, G. F. B., 'The Central Congregational Church in Sheffield' (typed booklet, 1971, Sheffield Local Studies Library).

Hopwood, P. G. S., 'The Gates of Zion: The Story of a Church' (unpublished, no date, Sheffield Local Studies Library).

Martin Hewitt, 'Society as Space: the Territoralisation of Social Knowledge in Nineteenth-Century Manchester' (unpublished paper, 2005).

Marshall, A. E., 'The Sheffield Mechanics' Institute: A Study in Educational History and Interpretation' (Sheffield City Polytechnic: unpublished MA thesis, 1981).

Pedley, S. J., 'The Sheffield Literary and Philosophical Society, 1822–1932' (University of Sheffield: unpublished MA thesis, 1970).

Plant, Helen, 'Gender and the Aristocracy of Dissent: A Comparative Study of the Beliefs, Status and Roles of Women in Quaker and Unitarian Communities, 1770–1830, with Particular Reference to Yorkshire' (University of York: unpublished DPhil thesis, 2000).

Price, Richard, 'Encounters of Empire: the British, the Xhosa and the making of an imperial culture at the frontier and at home 1830–1870' (unpublished paper, 2005).

——, 'Bad Education: how British humanitarians learnt racism in the Empire, 1840–1860' (unpublished paper, 2005).

Reid, Caroline O., 'Middle-Class Values and Working-Class Culture in Nineteenth-Century Sheffield' (University of Sheffield: unpublished PhD thesis, 1976).

Richardson, Sarah, 'Women, Philanthropy and Politics in early C19th Britain' (unpublished paper, 2003).

Rigby, Nigel, 'A Sea of Islands: Tropes of Travel and Adventure in the Pacific' (University of Kent: unpublished PhD thesis, 1995).
Ross, Ellen, 'Slum Journeys: Ladies and London Poverty, 1860–1940' (unpublished paper, 2003).
Seed, John, 'The Role of Unitarianism in the Formation of Liberal Culture, 1775–1851' (University of Hull: unpublished PhD thesis, 1981).
Stanley, Brian. 'Home Support for Overseas Missions in early Victorian England, c. 1838–1873' (University of Cambridge: unpublished PhD thesis, 1979).
Symes, Ruth A., 'Educating Women: The Preceptress and her Pen, 1780–1820' (University of York: unpublished PhD thesis, 1995).
Taylor, Norma, 'The Life of Mary-Anne Rawson' (Sheffield University: unpublished BA dissertation, 1972).
White, A. P., 'Formation and Development of Middle-Class Urban Culture and Politics: Sheffield 1825–1880' (University of Leeds: unpublished PhD, 1990).

Index